Virtuous Violence

What motivates violence? How can good and compassionate people hurt and kill others or themselves? Why are people much more likely to kill or assault people they know well, rather than strangers? This provocative and radical book shows that people mostly commit violence because they genuinely feel that it is the morally right thing to do. In perpetrators' minds, violence may be the morally necessary and proper way to regulate social relationships according to cultural precepts, precedents, and prototypes. These moral motivations apply equally to the violence of the heroes of the *Iliad*, to parents smacking their child, and to many modern murders and everyday acts of violence. *Virtuous Violence* presents a wide-ranging exploration of violence across different cultures and historical eras, demonstrating how people feel obligated to violently create, sustain, end, and honor social relationships in order to make them right, according to morally motivated cultural ideals.

Alan Page Fiske is Professor in the Department of Anthropology at the University of California, Los Angeles, where he has also served as Director of the Behavior Evolution and Culture Center, and Director of the Culture, Brain, and Development Center. He has worked abroad for eight years as a Peace Corps Volunteer, World Health Organization consultant, and Peace Corps Country Director as well as conducting ethnographic fieldwork. He is widely known for his relational models theory, the only comprehensive, integrated theory of human sociality, which has been tested and applied in numerous studies by hundreds of researchers.

Tage Shakti Rai is a Postdoctoral Research Fellow with the Ford Center for Global Citizenship in the Kellogg School of Management at Northwestern University. He is known for developing relationship regulation theory, which argues that morality cannot be understood independently of sociality, and that diversity in moral judgments and behaviors is driven by patterns in the social relationships within which they occur.

"With its wealth of eye-opening ethnographic and historical comparisons and its contrarian but well-argued analyses, this book is a fascinating exploration of violence and a major contribution to our understanding of the human condition."

Steven Pinker

"It's so hard for us to think clearly about violence because acts of violence trigger such strong moral condemnation. Fiske and Rai strip the moralism out of our own minds and put it where it belongs – in the minds of the perpetrators, who usually think their acts are justified. This astonishing book offers a unified approach to understanding the most ghastly events, from street crime and honor killings through war crimes and genocide. This book is essential reading for anyone who wants to understand and ultimately reduce violence."

Jonathan Haidt
NYU Stern School of Business and author of The Righteous Mind

"It's not possible to have a clear understanding of the past, present or future of war, terrorism and torture without knowing the basic message of *Virtuous Violence*."

Richard E. Nisbett
Distinguished University Professor, University of Michigan

"In our preferred world of liberal democracy, tolerance of diversity and distributive justice, violence – especially extreme forms of mass bloodshed – are generally considered pathological or evil expressions of human nature gone awry, or a collateral result of good intentions. Not so, argue Fiske and Rai, in this deeply reasoned and well-documented survey of violence, universally considered by its perpetrators to be mostly a matter of moral virtue. *Virtuous Violence* aims to explain the emotions and intentions that give rise to various kinds of human violence by understanding its generation in both our species-wide and culture-specific moral psychology, which is geared to regulate social life. Building on earlier ground-breaking work on the fundamental forms of social relationships in all cultures, the authors show that the most sustained and consequential forms of human violence – across history and cultures – result from beliefs that it is right and necessary to hurt and suffer harm, and to die and kill, to protect and foster those relationships. Through compelling analyses ranging from primeval forms of human sacrifice to contemporary torture, ancient wars to medieval jousts, contact sports to gang fights, violent revolutions to suicide terrorism and mass murder, *Virtuous Violence* lays bare the moral motives for murderous passions, as a sort of evolutionary impetus to manage the interpersonal and intergroup interactions upon which societies depend, often aided by gods, spirits and abstract causes to which no creature but man is subject. Happily, however, the authors also show that violence isn't always necessary to keep things in line, so that modern prescriptions for non-violence within and between societies increasingly have a chance, provided they are grounded in understanding social facts rather than in wishful thinking or pure reason."

Scott Atran
Directeur de Recherche, Anthropologie, CNRS / Ecole Normale Supérieure,
Paris and author of In Gods We Trust *and* Talking to the Enemy

"A provocative tour through the (long) world history of violence. You won't think about violence and its many manifestations – or read a newspaper – the same way again."

Dov Cohen
Professor, University of Illinois

"We have all watched movies where violent actions occur as part and consequence of social relations, and where the art of the movie consists of letting the audience share exactly the same emotions and motives that make that violence inevitable and feel right. At the same time, the mainstream social psychological arguments rarely pick up on these motives. This book provides a powerful argument in favor of scientifically considering these causes of violence. It is a scientifically important book, which touches on many issues we are concerned about as citizens, and will surely attract much attention and discussion as well as hopefully influencing future work in the social and behavioral sciences on this topic."

Thomas Schubert
University of Oslo

"The authors of this exciting book convincingly show that most individuals and groups engage in violence believing that what they do is right, moral and even obligatory. This well-written book shows the great challenge of preventing such righteous violence, and provides the knowledge base to engage with this challenge."

Ervin Staub
Author of The Roots of Evil, The Psychology of Good and Evil and Overcoming Evil.

Virtuous Violence

Hurting and Killing to Create, Sustain, End, and Honor Social Relationships

The social-relational, moral motivational psychology, cultural anthropology and history of war, torture, genocide, animal and human sacrifice, obedience to gods, religious self-torture, homicide, robbery, intimate partner conflict, rape, suicide and self-harm, corporal and capital punishment, trial by ordeal and combat, policing, initiation, castration, fighting for status, contact sports and martial arts, honor, the *Iliad* and the Trojan War, injurious mortuary rites, and homicidal mourning

Alan Page Fiske and Tage Shakti Rai

CAMBRIDGE
UNIVERSITY PRESS

CAMBRIDGE
UNIVERSITY PRESS

University Printing House, Cambridge CB2 8BS, United Kingdom

Cambridge University Press is part of the University of Cambridge.

It furthers the University's mission by disseminating knowledge in the pursuit of education, learning and research at the highest international levels of excellence.

www.cambridge.org
Information on this title: www.cambridge.org/9781107088207

First published 2015

A catalogue record for this publication is available from the British Library

Library of Congress Cataloguing in Publication data
Fiske, Alan Page, 1947–
Virtuous violence : hurting and killing to create, sustain, end, and honor social relationships / Alan Page Fiske and Tage Shakti Rai.
    pages   cm
ISBN 978-1-107-45891-8 (pbk.)
1. Violence.   2. Violence – Moral and ethical aspects.   I. Rai, Tage Shakti.   II. Title.
HM1116.F583   2014
303.6–dc23

2014023810

ISBN   978-1-107-08820-7   Hardback
ISBN   978-1-107-45891-8   Paperback

To Gwendolyn, Colin, Zoé, Kai, Wyatt, and Benjamin:
may your lives be forever full of love and free of violence.

To Arjuna:
Julia and I will carry you in our hearts until you return.

CONTENTS

FIGURES AND TABLE

FOREWORD

Moralization is the original sin of the behavioral sciences. Scientists of human nature – psychologists, sociologists, anthropologists, geneticists, neurobiologists – must be committed, as scientists, to describing the world as it is rather than as we wish it to be. But it's irresistible to read our morals into reality and describe the world as if it strove to implement our values. Nowhere has this fallacy been more damaging than in the attempt to understand violence. The harder-headed the scientist, the more rigorous he or she claims to be, the more likely that the scientist will assume that violence is the result of a defective gene, a damaged brain, a psychopathology, a contagious public health problem, or a societal malfunction.

The book you are now holding presents a rare escape from this conceptual prison. It presents one of those rare hypotheses that is both flagrantly contrary to expert belief (at first sight yet another example of the tedious "everything-you-think-is-wrong" formula) and at the same time very likely to be true. Having myself tried to make sense of 10 thousand years of human violence, I came to a conclusion that is very similar to the one that Alan Fiske and Tage Rai present in this book: most perpetrators of violence are neither pathological nor self-interested but are convinced that what they are doing is in the service of a higher moral good. As I put it in introducing the section on "Morality" in *The Better Angels of Our Nature: Why Violence Has Declined*:

> The world has far too much morality. If you added up all the
> homicides committed in pursuit of self-help justice, the casualties of

religious and revolutionary wars, the people executed for victimless crimes and misdemeanors, and the targets of ideological genocides, they would surely outnumber the fatalities from amoral predation and conquest. The human moral sense can excuse any atrocity in the minds of those who commit it, and it furnishes them with motives for acts of violence that bring them no tangible benefit. The torture of heretics and conversos, the burning of witches, the imprisonment of homosexuals, and the honor killing of unchaste sisters and daughters are just a few examples. The incalculable suffering that has been visited on the world by people motivated by a moral cause is enough to make one sympathize with the comedian George Carlin when he said, "I think motivation is overrated. You show me some lazy [bum] who's lying around all day watching game shows ... and I'll show you someone who's *not causing any [freaking] trouble!*"

(As George Carlin fans might guess, my brackets and ellipses here conceal saltier wording in the original.)

Though I came to conclusions similar to those of Fiske and Rai, the convergence is not completely accidental. I have long thought that Fiske's theory of relational models is the best – indeed the only – overarching theory of social psychology. For starters, the theory acknowledges the fundamental fact about human sociality, the first observation that the proverbial Martian biologist would notice about our species: we don't act the same way to everyone, but have radically different kinds of thoughts and feelings about people depending on the relationship that holds between us. We have different thoughts and feelings about our mothers and fathers than we do about our siblings, distant relatives, spouses, lovers, friends, rivals, enemies, and strangers. Yet, if you read the chapters on "social psychology" in the major textbooks, with their discussions of generic processes like stereotyping, attribution, and attitude formation, you would have no inkling that human beings treat each other differently depending on the qualitative nature of the relationship that binds them.

Relational models theory also tackles the paradox that social behavior varies radically from one society to another, and from one historical era to another, yet, throughout this variation, a few themes seem to pop up again and again in different guises. People in all cultures are obsessed with solidarity and warmth, with dominance and authority, with fairness and equity, and with complex rules and formulas, albeit to different extents and in different ways in different contexts. As with language, human relationships seem to conform to an abstract universal grammar that is instantiated in different ways in different cultures.

I like relational models theory for a third reason. Various subfields within evolutionary psychology have mapped out the distinct adaptive rationales of different kinds of social relationships. The inclusive-fitness calculus that selects for feelings of solidarity among kin is different from the hawk–dove game that results in dominance hierarchies, which is different yet again from the iterated prisoner's dilemma that gives us the sense of fairness which polices reciprocal altruism. And all of these evolved strategies differ in turn from the cool cognitive calculations by which we reckon and regulate our lives by formal rules. Relational models subsumes them all under a comprehensive theory and, more interestingly, shows how the choice among them gives rise to the complexity and variation in human social life.

I'm not only a fan of relational models theory but also a user. As a psycholinguist, I had long puzzled over the mysterious rituals of euphemism and innuendo that govern everyday conversation: why it's emotionally so much easier to say *Gee, officer, is there some way to settle the ticket here?* than *If I give you $50, will you let me drive away?* or why it eases feelings all around to ask *Would you like to come up and see my etchings?* rather than *Would you like to come up and have sex?* Fiske's theory that violated expectations of communality, authority, or equality are emotionally awkward was the missing piece in the puzzle of why we are so likely to sidestep and shilly-shally rather than blurt out what we mean, and I gave it pride of place in my analysis of these phenomena in *The Stuff of Thought* and subsequent papers.

My analysis of innuendo relied on the observation by Fiske and his collaborators that when one person violates the relational model that currently governs his relationship with another person and the violation is unintentional or transient, the response of that person and of third parties is typically one of awkwardness or puzzlement. But when the violation is deliberate and ongoing, the reaction can be one of shock and outrage, and, as Fiske and Rai elaborate in this book, it often leads to violence. That's why I found relational models theory so useful in solving a second problem, the role of the moral sense in violence, which was a major theme of *Better Angels*:

How can we make sense of this crazy angel – the part of human nature that would seem to have the strongest claim to be the source of our goodness, but that in practice can be more diabolical than our worst inner demon?

To understand the role of the moral sense in the decline of violence, we have to solve a number of psychological enigmas. One is how people in different times and cultures can be driven by goals that they experience as "moral" but that are unrecognizable to our own standards of morality. Another is why the moral sense does not, in general, push toward the reduction of suffering but so often increases it. A third is how the moral sense can be so compartmentalized: why upstanding citizens can beat their wives and children; why liberal democracies can practice slavery and colonial oppression; why Nazi Germany could treat animals with unequaled kindness... And the overriding puzzle, of course, is: What changed? What degree of freedom in the human moral sense has been engaged by the processes of history to drive violence downward?

Virtuous violence theory resolves these puzzles and more. With its wealth of eye-opening ethnographic and historical comparisons and its contrarian but well-argued analyses, this book is a fascinating exploration of violence and a major contribution to our understanding of the human condition.

Steven Pinker

WARM THANKS

Gabriel Rossman discussed nearly every chapter with us, providing novel suggestions, innumerable references, and cheerful support; his many contributions added new dimensions to the book, for which we thank him. For reading the entire manuscript and offering many wise and wonderful comments, we are extremely grateful to Maroussia Favre Carlen, Hans IJzerman, Steven Pinker, Linda Skitka, Diane Sunar, and Sven Waldzus. Clark McCauley and Thomas Schubert reviewed several chapters and offered suggestions that reshaped the whole book. We also greatly appreciate the perceptive comments on parts of the manuscript kindly contributed by Daniel Bartels, Vivian Bohl, Rodrigo Brito, Alan Ehrenhalt, Zoé Robin Fiske, Jeremy Ginges, Jesse Graham, Jon Haidt, Katharina Kugler, Brian Lucas, Francesco Orsi, Julia Ortony, Beate Seibt, Christopher Stephan, David Tannenbaum, Zsolt Unoka, and Adam Waytz. We also received many perspicacious perspectives on our basic conceptualization of violence from the audiences of colloquia Alan Page Fiske delivered at the University of Tartu, Würzburg University, Tilburg University, the University of Oslo, UCLA, the Rotterdam School of Management of Erasmus University, Ludwig-Maximilians-Universität, ISCTE-IUL (Lisbon), the Technical University of Munich, and the Sintra, Portugal, workshop on Embodiment and Relational Models. Following presentations by Fiske on our metarelational theorization of honor and the *Iliad*, we received many insightful comments from colloquium audiences at VU University, Amsterdam; the Max Planck

Institute for Evolutionary Anthropology, Leipzig; the University of Tartu; the University of Würzburg; Tilburg University; Erasmus University; UCLA; and participants in the Barcelona Workshop on Honor and Shame. Insights from audiences of colloquia Rai delivered to the Chicagoland Morality Researchers Group; the Cross-Cultural Perspectives on Moral Psychology Conference at Korea University, Seoul; the Research Centre for Human Values at the Chinese University of Hong Kong; and the Department of Psychology at the University of Iowa were also instrumental in refining our conceptualization of moral psychology and the implications of our theory of virtuous violence.

Participants in our seminar on moral motives for violence helped us develop our ideas and think about the data. Sheryl Fulgencio helped locate and review some of the hazing and initiation practices, Megan Mehany searched the literature on the corporal punishment of children in the contemporary United States, and Magaly Chavez reviewed much of the literature on female genital modification.

At Cambridge University Press, Rebecca Taylor, Carrie Parkinson, Hetty Marx, Joseph Garver, and Jonathan Ratcliffe magnificently transformed our work from manuscript to publication. Aras Karimi kindly created a beautifully intriguing design for the cover which unfortunately we could not use here.

In many respects this book is a conversation with all of these partners. Some sentences consist of our interpretations of ideas our colleagues contributed, while many passages and a few chapters are responses to points they raised. We look forward to continuing and widening this conversation.

Thank you, all!

THE POINT

How all occasions do inform against me
And spur my dull revenge! What is a man,
If his chief good and market of his time
Be but to sleep and feed? A beast, no more.
Sure he that made us with such large discourse,
Looking before and after, gave us not
That capability and godlike reason
To fust in us unus'd. Now, whether it be
Bestial oblivion, or some craven scruple
Of thinking too precisely on th' event, –
A thought which, quarter'd, hath but one part wisdom
And ever three parts coward, – I do not know
Why yet I live to say 'This thing's to do,'
Sith I have cause, and will, and strength, and means
To do't. Examples gross as earth exhort me.
Witness this army of such mass and charge,
Led by a delicate and tender prince,
Whose spirit, with divine ambition puff'd,
Makes mouths at the invisible event,
Exposing what is mortal and unsure
To all that fortune, death, and danger dare,
Even for an eggshell. Rightly to be great
Is not to stir without great argument,
But greatly to find quarrel in a straw
When honour's at the stake. How stand I then,

That have a father kill'd, a mother stain'd,
Excitements of my reason and my blood,
And let all sleep, while to my shame I see
The imminent death of twenty thousand men
That for a fantasy and trick of fame
Go to their graves like beds, fight for a plot
Whereon the numbers cannot try the cause,
Which is not tomb enough and continent
To hide the slain? O, from this time forth,
My thoughts be bloody, or be nothing worth!

Shakespeare, Hamlet, Act IV, scene iv

Violence is often considered the antithesis of sociality – people think that violence is the expression of our animal nature, breaking through when learned cultural norms collapse. Violence is also considered to be the essence of evil: it is the prototype of immorality. But an examination of violent acts and practices across cultures and throughout history shows just the opposite. When people hurt or kill someone, they usually do so because they feel they ought to: they feel that it is morally right or even obligatory to be violent. Moreover, the motives for violence generally grow out of a relationship between the perpetrator and the victim, or their relationships with third parties. The perpetrator is violent to make the relationship right – to make the relationship what it ought to be according to his or her cultural implementations of universal relational moral principles. That is, most violence is morally motivated. Morality is about regulating social relationships, and violence is one way to regulate relationships. That's our thesis.

Shakespeare expresses this in Hamlet's soliloquy: Hamlet berates himself as a rationalizing coward for not yet having done his moral duty to kill his uncle Claudius (his father's brother) to avenge Claudius' murder of Hamlet's father and Claudius' "incestuous" marriage to Hamlet's mother. Hamlet's moral sentiments grow out of the links among several interlocking social relationships: his duty as a son, his father's relationship to the brother who murdered his father to become king, his father's marriage to Hamlet's mother, and his mother's marriage to the usurper Claudius. Hamlet experiences his moral motives to kill his uncle as shame because he has not performed his duty as a son. He compares himself to the soldiers who are ready to die merely for fame, fighting over a prince's claim to a bit of land. With growing anger, he concludes that his thoughts must be violent or they are worthless.

This book systematically develops Shakespeare's point that violence is morally motivated by culturally informed variants of universal social-relational models. Our aims in this book are to establish beyond any doubt the ubiquity of virtuous violence, to reveal its moral motives, to show that people intend their violence to constitute four elementary forms of social relationships, and to illuminate the specific constitutive phases that people aim to realize through violence. We also show that much violence emerges from combinations of relationships, where specific configurations of relationships motivate moral violence that none of the component relationships would evoke on their own.

We do this for the most part ethnologically, by examining a great variety of violent practices in a great many cultures across the span of history. To explain *human* violence, it is essential to know about most of the kinds of violence people do – not just in one culture at one point in history, but everywhere, throughout history. While our primary goals are to understand the psychology and cultural meanings of violence, we also get invaluable perspective by comparing human violence with the violence other animals do, and we reach another level of understanding by considering the adaptive functions of violence. The pattern that emerges is clear, revealing something fundamental about violence, morality, and social relationships. At the same time, by comparing these diverse kinds of violence we illuminate each instance of violence. So we hope that this book and the theory we set forth in it will be interesting to all social scientists and humanists, as well as to anyone who wants to understand themselves and other humans.

Our theory of virtuous violence integrates aspects of many other theories of violence, and in doing so illuminates the nature of impulsivity, rationality, instrumentality, emotions, motives, and, above all, moral psychology and social relationships. While this book is a work of empirical science, toward the end we suggest that our characterization of the nature of the real world may have some profound implications for prescriptive morality and law.

Our goal in this book is to understand the motivations for violence: the emotions and intentions that give rise to violence. We want to explain why and when people are violent. So we have relatively little to say about the experience and consequences of fearing, expecting, suffering, surviving, or remembering violence. Those are important topics, but not our topics.

A theory of perpetrators' motives for engaging in violence must account for most of the violent practices that humans enact in every type of culture, in every historical period; the theory should make sense in comparative phylogenetic perspective, and there should be plausible evolutionary processes that would select not just for the propensity for violence but also for a propensity tuned to social systems and relational circumstances. Virtuous violence theory does all this. Our theory will certainly need to be refined and modified to fit future findings of studies specifically designed to explore the moral motives for violence. We simply hope that virtuous violence theory provides a solid framework to build on.

Readers may not find it absolutely necessary to read the whole book. Readers primarily interested in particular kinds of violence could get something worthwhile out of any of the topical chapters read by themselves, but then might find that they would develop a deeper understanding by reading some of the conceptual chapters (1, 2, 9, 10, and 20–4). Conversely, those with primarily theoretical orientations could read the conceptual chapters, browsing and sampling among the topical chapters. But the whole is more than the sum of the parts. It's not pleasant to consider so many of the gruesome things that people have done or now do to others, nor is it agreeable to recognize that people who do violence usually feel they should do it or absolutely *must* do it. But our view is that we should consider all this carefully if we wish to understand ourselves, our species, our communities, and our cultures. Or if we are committed to reducing violence.

Chapter 1 lays the foundations for the book, stating the theory in the simplest terms, then explaining what we mean by "violence" and what we mean by "moral," and then briefly comparing virtuous violence theory with previous approaches that address the morality of violence. Chapter 2 presents the analytic structure we will be employing throughout the book to understand the social-relational nature of violence: the four fundamental relational models, their essentially cultural implementation, their constitutive phases, and how they are linked into larger metarelational configurations. This completes the foundation and erects the framework of virtuous violence theory. Chapter 3 makes the crucial point that people often feel that it is right and necessary to use violence for defense, punishment, or retribution. Chapter 4 explores the moral motives for violent enforcement of legitimate authority, while Chapter 5 illuminates the moral motives for regulating relationships consisting of contests of violence such as jousts, martial and contact sports, or confrontations between gangs. Chapter 6 characterizes honor and shame as motives for violence in many cultures and subcultures, and we unpack the metarelational moral motives for violence that comprise the framework for the Trojan War and Homer's account of the violent regulation of relationships among the ancient Greeks. Chapter 7 describes national leaders' moral motives for going to war, and soldiers' moral motives for killing and dying. Then in Chapter 8 we consider how humans violently constitute social relationships with gods and spirits, including human sacrifice and excruciating self-torture.

After showing that these six types of violent practices are morally motivated to constitute critical social relationships, we pause to explicate virtuous violence theory more precisely. Chapter 9 considers more deeply the links between moral and immoral motives for violence, showing that morality is not defined by forms of actions or their material consequences. Rather, morality is culturally defined by local precedents, prototypes, and precepts for implementing the four universal relational models (RMs). We also show that both impulsive and reflectively considered violence are mostly morally motivated. This allows us in Chapter 10 to show how virtuous violence theory either encompasses or complements previous theories that violence results from sadism, psychopathy, rational cost-benefit calculation, or, conversely, failures of rationality.

Then we tackle forms of violence that people may be loath to acknowledge could be morally motivated, but, in fact, often are: in Chapter 11, intimate partner violence; in Chapter 12, rape, including gang rape and rape in warfare. Chapter 13 demonstrates that moral motives to constitute critical relationships with or among their children drive people to perform violent initiation rites on boys, to excise or infibulate girls, and to castrate boys. We discover in Chapter 14 that moral motives drive the leaders who order torture and their minions who enact torture on victims, as well as the wider public who condone torture. Chapter 15 investigates the motives of killers; we see that most homicides are morally motivated and the killers' peers and neighbors feel that they did exactly what they should have done. Even mass murderers and mentally ill killers typically kill because they genuinely feel that their victims deserve to die. Chapter 16 analyzes lynching and genocide, which sustain what the perpetrators and their reference groups perceive as legitimate, natural, and morally necessary relationships with their victims' ethnic group or race.

When we look at suicide and non-suicidal self-injury in Chapter 17, we discover that violence against the self is also intended to rectify critical relationships: the person who hurts herself feels that violence makes the relationship right. Chapter 18 illuminates the final constitutive phase of violence. In quite a few cultures in diverse parts of the world, people mourn the deaths of loved ones by seriously injuring themselves or others, or by going out to kill some random innocent person – and then, eventually, by also killing the witch or sorcerer or manifest assailant whom they hold responsible for the death. Then we conclude our empirical ethnological and historical investigations by considering robbery in Chapter 19. Though robbers have obviously instrumental motives, it turns out that often they are highly morally motivated to regulate relationships with victims who don't deserve what they have, or shouldn't have flaunted what they had.

We conclude the book with five chapters of further theoretical explorations building on virtuous violence theory. In Chapter 20 we consider whether the *way* people hurt or kill is a function of the particular kind of relationship they are regulating. In Chapter 21 we ask when and why people constitute their relationships *violently*, rather than in any of the other ways that people usually constitute relationships. Throughout the book we will see that metarelational models commonly motivate violence: perpetrators are often motivated to hurt or kill a victim in order to constitute one or more relationships with third parties, or because of the dynamic moral implications that any relationship has for other relationships linked to it. Chapter 22 considers the converse: how metarelational models known as cross-cutting ties can blunt, reduce, or prevent violence. Chapter 23 addresses how people can often quite effectively resist illegitimate state violence through non-violent interventions by catalyzing common knowledge of the metarelational ramifications of violence and disapproval of it by third parties and the larger community. Finally, in Chapter 24, we ask how "natural" virtuous violence is and consider the ethical, legal, and psychological implications of virtuous violence theory. We go on to discuss several empirical lines of research that emerge once it is understood that violence is morally motivated to regulate relationships.

The book ends with a very brief coda reflecting on the nature of theory and the merits of inductively generating theory and broad explanations by observing and comparing the widest possible range of naturally occurring phenomena.

1 WHY ARE PEOPLE VIOLENT?

We, the authors, must make clear at the outset that, prescriptively, we judge most violence to be immoral. But in every culture, some people sometimes feel morally entitled or required to hurt or kill others. Violent initiations, human sacrifice, corporal punishment, revenge, beating spouses, torturing enemies, ethnic cleansing and genocide, honor killing, homicide, martial arts, and many other forms of violence are usually morally motivated. The fact is that people often feel – and explicitly judge – that in many contexts it is *good* to do these kinds of violence to others: people believe that in many cases hurting or killing others is not simply justifiable, it is absolutely, fundamentally *right*. Furthermore, people often regard others' infliction of violence against third parties as morally commendable – and sometimes acknowledge or even appreciate the morality of violence inflicted on themselves. We wish this weren't true – we abhor it. But it is true, so to understand or reduce violence, we must recognize its moral roots. Most violence is *morally motivated*. People do not simply justify or excuse their violent actions after the fact; at the moment they act, people intend to cause harm or death to someone they feel *should* suffer or die. That is, people are impelled to violence when they feel that to regulate certain social relationships, imposing suffering or death is necessary, natural, legitimate, desirable, condoned, admired, and ethically gratifying. In short, most violence is the exercise of moral rights and obligations. Working within the framework of relational models theory (Fiske, 1991, 1992, 2004) and relationship regulation theory (Rai and Fiske, 2011), our thesis is that *people are morally motivated to do violence to create, conduct, protect, redress,*

terminate, or mourn social relationships with the victim or with others.
We call our theory virtuous violence theory.

Virtuous violence theory is not a theory about crazy people. It's about ordinary people trying to create, sustain, modulate, and repair the relationships that matter to them, to terminate relationships that become intolerable, or to mourn the loss of a partner. For the most part, agents of the violence fully appreciate that they are hurting fully human beings, and judge that it is right to hurt them. More specifically, we investigate normative cultural practices in which, in the subculture or reference group that practices violence, "everyone" in the relational situation of the perpetrator does it, everyone should do it, and people assume it's natural and necessary to do it. Virtuous violence theory is based on the observation that *people often judge that to constitute or regulate crucial relationships they are morally required to hurt or kill another person,* and that obligation makes local sociocultural sense. In other cases, violence may not be absolutely required in order to regulate important relationships, but it is condoned, praised, and admired.

What we mean by "violence"

We need some term that encompasses intentional infliction of pain, physical harm, and killing; "violence" seems like the most apt.[1] For the purposes of this book, "violence" *consists of action in which the perpetrator regards inflicting pain, suffering, fear, distress, injury, maiming, disfigurement, or death as the intrinsic, necessary, or desirable means to the intended ends.* To some degree, the perpetrator may perceive the pain, suffering, fear, distress, maiming, disfigurement, or death as ends in themselves – or at least as the appropriate medium for the perpetrator's purposes. This definition thus excludes action where pain or suffering is incidental, or necessary but undesired or irrelevant. For example, it is violence when boys being initiated are made to fear the pain of circumcision and, to prove their manhood, must stoically endure it without flinching; it is not violence when infants are circumcised for religious or

---

[1] "Aggression" would be a workable synonym, except that it, too, has been used to mean "wrongful or wanton harm," and seems even more evaluative than "violence," which is a bit more directly descriptive. But we intend virtuous violence theory to address essentially the same issues that others have studied under the rubric of "aggression." There is also some overlap with the wider concept of "force."

health reasons by adults who perceive the pain as unfortunate, or who would prefer to use anesthetics if they could be used. So virtuous violence theory does not explain and is not meant to explain actions whose purpose is not to hurt or kill. We also exclude from consideration here practices such as painful surgery and physical rehabilitation because the distress or injury involved is regarded as undesirable but necessary to achieve the aims *of the sufferer*. The goals of such practices are primarily practical, although people sometimes feel that it is virtuous to overcome the necessary suffering in order to achieve difficult goals. So the primary focus of this book is on actions meant to activate nociceptive neurons, to damage tissue, or to cause death. To maintain focus and to keep this book from being impossibly long, we do not investigate imprisonment, isolation, ostracism, shaming or humiliation, deprivation, and intentional evocation of high levels of fear and anxiety. While we imagine that virtuous violence theory could be directly extrapolated to encompass such practices, we simply could not include them in a book of reasonable length.

Violent action, like all action, varies in the agent's degree and explicit awareness of his intention, as well as others' attributions of the degree and the nature of intent. We exclude from our definition of "violence" action that "accidentally" results in harm to the extent that it was not the agent's intent to harm and the risk of harm was not readily foreseeable. We are aware that the concept of "intent" is extremely complex and problematic, while any doctrine of "due and reasonable care" is also tendentious. But since we cannot resolve the issues involved, pending further philosophical and empirical clarification, we will have to leave the meanings of those constructs to intuition. So let us just say that for the purposes of virtuous violence theory, "violence" is harm, suffering, or killing that people do on purpose. Hence, we do not address "structural violence" and the noxious externalities of everyday actions that result in harm, when the agents are largely oblivious or indifferent to the consequences of their actions. This is a real path to real harm, but it is outside the scope of our theory and our book.

Natural aversion to killing and hurting

[Aunt Polly, speaking of her foster son, Tom Sawyer]
    He 'pears to know just how long he can torment me before I get my dander up, and he knows if he can make out to put me off for a minute or make me laugh, it's all down again and I can't hit him a

lick. I ain't doing my duty by that boy, and that's the Lord's truth, goodness knows. Spare the rod and spile the child, as the Good Book says. I'm a laying up sin and suffering for us both, I know. He's full of the Old Scratch, but laws-a-me! he's my own dead sister's boy, poor thing, and I ain't got the heart to lash him, somehow. Every time I let him off, my conscience does hurt me so, and every time I hit him my old heart most breaks.

(*Mark Twain*, The Adventures of Tom Sawyer)

Now, for the most part, people hate hurting others. It is extremely distressing to directly kill or injure another person face-to-face, no matter how socioculturally justified or legally obligatory it is (Baumeister, 1997: 203–12; Chirot and McCauley, 2006: 52–3; Collins, 2008; Grossman, 2009; MacNair, 2002; Milgram, 1974). Like many other moral acts, killing or hurting others can be difficult, requiring training, social support and modeling, effort, practice, and experience before it becomes second nature. Few people become unambivalently dedicated to moral violence or do it easily, *but that is true of many difficult moral practices other than violence* – people often resist or fail to do what is morally required of them, even when they have no doubt about whether they *should* do it. Like many sorts of moral action, most people are able to commit only the moral violence they know they should commit because their moral motives are reinforced by fear of being shamed, fear of failing their loved ones, and fear of punishment (Grossman, 2009; Mathew and Boyd, 2011). When people fail to commit moral violence even though their moral sensibilities tell them they ought to do so, it is because they have countervailing moral or non-moral motives they cannot overcome. Conversely, people may feel guilt, shame, remorse, sadness, nausea, or horror before, during, or even after committing moral violence because of antiviolence motives that operate alongside the moral violence motives. Humans typically have multiple conflicting moral sentiments, derived from distinct aspects of their social relationships (Rai and Fiske, 2011, 2012).

But the fact that people have competing motives to refrain from violence, yet often overcome those motives to achieve virtuous violence, does not make their violence any the less moral. Moral motives may lead a person to jump into icy waves to rescue someone; the rescuer's horror at the waves and abhorrence of cold water do not make his heroic rescue any less moral – indeed, they make it *more* morally laudable, because they demonstrate that the rescuer overcame huge motives impelling him not to jump in. The fact that sometimes it is very hard to do harm to others, that in some important respect agents are averse to doing it, or that some people are unable to go through with doing what they should do, does not make a violent or harmful act any less virtuous. Violence is virtuous if the agent, her reference group, and her audience truly regard it as the right and moral thing to do, however difficult.

What we mean by "moral"

A definition is merely a declaration of intentions about the use of a word, but some ways of using words get in the way of understanding the world, while other ways of using words help us delineate and discriminate natural kinds in the world – real entities or processes that interact in consistent ways with other natural kinds. Suppose that, coming from a certain modern Western sensibility, we define polygamy as "immoral cohabitation among three or more persons." In most cultures through-out history, men or women have commonly had multiple spouses simul-taneously – but, empirically, the participants, their kin, and everyone else in those cultures have regarded having multiple spouses as natural, legitimate, and often admirable. So defining polygamy as "immoral cohabitation among three or more persons" would exclude from consideration, a priori, most instances of actual polygamy – and would impede understanding the motives or moral perspectives of the people involved. In short, we have to keep our ethnocentric values out of our scientific definitions; indeed, we have to totally separate ethics from ontology, even when we are defining "morality."

So we define morality in two ways, which we believe coincide and are indeed two sides of the same psychology. Morality consists of a certain set of evaluative emotions, as well as a certain set of intentions. The motives and emotions concern the feelings that something should or should not be done, while the intentions concern making relationships what they should be. When we posit that most violence is *morally motivated*, we mean that the person doing the violence subjectively feels that what she is doing is right: she believes that she should do the violence, and she is actually moved by moral emotions such as loyalty or outrage. At the same time, *moral* refers to the evaluation of action, attitudes, motives, or intentions with reference to an ideal model of how to relate. In the next chapter, we briefly review relational models theory, which characterizes the four elementary models that people use to generate, understand, coordinate, regulate, and evaluate all social relationships (Fiske, 1991, 1992, 2004). A core tenet of relational models theory is that people experience these four elementary types of relationships as intrinsically desirable, fulfilling, meaningful, and necessary: such relationships are motivating ends in themselves. People seek to create and participate in relationships that realize these four models, and evaluate all social action with reference to them: they are emotionally imbued moral ideals. They are the ways that people *must* relate. *Morality thus concerns the realization of ideal models for relationships.* What is morally good, what is right, what is obligatory is, therefore, relating according to the four ideal relational models (RMs) (Fiske, 1990). Morality is relationship regulation (Rai and Fiske, 2011, 2012), and *moral motivation is the motivation to make actual relationships correspond with culturally implemented ideals of the four RMs.*

Contrary to popular opinion, morality is not synonymous with pure altruism; it can be instrumentally rational and self-serving if the intended benefit is consistent with culturally appropriate realization of the right social relationship. Moreover, the social relationships that give rise to moral standards and motives need not be with other living humans: they can be relationships with deceased ancestors, spirits, or deities. Is it not moral if people know they should be peaceful, fair, and giving in their relationships with other people, but they only do so because they fear God's wrath and wish to be sent to heaven and not cast down to hell? Is it not moral if a child strives to be honest and obedient, but only because she wants to avoid ending up on Santa's "naughty" list? If you agree that moral motives can be instrumentally motivated by relationships with supernatural beings, then, logically, you must acknowledge that moral action can be instrumentally motivated by the culturally shaped social relationships among humans. If you don't acknowledge that people are morally motivated when they act in accord with their perceptions of the will of their ancestors, spirits, or god(s), then you are effectively excluding the moral lives of most humans throughout most of history. Actions that are motivated by culturally prescribed models for relationships within a community or culture, including actions intended to avoid being shamed or humiliated, actions that restore honor, and actions that enhance honor, respect, and status within a community, are still *morally* motivated if the actions are aimed toward realizing ideal models for relationships.

Moral action is also not restricted to thoughtful, reasoned, controlled action. Most of the time, people have strong, intuitive, emotional reactions to moral situations, which they rationalize only later, if ever (Haidt, 2001). In the moment of action, people may have no sense that their actions serve some selfish end; instead, they only feel the moral emotion and they act on it. If people experience intense moral emotions and they act on them in an uncontrolled fashion, such as by lashing out at someone who has insulted them, their actions are still morally motivated, regardless of whether they are acted upon "automatically" in the moment, or planned strategically for years (see Chapter 9).

When we use the term *moral* in this book we always mean *"moral from the perpetrator's point of view."*

That is, we use the term descriptively, not prescriptively. Prescriptively, we abhor all violence. But our prescriptive judgments – and the reader's prescriptive morality – are irrelevant to the scientific explanation we seek. We seek to understand what motivates violence; once we do, we can consider the prescriptive implications of our understanding. Understanding violence will help us to minimize it. To understand violence, it is essential to maintain a clear distinction between our own moral judgments and the motives of perpetrators at the moment they commit violence. Furthermore, for the most part, perpetrators' moral sentiments are consistent with the sentiments and judgments of their own cultural communities, however much they may differ from those of other cultures, including the writers' or readers' cultures.

Conflicting moralities and post-hoc justifications

The most fundamental finding of anthropological research is the descriptive fact that morals are culturally relative (Brandt, 1954; Edel and Edel, 1959; Fiske, 1990). Quite simply, many actions that people judge to be right in any given culture are judged wrong in many others.[2] A man walks into the yard of his neighbor, who is away, takes an ax, and tells no one that he took it. Is this wrong? Well, if the man and the neighbor are joking partners in West Africa, it's perfectly appropriate;

---

[2] We use the terms "judge" and "judgment" throughout the book without any implication about whether the moral evaluation is based on immediate emotional response or reflectively articulated reasoning; we simply mean "morally evaluate," in the broad sense of any attitude, value, emotion, or motive.

he didn't do anything wrong. A man sends a boy to ask another man for two chairs to seat important visitors, and then never returns them. Is this wrong? If the man who sent the boy is the chief of a Moose village in Burkina Faso, he "owns" everything in it and has a perfect right to expropriate whatever he wants within the boundaries of the village. So the chief of the village where I (ApF) lived kept my chairs, and everyone agreed that he was entitled to them. When he visited me and saw some rope lying on my wall, he just took it; it was his, after all. (I learned to keep my movable property out of sight; it would not have been right for the chief to search the house.) As these examples illustrate, an act that's "theft" in one culture, and therefore wrong, is "joking" or "taking what's rightfully his" in another culture, and therefore right. A married man arranges with a 17-year-old girl's parents to have his friends abduct her against her will, and then makes her have sex with him. Kidnapping and rape in one culture. Correct and legitimate polygamous marriage among the Moose and in many other cultures, where all concerned – including the girl – judge that her parents' giving her to the man was a virtuous, generous act of gratitude, requiting his years of generous gifts and service to them. Throughout this book we will describe actions that would be wrong in one culture (say, our own), but are right and even obligatory in others. None of the moral motives for violence we describe here will be intelligible without accepting the empirically irrefutable premise that actions that outsiders perceive as wrong are morally right from the cultural perspective of insiders. What is virtue in one culture is evil from the perspective of some other cultures – but the perpetrator is motivated by the morality of *his* own culture, not the moralities of other cultures he doesn't know or care about, or outsiders' standards that perhaps he may need to take into account pragmatically but that don't motivate *him*.

Diversity of moral perspectives is also common within a culture, a nation, or a community, and among the participants in a particular interaction. Is abortion murder, or a woman's right to choose and to control her own body? Is your partner's joking and dancing with that attractive man disloyalty, or just having innocent fun? If you grew up in an honor culture and feel morally entitled, indeed obligated, to threaten the man with violence and he doesn't back down, when you kill him you may be doing what you feel you had to do. Your conviction is that you just did what any self-respecting man should do. But your partner from a liberal culture may judge your action to be evil, the judicial system of a modern Western state may punish you for it, and, of course, we the authors and you the readers judge homicide to be wrong.

Our aim in this book is to show that when a person is violent, he is usually morally motivated to do what he does. Often, the victim shares the moral perspective of the perpetrator, and so do third parties from the perpetrator's subcultural reference group. But it's quite common for people to differ in their moral judgments. The person who violently retaliates for an affront to honor generally expects that others share his evaluation of the situation, and hence condone his acts. However, the honor motivation of the perpetrator is the same, regardless of whether or not his victim, his girlfriend, the other people at the party, the police, the prosecutor, the jury, the journalist, the public, or the law professor share his culture of honor perspective. If the potential perpetrator knows (and cares) that some of these other people do not share his sense of honor, he may restrain himself, or simply be more careful in planning to avenge his honor. But his honor is *his* honor, his motivation is *his* motivation, either way. His moral motivation may be more intense if he knows that all concerned will mock and disparage him if he fails to defend his honor, but will hold him in esteem and praise him if he does. Others' moral evaluations do matter to him – their evaluations affect his relationships with them. Moreover, as scientists, we can use the judgments of others from the perpetrator's subculture and reference group as one kind of evidence for *inferring* his motives (as we sometimes do in this book). But *a person may be sincerely and truly morally motivated to do something that many other people involved judge to be wrong.* If he doesn't take others' judgments into account, or his moral motives are so intense that he ignores others' condemnation of his act, he is nonetheless morally motivated. It is specifically the perpetrator's motives and intentions we are trying to explain, not everyone else's.

Of course, people may deploy moral language to justify violence that is actually motivated by amoral ends (Haidt, 2001; Tsang, 2002). However, justification presupposes relevant moral sentiments that others regard as legitimate: the actor seeking to justify his violence and those to whom he appeals take for granted that *if* his violence fits the moral standards to which he is appealing, it is moral. In other words, *justifications reveal the moral standards of those being appealed to* (Austin, 1956). So even if Machiavellian psychopaths are the perpetrators of some mayhem, any acceptance, legitimation, or praise of their violence is based on moral frameworks in which such violence can be construed as virtuous. Another way of putting this is that the moral justification in question could only have arisen and would only be accepted if it tapped into a valid framework for judging action and reflected a socially accepted moral motive in the local culture. Thus, even justifications are informative about the conditions under which some people would be morally motivated by culturally legitimate standards for relationships.

Pain and suffering are not intrinsically evil

In the present cultural historical context in which life, liberty, and the pursuit of happiness are the ultimate goals that humans "naturally" pursue, and should pursue, and hence are the most fundamental human rights, virtuous violence theory's proposition that most violence is morally motivated seems a contradiction in terms. It is axiomatic to contemporary Western folk psychology and folk ethics that the core of morality, reciprocity, and social reason consists of minimizing harm, especially to others. For example, Mikhail (2007) suggests that humans have a universal moral grammar, one of whose principles is a prohibition against "intentional battery." Gray et al. (2012) go further, arguing that all moral judgments derive from a cognitive template that involves a prohibition against one person intentionally harming another person.

Pain and suffering are aversive, by definition. But being aversive does not logically or empirically imply that experiencing them is evil. Pain and suffering can be morally commendable. In certain cultures in certain periods of history, and in certain contexts in a great many cultures, it is good to accept naturally occurring pain and suffering, to seek them out, or even to inflict pain and suffering on oneself. And throughout most of history people expected suffering – it was taken for granted as a natural, intrinsic, inevitable aspect of life.

> Late medieval European culture, for example, was notable for the tremendous *positive* significance identified in pain. Suffering was not to be dismissed, vanquished, or transcended: suffering was to be felt with an ever-deepening intensity... The use and application of pain ... were considered aspects of a teleological, all-embracing civilizing process. By approaching what one wished to avoid, argued medieval thinkers, one could perfect one's self.
>
> *(Cohen, 2010: 4)*

Across all domains of life,

> The logical conclusion deriving from the utility of pain was that the more it was inflicted, the better. What we now consider cruelty, such as slow, painful executions ... was often viewed as a force for betterment.
>
> *(Cohen, 2010: 260).*

Still more wonderfully, earthly pain, like the fires of Purgatory, purified the body to prepare and qualify it for Paradise. William of Auvergne, for example, asserted that pain can cleanse by burning away vice and cauterizing against temptation. Fire is ideally suited for this.

> Vice is too deeply embedded to be washed off, for it alters the very nature of mankind. To be removed, it must be destroyed, totally annihilated ... Like a surgeon's knife, it [fire] removes the sickness [sin] with all that surrounds it. Pain is therefore destructive of vice and constructive of internal strength. Working inward, so to speak, it obliterates evil.
>
> *(Cohen, 2010: 33)*

Late sixteenth- and early seventeenth-century Protestant religious manuals explained to and persuaded readers that suffering is good because it purifies, purges, and perfects; these manuals instructed readers that pain is "useful, refining, elevating, reassuring and even delightful" (Mayhew, 2009: 321).

If the experience of pain and suffering can be praiseworthy, can indeed be morally exalting, then it is logically and empirically false to posit that the foundation, source, or core of morality must be, or even could be, that inflicting pain and suffering is intrinsically evil. On the contrary, in some contexts they are good, and people are praised for suffering, even seeking and inflicting pain or suffering on themselves. Pain and suffering can be admired, praised, and revered as morally meritorious. Pain or suffering may provide opportunities to be virtuous, may be inherently virtuous, or may indexically demonstrate virtue. It is just a fact that pain, suffering, and moral goodness are not mutually exclusive; on the contrary, pain and suffering can be essential media for moral virtue. In contemporary Yap (Micronesia), for example, willingly assumed pain and the acceptance of suffering are indices of love and the capacity for compassion: suffering in the service of others is good because it shows that one sacrifices, and at the same time can appreciate others' suffering (Throop, 2010). To be a good person, one must suffer – suffering is necessary to make a person virtuous.

Our central concern in this book is with the moral motives for and virtuous evaluations of *perpetrating* pain and suffering on others or the self, not with the virtue of experiencing pain or suffering. But to make sense of our thesis, it is essential to acknowledge right off that people do not necessarily perceive pain and suffering to be inherently evil. To appreciate the plausibility of virtuous violence theory, it is necessary to realize that the painfulness of pain does not imply that the person experiencing the pain, the person causing the pain, or impartial third parties perceive that it is morally *evil* to experience pain, let alone immoral to cause the pain. The same is true of any kind of suffering, and even death: in many salient respects they are intrinsically aversive, but that does not mean they are judged as morally wrong, nor does it imply that causing suffering or death is intuitively felt or reflectively judged to be morally wrong. Pain is noxious, suffering is aversive. But that doesn't mean that pain or suffering must be psychologically, socially, or culturally evaluated as moral *evils*. The fundamental core of human moral psychology and most cultural-historical standards of virtue do *not* revolve around, let alone reduce to or develop out of, an ethics of not harming anyone.

Forerunners of virtuous violence theory and how it goes beyond them

More than a century ago, Westermarck (1908) surveyed what was known at the time about the world's cultures to catalog culturally legitimate practices involving moral sentiments condoning killing strangers (vol. I, p. 338); killing the aged and ill (vol. I, pp. 386–93); killing infants, including ancient Greek and Roman practices (vol. I, pp. 393–413); human sacrifice to the gods of the Greeks, Hindus, and many other cultures (vol. I, pp. 434–72); human sacrifice to accompany the dead (vol. I, pp. 472–6); and suicide (vol. II, pp. 229–64). However, Westermarck aimed to describe moral cultural practices and evaluative *responses* to actions – he was interested in how people *evaluate* violence. But virtuous violence theory goes further, positing that most violence is *motivated* by moral sentiments. Pinker (2011) made a similar suggestion, but his focus was primarily on the decline in violence over time. Hence, he did not investigate in depth what violence may be morally motivated *toward* – what its *aims* are. Our thesis is that moral sentiments are the most common proximate *motivations* for engaging in violence: the perpetrator's *intentions* are to realize ideal models for social relationships.

In this regard, our thesis converges with that of Black (1998; see also Cooney, 1998), who posits that most violence is moralistic insofar as it is "self-help," a form of "social control" that functions to restrict morally deviant behavior. However, Black's "pure sociology" explicitly excludes psychology and indeed acknowledges no persons at all, so he entirely and purposefully disregards motives, emotions, sentiments, judgments, or any sort of cognition, addressing violence purely in terms of societal structures and processes. His account is functional, addressing the social system-maintaining *effects* of violence. In contrast, virtuous violence theory is an account of the motivational *sources* and aims of violence. Moreover, whereas Black focuses on violence as moralistic punishment for transgression, we will demonstrate that beyond redressing wrongs, much violence creates or enhances social relationships, sustains or modulates social relationships, mourns the loss of a relationship, or simply *is* the relationship – is the substance, conduct, practice, process, or performance of the relationship.

Our approach is also congruent with that of Gould (2003), who argues that conflict – and violence in particular – occurs when people contest dominance and submission. Drawing on European historical records, Gould argues that conflicts are more frequent when social rank is contestable. Hence, formal organizations, precedence rules, well-established traditional cultural cues, and other explicit semantically formulated ranking principles reduce violence. Whereas Black (1998) is limited by his focus on violence as a form of redress, ignoring violence tied to the constitution, conduct, modulation, and termination of relationships, Gould (2003) is limited insofar as he only focuses on one kind of relationship – dominance. We will show that violence grows out of all four of the fundamental types of social relationships (Fiske, 1991, 1992) and that people are violent to constitute relationships in many ways, not merely to contest them. Similarly, Baumeister and colleagues (Bushman and Baumeister, 1998; Baumeister *et al.*, 1996) have argued that one motive for violence is "threatened egotism," and have found that people high in narcissism are especially prone to respond with violence to ego threats. As we will demonstrate in the book, in many cultures a great many people are often morally motivated to engage in violence in order to maintain their status. To the extent that narcissists believe they are particularly deserving of high status, they will be particularly sensitive to any provocation that threatens that status.

Research on a few specific kinds of violence have anticipated specific elements of virtuous violence theory's global claim that violence is morally motivated. Both Haidt (Graham and Haidt, 2011; Haidt and Bjorklund, 2008) and Baumeister (1997; Baumeister and Vohs, 2004) have argued that, within large groups, violence can take on moral or idealistic dimensions and overwhelm motives that would have previously restrained violence if it were built into an ideology, leading to many cases of mass killing and intergroup violence. Chirot and McCauley (2006) have argued that when people genocidally kill, rape, or drive out a whole category of persons, the perpetrators' motives are usually moral. In particular, they observe that perpetrators may feel that another group's presence or intermarriage pollutes their collective essence, making it necessary to wipe them out to purify and cleanse the endangered essence of the perpetrating group. Baumeister also argues that individual violence often occurs in response to perceived insults or slights, but he stops short of referring to these motives as "moral." Finkel has referred to these as "provocations" and "instigating triggers" in his work on intimate partner violence (Finkel *et al.*, 2012; Slotter and Finkel, 2011). Other studies of intimate partner violence have suggested that it is more likely to occur in societies that valorize violence by men against their partners and have established social norms to morally exculpate it (Dobash and Dobash, 1979; Jewkes, 2002). Researchers who study honor cultures have argued that aggression in these settings is the result of perceived affronts or threats to one's honor that must be rectified in order to salvage important social relationships (Nisbett and Cohen, 1996; Schneider, 1971). Jeremy Ginges and Scott Atran have argued that the motives of terrorists are quintessentially moral. They commit violence because they believe it is the right thing to do (Atran, 2010; Ginges and Atran, 2009; Ginges *et al.*, 2011). Virtuous violence theory expands on these works to describe the role of moral motives and how they function to regulate relationships across the entire spectrum of violent acts, ranging from everyday acts of harm to large-scale atrocities. The present book is the first to consider a wide range of violent practices across cultures and throughout history from a moral psychological perspective, describing in detail the psychosocial motives and relationship-regulating functions of violence.

Scope: what we are and are not discussing

Virtuous violence theory focuses on the intrinsic psychosocial motivation and cultural valuation of violence, not on environmental, technological, political, economic, or social structural factors. It is probably true that the frequency, intensity, and lethality of violence are greater the more people are accustomed and exposed to and intimately involved with guns and other weapons, hunting, butchering, childbirth, death, and burial; and the higher the local morbidity and mortality rates. Violence is more prevalent in the absence, inefficacy, or unruliness of police and judicial systems; in the face of desperate poverty and hunger; and when violent predation is the most feasible means of survival. But our concern here is the sociocultural relational psychology of violence, not its systemic social structural, political, economic, or environmental contexts. Once we understand the immediate moral motivations and social-relational functions of violence, future research will be needed to connect this sociocultural psychology to the environmental, macrostructural, historical, and technological factors that facilitate it.

Although this book looks at physical violence, we suspect that people have the same moral aims when they inflict other sorts of harm. Insults, taunting, and cursing often precede violence and are motivated by the same relational intentions that motivate the subsequent violence. Before or after harming a victim, perpetrators often take or destroy the victim's property. And violence is often intended to evoke fear, humiliation, and shame. So we think that most of our analyses could be extended to morally motivated non-corporeal harm. But our scope is large enough already – we cannot possibly encompass in this book all the distress that people intentionally inflict on each other. So we do not specifically address economic, material, emotional, or reputational harm, although we believe that future research will show that all sorts of harm can readily be encompassed by our framework.

Illegitimate, immoral violence

In this book we will show that most violence is intended to regulate relationships, and that perpetrators and most others perceive most of their relationship-regulatory violence to be consistent with their cultural rules. But not *all* violence is intended to regulate a relationship. If I desperately want a drink and I see that you are carrying a bottle of whisky, and so I stab you purely and simply in order to get the bottle, my assault is *not* morally motivated. There is no moral motivation for the criminal violence that drug addicts, starving people, and psychopaths do simply in order to get substances they want to satisfy their purely individual appetites. But even most criminal violence is morally motivated, and in every culture it turns out that only a tiny fraction of all violence is criminal. Across cultures and history, most violence is morally motivated to regulate relationships in a culturally prescribed manner.

People are human, and sometimes transgress relationships. Whether returning gifts or evenly matching an eye for an eye, people aren't always saints: sometimes they don't give back something that fairly matches what they received. People violate all facets of relationships, including rules for violence. Undetected or when circumstances prevent enforcement, the perpetrator of illegitimate violence may get away with it for a longer or shorter period of time, but the illegitimacy of the violence jeopardizes the relationship. Indeed, people often refuse to relate to cheaters, excluding and shunning them. Hence, illegitimate violence is a problematic, tenuous, risky way to regulate relationships. It does occur sometimes. But our goal in this book will be to convince you that, most of the time, the motives for violence are moral, and that most perpetrators aim to regulate relationships in accord with the implementations of the four RMs that are prescribed in their (sub)culture, reference group, or primary group.

People kill because they feel that the victim deserves to die. Usually, the motivation to harm or kill someone is moral: the perpetrator is moved by his or her sense of moral necessity. In short, most violence is virtuous, in the eyes of the perpetrator. It is difficult and traumatic to kill or maim, but people sometimes feel that they may or must hurt someone in order to create or regulate a vital social relationship with the victim, or with someone else. In short, people are violent when they feel that violence is necessary to constitute essential social relationships. This surprising discovery violates our intuitions about morality and violence, and it certainly contradicts most theories of morality, along with most theories of violence. But in this book we will analyze a great many kinds of violence that are morally motivated, in the sense that perpetrators mean to constitute or regulate the social relationships that are at stake, and they feel that violence is the right way to do so.

2 VIOLENCE IS MORALLY MOTIVATED TO REGULATE SOCIAL RELATIONSHIPS

Virtuous violence theory proposes that the perpetrator intends to harm or kill in order to constitute a social relationship to make it correspond with a prescriptive model of what the relationship ought to be – what it *must* be made to be. For our purposes, a social relationship consists of complementarity between the actions of the participants: each participant's actions fit previous actions by the other and presuppose "fitting" actions by the other(s), such that the actions of each are incomplete without the congruent action by the other(s). That is, the acts of each are part of a whole that none of them can bring off alone. We encompass in the terms "act" and "actions" not simply the morphology of movements, but also, crucially, the participant's intentions, moral judgments, and motives (often consciously experienced as emotions). Furthermore, each participant implicitly or explicitly aims to induce completion of her acts: she intends to motivationally *evoke* and morally *invoke* the congruent actions that will complete or dynamically sustain the jointly constructed pattern. That is, a participant *expects* the other(s) to do their part, in the predictive sense, in the hopeful sense, and in the evaluative sense of judging the others' actions according to how well they complete the intended gestalt. A football game is only football if the opposing players hit each other as hard as they can; the offense can only play offense, blocking and knocking down defenders, against a tackling defense.[1]

---

[1] Note that this definition allows for a person to perceive herself to be a participant in a social relationship with an imagined being, a deceased person, an animate, non-human

Fundamental ways of relating: the four elementary relational models

Relational models theory (RMT) posits that people in all cultures coordinate nearly all aspects of most social activities by four fundamental relational models (RMs) (Fiske, 1991, 1992, 2000; Fiske and Haslam, 2005). People use these implicit, intrinsically motivated RMs to generate, understand, and evaluate interaction. The models are communal sharing (CS), authority ranking (AR), equality matching (EM), and market pricing (MP). At this point, over 275 researchers have used a great variety of methods to study many social and cognitive phenomena in diverse cultures, and have published hundreds of experimental, ethnographic, interpretive, theoretical, analytic, and philosophical papers, dissertations, and books supporting, extending, or applying RMT (www.rmt.ucla.edu). An essential aspect of these models is the four fundamental motives that underlie most moral judgment, emotions, and behavior: unity, hierarchy, equality, and proportionality (Rai and Fiske, 2011).

Communal sharing: unity

We use CS models when we perceive people in the same group or dyad as undifferentiated and equivalent in a salient feature, while others are not. Families, teams, brotherhoods, military units, nationalities, ethnicities, and some close friendships are often organized by CS. The moral motive guiding CS models is unity. Unity is directed toward caring for and supporting the integrity of in-groups through a sense of collective responsibility and common fate. If someone is in need, we must protect and provide for that person; if someone is harmed, the entire group feels violated and must collectively respond. If an in-group member is contaminated or commits a moral violation, the entire group bears corporate responsibility and feels tainted and shamed until it cleanses itself. A threat to the group or its integrity, or to any member of it, is felt to be a threat to all. Unity is partially captured by conceptions of a moral circle (Singer, 1981) and the construct of moral inclusion–exclusion (Clayton and Opotow, 2003; Opotow, 1990; Staub, 1990), whereby only those who are included in the group are within the scope of moral concern.

being (e.g., a pet snail), or an inanimate object. All that is required is that the person expects the imputed partner to complete the relational gestalt.

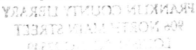

When motivated by CS unity, violence is morally praiseworthy if the victim is perceived as a potential threat or contaminant to the in-group. In other cases, violence creates the CS relationship, as when urban gangs and African militias "beat in" new members, or men violently initiate youths.

Authority ranking: hierarchy

When we rank or order individuals along a dimension, we are using an AR model. AR is a linear ordering of the relative position of individuals in a linear hierarchy, such as between dominant and subordinate individuals, between adults and children, among military officers, and among people of different castes, ages, or genders in many societies. The moral motive guiding AR models is hierarchy. Hierarchy is directed toward creating and maintaining linear ranking in social groups. Subordinates are motivated to respect, obey, and pay deference to the will of superiors, such as leaders, ancestors, or gods, and to punish those who disobey or disrespect them. Superiors, in turn, feel a sense of pastoral responsibility toward subordinates and are motivated to lead, guide, direct, and protect them. Unlike theories of social dominance (Sidanius and Pratto, 1999) or system justification (Jost et al., 2004), RMT does not take the position that hierarchies are inherently immoral, exploitive, or even undesirable. Nor do legitimate hierarchies emerge out of pure force or coercion. In many cultures, people perceive hierarchy as natural, inevitable, necessary, and legitimate (Fiske, 1991; Nisbet, 1993; Tiedens et al., 2007; Tyler and Lind, 1992). In our own lives, Hierarchy is experienced when we expect our edicts to be followed by those under our care, such as our children, students, or followers, or simply when we expect subordinates to show us the respect we deserve as their parents, teachers, or leaders. In turn, we feel morally obligated to guide, stand up for, look out for, and protect them. AR hierarchy motivates people to judge that superiors committing violence against subordinates is often acceptable and may even be praiseworthy if done to instruct or punish. For example, European and American schoolmasters used to consistently perform their instructional duties by striking pupils for errors or omissions; two hundred years ago, naval captains had crew members severely flogged for disobedience. The pupil's parents might fire a schoolmaster who did not discipline their children, while admirals might remove from command captains who failed to flog their crews to keep them in line. Conversely, subordinates' violence against superiors was very harshly punished: an eighteenth- or early nineteenth-century sailor who struck an officer might be executed.

AR consists of asymmetrical relationships that participants experience as natural, good, legitimate, and even necessary. Furthermore, like the other RMs, AR relationships are intrinsically motivated ends in themselves. Hence, AR is quite distinct from purely coercive instrumental relationships in which people pursue non-relational ends by controlling or manipulating others through force or control over resources. AR is also entirely different from power, if "power" only refers to the ability to get what one wants, even when others also want it, or despite others' resistance.

Equality matching: equality

When people use EM they keep track of whether they are even, or how many of something one owes the other. More technically, participants attend to additive interval differences in order to balance the relationship. EM is manifest in activities such as turn taking, in-kind reciprocity, even distributions and randomization procedures such as coin flipping. The moral motive guiding EM models is equality. Equality is directed toward enforcing even balance and in-kind reciprocity in social relations. It requires equal treatment, equal voice, equal opportunity, equal chance, even shares, even contributions, turn taking, and lotteries (e.g., for conscription, for a dangerous assignment, for choosing ends of the field in sports or in a duel). Equality provides the moral motivation for maintaining favor-for-favor forms of reciprocity and pursuing eye-for-an-eye forms of revenge. Thus, equality accounts for the sense of obligation we feel both in inviting people to our home after they have invited us to theirs, and in seeking to hurt people in exactly the same way they have hurt us, an eye for an eye, a tooth for a tooth. When terrorists attack Americans, the American military strikes back at the terrorists – and at those who harbor them.

Market pricing: proportionality

MP relations involve the use of ratios and rates to compare otherwise non-comparable commodities on a common metric, such as in the monetary exchanges between buyers and sellers in a marketplace, costs and benefits of a social decision, or utilities in a moral issue. The moral motive guiding MP models is proportionality. Proportionality is directed toward calculating and acting in accord with ratios or rates among otherwise distinct goods to ensure that rewards or punishments for each party are proportional to their costs, contributions, effort, merit, or guilt. Unlike our earlier example of the retributive equality of vengeance, US law does not prescribe that someone convicted of assault be assaulted in turn. Rather, the sentence should be proportionate to the crime in terms of the time the defendant must serve or the fine that must be paid. Similarly, in a number of cultures (e.g., ancient Egypt), people expect their fate in the afterlife to depend on the weighing of all their good and bad deeds on the scales of justice, implying a belief that the morality of acts of all kinds could be weighed on the same scale (Pritchard, 1954). The primary violation of proportionality is cheating, which we strictly define as referring to instances in which individuals attempt to gain benefits that, according to cultural standards, are not proportional to what they deserve. In the framework of proportionality, it is morally correct to inflict harm or to kill if the benefits outweigh the costs. In World War II, President Truman was advised that exploding atomic bombs over Hiroshima and Nagasaki was morally necessary in the cost-benefit calculus of winning the war with the fewest American casualties.

Cultural implementations of universal models

The universally shared, innate structures of the RMs are necessary but not sufficient to coordinate any aspect of any activity or to make any evaluation (whether intuitive and immediate, reflectively analyzed, or explicitly discussed). To realize any RM in any given situation people must have guides that specify which RM to use, and how, with whom, when, and with respect to what the RM operates. So, for example, to use CS to organize consumption, participants in an interaction must all know what resource is to be shared and who may share it, among many other specifications. Coordination according to AR depends on agreement as to the relative positions of each person in the rank ordering, when and how ranks are determined, and a great deal more. To use EM to coordinate work, people need to know who is participating; whether to divide the work evenly, take turns, or assign the work by lottery; what counts as a turn; the temporal intervals between turns; and so forth. MP cannot be implemented without specifying what is to be compared to what, in what proportion, and much more besides. The implementation of any RM is guided by cultural precedents, praxis, prototypes, paradigms, precepts, propositions, prescriptions, pronouncements, proverbs, and the like. The technical term for these cultural guidelines that specify how to implement a RM in a particular contest is *preos* (Fiske, 2000). No RM can be realized except with reference to preos.

What this means with respect to morality is that when people are realizing a RM, they are always realizing the RM according to cultural preos. Thus, *morality consists of intentions, motives, emotions, and judgments about realizing RMs according to cultural preos.* In other words, morality is regulating relationships to make them correspond to cultural implementations of RMs.

The same dyad or group may use different RMs at different times to organize different activities. For example, they might decide by CS consensus that it would be most efficient (MP) to take turns doing a task (EM), under the supervision of an expert (AR). Even at any given moment in time, different RMs may operate in the coordination of different aspects of the same interaction. So when a chief leads his men to kill an enemy to avenge a death, AR and EM are operating simultaneously with respect to different aspects of their action. If they hold everyone in the enemy group collectively responsible, so that they are indifferent to which individual they kill, CS is also operating at the same time. Then a judge (AR) or a jury of EM peers who have to reach a unanimous consensus verdict (CS) might encompass the entire event by sentencing the individual killer to a prison term proportionate to his crime (MP). As this example illustrates, the same RM may operate according to different cultural preos to organize distinct aspects of the social interaction.

Constitutive phases

The moral motives of each RM generate, shape, and preserve the social relationships a person needs in six ways. People usually perform these functions non-violently, but each function can also be performed by harming or killing someone, so for our present purposes we formulate these constitutive phases in terms of violence. Each of these six functions may be oriented toward first, second, or third parties. For example, you can redress and rectify a relationship by punishing yourself, punishing someone for something they did to you, or punishing someone for something they did to someone else.

1. **Creation:** violence that is intended to form new relationships, either between strangers or in a way that fundamentally changes a pre-existing relationship. Creation-based violence may establish a relationship among the perpetrators, between the perpetrator(s) and the victim(s), or between the perpetrator and one or more third parties.

2. **Conduct, enhancement, modulation, and transformation:** violence that comprises the relationship itself – enacting, testing, enforcing, reinforcing, enhancing, honoring, attenuating, or transforming it. In some cases, the relationship consists of violence. Examples are martial arts, contact sports, jousting, dueling, feuding, and religious self-torture. In feuding and related practices, each homicide or other act of violence reverses the "debt" or "balance." Conduct enhances the relationship when it brings the relationship closer to its ideal state, such as when partners in a CS relationship harm themselves in order to prove their love for one another. Conduct that changes the nature of an existing relationship in ways that do not create a fundamentally new relationship, such as when subordinates and superiors legitimately contest rank in an AR hierarchy, represents cases of modulation and transformation.

3. **Protection:** people's belief that they have a moral entitlement to protect themselves and their relationship partners. Defense-based violence in the context of an important relationship may be directed toward anyone who threatens the relationship, including the relationship partner. Pre-emptive violence to prevent people from threatening a relationship is protective of relationships in the same manner as defense-based violence, and pre-emptive violence can be used to signal future relational intentions or establish a strong reputation as a relational partner to be reckoned with. It is a warning. Such violence may also be aimed to make a person cease doing something that threatens the relationship, in which case its function is close to rectificatory violence. It may be aimed at second or third parties, and often both.

4. **Redress and rectification:** punishment, making someone "pay a penalty," retaliation, revenge, purification, restoration of honor,

violent sacrificial offerings, or self-punishments in response to transgressions that threaten relationships. The function is restorative, to
return the relationship to its ideal or equilibrium state. Along with
protection, this is probably the most common moral motivation for
violence.

5. **Termination**: unlike the previous relationship functions, violence not
   meant to create, protect or restore the relationship but to have it
   permanently cease. In some cases, this violence is meant to free someone from relational obligations that they can no longer fulfill, such as
   in cases of euthanasia or Japanese *seppuku*. In other cases, terminative violence is metarelational, meant to fulfill the perpetrator's obligations to one party by terminating a third party. Termination may
   also occur in cases where transformation cannot occur without the
   death of one of the parties, such as when the former subject becomes
   king by killing the incumbent. People may kill and die to end an
   unbearable relationship, such as love that cannot be fulfilled. Honor
   killing to eliminate a family's shame terminates the woman's relationship with her family but redresses the family's relationship with
   everyone else in the community. In some instances, potential future
   relationships may be terminated through violence, such as in cases of
   clitoridectomy or castration that reduce sexual pleasure or desire.

6. **Mourning**: action in response to the loss of an important relationship
   due to the other's departure, defection, or death. As we will discuss
   in Chapter 18, in many cultures people do violence to the self or
   others that is cathartic, convulsive, transcendent, or a generalized
   rage response to the loss of an important relationship. This is distinct
   from punitive violence; it has no rectificatory function. The persons
   being injured or killed are *not* being attacked because of any sense
   that they are in any way responsible for the death.

Each of these relationship-constitutive phases may motivate
relationship-regulating violence if cultural implementations of the relationships condone appropriate violence, and if countervailing social
bonds together with cultural, social, and practical factors do not outweigh the motivation to commit relationship-regulating violence. For
example, the members' infliction and the initiate's experience and stoic
endurance of the pain of a severe initiation *create or transform* a previous
relationship into a CS relationship between the initiate and the group
that initiates him, and/or an AR relationship between initiators and

initiates. Opponents in a feud, duel, or martial arts competition *conduct* their EM relationship by hurting or killing each other and *modulate* their AR rank through the results of the contests. The soldier or the parent who shoots an intruder and pre-emptively establishes his reputation for violent action is *protecting* his CS relationship with those he loves most. When a schoolmaster strikes a pupil for failing to follow instructions, he *redresses* and *rectifies* the AR relationship that the pupil transgressed. When a woman kills her partner to be with her new lover, she does so to *terminate* the old CS relationship that is preventing her from *creating* a new one. *Mourning* the death of a loved one, a Warramunga man would cut his own thighs deeply, and a Kwakiutl man would kill anyone of the same rank as the family member he mourned. As these examples indicate, a single act of violence may be motivated to perform multiple constitutive phases.

Depending on the cultural implementations of a relationship, violence may be essential for any of these constitutive phases, or it may be facultative. In most martial arts, participation in the relationship is inherently violent: the conduct of the relationship *is* violence. Likewise, in many societies the initiations of warriors absolutely entails inflicting pain on the initiates. Toward the middle of this continuum, nineteenth-century American and European parents and schoolteachers were fully entitled and expected to rap children's knuckles, twist their ears, or beat them (e.g., Muir, 2009), but, presumably, some parents and teachers shirked these duties without major repercussions. At the optional-permissive end of this continuum, a romantic couple could consensually agree to the mutual infliction of pain during love-making if they felt that it enhanced their bond (so to speak), but no one would hold it against them if they were gentle.

Metarelational models

In the simplest case, the social relationship that motivates violence is just a dyadic relationship between the agent and the victim of violence. But generally the links among multiple relationships are crucial to generating the violence, or suppressing it. For example, A does violence to V or refrains from violence to B in order to regulate A's relationship with C, or to regulate V's relationship with C. Prescriptive or proscriptive links among social relationships are called metarelational models (Fiske, 2011).

Metarelational models may involve many entailments or prohibitions other than violence, but in every case the configuration of relationships defines moral obligations imbued with regulative emotions. In a metarelational model, what people do or don't do in one of the component relationships has emotional, motivational, and moral implications for the other relationships. Some metarelational models involve configurations of four or even many more relationships that have strong implications for each other. Examination of many violence practices will show that certain metarelational models require a person to harm another in order to create, conduct, protect, redress, terminate, or mourn relationships with others. Conversely, many other metarelational models restrict violence from occurring in a given dyad because of its implications for the other relationships linked to it.

For example, when X is Y's enemy, Z's violence against X enhances Z's relationship with Y. That is, it makes Y and Z allies or even "brothers" in common opposition to X. On the largest scale, joining in the patriotic defense of the nation (or in the nation's grand aggression) bonds the fighters. Any wounds or disabilities the warriors suffer in fighting for the nation binds them still more strongly together as patriots. On the other hand, when X is Y's kin, friend, or ally, if Z is Y's kin, friend, or ally, this combination of relationship morally inhibits Z from harming X – even if Z has other moral motives to do so, such as motives to regulate his own dyadic relationship with X.

It is helpful to represent metarelational models graphically, along with their verbal articulation. We use an arrow to represent violence in a relationship, and parallel lines to represent other relationships metarelationally linked to the violent relationship. (To be accurate, the arrows should be shown within parallel lines indicating the relationship in which the violence occurs, but, for simplicity in the first four figures, we let the arrow represent violence understood to occur within a relationship.) P stands for perpetrator (or potential perpetrator); V, for victim (or potential victim); O, for other; and A, for another person in the metarelational model. Hence, Figure 2.1 depicts a dyad in which a perpetrator is violent to a victim. For example, if the victim V stole money that belonged to a partnership with the perpetrator P, then P might be morally motivated to assault V to rectify the relationship.

A person's relationship with someone may motivate him to harm or kill someone else. Figure 2.2a graphs this: if the perpetrator, P, is motivated to regulate a relationship to the other, O, and doing so

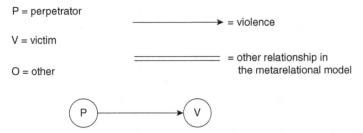

Figure 2.1: The primary motivation for violence is to constitute a social relationship

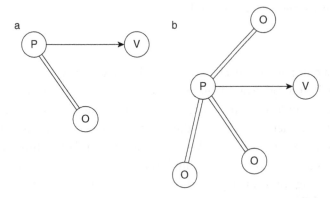

Figure 2.2: Relationships with others may motivate violence against a third party

a: A metarelational model in which P's relationship with O is constituted by P's violence against V.

b: Multiple or complex metarelational models may magnify A's propensity to violence against V.

requires P to do violence to the victim, V, then P may hurt or kill V for the sake of P's relationship with O. For example, a soldier may obey a superior officer who commands her to shoot someone, or an ice-hockey player may fight an opponent to impress his girlfriend. The more critical P's relationship is with O, and the more numerous such relationships P has with others that demand violence against V, the more likely it is that P will resort to violence and the more severe the violence will be. Figure 2.2b can represent two distinct configurations: first, it can depict multiple independent metarelational models, each of which makes P's relationship with a single O morally contingent on P's violence against V. Second, it can represent one complex metarelational model in which P's relationships with each and all of the Os are contingent on P's violence against V. For example, suppose that P has joined with all of

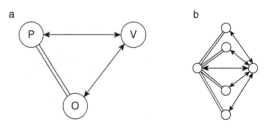

Figure 2.3: Indirect ties may potentiate multiparty violence, or inhibit violence
  a: A metarelational model in which P's bond with O together with O's enmity to V prescribes that P be violent to V.
  b: The effects are enhanced when there are multiple or complex metarelational models.

the Os in a compact that each of them will kill one enemy soldier, or each of them will fight one round against V in a martial arts contest.

A person's allegiance to a kinsman often motivates him to fight the kinsman's enemies. That is, there may be a metarelational model linking violence between O and V with a communal relationship between O and P such that P is morally bound to attack V. My friend's enemy is my enemy. Figure 2.3a depicts this. If P has many allies who are all fighting with V, either separately or within an integrated metarelationship, P is even more likely to feel morally motivated to harm or kill V. On the other hand, the friend of my friend(s) is my friend – even if I am angry at him. Although he has committed a grave offense against me, I don't want to kill my daughter's husband, especially if he is also my brother's godfather and my priest's son. That's what Figure 2.3b graphs.

Figure 2.3 also helps us consider the nature of alliances. A potential perpetrator's capacity and propensity to successfully use violence against a victim depends on whether others will support her against her victim, or vice versa (Gould, 2003: 61). One important case is that in humans and many non-human species, dominance rank depends on the rank and number of allies that an animal can count on to support him in conflicts with competitors (de Waal, 1982; Fiske, 2011). Conversely, the outcomes of contests of rank between any two persons – especially the leaders of opposing coalitions or groups – spread to the AR relations between their respective allies: when a leader falls, his supporters fall with him (Gould, 2003: 150–61). Hence, violence often propagates through interlocking metarelational models. Gould, (2003: 155–61) demonstrates that Corsican homicides in 1835–1914

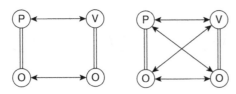

Figure 2.4: Violence-enhancing metarelational models involving four to six relationships among four persons

and twentieth-century homicides in France, Italy, and Finland correlate highly with regime changes; when a leader falls, his followers become vulnerable to vendetta killings by everyone they have harmed or offended.

These metarelational moral motives concatenate and extend recursively, so that, for example, my brother's enemy's brother is my enemy, as depicted on the left-hand side of Figure 2.4. At the same time, usually my brother's enemy is my enemy and my brother's enemy's brother is my brother's enemy. The right-hand graph in Figure 2.4 depicts this.

A person may be motivated to violence with the intention to perform any of the six constitutive phases of any of the four RMs and their corresponding moral motives. Furthermore, a person's relationship-constitutive moral motives may be aimed at the relationships of the person herself, her partner(s), or her partner(s) partners, and so on (see Black, 1998: ch. 7).[2] Figure 2.5 illustrates some of the possibilities. (In this figure we show the parallel lines around the arrow to remind us that the violence regulates the relationship between perpetrator and victim.) Figure 2.5a represents a person who harms himself in order to constitute a relationship with another person; for example, a suicide intended to terminate a relationship that the perpetrator dishonored. Another example is self-injury intended to elicit a partner's care or evoke the partner's guilt. Figure 2.5b represents a perpetrator committing violence against a victim to constitute the relationship between the two of them; for example, a knight doing battle against another knight to create an AR relationship between the two of them and establish their relative positions, or a man attacking someone who insulted his honor, in order to rectify their EM relationship.

---

[2] In principle, this recursion need not end with the third person; it could go on indefinitely, and probably sometimes does extend to the fourth or even fifth step. But the moral motivation rapidly grows weaker with each step.

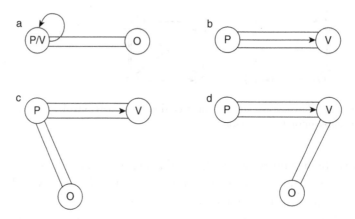

Figure 2.5: Violence to constitute the perpetrator's relationship with another, and with a second or third party

Figure 2.5c shows a perpetrator motivated to regulate the relationship between himself and the victim, and at the same time regulate the relationship between himself and another person. For example, a man might whip his son for disobedience to redress the father's relationship with his son, while enhancing the father's relationship with his pastor, who approves of discipline enforced by corporal punishment. Along with regulating the relationship between perpetrator and victim, the aim of violence may also be to regulate the relationship between the victim and another person, even when the perpetrator has no relationship with the other person (Figure 2.5d). For example, a father could whip his son to punish him for taking a stranger's horse, rectifying his son's relationship with the stranger. In such cases, the perpetrator simultaneously intends his violence to constitute his relationship with the victim: the father is reasserting his authority over his son.

Violence often regulates the perpetrator's relationship with the victim, the perpetrator's relationship with another, and the victim's relationship with that other, as Figure 2.6a graphs. For example, a father whips his son for taking his brother's horse, rectifying the relationship between the brothers and enhancing the father's relationship with the son who took the horse and at the same time the father's relationship with the son whose horse was taken. Or a man may whip his son because his son has disobeyed the man's wife.

The same act of violence can regulate any number of relationships; Figure 2.6b shows, for example, violence that metarelationally

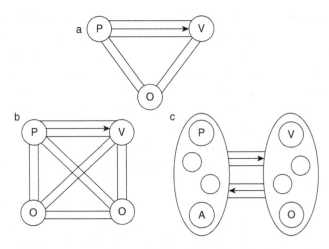

Figure 2.6: Violence to constitute multiple relationships simultaneously

constitutes P's relationship with V, P's relationship with an O, that O's relationship with a second O, that second O's relationship with V, and V's relationship with the second O. This is the configuration that motivates a woman to kill her husband's lover; this terminates the wife's competitive relationship with her husband's lover, reconstitutes the killer's own relationship with her husband, terminates the husband's relationship with his lover, and rectifies the husband's relationship with his lover's husband, the lover's relationship with *her* own husband, and the killer's relationship with her friend, the lover's husband. The same graph could diagram the motives for a man initiating his son into manhood: the violence creates a CS relationship bonding his son and himself, while bonding each of them with other adult men and initiates, while at the same time transforming the mother's relationships with all of them. Likewise, a naval captain who has a sailor lashed for disobeying a lieutenant is rectifying the AR relationship between the lieutenant and the sailor, while enhancing the AR relationship between himself and the lieutenant, sustaining the AR relationship between the sailor and himself, and sustaining the AR relationship between the punished sailor and other officers and between other sailors and other officers, while evoking the sailor's solidarity with other sailors who have been lashed for similar offenses, and so forth. When he orders the bo's'n to flog a man, a good early modern naval ship captain aims to regulate many relationships, all critical to his legal and moral mandate to maintain discipline and make his crew into an effective fighting force. Many moral motives and obligations converge to impel him to order the flogging, even if he hates to do it. Whether the wife or the husband kill immediately – let us say, "impulsively" – without self-conscious reflection, or whether they carefully and thoroughly articulate all of the relational considerations and metarelational implications involved before they kill, they may have multiple convergent or divergent motives, most of which are moral.

As everyone knows, and as we shall consider in Chapters 7 and 16, people are often morally motivated to do violence on behalf of their own group against another group. Rugby and ice-hockey teams are hitting opponents with whom they typically have no personal dyadic relationships: it's one team against another. Nazi officers killing Jews were acting as group to group, motivated by the relationships they perceived between the groups. It's the same with feuding clans or warring nations. Figure 2.6c depicts this. For example, violence between groups is predicated on the EM relationship between the two groups, and at the same time the CS relationships within each group, so that the violence of a P against a V in the other group balances out the violence of an other (O) in V's group against another (A) in P's group, because the actors within a group are interchangeable due to their CS equivalence. At the same time, P's vengeance enhances his CS unity with A, and V's CS unity with O, while rectifying the EM equality between O and A and between P and V.

Obviously, in the dynamics of the cycle of EM vengeance, each successive act of violence may motivate a further, reciprocal act that the agents each perceive as rectifying what they regard as a previous imbalance in the relationship. This recursion is a kind of serial metarelational model extended over time. These diagrams are merely static images of what is actually a dynamic process in which successive actions transform relationships sequentially and without end.

Any social action, including violence, may be motivated with the aim of performing any one or several of the six constitutive phases of any of the RMs *for any number of relationships*. Any act, including a violent act, may have constitutive phases that differ across relationships: for example, the same act may create one relationship while sustaining a second relationship, rectifying a third, and terminating a fourth. For example, a soldier who kills enemies attacking his unit sustains his AR relationship with the officer commanding the unit, modulates his EM relationship with the enemy by avenging their killing of his comrades the day before, enhances his CS relationship with his fellow soldiers in the unit (both the dead and the living), wins a medal and is promoted over them to create a new AR relationship with them and the replacements who join the unit, but terminates his relationship with his pacifist girl-friend who is appalled and disillusioned by his violence. Or consider a knight in the age of chivalry who, inspired by pride and love for the lady he champions, violently overcomes an opponent, thereby creating an AR relationship of superiority over the defeated opponent, enhancing his CS relationship with the lady whose ribbon he carries, paying off his MP creditors with the purse awarded to him as victor, being awarded a position as EM peer of his fellow knights, who admire his valor and skill, and setting in motion EM vengeance by the brother of the defeated knight, who feels humiliated by the knight's excessive display of pride in his victory.

These diagrams illustrate the nature of the moral motivations for violently constituting relationships, and demonstrate a simple analytic tool for exploring motivations for violence. But they certainly do not exhaust the metarelational model configurations that motivate violence. Many of the diagrams simplify the metarelational psychology of virtuous violence by representing violence occurring in only one direction, or in only one or two dyads. And these diagrams are limited to depictions of only four persons (and just two groups), while the psychology of metarelational models may connect quite a few persons in many relation-ships – as we shall consider in Chapter 6 on honor violence and its exemplification in the *Iliad*. In any case, it is abundantly clear that the aim of violence is often to regulate relationships not just with the victim but also with others. We can't understand violence without recognizing the metarelational configurations that morally motivate it. In Chapter 22 we return to metarelational models, showing that other metarelational models have the opposite effect: they generate moral motives to inhibit violence.

By reconceptualizing violence as morally motivated, virtuous violence theory enables us to better describe and explain a diverse array of violent acts, including war, terrorism and self-sacrifice, suicide, violent sports, execution, corporal punishment, torture, vengeance, honor-related violence, retributive justice, violence during initiation rites, self-mortification, violence committed under orders, execution, mass killing, human sacrifice, and headhunting, as well as the valorization of the violence committed or commanded by gods and heroes. In these culturally informed relationships, by killing and by being killed, as well as by being liable to be killed or obligated to kill, participants constitute and vividly display their social relationships. In the sources describing these particular practices, there is ample evidence that the primary motives for violence are at the same time subjectively moral – people feel they *must* harm or kill others simply because it's the right thing to do – and also moral in the framework of relationship regulation theory, where morality is the regulation or constitution of vital social relationships.

3 DEFENSE, PUNISHMENT, AND VENGEANCE

[Injun Joe and the Spaniard, hiding in the dark outside the home of the Widow Douglas – Injun Joe speaks first]

"I tell you again, as I've told you before, I don't care for her swag – you may have it. But her husband was rough on me – many times he was rough on me – and mainly he was the justice of the peace that jugged me for a vagrant. And that ain't all. It ain't a millionth part of it! He had me *horsewhipped*! – horsewhipped in front of the jail, like a nigger! – with all the town looking on! *Horsewhipped*! – do you understand? He took advantage of me and died. But I'll take it out of *her*."

"Oh, don't kill her! Don't do that!"

"Kill? Who said anything about killing? I would kill *him* if he was here; but not her. When you want to get revenge on a woman you don't kill her – bosh! you go for her looks. You slit her nostrils – you notch her ears like a sow!"

"By God, that's ———"

"Keep your opinion to yourself! It will be safest for you. I'll tie her to the bed. If she bleeds to death, is that my fault? I'll not cry, if she does."

Mark Twain, The Adventures of Tom Sawyer

Defense and punishment

Most contemporary theories of violence implicitly limit their scope to violence that the theorist unreflectively construes as illegitimate: that is, most are attempts to explain "bad" violence (Betz, 1977). But there are two constitutive phases of violence that, in varying forms and degrees, are almost universally recognized as morally acceptable, justified, and even obligatory: protection in the form of defense and redress in the form of punishment. Yet most theories of "violence" exclude or simply ignore defense and punishment, providing no explanation for them or not integrating the account of them into the overall theory of "violence," which is a priori defined to exclude them.

When someone threatens a person's life, property, or domain, it is generally agreed in most cultures that the person may use violence to defend herself. Insofar as the victim is simply protecting her life and body, in important respects her violence is not virtuous – it is simply self-preservation. However, people always recognize some rights in their persons and property, rights that entitle a person to protect what is theirs. Hence, threats or harm to herself, her family, or her property are transgressions against the victim, and defensive violence is virtuous. Thus, when humans violently defend their children, spouses, family, buddies, or allies, this defense is virtuous violence. It is virtuous because protecting partners is the core of the relationship. It is a moral obligation to protect one's partners, and throughout history humans have accorded great honor to heroes who aggressively defend themselves, their families, or their communities. A nation invaded is entitled to violently resist its attackers, and might be justified in aiming to destroy the invading nation to avenge the invasion and ensure its future safety. Defense is a very common moral motivation for violence.

The other most common constitutive phase of violence is redress and rectification of the transgression of a relationship. People often feel compelled to respond with violence when they feel that they have been violated. Moreover, when someone commits a transgression against another person, most third parties feel that the transgressed party is entitled to retaliate and punish the transgressor. The proximate cognitive and social psychological emotions and motives for punitive violence have little to do with practical considerations of deterrence functions. That is, as far as conscious intentions go, we generally do not punish people who harm us in order to prevent them from harming us in the future, or to signal to others that they will be punished for the same actions. In a series of experiments, Kevin Carlsmith, John Darley, and Paul Robinson (Carlsmith, 2006; Carlsmith *et al.*, 2002; Darley *et al.*,

2000) found that laypeople's judgments of how much to punish were largely insensitive to factors that would be important for deterring future crime, such as the likelihood of the crime being detected when committed or the likelihood of the perpetrator repeating the crime in the future. Instead, judgments of appropriate punishment were primarily driven by factors such as the seriousness of the crime or whether the perpetrator had good or evil motives for committing the crime. These data suggest that people are retributive. We punish harm-doers when we believe that it is fundamentally just to do so and when we are morally outraged by what they have done – not when it is rational to do so in terms of preventing future harm.

In many cases, defense and punishment coincide. Police, body-guards, security personnel, and peace-keeping "forces" have a duty to stop criminals and defend civilians, even when they have to use force to do so. Prosecutors, judges, juries, jailors, and executioners have a duty to impose penalties on criminals, including violent penalties. When a police sniper shoots an armed kidnapper, or a jury sentences a serial killer to death, they are following their civic duty to enforce the law. When peace-keeping forces shoot a suicide bomber driving through a checkpoint, they are protecting the innocent. When a homeowner shoots a threatening intruder in order to protect his wife and children, his motivation is moral and most third parties would approve of his violence. Harming transgressors to "enforce" the law is virtuous when necessary or required by law. If someone starts to hit you, you are entitled to defend yourself and retaliate by hitting back – and you are likely to be quite morally motivated to do so. In many cultures, if someone kills a man's brother, he is absolutely obligated to avenge the death by killing the killer, or killing one of the killer's brothers – and his moral motivation to do so will be ferocious, since his family's honor and safety depend on his unmitigated vengeance.

Vengeance

In 1991, a fight between children of the El-Hanashat and Abdel-Halim clans in Egypt ended in two deaths, sparking a blood feud. The most recent murders were in 2002, when twenty-two El-Hanashat members were gunned down. In response, a surviving El-Hanashat stated,

"No matter what sacrifices it takes, we are determined to kill as
many of them [Abdel-Halims] as were murdered."

(Halawi, 2002)

"Vengeance" is simply a term used to describe retributive punishment
that either observers or the modern state deem as illegitimate. Persons
who perceive themselves to be the victim of a transgression often want
to hurt the transgressor in retribution. Typically, allies and other third
parties also want to violently punish major transgressors. The desire to
punish transgressors is universal and usually intense, though at times
other motives may counteract or prevail against punitive moral
motives. In most cultures, in many relationships, the most natural,
intuitive, satisfying punishment for the grave transgression of any
relationship is corporal violence, such as flogging or execution for
theft, heresy, or homicide. And in many cultural implementations of
many relationships, it is common for people to be morally motivated to
hit people to punish them for even relatively small infractions, such as
damaging property or failing to learn a school lesson. In stateless
societies, honor-based retaliatory violence and retribution by kinship
groups and alliances are major causes of morbidity and mortality. In
contrast, the modern state prohibits or restricts self-help retaliatory
violence, claiming for itself the authority to violently enforce the laws
that delimit relationships among citizens and between citizens and the
state. But modern Western states, especially, are diminishing their use
of violence to enforce the law and increasingly restricting citizens' rights
to use violence to regulate their relationships with each other; this is one
of the major causes of the decline of violence (Durkheim, 1973, 1997;
Pinker, 2011).

Yet across human societies and history, the moral obligation to
violently rectify transgression is widespread. For example, in ancient
China, "The Confucian school identified proper vengeance as a highly
moral act that was obligatory to uphold or validate the personal ties that
created human society... The violence of revenge was considered to be a
fundamental constituent of the Confucian moral order and closely identified with the violence of legal punishments" (Lewis, 1990: 87). Anyone
who reads novels or plays, watches television, or sees movies constantly
encounters psychologically plausible depictions of moral motives for
vengeful violence: violent retributive justice in response to previous
transgressions is one of the most common themes in human stories.

Indeed, morally motivated violent vengeance and retributive punishment are so ubiquitous that they deserve a book of their own; fortunately, that book has already been written (twice: Henberg, 1990; Zaibert, 2006; see also Cottingham, 1979).

Metarelational retribution

> Well my homeboy had bought some coke, and he said it wasn't good. So I told him I would go and fix it. I met the dude [who sold the bad cocaine] in my neighborhood, and it all went to shit. I told him, "Hey, if you're going to buy drugs to sell, you need to get good shit. You don't fuck around with this shit." He then pulled out a small gun, I think it was a .380. But I had the advantage because I think he was all fucked up on coke. I told him, "vato (man), what you did, I'm just coming over to fix it." That's when I slapped the gun and I already had mine on him and boom.
>
> *(Valdez* et al., *2009: 299)*

As this example illustrates, a third party in a metarelational model may be the perpetrator of violent punishment; in this case, the gang leader took AR responsibility to look out for and stand up for his "homeboy" (gang member), killing a drug dealer for violating a MP relationship with the homeboy. At an abstract level, the metarelational configuration operating here is similar to that which generates punitive violence when a chief, a king, or a modern state enforces laws protecting citizens from being cheated in business or sales.

Likewise, in certain cultures, AR relationships are defined by the obligation of subordinates to avenge the killing or humiliation of a master. Warring-States China was an example: in one indicative text, "the obligation to avenge a murdered lord is treated as so absolute that to fail to do so is tantamount to killing him oneself... The obligation to avenge is one of the basic elements of the bond between lord and retainer or father and son, and the man who fails to perform that obligation dissolves the ties that linked him to the deceased" (Lewis, 1990: 81–2). Thus, "avenging an ancestor is a moral obligation and a supremely worthy act" (Lewis, 1990: 83). Conversely, Qin law defined a moral principle of "mutual implication" or collective responsibility (*lian zuo*), according to which "punishment for certain serious crimes did not end with the individual but was extended to his family, neighbors, and in the case of an official to his immediate superiors, subordinates, or the man who recommended him to office" (Lewis, 1990: 91). Anyone implicated in a serious crime in any of these ways was liable to be executed. In other words, the AR relationship defined and constituted a CS group that was collectively obligated to undertake violent retribution for killing their superior, and, conversely, to be collectively punished for rebellion or malfeasance.

Violence due to conflicting models

There are many reasons for people to violate a relationship, potentially evoking violent retribution from the person whom they have trans-gressed against. One of the most interesting to consider here is that the partners in a relationship may each be using a different model to generate his own action and evaluate the relational coordination. In such cases, each participant perceives his own action as moral, but the other's as transgressive. If A perceives a road as a public right of way, in CS, while B perceives the road as on his purchased property, under MP, they might come to blows when A uses the road. One such conflict between disparate RMs generated the violence between nineteenth-century cattlemen in the United States who saw the land in CS terms as open range, and farmers who homesteaded and fenced the land. Similarly, when an imperial official perceives himself as a rightful AR authority over his colonial subjects, while those purported "subjects" see themselves as his human equals in EM terms, the result may be mutual violence. In such instances, each sees his own violence as prop-erly punitive of the perceived violation of the RM he is using, while seeing the other's violence as a flagrant further violation. Or two people may be interacting using the same model, but implemented differently. Suppose that A perceives that it's his turn to channel the water into his field to irrigate it, but B perceives that it's *his* turn; the contention may escalate to violence. Thus, sometimes *both* participants in a relationship may be morally motivated to violently punish the other because their perceptions of the relationship are discordant, and hence each perceives the other as the transgressor whose initial misdeed is further com-pounded by his illegitimate violence.

Protection and redress are the most common constitutive motivations for moral violence, yet it seems to be precisely because defense and punishment are so clearly moral that they are often excluded or mischaracterized when philosophers and social scientists define violence as the "immoral" or "illegitimate" use of force or harm. Meanwhile, vengeance is also misunderstood when it is a priori distinguished as immoral.

We will see in subsequent chapters that the constitutive phases of protection and redress are common components of motivations for violence. But these are only two of the constitutive phases that generate moral violence – there are four others. The crucial conceptual point that has not been widely acknowledged is that once one recognizes that people are morally motivated to violently protect and redress relationships, it becomes clear that people are also morally motivated to do violence to perform the other constitutive phases: creation, conduct, termination, and mourning. Every aspect of relationship regulation may motivate violence. Although in this book we will focus on violent practices whose motivation is less obviously moral than defense, punishment, and vengeance, these obviously moral aspects of constituting relationships should be kept in mind throughout.

4 THE RIGHT AND OBLIGATION OF PARENTS, POLICE, KINGS, AND GODS TO VIOLENTLY ENFORCE THEIR AUTHORITY

Here is a Chinese story that takes place in the Zhou dynasty (1256–1046 BCE), as set down in the third century CE:

> A man, Ho, offered a jade matrix as a gift to King Li, and later again to King Wu. Each king's jeweler failed to recognize the gem in the matrix, and each king ordered one of Ho's feet amputated for the apparent insult. Hearing that Ho was weeping, King Wu sent a retainer to discover why. The retainer inquired, "Many people in the world have had their feet amputated – why do you weep so piteously over it?" He replied "I do not grieve because my feet have been cut off. I grieve because a precious jewel is dubbed a mere stone, and a man of integrity is called a deceiver. This is why I weep."
>
> *(Han Fei Tzu, c. 235 CE; quoted in Collins, 1974: 415–16)*

Ho grieved that an act of deferential respect had been mistaken for an offense, while taking it for granted that a king may order his foot amputated for insulting him.

Cultural implementations of AR very often empower and obligate superiors to hurt subordinates. For long periods of history, men have been entitled to strike or beat their wives and force them to have sex; parents have been entitled to whip their children; schoolmasters have exercised the right to rap their pupils' knuckles, twist their ears, or cane them; military officers have been authorized to strike or flog soldiers and sailors; slave-owners have been freely permitted to beat and rape slaves; and, in general, elites have had a great deal of latitude to inflict physical abuse on lower social classes. Often superiors have the authority to harm at their whim, merely to enact their authority: violence is an integral component of the conduct of these AR relationships. Much more widespread is the authority for the corporal punishment of disrespect and, especially, disobedience: violence is the crucial, prototypical, traditional means for redressing transgressions of AR. These are not just permissions: superiors are often *required* to inflict corporal punishment as part of the correct performance of their duties. That is, in many AR contexts in many cultures, the necessary, natural, and proper exercise of authority entails inflicting pain on subordinates, sometimes to the point of severe distress – and sometimes so as to inflict permanent injury or death.

Durkheim (1973/1899–1900) posited that the more absolute the authority of the ruler, the harsher the punishments he imposes. Subsequent research has supported and extended his thesis. The greater the difference in rank, the stronger is the moral support for violence against those far below and the stronger the moral condemnation for violence against those far above (Cooney, 2009: 186). In post-Han ancient China, for example, "the power of emperor, mandarin, family head, were indeed upheld by force – above all by beating (even to the point of death), with bamboo sticks" (Collins, 1974: 430). Although in modern states all citizens are legally equal, in fact, violence committed against low-status people by high-status people, against outsiders by insiders, or within "close" relationships, is punished by the judicial system much less severely than violence by low-status people against high-status people, by outsiders against insiders, or toward people in more "distant" relationships (Cooney, 2009). In some cultural contexts, violence by high-status insiders against low-status outsiders with whom the perpetrator has an intimate relationship, such as by masters against slaves, is often applauded. Moreover, people commonly judge that superiors have considerable moral license to harm or kill subordinates at will, and especially to order subordinates to put themselves in harm's way. Conversely, any violence by inferiors against their masters is severely, immediately, and brutally punished (Cooney, 2009: 36–62). Indeed, the least violence by a subordinate against a superior is a profound and fundamental violation of the AR relationship (Rai and Fiske, 2011), meriting extreme and often immediate punishment.

Of course, it is a fact that sometimes people – especially psychopaths – use violence purely instrumentally to control others. But amoral coercive force is not especially common and is not what we are analyzing here. Rather, we are illuminating culturally informed AR relationships in which authorities have the *right* or the *duty* to violently conduct and enforce their authority.

Corporal punishment of children

The earliest and most basic AR relationship is between children and adults, particularly their parents. In early civilizations such as Shang China, ancient Mesopotamia, Old and Middle Kingdom Egypt, pre-colonial Yoruba and Benin, Classic Maya, pre-conquest Aztec and Inca, adults physically punished children for disobedience and for sub-standard performance (Trigger, 2003: 668). Likewise, US parents have long used punishments such as whipping, isolating, and depriving children of food (Greven, 1977; McLoughlin, 1971). In contemporary America, many parents, especially conservative Christians, believe that some forms of corporal punishment of children are appropriate and indeed good for children (Ellison *et al.*, 2011; Gershoff *et al.*, 1999; Guarendi, 1991; Knox, 2010; Martin, 2009; Strauss and Donnelly, 2001; Vittrup and Holden, 2009; Wilcox, 2004). Moreover, in their eyes, corporal punishment is essential to upholding parental authority, where respect and obedience are core moral values based on tradition and the Bible. It fact, as recently as the year 2000, corporal punishment was the modal practice in America: In various nationally representative samples of contemporary Americans, 94% of parents of 3- to 5-year-old children reported that they had hit their child in the past year, and 67–85% of mothers of 2-year-old children said they had spanked their children in the previous week; those who had spanked their children reported a mean of 3.2 times the previous week (Straus, 2000). In 1968, 94% of Americans believed that "a good hard spanking is sometimes necessary," and in the 1990s, more than two-thirds still believed that (Straus, 2000). Analyses of large representative samples of ethnographies show that in about three-fourths of the world's cultures, parents or other adults physically punish children by slapping, spanking, hitting, beating, scalding, burning, pushing, pinching, or switching (Levinson, 1989: 28). And these parents feel it's what they *should* do to raise morally responsible children.

It was routine for schoolmasters in Europe and America to casually strike or formally whip their pupils, even young children.

"From antiquity to the early modern period, the methodical infliction of pain was conceived as a helpmate to learning and memorizing" (Traninger, 2009: 53). To help children remember the consequences of felony, seventeenth-century French parents brought children to public executions and caned them there; in Brandenburg, people beat children on the parish borders to help them remember where the boundary lay (p. 55). And in early modern Europe, it was still widely taken for granted that learning Latin necessarily entailed whipping (Traninger, 2009). But this was not limited to Latin.

> For the beating of children outside the home there was a clear tendency to grant general license: it was numbered among the typical duties of the *magistri* [teacher] or the school master. . . The use of violence in the school was the expression of *potestas* [legitimate authority], which had been invested in the schoolmaster, and not the application of illegitimate *violencia*. . . Both the *ferula* [cane] and *virga* [switch] became the stock items of any European classroom. They became the insignia, the iconographical attributes of the pedagogue as well as the emblems of scholastic discipline.
>
> *(Traninger, 2009: 42)*

While observing the caning of young pupils, other students were sometimes required to sing hymns to the rhythm of the beating (p. 55). Well into the twentieth century, many European and American teachers struck pupils on the knuckles for inattention or failure to learn their lessons; teachers and parents caned or whipped children for disobedience or disrespect (e.g., Muir, 2009; Wilcox, 2004).

This AR violence consists of more than just punishment for infractions – it is felt to be the morally necessary and natural assertion of authority. In these culturally informed AR relationships, a superior is or was entitled to inflict pain to show his displeasure, or simply to exercise his arbitrary authority. Even today, drill sergeants and coaches exercise legitimate power to inflict pushups, laps around the track, or climbing the stadium steps until recruits or players suffer from excruciating cramps, and beyond.

The AR relationship between parents and their children is re-enacted in other social contexts, licensing and requiring violent enforcement of quasi-parental authority. In the Eastern Congo,

Mai Mai militiamen say that their commanders are morally entitled to punish them for disobedience, at least when their commands are legitimate. Many of the soldiers consider the command structure to be paternalistic. Commanders are like fathers and as such have to be obeyed implicitly. Speaking about his superiors, one respondent said,

> "I am like his son. . . [The higher ranking officer] has become like my father and my mother at the same time. If I make a mistake, it is normal that he punishes me and I cannot complain. I have to tell myself if I am punished, I deserve it. . ." Punishment for disobedience is harsh and includes imprisonment, flogging, and possibly death.
>
> *(Kelly, 2010: 7)*

In short, around the world, parental authority and its analogs often encompass the right and indeed the obligation to use corporal punishment to enforce the AR relationship. Corporal punishment is morally motivated in both the subjective and the theoretical sense: subjectively, fathers *feel* that they should hit, spank, or paddle their children; others in the community regard this as right and necessary. Theoretically, parental corporal punishment is moral insofar as it sustains or redresses the AR relationship between parent and child. Moreover, it is nearly always metarelational. One widespread American script is that a child transgresses in an interaction with the mother, who tells the child that when his father comes home he will take the child out to the woodshed and whip him. The father thus not only validates his wife's verdict in the particular instance but he also reinforces the mother's authority over the child – and over the siblings of the child he whips. Furthermore, accepting her judgment that the child should be punished and backing her up accordingly, he enhances his relationship with his wife. In addition, fathers commonly whip children to sanction the child's transgression of relationships with other third parties, including siblings and neighbors (e.g., Muir, 2009). Especially devout Christian fathers may feel that in corporally punishing a child, they are obeying God's will. All in all, like most violence, the moral motives for violently disciplining children grow out of a number of metarelational models linking many other relationships to the relationship between the perpetrator and the victim.

Violence in the military

Until late in the nineteenth century it was common, legal, legitimate, and even praiseworthy for military superiors in Western and other cultures to strike subordinates at their whim. Petty officers in the British Royal Navy in the Napoleonic Wars carried "starters" – ropes with hard, heavy knots at the end – with which they routinely struck sailors who displeased them in any way, such as being slow to obey (the novels of C. S. Forester and Patrick O'Brian depict this vividly). In his role as chief disciplinarian of the ship, the bo's'n wielded a cane with which he struck the posterior of any sailor whose performance or lack of alacrity displeased him. Conversely, the Royal Navy Articles of War of 1749 decreed:

> 22. If any Officer, Mariner, Soldier or other Person in the Fleet, shall strike any of his Superior Officers, or draw or offer to draw, or lift up any Weapon against him, being in the execution of his Office, on any Pretence whatsoever, every such Person being convicted of any such Offence, by the Sentence of a Court Martial, shall suffer Death; and if any Officer, Mariner, Soldier or other Person in the Fleet, shall presume to quarrel with any of his Superior Officers, being in the execution of his Office, or shall disobey any lawful Command of any of his Superior Officers; every such Person being convicted of any such Offence by the Sentence of a Court Martial, shall suffer Death, or such other Punishment as shall, according to the Nature and Degree of his Offence, be inflicted upon him by the Sentence of a Court Martial.

Note that there is no possible lesser penalty for striking an officer or threatening him with a weapon: death is absolutely mandated. "Violence done by officers to men was seen as almost unequivocally good; and violence done by men to officers just as unequivocally bad" (Nicolson, 2005: 56).

The British naval Articles of War also prescribed death for sleeping on watch, negligence in performance of duty, failing to engage and pursue the enemy, cowardice or flight, desertion, enticement to desertion, and arson. Mutiny, of course, was a capital offense, as was sedition (inciting to mutiny), as well as concealing mutinous "practice or design" (Article 19). Orders had to be obeyed, of course.

> 11. Every Person in the Fleet who shall not duly observe the Orders of the Admiral, Flag Officer, Commander of any Squadron or Division, or

other Superior Officer, for assailing, joining Battle with or making Defence against any Fleet, Squadron or Ship, or shall not obey the Orders of his Superior Officer as aforesaid in time of Action, to the best of his Power, or shall not use all possible Endeavours to put the same effectually into execution, every Person so offending, and being convicted thereof by the Sentence of the Court Martial, shall suffer Death, or such other Punishment as from the Nature and Degree of the Offence a Court Martial shall deem him to deserve.

14. If when Action, or any Service shall be commanded, any Person in the Fleet shall presume to delay or discourage the said Action or Service, upon Pretence of Arrears of Wages, or upon any Pretence whatsoever, every Person so offending, being convicted thereof by the Sentence of the Court Martial, shall suffer Death, or such other Punishment as from the Nature and Degree of the Offence a Court Martial shall deem him to deserve.

For lesser offenses, sailors in the Royal Navy (many or most of whom were conscripts legally kidnapped on the streets by official "press gangs") were flogged: with their shipmates assembled to observe, they were tied to a grating and lashed with heavy whips that cut through skin and flesh to the bone. Sentences of 10 or 20 lashes were entirely routine, and for desertion, failure to obey an order, or homosexual acts, sailors were sentenced to floggings that were certain to kill them. In the British ship of the line *Victory* with a crew of about 850, during the course of the year 1804, Captain Thomas Hardy, Horatio Nelson's flag captain and a British hero, ordered 4,560 blows of the lash (flogging sentences were denominated in units of a dozen lashes) for over 150 "acts of insubordination," especially drunkenness but also contempt, disobedience, insolence, neglect of duty, sleeping at one's post, or theft (Nicolson, 2005: 139). Nelson himself, Britain's greatest naval hero in history, universally loved by his officers and men and indeed by all England, while commanding the warship *Boreas*, over the course of 18 months ordered floggings for 66 of its crew of 142 (Nicolson, 2005: 233). Nelson was renowned for his humanity.

Violent policing

In modern societies, violence that is morally motivated to sustain AR relationships is evident in moral standards regarding violence committed *against* police compared to violence *by* police against civilians, especially lower-class civilians. Even in modern democracies, police who harm or kill civilians, especially lower-class civilians, are rarely sanctioned by their superiors, very rarely indicted, and hardly ever convicted (Cooney, 2009: 62–78). In the infamous Rodney King beating case, Officer Koon admitted that the action of the police was "violent and brutal" but justified, stating "it followed the policy and procedures of the Los Angeles Police Department and the training" (Linder, n.d.). In American culture, violence against criminals and suspects is integral to the authority of police (Carmichael and Jacobs, 2002: 26). Police forces train officers in the use of violence, which is taken for granted as natural, necessary, and morally salutary (Geller and Toch, 1996: 183; Stark, 1972: 68). Violence is a potential means of conducting AR relationships with anyone stopped by the police; the threat is evident in the guns and clubs carried by police officers, along with everyone's knowledge that police are rarely convicted of assault or homicide against anyone they apprehend. Indeed, the police force commonly valorizes and glorifies violence against criminals (Baker, 1985: 145, 159; Middleton, 1994: 66). Police also feel that violence enhances respect for their authority, and hence is integral to their AR relationships with civilians in general, not just suspects (Lester, 1996: 183; Stark, 1972: 60; Westley, 1953: 38). Referring to clashes between officers and protesters in Berkeley, California, one officer said, "if the parents of these cocksuckers had beat 'em when they were young, we wouldn't have to do it now... There's a whole bunch of these assholes who've learned some respect for law and order tonight" (Stark, 1972: 61). A policeman who beat two youths who threatened another officer told an observer, "on the street you can't beat them. But when you get them to the station, you can instill some respect in them" (Stark, 1972: 81). Thus, officers are enforcing moral values that support the AR relationship that they believe must be sustained between civilians and the police force charged with protecting them.

Some police think the criminal justice system is too lenient on offenders, or is ineffective in deterring criminals, so they dispense their own justice on the street (Lester, 1996: 183). A veteran detective who shot an armed robber before giving him a chance to surrender remarked, "[A]fter what I've seen people do to one another, it doesn't bother me a bit to shoot one of these people" (Waegel, 1984: 149). One officer expressed his lack of faith in the criminal justice system, stating; "I no longer believe in the jury system after some of the cases I've seen...

We get a guy off the streets and within three or four days he's back committing more crimes" (Waegel, 1984: 149). Police also engage in pre-emptive violence as a deterrent for prospective criminals (McNamara, 2002: 54; Waegel, 1984: 149). In short, when police violently take justice into their own hands, they reinforce their AR superiority over subordinate victims as they believe they must, and their violence is morally motivated. Of course, they are violating some other citizens' cultural preos regarding their AR relationship with civilians, and so their violence is immoral from the perspective of those others. But *their own motives* are nonetheless moral.

Some police sometimes seem to be motivated to be violent to maintain AR relationships between races, or possibly to cleanse the CS essence of the community of polluting elements. McNamara (2002) argues that police see themselves as representatives of a higher morality and believe they are meant to rid society of "deviants," and this justifies their use of force against subjects who they think are morally inferior, and deserve punishment (Crank, 1998). Such judgments of moral inferiority are often based on criminal actions, but they may also be based on group-based boundaries, such as race (Lester, 1996: 184; Stark, 1972: 80). Here, violence is intended to humiliate the "scum" who must be put back in their place or even eliminated to purify the community. Moreover, in some police subcultures, shooting "scum" enhances the prestige of the officer who kills the suspect, and enhances his solidarity with fellow officers. In the Los Angeles Police Department, the "Jump Out Boys" had tattoos celebrating their killings (Faturechi, 2012a, 2012b). Their pamphlet proclaimed, "We are alpha dogs who think and act like the wolf, but never become the wolf," and stated that sometimes the police "need to do the things they don't want to do in order to get where they want to be" (Faturechi, 2013).

Violence by gods

Gods, the supreme, absolute authorities, administer the greatest punishment; they may, must, and do inflict the most terrible violence. In early civilizations,

> Deities were easily offended and capable of great severity in their
> dealings with human beings... [They] killed and injured
> [individually] innocent and guilty people alike. Moreover, while

gods might punish individuals, ethnic groups, or all humanity for immoral or disrespectful behavior, they attacked them for more trivial reasons. Mesopotamian kings dreaded that some inadvertent mistake they made in performing rituals might result in tutelary deities' abandoning their city-states to their enemies.

(Trigger, 2003: 438)

The Vedic god Rudra and his Hindu successor Shiva are creators and preservers, but, equally fundamentally, destroyers. One avatar of Shiva is Bhairava, the annihilator (Kramrisch, 1981), who, according to legend, cut off one of the five heads of Brahma (Sehgal, 1999). Another form of Shiva is *Mahākāla* (Sanskrit: महाकाल), "great time," which ultimately destroys all things (Kramrisch, 1981).

The violence that the Abrahamic God does is good by definition: whatever Yahweh does *is* right, ultimately and absolutely moral because it is He who does it. Indeed, in many religions, the gods may legitimately harm humans to test them, or just because it pleases them to do so, without any humanly comprehensible reason. Plagues, starvation, and genocide; burning and torture; it's all moral when a supreme god does it. Indeed, in some religions, God justly condemns most humans to the most horrible perpetual pain because their ancestors were disobedient to Him. God is also not gentle with whiners. After the Israelites have escaped from Egypt, they complain to Moses about the lack of water and the meager, detestable food, so the Lord sends venomous snakes among them, biting and killing many (Numbers 21).

Because humans were too noisy, the Mesopotamian god Enlil destroyed humanity in a flood. Likewise, Yahweh wiped out the entire human race in a flood – possibly the same one – saving only Noah and his family. And beyond that massacre, all sinners are doomed to eternal hellfire (Matthew 13:36–43). Likewise, the Koran (4:56) specifies that

> Indeed, those who disbelieve in Our verses – We will drive them into a Fire. Every time their skins are roasted through We will replace them with other skins so they may taste the punishment. Indeed, Allah is ever Exalted in Might, and Wise.
>
> *(Sahih International)*

Of course, virtuous violence theory is a theory of *human* motivation for violence, not divine motivation. But if gods are idealizations of human beings and models for conduct, then the behavior of a society's gods toward humans represents an important aspect of that culture's moral ideals for human interaction. Gods' morality is a model for human morality, motivating analogous violence.

Explanations of accidents, misfortune, and suffering

Throughout history in most cultures, most people have attributed most misfortune, suffering, and death to the sociomorally motivated actions of either living humans acting supernaturally (i.e., sorcerers and witches) or the sociomorally motivated actions of immaterial supernatural beings (i.e., those whom we social scientists call "deities," "spirits," and "ancestors"). When things go wrong (an accident, a natural disaster, a disease or death), people infer that someone has done something wrong: either the unfortunate or dead person is suffering as a punishment for what he did wrong, or he is the more or less innocent victim of a (supernaturally perpetrated) crime. Or else he is a member of a CS group whose members are collectively responsible for any of its members' transgressions of relationships with supernatural beings. In short, most people in most cultures at most times have experienced most of their setbacks, failures, illnesses, injuries, and deaths as morally motivated violence intended to regulate their social relationships with supernatural beings or human beings acting supernaturally.

This is relevant to virtuous violence theory because people understand supernatural beings to be motivated by the same morals – albeit sometimes more perfect or extreme – that move humans. So the motives people attribute to such beings provide unique evidence about the attributors' own motives. Ironically, people also *model* their own motives on the ideal motives attributed to ideal supernatural beings. Hence, informants' statements about the morality and motives of ideal beings are declarations about the informants' own prescriptive morality, while their statements about the social-relational motives of all supernatural beings are reflections of the informants' implicit perceptions of their own and others' social-relational motives. The crucial fact for us here is that this shows that, extrapolating from their introspection and intuitive folk social psychology, *people expect social beings to violently regulate their social relationships*. That is, people think it is natural, almost inevitable, that social beings, whether human or superhuman, are morally motivated to harm or kill their relational partners when their partners transgress a vital relationship. People feel that it is deeply intrinsic to the nature of social beings that they regulate their relationships violently. It's virtually inevitable: to participate in a social relationship is to be the potential victim of moral violence, and to be prone to inflict it. The gods do it, the ancestors do it, witches do it, sorcerers do it, and even the mountains and rivers do it: everybody regulates their relationships violently.

Trial by ordeal and combat

Gods and other supernatural authorities kill humans to express, exhibit, and establish their supremacy, and, of course, to punish failure to obey their will. In addition, gods and supernatural beings can be invoked to adjudicate the social relationships of ordinary mortals. They do this by maiming or killing the person who is in the wrong. Thus, death settles the conflict between the human parties, while providing a dramatic demonstration of the moral authority of the gods, carried out through the edicts of their human delegates on earth. Especially when accusations cannot be refuted by reliable oaths supporting the accused's character, nor can the accusations be sustained by solid material evidence, judicial ordeal or combat provides an indisputable verdict: the wounded or dead person was morally culpable, and hence, more or less incidentally, deserved to die. From a practical point of view, the torture, maiming, or combat is morally necessary and sensible, since it establishes guilt or innocence. A priori, if a person who undergoes a trial by combat or an ordeal does not suffer or die, he is innocent, and if he is injured or dies, it is all well and good because the suffering or death is deserved – God has ordained it.

In medieval Europe, ancient India, and elsewhere, courts of law often determined the accused's guilt or innocence by ordeal (Bartlett, 1986; Hara, 2009; Kerr *et al.*, 1992). "The Christian supporters of ordeal in the Middle Ages believed that God would sustain the righteous and put down the wicked if requested under the proper circumstances" (Bloomfield, 1969: 553).

> For 400 years the most sophisticated persons in Europe decided
> difficult criminal cases by asking the defendant to thrust his arm into

a cauldron of boiling water and fish out a ring. If his arm was
unharmed, he was exonerated. If not, he was convicted.

(Leeson, 2012: 1)

Another ordeal was carrying a red-hot iron (weighing one to three
pounds, depending on the crime) nine paces, and days later the
accused's hands were examined to see if they were burned.
Alternatively, authorities sometimes ordained that suspects walk on
hot plowshares. In either case, defendants whose burns showed them to
be guilty were mutilated or executed. Bishops and priests blessed the
proceedings and equipment, and clerics typically were the ones who
examined the hands or feet three days after the event to determine
whether there were suppurating burns, and hence guilt. The other
common European ordeal was lowering the accused into a deep pool
of water; those who floated were guilty, while those who sank were
innocent (and were pulled out before they drowned). Courts used these
ordeals to adjudicate cases of murder, arson, robbery, disputed property ownership, adultery, disputed paternity, religious heresy, treason,
and, especially in seventeenth-century Europe and America, witchcraft
(Bartlett, 1986; Leeson, 2012).

People believed that God adjudicated the ordeal: the outcome
was divinely ordained, and hence the result silenced any further dispute
(Hyams, 1981). In important respects, early medieval European judicial ordeal was a way of obtaining communal consensus about guilt
where a small community would otherwise be divided (Brown, 1975:
Hyams, 1981; see discussion of the issue in Bartlett, 1986). In other
words, ordeals sustained CS solidarity that would otherwise be
breached by dispute. By the time of Charlemagne (reigned 768–814),
however, judicial ordeal became an instrument of royal authority,
imposed and required by rulers and administered exclusively by
their appointed officials (Bartlett, 1986: 36–42; Langbein, 2006; Lea,
1870; Peters, 1985; Ruthven, 1978). Ordeal was "an exercise of
power, yet represented submission to that power as submission to
the deity" because the outcome showed God's will (Bartlett, 1986:
36; Hyams, 1981). Bishops and priests had key roles in administering
ordeals – and were exempt from trial by ordeal. (Jews were also
exempt, because the accused in a trial by ordeal ordinarily had to
perform a vigil in church and take communion before the ordeal
(Bartlett, 1986: 54–5)).

Many other cultures, particularly in Africa but also around the Mediterranean, also used judicial ordeals (Roberts, 1965; see also references in Bartlett, 1986: 2, note 4). In India, a god or other divine being not only determined the outcome of a fire or floating ordeal but was invoked as a witness (Hara, 2009). In Africa, people such as the Azande of South Sudan administered strychnine poison to accused witches or adulterers (Evans-Pritchard, 1937; Roberts, 1965; Singer and Ryle, 1981). The poison, *benge*, was a judicial being or entity to whom the person administering the *benge* addressed a request to kill the recipient if he or she were guilty, but let the suspect live if innocent of the accusation. Analysis of a sample of world cultures shows that ordeals are closely associated with social stratification, with political integration (i.e., chiefs and kings), with hierarchically organized judicial authority, with religions oriented toward high gods, and with child socialization emphasizing obedience (Roberts, 1965). In other words, judicial ordeal is an exercise of human authority in the name of divine authority – implementing a metarelational model.

Ancient Greeks and medieval Europeans (especially Germanic peoples) also resolved wars, disputes, and accusations of moral transgressions by judicial combat, which was regarded as virtually equivalent to trial by ordeal (Armstrong, 1950; Bloomfield, 1969; Medieval Sourcebook; Ziegler, 2004). Among the Homeric Greeks,

> trial by battle is an appeal to the judgment of the gods, a form of ordeal. It is a form of ordeal befitting nobles... All disputes between nobles are disputes ultimately of honour, and what is intended to be decided by judicial combat is who is the better man.
>
> *(Armstrong, 1950: 74)*

Likewise in medieval Europe, kings or nobles presiding over a dispute could dictate that judicial combat determine the will of God when there was no other valid way to determine guilt or truth (Bloch, 1977; Bloomfield, 1969: 550; Hyams, 1981). The Normans brought to England the practice of trial by battle, as well as the principle (if only a principle) that only the king or those he licensed could order it (Hyams, 1981: 111–21; Leeson, 2011). Indeed, it was thought to be "essential to baronial dignity" to hold a royal grant authorizing the baron to order an ordeal or trial by combat (Hyams, 1981: 113). Staging ordeals was an important prerogative of major churches, as well. By the middle of the thirteenth century, trial by battle became rare in English criminal trials, being largely restricted to civil cases such as land ownership disputes; however, for some time trial by battle continued to be used to resolve criminal cases in Scotland (Hyams, 1981: 124). Like a sport or game, the rules and concrete conditions of judicial combat were EM while the outcome made the victor socially superior in an AR relationship to the loser (see Bloomfield, 1969: 551).

Trial by combat redresses disputed transgressions of any RM while at the same time reasserting the authority of the human rulers acting on behalf of divine authority. That is, in all of these cultures, divinities are fourth parties adjudicating the relationship between the parties to the case, and with human third-party kings, nobles, and ecclesiastics overseeing the ordeal or combat. So, the right to invoke trial by ordeal or combat was an expression, display, and performance of royal authority, and, when administered by a noble, was also an expression, display, and performance of the royal backing for the noble's authority. The participants' prayers in the church and then their vindication or conviction expressed their respective relationships with God, as He adjudicated their relationship with the other parties. Church blessing, supervision, and above all the church's examination and certification of the result of an ordeal – was the accused burned or miraculously preserved? – asserted and enhanced the authority of the church, and perhaps to some degree of the particular churchman involved. The outcome evinces God's ruling in the case, demonstrating his authority over all human relationships.[1]

Metarelational aspects of authority-ranking violence

The AR relation of supreme and often lesser authorities with their subordinates typically extends to regulation of aspects of many of the subordinates' social relationships with others. In other words, the AR relationship is the pivot of a metarelational model in which transgression of a subordinate's relationship with another constitutes a transgression of the subordinate's AR relationship with the superior. We see this when

---

[1] Implementing another complex metarelational model, female disputants and others who were not knights often selected champions to do battle for them; sometimes both sides were represented by knightly champions.

a parent intervenes to control a child's interactions with playmates or neighbors, when a playground supervisor comes over to make sure kids take turns, when a military court punishes an officer for adultery, or when God damns a person to hell for committing a sin such as worshipping another god or coveting a neighbor's ox or donkey. The very idea of "the state" and "crime" is that the state assumes jurisdiction over the social relationships of subjects and, in particular, reserves to itself the exclusive right to use violence to enforce relationships. That is, citizen subjects of a state cannot violently punish transgressions of their own or third parties' relationships: only the state may do that. Looked at from the other way around, the authority's motive for punishment (violent or not) is the subject's transgression of a relationship with a third party. In effect, the state authority is the guarantor of certain aspects of certain of its subordinates' relationships. This third-party enforcement is a moral and legal obligation of the authority.

Conversely, authority also entails responsibility to stand up for and protect subordinates. A threat or injury to my children is an attack on me, and, if necessary, I will resort to violence to protect my children. The same metarelational model operates at the level of the state, which may use violence to protect its citizens – for example, against piracy or kidnapping by terrorists. The metarelational moral motive may be emotionally experienced by authorities as a feeling that harm to those they are protecting is an affront to their own dignity and honor. Harming the authority's subordinate is a challenge to and offense against the authority itself. So, when members of Al-Qaeda flew airliners into the World Trade Center and the Pentagon, the US government proclaimed moral outrage and claimed the right and obligation to strike back at Al-Qaeda. Indeed, according to official pronouncements, the United States invaded Afghanistan and is still at war with the Taliban because the Taliban protected Al-Qaeda: an apparent metarelational model operating at the international level.

Acts of punitive and protective violence are warnings to others. When an authority violently protects or violently punishes a subordinate, an important part of the authority's motivation is to warn others of the consequences of harming one of its subordinates or violating its edicts about relationships among or with subordinates. The authority is acting pre-emptively to preserve or enhance its moral reputation so as to prospectively preserve and enhance relationships with fourth parties who observe or learn of its actions. Indeed, apparently irrational,

hotheaded violence that yields a reputation for extreme, excessive, reckless rage may be extremely effective in persuading others not to transgress against the hothead (Frank, 1988; Hirshleifer, 1987; Nesse, 2001;
Schelling, 1960). Thus, the authority's moral motivation for violence
may be the product of a RM between itself and a subordinate, a
metarelational model involving three social persons in three relationships, or a more complex metarelational model involving four or more
persons in several present and future relationships.

High rank does not always confer authority to violently sustain and
enforce the AR relationship, but across cultures and historical epochs it
often does. In innumerable societies, political and religious authorities
and judiciaries have imposed corporal and capital punishments on traitors, heretics, rebels, and criminals. "Crimes" are defined as violations of
the will and edict of the ruler, or as affronts to the gods themselves, and
are punished by imprisonment, torture, and execution. In all kinds of
premodern and early modern societies, it was legitimate and sometimes
common for chiefs to execute witches or sorcerers who were blamed for
deaths and other misfortunes (e.g., Evans-Pritchard, 1937).

The moral motivations for violence grow out of the dyadic
relationship between the perpetrator and the victim; but also, and sometimes even more strongly, out of metarelational models linking the
relationship between perpetrator and victim to their relationships with
third-party nobles, ecclesiastics, and deities; and, in turn, they grow out
of those first, second, and third parties' relationships with fourth parties
such as the king, and to an important degree with other subjects of the
nobles, congregants of the church, and worshippers of God. So, for
example, a schoolmaster may hit a pupil to sustain their relationship,
but at the same time the schoolmaster is hitting the pupil in obedience to
the headmaster, who expects the schoolmaster to properly control and
motivate his pupils so that the headmaster will satisfy the pupils' parents
and remain in the good graces of the bishop.

One final caveat: even when a person is universally regarded as a
legitimate superior in a legitimate relationship, it is not always clear to
the superior, his subordinates, or others just when and to what extent
he is using violence to enforce the relationship as such – which all regard
as morally valid – and when he is merely taking advantage of the
opportunity the role affords him to use violence instrumentally to exploit

his subordinates, or simply to enjoy his coercive control over them, or even to sadistically make them fear him. In other words, legitimate authorities can abuse their superior position and exert amoral power. However, the empirical difficulty in discriminating moral from amoral motives and assessing their relative influence on action should not lead us to falsely assume that all violence is amorally instrumental. Duly constituted authorities often dutifully mete out proper violence to regulate their legitimate relationships with subordinates, acting from deeply moral AR motives. Such morally motivated AR violence is common, and should not be overlooked, discounted, or disregarded. The available evidence suggests that morally motivated violence is much more common than purely instrumental, amoral, coercive violence.

5 CONTESTS OF VIOLENCE: FIGHTING FOR RESPECT AND SOLIDARITY

Neither boy spoke. If one moved, the other moved – but only sidewise, in a circle; they kept face to face and eye to eye all the time. Finally Tom said:

"I can lick you!"

"I'd like to see you try it."

"Well, I can do it."

"No you can't, either."

"Yes I can."

"No you can't."

"I can."

"You can't."

"Can!"

"Can't!" ....

"Well, you *said* you'd do it – why don't you do it?"

"By jingo! for two cents I *will* do it."

The new boy took two broad coppers out of his pocket and held them out with derision. Tom struck them to the ground. In an instant both boys were rolling and tumbling in the dirt, gripped together like cats; and for the space of a minute they tugged and tore at each other's hair and clothes, punched and scratched each other's nose, and covered themselves with dust and glory. Presently the confusion took form, and through the fog of battle Tom appeared, seated astride the new boy, and pounding him with his fists. "Holler 'nuff!" said he.

The boy only struggled to free himself. He was crying – mainly from rage.

"Holler 'nuff!" – and the pounding went on.

> At last the stranger got out a smothered "'Nuff!" and Tom let
> him up and said:
> "Now that'll learn you. Better look out who you're fooling
> with next time."
>
> *Mark Twain*, The Adventures of Tom Sawyer

A number of widespread practices consist of culturally organized violence: the relationship between the participants consists of violent acts
directed at each other. The violence itself is typically regulated by EM,
while the result created is AR of victors over vanquished. The first-person
relationship constituted by the violence also extends to the participants'
relationships with second persons such as fans and admirers, as well as
these second persons' relationships with third parties, such as supporters
of the opponent. That is, the allies, teammates, family, coaches, peers, or
fans of the combatants are communally identified with them, so that the
combatant's victory is shared by them all.

For example, analyzing how feuding mediates honor around the
Mediterranean and in the Middle East, Black-Michaud (1975) found
that like a sports contest, equality is the default initial position of the
competitors, but the outcome of the confrontation determines their
relative AR ranking. "Feud constitutes not only a relationship between
equals, but also – paradoxically – a means of affirming authority in the
absence of an institutionalized power structure... The party in a feud
which has inflicted more deaths than it has received is 'winning'" (Black-
Michaud, 1975: 24–5). He goes on to say that

> the reason for indulging in feuding relations is not so much the
> desire to inflict a loss on a given [Cyrenaican lineage] section, as to
> use this victory to enhance individual and group prestige within the
> home community and in the eyes of the world. The prestige thus
> acquired is the foremost ingredient of leadership in a situation in
> which egalitarian ideals and a lack of opportunity for economic
> differentiation prevail.
>
> *(Black-Michaud, 1975: 26–7)*

Whereas in the last chapter we observed that high status confers the right
or obligation to magisterial violence, in the cultural contexts we explore
here, heroic violence in warrior combat establishes high status. The
moral arrows go in opposite directions. Magisterial violence is the

moral prerogative of high rank, whereas victory in warrior combat raises rank. Warriors gain respect, deference, admiration, and fame by skill-fully, fearlessly inflicting violence. A warrior's rank is determined by how well he fights: the better his violence and the more harm he inflicts, the higher he rises. Combatants rise in AR status especially by defeating their opponents, but even deft and determined ferocity in defeat earns others' respect. Thus, violence constitutes AR relationships that are vital to the participants, their allies, and their admirers.

Fighting for respect and inclusive solidarity is crucial to Indo-European warrior societies; Mediterranean, Near Eastern, and Hispanic societies; premodern northern European and East Asian societies; pastoral societies in many parts of the world; the US South; contemporary urban gangs; and many other social systems. It can be traced back thousands of years.

> Orthodox Hinduism, in fact, makes a special place for the warrior, the (Kshatriya) caste; the famous Bhagavad-Gita's central concern is to justify a battle, even against kinsmen, as part of the ordained karma of that particular station.
>
> *(Collins, 1974: 428)*

Meanwhile, early Greeks, particularly aristocrats, were highly focused on *eris*, conflict, or competition to establish and reinforce honor.

> In the Homeric poems competition can be socially integrative because it creates, or at least affirms, hierarchies of prowess and so of honor and social standing: in war, when one hero kills his opponent, or when one community defeats another, or when warriors on the same side compete in doing service to the army as a whole; in speaking persuasively in council; or in athletic games and other contests.
>
> *(Thalmann, 2004: 366)*

Likewise among British football hooligans today, men gain prestige by proving themselves as fighters (Dunning *et al.*, 1986).

> Correlatively, there is a tendency for such males to enjoy fighting and to regard openly aggressive behaviour in certain contexts as both appropriate and desirable. They also view it as a means of gaining status and prestige. As a result, their identities tend to be

centered around what are, relative to the standards that are dominant in Britain today, openly aggressive forms of *macho* masculinity. Many males of this kind also have a high emotional investment in the reputation of their families, their communities and, where they are into the "football action", their "ends" or "crews" [hooligan gangs], as aggressive and tough.

(Dunning et al., 1986: 176)

In these warrior cultures, subcultures, and practices, violent combat is not merely morally tolerable – it is the ultimate virtue. The only thing more noble than bravely defending oneself and one's primary CS group is fiercely attacking and defeating rivals. In these systems of social relations the moral focus is on fearless bravado, skill, and victory in battle: the courageous warrior is the paragon of virtue. In more regulated, generally non-lethal forms of combat, this is the ethos of martial arts and contact sports.

Defeating another man raises the winner's status and lowers the loser's: combat establishes relative rank in an AR relationship. So men seek combat to raise their AR status in the within-group hierarchy while raising their group's status in between-group hierarchies. More ignominious than defeat is cowardice: refusal to fight or fleeing from battle not only lowers the status of the coward, but makes him an outcast, an object of derision. Bravely going into combat with courageous joy preserves the fighter's CS relationships with his peers, family, neighbors, and community: even if he loses or is killed, he preserves his honor, and the honor of his family. For the honor of each is the honor of all in the CS group: the patrilineal family, the gang, the community, the army, or the nation. The man who backs down not only lowers his own status, but he also dishonors his CS group, lowering their status *vis-à-vis* other groups. Such cowardice disintegrates the coward's CS relationship with his primary honor group while it tends to dissolve his honor group's CS relationship with the larger community.

Teammates, coaches, family, friends, lovers, peers, fans, rivals, opponents, enemies, and wise arbiters of morality approve of such violence, and admire, praise, foster, and encourage it. Inflicting violence well wins the praise of others – but it does more. It shapes the combatants' relationships with their teammates, coaches, family, friends, lovers, peers, fans, rivals, opponents, and enemies. Each combatant is morally motivated not only to vanquish his opponent but also to enhance his relationships with others. The more wonderfully violent he is, the more others esteem him, identify with him, imitate him, wish to associate with him, and offer him opportunities for fruitful new relationships. Victory or defeat determine the relative rank of the combatants, but also determine the quality, intensity, and number of their relationships with many others who care about their violent performance. A warrior may fight vigorously not simply to defeat his opponent, but to win the love of his lady, the envy of his peers, the gratitude of those he rescues, or the approval of his lord.

Knighthood in medieval Europe

Medieval Europeans honored knights for their prowess in battle: the greater the valor, the greater the honor (Brown, 2011; Kaeuper, 1999). A knight's honor depended on his demonstrating unflinching courage. But the essence of honor was killing: "knighthood was defined by violence" (Brown, 2011: 258). The more and the worthier were the opponents he killed, the more honorable the knight. By defeating other knights or by showing greater prowess in killing, knights rose in status and won the "worshyppe" of all. Medieval morality was based on honor won in battle, and there was no greater merit than that of the supreme killer. Knights tirelessly competed for honor. "In the end, fine feats of arms are their own justification, especially when performed in the service of love" (Brown, 2011: 272). The more of his own and especially others' blood a knight spilt, the greater the honor. To be covered in blood was heroic, and chivalric literature ceaselessly relishes the gore (Kaeuper, 1999: 147–56).

> Clearly, the personal capacity to beat another man through the accepted method of knightly battle – in fact, the actual physical process of knocking another knight off his horse and, if required, hacking him down to the point of submission or death – appears time and again as something like the ultimate human quality; it operates in men as a gift of God, it gives meaning to life, reveals the presence of other desired qualities, wins the love of the most desirable women, determines status and worth, and binds the best males together in a fellowship of the elect.
>
> *(Kaeuper, 1999: 143)*

Medieval lords organized tournaments to provide men the opportunity to show off prowess in battle, quite often by killing opponents. In between tournaments, knights commonly roamed about in search of glory, simply challenging and fighting any strange knight they encountered. Defeated knights often refused to ask for mercy, but if a knight survived an encounter, he gave honor to the one who defeated him, just as martial arts fighters do today. Honor also required loyalty to superiors and inferiors, including keeping one's word – another aspect of AR (Kaeuper, 1999: 185–8). Furthermore, "when a king declared war, all manner of typical knightly behavior – plundering, pillaging, capturing, ransoming, killing, and raping – became *ipso facto* legitimate" (Brown, 2011: 282).

Although honor through victory is the AR core of knightly chivalry, sometimes the blood mutually shed in combat also binds men in CS relationships. After fighting fiercely for several hours, two knights might each tear his own shirt to bind the other's wounds, express their undying love, kiss, swear to always stay together, and, later in life, ask to be buried in the other's tomb (Kaeuper, 1999: 215–19).

Gang and criminal cultures

> **Tio:** It's a myth that most of the violence is gang-related because a lot of the violence is interpersonal conflict. Guys get into it for the most pettiest reasons out here... So it's all about respect and disrespect. Not being accepted in the overall society, a lot of people feel ostracized, so what they do? They try to dominate their surroundings.
>
> (The Interrupters, *documentary film (James, 2011)*)

Contemporary youth street-gang members often orient to a morality of violent confrontation, esteeming aggressive confrontation and resolute refusal to be cowed by others' threats (Horowitz and Schwartz, 1974). In these cultures, maintaining one's reputation and honor are crucial.

> **Tio:** I really understand why it's not easy for people to back down for one reason. Because you've been taught all your life ... in the community where I grew up in, you know, like, you know you got to stand up. No matter what happens. Death before dishonor.
>
> (The Interrupters, *documentary film (James, 2011)*)

Even when violence is gang-related, it is inherently interpersonal. Often the battles are over gang status:

> It all started in high school. They [the offender's gang] were all jocks, and we [the victim's gang] were just ordinary people. They were all older than us and were in the 12th grade [ages 17–18]. We were only 9th graders [ages 13–14]. What started it all was because we knocked them down [in status] at school. We just took over, and they didn't like that. That's what started it all. The day it happened, we were going to a party. It was me, Patrick, Allen, Marc, and two other of my friends. We were getting ready to leave; we were in front of Marc's house. All of a sudden the AOS, they just started shooting at us, killing two and wounding one.
>
> *(Valdez et al., 2009: 297; see also Katz, 1988: 117ff.;*
> *Papachristos, 2009)*

In addition to combat over the status of the gang *vis-à-vis* other gangs, individuals also kill over personal status:

> We were in the neighborhood hanging out. T-Man was there, and then this guy showed up and started talking shit, saying he was a big time member of the adult prison gang. T-Man told him, "You're nobody" and shit, and then he kicked his ass in front of everybody. He told him to split, and the man didn't want to leave. He was with his girlfriend. T-Man told him to leave again, but he didn't want to. Then T-Man just took out a gun, and he just shot him with a gauge [shotgun].
>
> *(Valdez et al., 2009: 298)*

On the street, extreme, "excessive" responses to affronts to honor are essential to preserving or elevating one's AR status: Jacobs and Wright (2006: 42) argue that ranking is based on accumulated reputation and that "bringing someone down for what he did to you" raises your peers' esteem for you. Reflexively, some readers may feel that violence of this sort isn't moral at all, but the violence earns the praise, admiration, and respect of gang members' peers. Within these cultural contexts, violence in response to affronts to honor and to elevate status is virtuous.

Gangs are unforgiving of conflicting CS loyalties that compete with the CS solidarity of the gang. A gang member may be killed for his

CS disloyalty in choosing his relationship with his girlfriend over his gang membership:

> He was a homeboy, he wanted to get out. He told us that he wanted to get out because of his chick [girlfriend]. We told him, all right, well, we are going to have to roll you out because you don't dis [disrespect] a homeboy for a ho [girl]. We were all drunk, and he was dissing us for just to go with his chick. So they kicked his ass. He was just laying there, then they just cracked his head open with a rock. They killed him.
>
> *(Valdez et al., 2009: 298)*

Likewise, gangs maintain a CS identity with their "turf" and the violent defense of their territory.

> Interviewer: What kind of things does the gang have to do to defend its turf?
> Gang member: Kill. That's all it is, kill.
> Interviewer: Tell me about your most recent turf defense, what happened, a guy came in?
> Gang member: A guy came in, he had the wrong colors on, he got to move out. He got his head split open with a sledgehammer, he got two ribs broken, he got his face torn up.
>
> *(Decker, 1996b: 259; see also Katz, 1988;*
> *Papachristos, 2009)*

In interviews with 160 male gang members between 14 and 25 years old in San Antonio, Texas, 82% said they had fired a gun in a gang-related fight (Valdez *et al.*, 2009). Many reported attacking members of other gangs who trespassed in their gang's territory, or being attacked for appearing in another gang's territory. In other words, protective CS motivates gang members to shoot others who impinge on their territorial integrity.

Violent confrontation is still a cardinal virtue in the Mafia of Calabria, Italy. Honor accrues to the man who is

> capable of revenging by his own force any sort of offense done to his own personality and capable equally of dealing out offense to an enemy. Such behavior, be it defensive or aggressive, was not only justified but encouraged and even idealized by the society ... even if

it risked a frontal clash with the authority of the state... [The ideal was that people would say of a man] 'He was truly valiant and nobody could face up to him.' 'Usually he was not violent but on the occasions when he was forced to it, he stunned people and astonished his enemies. It happened six or seven times and people still talk about it as if it were a legend.' .... The word 'honorable' denoted little more than an affirmation of superior force... An honorific act was, in the last analysis, an extremely successful act of aggression, and it made no difference if it was in response to a previous act or was an autonomous initiative of the aggressor... All means were good ... robbery with violence, devastation, kidnapping and slaughter. Aggression became the accredited form of action and the booty the most immediate proof of victorious aggression... Taking a life, especially killing a fearful enemy, was honorific in the highest degree. 'X is an exceptional man; he "has" five killings.' 'Y is a man of respect; he has "stubbed out" four Christians.' These sort of phrases recur in mafia conversation. Among the *mafiosi* of the Plain of Gioia Tauro the act of homicide, if carried out in a competition for supremacy of any sort whatever, indicated (and still does, for these attitudes persist in the flourishing mafia of today) courage and the capacity to impose oneself as a man. It brought an automatic opening of a line of credit for the killer. The more awesome and potent the victim, the more worthy and meritorious the killer... The honorific dimension of murder, as an expression of the arrogance and capacity for revenge of the killer, wrapped in an aureole of glory every act of homicide.

(*Arlachi, 1983: 111–13*)

Fighting among and alongside the gods

Gods of the earliest civilizations, as well as those of smaller-scale societies, often fought, wounded, dismembered, raped, and killed each other (Trigger, 2003: 437). In Norse religion, the cosmos begins with the killing of the proto-giant Ymir, continues with the battles between the gods and the frost-giants, and ends with the final battle of Ragnarök, in which the gods and men will fight together against the frost giants (Dumézil, 1959; Lindow, 2002). Odin himself gave one eye for the magical mead that gave him all wisdom; he also hanged himself from the World Tree and was pierced by a spear, giving him further wisdom.

Norse human male fame and status were based on prowess in raiding and fighting. Men who fell in battle, killed themselves rather than surrender, or hanged themselves at home were thereby eligible to become the *einherjar* selected by Odin to feast forever with the great gods in Valhöll (Batey *et al.*, 1994). The greatest of the *einherjar* hoped to sit at Odin's own table and eat with him. In Valhöll the *einherjar*, paragons of Norse society, perpetually fight.

> All the einherjar in Odin's fields
> Hack each other each day.
> They choose slaughter and ride from the field
> Later sit reconciled together.
> *(Vafthrúdnismál 41, quoted in Lindow,*
> *2002: 104)*

What would be more glorious than an eternity of hacking and slaughter? Moreover, the *einherjar* will join the gods in the final battle of Ragnarök. In some Norse myths the goddess Freyja divides fallen warriors with Odin; those she selects join her in Fólkvangr, where they, too, fight every day in the eternal combat called *hjadningavíg* and feast every night until the end of time.

Sports

Combat for status and solidarity constitutes AR and CS relationships. At the same time, such combat is often governed by EM frameworks such that the combat is only legitimate and the outcome only valid if the combatants are evenly matched, have equal opportunities, and face the same constraints. This is especially true of, and defines, what we call sports. In many cultures throughout history, people have fought under controlled EM rules (Ingle, 2004). Today, many people engage in or are fans of boxing, martial arts, ice hockey, football, rugby, and lacrosse. Playing these games means hitting and hurting opponents, who in turn hit and hurt you. The harder you hit, the better you do and the more admired you are by teammates, opponents, coaches, and fans. So long as the opponents in martial arts and contact sports are evenly matched according to the rules of the sport, hurting others is not only condoned – it's praised, admired, and respected.

People who do martial arts and contact sports usually are not "aggressive" in other contexts, but such sports demand violence in the ring or on the field. For example, the sports columnist and writer Buzz Bissinger (2011) wrote that if football rules are changed to reduce violence, "It will no longer be football." Football *is* violence. Players say, "[I]t's like a way to test yourself against someone else and see what you have to get better with." Violence is not an unfortunate side effect, it's the point. Players say, "I kinda like it," "I love the feeling," "[I]t feels good, like a train wreck," and "[I]t makes you play harder" (Quebedeaux, 2012).

Q: How do you view or feel when tackling an opponent?
A: I feel really good. It's an adrenaline, dominance thing. You're completely trying to dominate someone else's will by hurting them and crushing their spirit.
Q: What are your intentions when hitting an opponent?
A: Trying to get the ball ... injure him, take him out of the game. Demolish him. Make him fumble ... make a big play.
   Another football player:
Q: How do you view or feel when tackling/hitting/etc. an opponent?
A: It is so much fun, blind siding is the best, knocking someone on their ass. It feels good and bad at the same time.
Q: What are your intentions when hitting an opponent?
A: It's bad to say, but it's in everyone's head, take them out of the game.
Q: What do you believe your opponents intentions are?
A: Hahaha, the same as mine.
Q: Do players, to your knowledge, ever intentionally hurt/injure another player? Why or why not?
A: Yes; all the time. It is because of the coach most of the time. They tell you to play fair, but, if you can, hurt someone so they can't play the best game.

(Quebedeaux, 2012)

In short, for football players, coaches, and fans, legal violence is essential to constituting AR relationships between opponents and competing teams. At the same time, good violence is a vital contribution to the team, cementing your place in the CS relationship that is the team and the school or the community of fans. In contact sports and martial arts, good violence is exalted – it makes you a winner and a hero. In ice hockey and baseball, too, violence – including CS fighting to display team solidarity – is universally understood to be intrinsic to the morality of the game (Bernstein, 2006, 2008; Munger, 2013: 21, 31ff.). For example, if a professional pitcher hits a batter, the pitcher on the batter's team selects a player of equal talent and stature to hit in EM retaliation. A professional ice-hockey or baseball player who failed to join a fight would lose honor and, indeed, "if you stayed in the dugout you would be shunned ... that would be an outrage"; in baseball, fighting is "a way of preventing people from showing you up, from disrespecting you – and to ensure that the other team doesn't get to harm your best players" (Munger, 2013: 21, 31ff.). The specific role of professional ice-hockey "enforcers" is to intimidate opponents, punish those who hurt your teammates, and humiliate opponents to damage their honor (Bernstein, 2006; Munger, 2013). Violence is intrinsic to the contests of violence that comprise contact sports and martial arts – and modern Western sports are mild versions of the combat of earlier times in the US Old West, and of many other cultures. There were many injuries in American Indian lacrosse, in public faction fights for fun in nineteenth-century Ireland, in organized fights among groups of frontier American loggers, in Renaissance Venetian bridge fights, and in early twentieth-century bare-knuckle boxing, to name just a few (Ingle, 2004). Violence was considered essential and intrinsic to these practices.

In boxing, the goal is to knock down or knock out the opponent; in other martial arts, the goal is to cause the opponent so much pain that he taps out, conceding defeat. The winner gains status over the loser, but so long as the loser fights hard, he is still respected. In fact, fighters respect opponents who can and do hurt them, and also respect them for taking the pain and carrying on.

Fighting among youths

Beyond organized sports, in many cultures it is accepted practice that "boys will be boys," so there is a long history of fighting for dominance in the streets and on the playground. And boys being boys, teachers and parents have "had to" whip them to instill obedience to their authority – where every failure to learn or to remember one's chores was construed as disobedience. John Muir (2009) describes boyhood in Scotland where boys were whipped for every failure, and it was natural and necessary for boys to establish their relative superiority to each other by fighting. Every new boy had to fight his way to whatever position he could reach.

> All these various thrashings, however, were admirably influential in developing not only memory but fortitude as well. For if we did not endure our school punishments and fighting pains without flinching and making faces, we were mocked on the playground, and public opinion on a Scotch playground was a powerful agent in controlling behavior; therefore we at length managed to keep our features in smooth repose while enduring pain that would try anybody but an American Indian. Far from feeling that we were called on to endure too much pain, one of our playground games was thrashing each other with whips about two feet long made from the tough, wiry stems of a species of polygonum fastened together in a stiff, firm braid. One of us handing two of these whips to a companion to take his choice, we stood up close together and thrashed each other on the legs until one succumbed to the intolerable pain and thus lost the game.
>
> *(Muir, 2009: 36–7)*

In the United States and Europe today, many studies show that bullying often involves an admired, high-status adolescent egging others on to combine together against the victim; especially if the others feel that their inclusion in the group is at risk, they may be motivated to bully the victim to ensure their own continued inclusion (Garandeau and Cillessen, 2006). Furthermore, bullying an outsider enhances the cohesion and attitudinal homogeneity of the group. People defer to the leader because they perceive that *others* admire him. Within the group, bullying lower-status members enhances the AR position of the bullies; the target may be someone the leader envies, or regards as a competitor for his status position.

Even among girls, physical fighting for reputation may occur. Campbell (1982) found that British working-class, 16-year-old girls often fought over insults to them, or to relatives or friends. Many of the insults that provoked fights were pejorative attributions about sexual behavior (especially promiscuity) or direct sexual curses; others were derogatory remarks about intelligence or delinquency, or concerned competition or jealously about boyfriends or threats to property, or were simply taunts challenging to a fight. Girls fought about what an informant called "pride" or, as the author puts it, "loss of face." Fighting, even losing, earned a girl "some level of status" because it demonstrated courageous determination to uphold her self-respect.

Metarelational aspects of fighting for respect and solidarity

In these contests of violence, the social relationships that warriors, sportsmen, and boys create and conduct through violence are not just the relationships between the violent actors themselves. Combative violence sustains and enhances the combatants' relationships with their lovers, their teammates, and their fans. The combatants are motived by loyalty and love of glory. To fight well and especially to be victorious is to attract and excite lovers, to be admired and envied by peers, and to evoke the gratitude of teammates and the pride of fans. The violent victor is honored by all. To fall to defeat, to fight poorly, and, most shamefully, to show cowardice is to disgrace oneself, degrading the coward's relationships with everyone.

Thus, the relationship *between* the combatants has moral implications for the respective combatants' relationships with others. For example, the warrior is obligated to valiantly defend his fellow warriors and to achieve victory for their sake: his relationships with his fellows depend on his performance in battle against the enemy. He is motivated to defeat his opponent not only to achieve superiority over him but also to honor his loyalty to his fellow warriors and his community. His CS and AR relationships with many others morally entail that he do his utmost to vanquish his opponent: ardent violence against his opponent is a moral duty to his fellows. If he fails to achieve victory, he will have failed in his duty to his family and his community. The social systems of chivalry, honor, and sportsmanship are all fundamentally metarelational because all of the combatants' relationships impel and require him to engage in violence against his opponents. Conversely, his victory or defeat, his courage or cowardice, is morally consequential for all of his relationships with those for whom he is fighting: his relationships with these third parties will be reinforced or stressed by his victory and valor or disgrace in battle. Extending beyond that, his victory and valor or disgrace will be shared by his team, his family, his community: *their* moral relationships with the team, the family, and the community of his opponent depend on how he and his opponent fight, and bear their pain and injuries.

These metarelational motives are moral in both the subjective and configurational sense. First, the combatants and their reference group subjectively experience violence as an obligation they must and should perform, whose excellent performance creates, sustains, and enhances, or jeopardizes, their relationships with their opponents, and with third parties. For example, a coach *ought to* respect and promote to starter a player who impressively excels in violence – the player, the coach, and observers feel that the player deserves the starting position. Everyone feels that the opponents in these contests of violence *should* be effectively and elegantly violent. Second, the motives are metarelational in the configurational sense that they are based on the moral implications of the quality of the violence between combatants *for their relationships with others*, and *for the others' relationships with certain partners*. Violence in these combative practices constitutes and regulates the metarelational models in which it occurs. Configurationally, for example, teammates are motivated to praise and admire the hero of the game, while the hero's girlfriend may feel she should have sex with him. In turn, the teammates and fans of the valorously violent hero can lord it over the team and fans he defeated, while the hero's girlfriend becomes the envied leader of her clique. The teammates, fans, and girlfriend are *entitled* to their newly enhanced status: their associates owe *them* respect for the hero's valorous violence, because of their relationship with him in conjunction with his violent triumph over their opponents.

In heroic combat, excellence in violence is the legitimate, laudable virtue that people resolutely strive to perfect. Disciplined, diligent dedication; patient, persistent practice; and arduous, assiduous sedulity are essential to perfect the valiant virtuosity of violence necessary for victory – and, failing that, for respectably valorous defeat. In these practices, people feel they *should* be violent: they intend to hurt their opponents, whom they understand to be fully human persons morally entitled to try to hurt them in turn. Indeed, the more skilled and determined a fighter's opponents are to inflict harm, the more the fighter respects and admires them. Everyone in the subculture of heroic combat makes the same judgment: it is virtuous to harm opponents in the prescribed manner, and merit accrues to the fighter who harms fiercely and courageously. The warrior *must* be ferocious, and the more ferocious, the more heroic. The warrior must also bravely accept the moral entitlement of his opponent to hurt him, stoically accepting bruises, wounds, or death without recrimination. These are practices in which it is *good* to be violent.

All of this combat for respect and solidarity is subjectively moral: participants and observers in their cultural or subcultural reference groups *feel* that they should do it, indeed that they must do it. The combatants – along with those who sustain a CS identification with them – feel shame if the combatants fail to do their utmost to inflict violence, or if they shy away from combat. In other words, the phenomenological experience is moral: in these practices, a person feels that he simply must be violent, whatever the pain, risks, and costs, and regardless of whether he personally *wants* to be violent. Inflicting violence is felt to be a duty.

This combative "warrior" violence is also moral in the functional constitutive sense we established when we characterized morality as the regulation of social relationships (Rai and Fiske, 2011). The violence creates AR and CS relationships: victory and defeat rank combatants and their respective CS groups as superior and inferior. At the same time, these combative practices consist of violence: the EM performance of the activity *is* violence. That is, while the violence functions to create and enhance the CS and AR relationships, the activity of combat *consists of* the reciprocal exchange of harm, in which each side ardently aims to match the violence it receives by returning violence in equal measure – or, if possible, overmatching the violence it receives by inflicting greater violence. Violence is what a person *does* – what he has to do – if he is a warrior, a knight, a man of honor, a macho Crip or Blood (US gang member), a boxer or an ice-hockey player, or even a boy on the playground in nineteenth-century Missouri or early twentieth-century Scotland. To be a true and good knight or mixed martial arts fighter is to be violent in the prescribed manner. In violent and contact sports, the combatants are under the AR control of a referee who enforces the EM rules that control admissible violence. Even when participants break the formal rules of combat and contact sports, or when spectators do violence, they are responding to what they perceive as injustice; the players or fans feel they have been wronged, so they retaliate (Mark *et al.*, 1983).

A person may attempt to enhance his position in any relationship by cheating – by covertly violating the moral framework of the relationship, while appearing to abide by it or, in certain cases, flagrantly committing a foul he thinks he can get away with. This is particularly salient in AR relationships, where, for example, a warrior or athlete may use "dirty" (transgressive) tactics in order to defeat an opponent. When a combatant makes a dirty violent move in order to gain status, his motive is relational but not moral if the combatant is aware that what he is doing violates the moral framework of the relationship. Violent breaches of the rules of combat are just outside the scope of our theory – they are one kind of violence that our theory only dimly and indirectly illuminates. But, as we will discuss later, perpetrators may be motivated to breach the explicit, technical rules of the immediate event in order to morally regulate relationships of greater scope.

6 HONOR AND SHAME

In diverse cultures around the Mediterranean basin and east though Arabia, Afghanistan, and Pakistan, there are variants of the honor and shame complex (Schneider, 1971). In the traditional Mediterranean, honor is synonymous with never backing down when threatened, forcing others to back down by threatening violence, avenging insults and homicides, and, to a somewhat lesser degree, killing rather than being killed. Honor and dishonor are shared among brothers, fathers, and sons, who are collectively responsible for avenging the death of any of them, and who are collectively liable to be killed in revenge for a homicide any of them have committed (Black-Michaud, 1975: 54). As Pitt-Rivers (1966a) points out, "The ultimate vindication of honor lies in physical violence" (p. 29), and in the extreme case, the final proof of superiority is that the individual is able to take the life of another (Marvin, 1986: 125).

Variants of this complex are salient in many other cultures with roots in this region, including much of Latin America and many societies strongly oriented to Roman Catholicism or Islam. While there are many differences and peculiarities of particular cultures, a number of common elements co-occur (or co-occurred) in most of the traditional cultures of this region; indeed, *all* of the following features occur together in many Mediterranean cultures and many cultures elsewhere that have been historically influenced by this region. These elements include:

- patrilineal kinship units (often very small) characterized by strong CS bonds;

- moral obligations largely limited to kin, affines, compadres, patrons, clients, and guests, along with distrust of all others;
- atomistic male individual autonomy and freedom from – indeed, defiance of – any constraints imposed by others except elder kinsmen;
- an orientation toward reputation, insults, slander, and gossip: a group's honor or shame is largely a function of how the community perceives the group – especially what other people say in public;[1]
- the duty to provide hospitality, along with special bonds resulting from the host–guest relationship; this ranges from "treating" others to drinks in cafes to extravagant feasting and other kinds of generosity or ostentatious gift giving; in some regions people receive guests in communal men's guest houses;
- in many societies, the hosts' obligation to harbor and protect suppliants – even enemies – who are incorporated into the hosts' collective honor as long as they remain in the host's sanctuary;
- augmentation of the honorific prestige of the hosts, with some diminution of the honorific prestige of dependent guests;
- concern about the vulnerability of women, their sexual desire, and the shamefulness of their sexuality, so that it is often required that women be veiled, secluded, subjected to clitoridectomy or infibulation, or all of these;[2]
- strong requirement of premarital virginity and, especially, the abstinence of women from sexual relations outside marriage, or any imputation of such;
- the *collective* dishonor to the men in the kin groups (natal or marital or both, including father, brothers, sons, fiancé, or husband) of any woman who violates this norm, or any woman who is reputed to have done so, or any woman whose chastity is impugned without retaliation; typically, once a woman is married the loss of honor focuses on the husband north of the Mediterranean, while south and

---

[1] See Farès (1932: 196–202) on the vulnerability of pre-Islamic Arab honor to public defamation by poetic satire. This dimension of honor may be related to the intensity of the reaction of contemporary Moslem clerics to the authors of works deemed blasphemous.

[2] For example, see Giovannini (1981) for a detailed analysis of conceptions of women in Sicily, and Gilmore (1983: 242) for specific references on this prominent Mediterranean ideology.

east of the Mediterranean her purity continues to be the primary responsibility of her brothers and father;[3]

- in many instances, a loss of honor for the female kin of a dishonored woman;
- in some cultures (especially in the Arab and Muslim world) the ideal that a woman's brothers or father should kill their sister and her paramour if she violates this norm (even if she is raped) in order to partially restore their honor; in many cultures, abortion, infanticide, or putting out to adoption in the event of non-marital pregnancy;
- the shame of men who are dishonored and their vulnerability to gossip, ridicule, and ostracism from all sorts of crucial social interaction, especially the sharing of food and drink;
- the extreme insult to the honor of a man that occurs when another man impugns the virtue of his mother, his sister, or wife;
- a tendency toward acceptance of male pre- and extramarital sexual relations, often extending to a certain admiration of sexual advances toward women and sometimes approval of men who dishonor other men by seducing their women.[4]

Many of these features appear in Andalusia (Spain) (Gilmore, 1987; Pitt-Rivers, 1966a, 1977: 77–80, 105, 165, and *passim*; see also Press, 1979 for the comparable urban norms); in Aragon (Spain) (Lison-Tolosana, 1983); in Naples, Italy (Parsons, 1969: cf. Giovannini, 1981 on Sicily);[5] among the Sarakatsani shepherds of northwestern Greece (Campbell, 1964, 1966); in central Greece (Friedl, 1962: 87, 104–5); among Greeks in the mountains of Cyprus (Pitt-Rivers, 1966b); in Crete (Herzfeld, 1985); in Turkey (Delaney, 1987; Meeker, 1976); in northeastern Jordan (Antoun, 1968); among Palestinian Arabs (Canaan, 1931; Cohen, 1965; Ginat, 1982: 177–85; 223–4); among Awlad 'Ali Bedouins of the western Desert of Egypt

---

[3] Meeker (1976) perceptively discusses the implications of this contrast between the disgrace of husbands among Turks and of brothers among Arabs. He links the disgrace of the Arab agnates of a fallen woman to their deep love for her – the very strong CS bond between brother and sister.

[4] "Honor" and "hospitality" are our analytic terms. In many of the languages and cultures of this region, there are corresponding folk concepts: often there is a narrow term for sexual virtue or honor (e.g., the Arabic *'ard*, Turkish *namus*) and its loss, along with a broader term for honorific prestige or precedence based on hospitality, independence, pride, vigilance, virility, and vengeance.

[5] In Venice during the fourteenth and fifteenth centuries, the sexual purity of women was very important to the honor of their fathers and husbands, and to the masters of slaves and servants; see Ruggiero, 1985: 17–22, 46–9.

(Abu-Lughod, 1986; Zeid, 1966, cf. Patai, 1971: 121); and among the
Kbyles of Algeria (Bourdieu, 1966; see "Outline" and Algerians), the
Iqar'iyen Berbers of Morocco (Jamous, 1981), and many other societies
in this region (see Antoun, 1968; Bates and Rassam, 1983: 213–18, 244;
Patai, 1971: 19, 79, 125, 287, 299). A very similar constellation of norms
and practices is salient in Moslem and Hindu (including Sikh) communities
across northern South Asia and elsewhere (e.g., Jeffrey, 1979, especially
pp. 29, 99–100; Keifer, 1991; Lindholm, 1982; for an overview, see
Mandelbaum, 1988 and references in Jeffrey, 1979: 35–6, notes 30–1).
With some modifications, most of the essential features of this constellation
were also present in the American South (Nisbett and Cohen, 1996; Wyatt-
Brown, 1982, see especially pp. 34, 44, 50–4, 90, 112, 295, 331, 334, 337–
9, 350, 368–9, 371, 373). Many of these features also occur in Latin
America and in Latino gangs in the United States, as well as in other
societies. (For a good review of honor-motivated violence in modern
Western cultures, see Copes *et al.*, 2013.)

Honor was already at the core of Arab society before the sixth
century (Farès, 1932). All of the essential elements were present. Honor was
an attribute of a group, defined in terms of the vigorous pursuit of vengeance against anyone who injured or insulted a man of the group, or who
fornicated with or impugned the virtue of its women. The father, brothers,
and sons of a woman were dishonored by violations of her chastity, by her
abduction, or by imputations of inchastity; they would kill the seducer,
rapist, or abductor, along with their own kinswoman (Farès, 1932: 76–81,
147). The kinsmen of a dishonored woman took collective action to avenge
themselves, or had to go into exile to hide their shame.

All of the features on our list are also prominent in a number of
Moslem societies outside the Mediterranean region, including, for example, in the Hindu Kush of northern Pakistan, among the Swat Pukhtun
(Pathan) (Lindholm, 1982) and the nearby Kohistani (Keifer, 1991). Swat
Pukhtun are aggressively atomistic; even brothers, fathers, and sons are
mutually antagonistic. They violently defend the honor of their women,
whom they keep in strict purdah; men sometimes kill a wife who commits
adultery, and do not hesitate to attack any man who dishonors them. The
honor of a group of agnates is collective, and all assume full and equal
responsibility for violently avenging any dishonor to any of them, whether
it results from insult, injury, or homicide, or fornication or adultery with a
wife, sister, or mother (Barth, 1965: 81–6, 137).

Very similar complexes of honor and shame exist or have existed
in many other cultures without historical connections to this region. For

example, honor based on the moral commitment to fight anyone who insulted and shamed a person or his dependants was crucial in ancient China (Lewis, 1990: 36–43). During the Warring-States period,

> honor was supremely important to the aristocracy and ... military prowess was absolutely central to the idea of honor. Warfare was one of the two great services of the state, and it was devoted to winning glory for the self and the lineage through victory in battle. In addition, a man's honor could be guaranteed in daily life only if he were ready to fight and conquer whoever slighted him. As the *Mozi* argued ... men demonstrated that they treasured honor and duty by fighting to the death over a single insulting word, so the only honorable man was the warrior.
>
> *(Lewis, 1990: 42)*

Guest-host relationship

This culture area constellation can be seen as representing a very diffused and extended form of CS among all men in the region of potential social interaction (excluding some outsider categories, such as musicians). All such men are potential hosts and guests, and any non-aggressive, sociable interaction between men requires selfless generosity. Participation in this loose and fluid network of weak CS relationships is contingent on honor – only honorable men are included. Honor is constituted and augmented by the many factors listed above, but the *sine qua non* of honor is the sexual purity of the women associated with the basic kin group. A man cannot participate in society if the purity of his mother, sisters, wife, and daughters is impugned or in doubt.

In these communities the world at large is a Hobbesian war of all against all. But in cafes, men's houses, churches, or mosques, all men in a community relate to each other communally, sharing food, drinks, tobacco, and religious brotherhood. This CS relationship is most obligatory and intense when hosts receive guests. Protection of the home is crucial to men's autonomous, assertive control; men's self-identity and social status are constituted by the inviolability of their home, their women, and their livestock. By the same token, when a stranger/guest comes into his host's domain, the host incorporates the guest into his communal identity by sharing food with him. These are complementary aspects of the same, highly marked boundary: the boundary must be protected at all costs, but, once inside, the other enters into the CS relationship of those who belong there. Men are like elementary particles that electrically repel each other with great force, unless they approach so closely that a still stronger nuclear force – operating at much closer range – bonds them together even more tightly. Indeed, Herzfeld (1987) suggests that the analytic term "honor" should be replaced by the term "hospitality."

Honor killing

Beyond restoring a family's honor by fighting anyone who impugns the chastity of a woman in the family, and killing anyone who fornicates with her, in many honor cultures men may, should, or must kill the woman herself if she has been tainted in any way. It is felt to be unfortunate and grievously difficult to have to do this, but in some honor cultures it is felt to be morally necessary. Nothing else fully and adequately purifies the family honor. A woman who has had sexual relations outside marriage, has eloped, has been alone with a man, or has been raped is irretrievably shamed – and so long as she is alive her existence is a disgrace that deeply dishonors her parents, siblings and cousins, or husband. Even if she did everything in her power to resist being alone with another man, and even if she believably insists that she has not been touched, the mere fact that her men failed to protect her, that she *could* have been sexually impugned, that at any time in any way there was no barrier between her and other men, means that she is irretrievably shamed (Gilmore, 1967; Herzfeld, 1980; Mandelbaum, 1988). There are no matters of degree in this: she is shamed, and the family dishonored so long as she lives.

Consider the commensal bonds among all men in a community of Sarakatsani shepherds in the western Greek mountains, who are an excellent example of the Mediterranean honor complex (Campbell, 1964). There are very strong CS bonds of solidarity among brothers and between father and sons in a *stani*, or family (e.g., p. 319). Adult men in the *stani* make decisions by unanimous consensus, hold their property in common, and stand ready to support and defend each other, right or wrong. Among the men of the *stani*, and to a lesser degree among other close kinsmen, there is trust, confidence, and altruistic concern about each other's welfare (p. 38). The honor of the *stani* depends absolutely on their daughters, sisters, mothers, and wives: if any woman has sexual relations outside marriage, the *stani* is dishonored, and her father, brother, or husband must kill her, and then her lover (pp. 169, 199–201, 303). "The worst insult that can be aimed at a man is to use the name of his sister, or mother, in an unpleasant sexual context" (p. 271), and "there is no more certain way of defiling the honour of another family than by seducing one of its women" (p. 270). Sarakatsani men spend their free time in coffee shops, buying rounds of drinks for each other. A man without honor is ashamed to appear there, and no one is likely to offer him a drink if he does appear (Campbell, 1964: 273, 284, 292, 296). Only the woman's death can restore the family honor, so some male in the family must kill her. It is a fundamental moral necessity.

Honor violence in the United States

In early modern Europe and America, a variant of the honor-shame complex gave rise to dueling. To avenge an insult against himself or a dependant, a gentleman challenged the offender to a duel whose structure was very precisely balanced EM. Andrew Jackson fought numerous duels and was later elected president (Buell, 1904: 164). However, dueling was not a simple dyadic interaction; duelists were restoring or sustaining their honor in the eyes of their peers, the honor of their seconds was at stake as well, and duels were performed for, and with various levels of involvement of, the immediate and indirect audiences (Falk, 2004). Alexander Hamilton abhorred dueling but he nonetheless accepted Aaron Burr's challenge because he knew that his capacity as a statesman would be diminished were he to refuse (Lodge, 1904: 474). He was killed in the duel.

Today, still, some contemporary white, working-class Southern men in small cities subscribe to a code that condones and requires violence to maintain honor and preserve respect (Copes *et al.*, 2013). There, as a matter of principle, a man who is insulted or disrespected should physically attack his opponent – or else he's not really a man. While there are strict EM limits to honorable fighting and a fighter should give quarter as soon as he has clearly won, even breaking an opponent's jaw or knocking out his teeth "may lead to local acclaim" (Copes *et al.*, 2013: 28). Men are proud of fighting to defend their character – it is admirable to do so. Conversely, it is shameful not to fight when a man or those he should protect are disrespected. Explained one man, if he failed to fight when he should have stood up for himself,

> I'd feel guilty. I'd feel weak. I'd feel like I let myself down. I'd feel like I let anybody else that was involved down. I'd feel like the other person involved got the upper hand. I'd feel like I lost something. And most of all I wouldn't feel like a man.
> *(Copes et al., 2013: 12, quoting informant "Kevin")*

Fights resolve the moral status of a conflict

> that's how you figure out dominance and who's right and who's wrong.
> *(Copes et al., 2013: 15, quoting informant "Fred")*

In their book, *Culture of Honor: The Psychology of Violence in the South* (1996), Richard Nisbett and Dov Cohen detailed how rates of homicide and violent crime are much higher in the southern states than in the northern states, but that this discrepancy in rates of violence is particularly pronounced for violence that occurs in response to insults to reputation and threats to property. When questioned, southern men were more likely to approve of violent retaliation in response to insults than northerners, and southern women were more likely to claim that boyfriends and husbands have a moral duty to use force to avenge an insult directed toward a girlfriend or wife. In a famous set of experiments, Nisbett and Cohen invited male students from northern and southern states to their lab at the University of Michigan. Unbeknownst to the students, the key part of the experiment actually took place in the narrow hallway outside the lab. In each experiment, students were physically bumped shoulder to shoulder and called an "asshole" by someone whom they thought was a stranger, but who was actually an assistant to the researchers. Nisbett and Cohen were interested in how the bump and insult would affect the subsequent behavior of the northern and southern students.

What they found was that when compared to a control group of southern students who were not bumped and insulted, southern students who were bumped and insulted were more likely to assume that hypothetical confrontations would end violently, and they were more dominant in their interpersonal behavior during interviews with experimenters. Even more interestingly, the experimenters measured cortisol and testosterone from the participants' saliva following the bump and insult. They found that southern students who had been bumped and insulted showed a significant increase in their levels of cortisol and testosterone compared to the control group of southern students. In a final version of the experiment, following the initial bump and insult, a new, larger confederate walked down the narrow hallway toward the students. In what was essentially a game of "chicken," the southern students who had been previously bumped and insulted waited longer before eventually getting out of the way than southern participants who had not been bumped and insulted. No such differences were found among northern students on any of the measures. The authors concluded that honor norms are more prevalent in the south and may explain some of the differences in rates of violence between the two regions.

Honor among thieves

In other cultures, violence is recognized as a morally valid way to enforce commitments, or to establish status. This is characteristic of criminal cultures, in particular, which share with Mediterranean honor cultures and many pastoralist societies the necessity for self-help. There is no chief or government third party to regulate relationships; the participants themselves must do so. A British man serving a 26-year prison sentence, having written an academic thesis on violence, describes how criminals, unable to turn to authorities to enforce their commitments to criminal conspiracies, adopt a strict moral principle of not "informing" on each other and, more generally, not cooperating with law-enforcement personnel – a moral principle that becomes a core of their identity. This also means that they themselves must enforce the commitments they make to each other.

> Criminals cannot draw on the facilities of the state to settle disputes with their own kind, but must settle their differences themselves. They can involve such sanctions as gossip, ridicule, contempt, ostracism, monetary penalties and so for forth; but also in the criminal's armory is violence. He lives in a culture in which violence is a *legitimate* and *proper* and *manly* sanction to invoke. This follows from the pattern of relations in which he is enmeshed, the

sort of bonds that typically bind him to other criminals, and the
kinds of sanction that necessarily underpin the criminal's morality.

(McVicar, 1982: 208; italics in original)

How the metarelational honor model organized the violence of the Trojan War

The moral motivation for violence to preserve and enhance honor is a
core element in the plot of the *Iliad*, indicating that this metarelational
configuration was already salient 2,700 years ago. It is well worth a close
examination of the moral motives for violence that Homer recounts,
because the *Iliad* illustrates how fundamental and how intense these
motives were in the society he depicts, and how complex were the
metarelational models that generated moral violence. The Trojan
Chryses, priest of Apollo, prays to Apollo to get his daughter Chryseis
back from Agamemnon, who has enslaved her as a concubine. So Apollo
causes a plague to descend on the Greeks, which leads the other Greeks to
persuade Agamemnon to release Chryseis. Then Agamemnon compen-
sates himself for his loss of Chryseis by taking Achilles' concubine Briseis.
This offends Achilles' honor (τιμη), so he withdraws from the battle and
refuses all offers of compensation and, for some time, any reconciliation –
until the Greeks are near defeat (Friedrich, 1977; Yamagata, 1994: 242).
Friedrich shows that, like later societies in this culture area, ancient
Greek honor focused on the sexual purity of women, such that a loss
of honor was experienced by the woman's consort as shameful, defiling,
polluting. The ancient Greek concept of honor was closely linked to the
sacred duty of hospitality and the enduring CS bond of guest-friendship,
xenia (ξενιη), created when host and guest exchanged gifts and vows
of mutual loyalty. This pair of norms forms the framework of the *Iliad*,
where the Trojan War has resulted from the terrible affront that Paris
commits against the honor of Menelaus and the Spartans when Paris
violates their hospitality by abducting Helen; this is ultimately avenged
when the Greeks kill the Trojan men and rape their women
(Yamagata, 1994: 12, 21).

King Menelaus gave hospitality to Paris; they formed the host–
guest bond of *xenia*. But Paris formed a liaison with Helen and took her
back to Troy. This doubly dishonored Menelaus, since not only had his
wife been in contact with a man but also that man was his *xenos;*
Menelaus was then bound to avenge himself by killing Paris

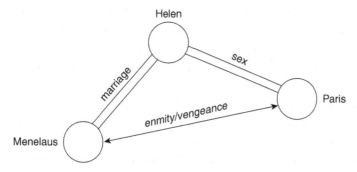

Figure 6.1: The core metarelational configuration at the root of the Trojan War

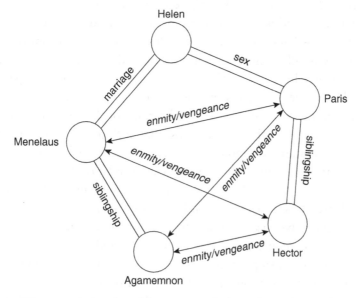

Figure 6.2: The metarelational model connecting the key relationships in the Trojan War (leaving out relationships with Achilles)

(Figure 6.1). The honor of a man and his brother are one, so King Agamemnon must support Menelaus, joining him in vengeance against Paris. So Agamemnon invoked his patronage and other relationships to persuade his allies to join his army. Likewise, the honor of Paris' father Priam, king of Troy, depends on Priam's supporting his son, as does the honor of Priam's other son (Paris' half-brother), Hector. Their allies are honor bound to fight against Menelaus, Agamemnon, and their allies. Figure 6.2 diagrams this metarelational configuration, for graphical simplicity leaving out Achilles and the other allies of both sides and depicting Hector but not Priam.

The moral sentiments, emotions, motives, and actions of the characters in the *Iliad* – or of anyone involved in an honor metarelationship – are oriented to a wider configuration, extending beyond the principals. We cannot comprehend their understanding of the situation, their motives, or their aims unless we take into account the implications of the relationships among the principals for their relationships with everyone else in their society. As we described in the preceding pages, crucial CS relationships consisting of commensal conviviality and hospitality are a function of the participants' honor. People of honor are welcome to join in feasts, and everyone will accept their invitations. People of honor are sought after as hosts and warmly received as visitors, where again they share food and drink. A dishonored person is avoided, excluded, reviled, and mocked – that is, shame means the loss of all CS relationships. No one will marry or ally themselves with dishonored families. In addition, dishonor greatly lowers status in AR relationships; a disgraced person is degraded. So the sentiments, emotions, motives, and actions of the principals in the *Iliad* encompass the implications of their relationships with each other for all of their CS and AR relationships with everyone else in their communities. To simplify, we can graph each of the principal actors' many relationships with all others as a single relationship with "others." Then Figure 6.3 depicts the full metarelational honor model that motivates the violence of the Trojan War, and all honor violence. Well, it's not really the full model, because it ignores the central figure in the *Iliad*, Achilles. And Homer represents the heroes, women, and gods as morally motivated to regulate relationships among the gods and between gods and men. So the *complete* metarelational model of the moral motives of those involved in the Trojan War would require a much bigger sheet of paper. But many real human interactions are motivated by huge configurations of recursively extended and reciprocal moral implications among many linked relationships. Complex metarelational motives drive violence everywhere. And, as we shall consider in Chapter 22, other metarelational configurations keep the peace.

An intriguing final dénouement of the story of the Trojan War is that it *should* conclude in an honor killing. The Greeks having defeated and killed the Trojans, Menelaus must kill Helen, and has indeed demanded that she die by his own hand. But he cannot – she is too beautiful and he still loves her (thanks to the final intervention of Aphrodite and Eros, apparently!). Accordingly, the figures do not show the prescribed violence by Menelaus against Helen.

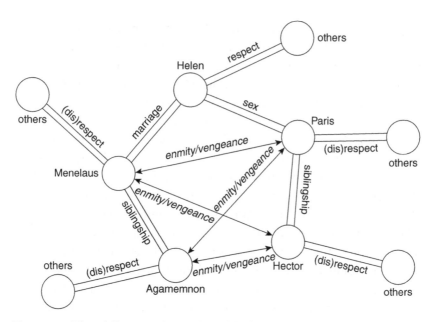

Figure 6.3: The "full" metarelational model of the Trojan War (leaving out the relationships with Achilles, among the gods, and between gods and humans)

The metarelational model that generates the *Iliad* is not restricted to social relationships among humans: humans relate to the gods through kinship, prayer and sacrifice, sex, envy, and other media (Lefkowitz, 2003). Some gods back the Greeks, some back the Trojans, others are more neutral, and a number of minor gods are involved in diverse ways. The gods intervene in the battles between humans, especially by rescuing their favorites or exhorting them to fight. Moreover, the gods' relationships with each other shape and are shaped by their respective relationships with their favored humans and the humans' relationships with each other. For example, Paris judges Aphrodite to be more beautiful than Hera or Athena, so Aphrodite "gives" Helen (Zeus' daughter) to Paris, and helps the Trojans throughout – while Hera and Athena support the Greeks because they are angry that Paris does not rank them as more beautiful than Aphrodite. However, Paris' seduction and abduction of Helen violates the *xenia* host–guest hospitality relationship, which is backed by Zeus, who therefore determines that Troy will eventually fall to the Greeks.

Recall that the core events actually related in the *Iliad* itself are motivated by Agamemnon's refusal to grant Chryses' request to ransom his daughter Chryseis, a war captive. Chryses is the priest of Apollo at a temple near Troy, so Agamemnon's refusal of his request is an affront to Apollo. Chryses prays to Apollo, who, angered by Agamemnon's disrespect of his priest Chryses, sends a plague on the Greeks. When a seer reveals to the Greeks why they are afflicted by the plague, Agamemnon is persuaded to return Chryseis, but says that he is entitled to some other female captive to replace her. Achilles says that he should wait until they capture more prisoners, angering Agamemnon, who feels disrespected. So Agamemnon demands that Achilles give up *his* beautiful war captive, Briseis. This greatly offends the honor of Achilles, who expects an EM relationship and does not accept Agamemnon's assertion of an AR relationship over him. But at Athena's command Achilles refrains from killing Agamemnon to redeem his honor. Instead, he refuses to join with the Greeks in fighting the Trojans, sitting out the ensuing battles – with disastrous results for the Greeks – until the Trojans kill his close friend Patroclus. Why has Zeus allowed the Trojans, whose prince, Paris, has violated Zeus' protection of the sacred *xenia* relationship, to resist the Greeks for so long?

> Even though Hera and Athena oppose him, Zeus is prepared to let
> many of the Greeks die because he owes a favor to another
> divinity, Achilles' mother, Thetis ... Thetis wants Zeus to make
> Agamemnon and the other Greeks realize that her son is the best
> fighter and the most worthy of honor.
>
> *(Lefkowitz, 2003: 56)*

Thetis has appealed to Zeus in response to the prayers of her son, Achilles, to let the Greeks suffer until they recognize his supremacy as a warrior. Zeus consents because Thetis once helped Zeus defeat Hera, Poseidon, and Athena. However, when Zeus has forbidden the gods to intervene in the war, Hera seduces Zeus so that he falls asleep, allowing his brother Poseidon to help the Greeks. This metarelational model motivating the violence of the *Iliad* is complex, indeed.

Many Greek myths portray the gods punishing humans for disrespect, including the hubris of acting like a god. In short, the gods violently enforce AR, killing humans who challenge them. And it is not only the person who angers the god who suffers the god's displeasure:

> In the myths, each crime, each refusal to do what a god commands,
> each failure to give due honor to a divinity, has consequences.

> Wrong actions can cause problems for succeeding generations in a
> family, or for a whole city or army.
>
> *(Lefkowitz, 2003: 11)*

In particular, the Greeks perceived the outcome of battles as morally ordained metarelational consequences of their parties' relationships with the gods: the defeated died because someone else, with whom the defeated was communally equivalent, had transgressed an AR relationship with the gods.

The *Iliad*, Greek myths, and religion more generally are relevant to virtuous violence theory in two opposite but reciprocal respects. Looking up, Greeks perceived their gods as models *for* human virtue – humans modeled themselves *after* the gods, paragons of honor. Among the gods, violence was moral action motivated to constitute social relationships, particularly honor-based status in AR relationships. What motivated the gods should motivate humans: the honor metarelationship. Conversely, from our perspective we recognize that the Greek gods were *projections of* ideals for social relations and moral motives among human Greeks. As in most religions, Greek gods were essentially representations of social relationships: they consisted of little more than nodes in relationships with humans and among themselves. They had few, if any, non-relational features, and their only actions were social actions. Much of the gods' action was violence motivated by honor metarelationships, reflecting the Greeks' experience and perception of their own human lives. Life was about honor, a metarelationship that entailed killing anyone who threatened one's honor. Honor was a property of one's patrilineal kin group, such that each person's honor was everyone's honor – their CS bonds made them all honorifically equivalent. They were collectively responsible for upholding and enforcing their shared virtue, and, whether punished by the gods or ostracized and ridiculed by peers, for each of their transgressions all suffered as one across the generations. Morally motivated to kill to sustain, enhance, and redress their most sacred relationships, the Greeks lived in a world of virtuous violence.

Many cultures across history and society have regarded violence as morally essential to the preservation of their most basic CS relationships – the intense primary group relationships of the family or minimal patrilineage – and also to the more diffuse CS relationships among men and families throughout the community. In these contexts, killing someone who insults a person or his women is good, right, necessary, and natural. A man *must* use violence to sustain the CS relationships crucial to his life. Each man is an autonomous, aggressively hostile, and proudly self-interested individual, suspicious of other individuals who would injure, exploit, slander, or humiliate him. But at the same time, every man has a strong identity as a member of an autonomous, aggressively hostile, and proudly self-interested patrilineage, suspicious of other communities that would injure, exploit, slander, or humiliate his patrilineage. At the same time, the communal guest–host bond is the complement and reflection of the agonistic relations among all men in honor cultures: every man is potential guest and host to every other honorable man. Nothing is more important than maintaining the honor of the patrilineage, and violence is the morally motivated and culturally necessary response to any affront to honor.

7 WAR

Duty, Honor, Country: Those three hallowed words reverently dictate what you ought to be, what you can be, what you will be ... Duty, Honor, Country: The code which those words perpetuate embraces the highest moral laws and will stand the test of any ethics or philosophies ever promulgated for the uplift of mankind. Its requirements are for the things that are right, and its restraints are from the things that are wrong. The soldier, above all other men, is required to practice the greatest act of religious training – sacrifice. In battle, and in the face of danger and death, he discloses those divine attributes which his Maker gave when He created man in His own image. No physical courage and no brute instinct can take the place of the divine help which alone can sustain him. However horrible the incidents of war may be, the soldier who is called upon to offer and to give his life for his country is the noblest development of mankind... Yours is the profession of arms, the will to win, the sure knowledge that in war there is no substitute for victory; that if you lose, the nation will be destroyed; that the very obsession of your public service must be: Duty, Honor, Country.

General Douglas MacArthur (1962)

It is not only warrior cultures, honor cultures, or street gangs that require men to be violent: in war, people in most cultures and subcultures deem it a moral duty to kill the enemy – and in many cases soldiers feel that they *should* kill, enslave, torture, rape, or starve enemy captives or civilians. Philosophers and religious leaders often exhort men (and sometimes women) to fight, extolling the noble virtues of warfare. In the twentieth century, soldiers killed approximately 140 million people and wounded far more; in most cases they were morally motivated to do so out of solidarity in support of fellow soldiers, obedience to officers, military honor, or patriotism (Leitenberg, 2006; this number includes deaths in German and Japanese concentration camps).

This is nothing new in human history; morally laudatory warfare has been common and bloody since early civilizations such as Shang China, ancient Greece, ancient Mesopotamia, Old and Middle Kingdom Egypt, pre-colonial Yoruba and Benin, Classic Maya, and pre-conquest Aztec and Inca (Lewis, 1990; Trigger, 2003: 240–63). All of these early civilizations regarded war as virtuous and greatly honored their warriors.

As recently as the eighteenth century and early nineteenth century in Europe, monarchs were motivated to fight in order to affirm their status as monarchs and to regulate their relationships with other monarchs (Whitman, 2012). This warfare was a legal proceeding: international law recognized the legitimacy of property claims based on winning a battle. For monarchs, victory was a "verdict" that validated rights to territory, and soldiers were legally entitled to the personal property of the enemy they killed.

In this chapter, we first focus on the moral motives of nations, and the decision-makers and public opinion that guide them. We then consider the moral motives of soldiers. Finally, we address the motives for war of radical political and terrorist groups.

The motives of leaders and nations

> When they start talking moral violation, it is time to get out the body bags.
>
> *(McCauley, 2000: 39)*

Nations often go to war to redress threatened AR relationships. That is, decision-makers and public opinion are motivated to declare war to maintain or raise the rank of their nation *vis-à-vis* other nations, particularly when they feel that they have been unjustly pushed down to a low rank among other nations. According to Lebow (2010), national honor is competitively contested and nations are vulnerable to humiliation if they are not violently assertive. In his terminology, "standing" is hierarchical rank in the eyes others, and slights to a nation's standing provoke revenge. Analyzing the motives for starting all 94 wars that involved a dominant, great, or rising power since 1648, Lebow found that standing motivated 58%, security 18%, revenge 10%, interest 7%, and other motives 7%.

So when a nation perceives that it has been unjustly pushed down to a low rank among nations, it may fight its way back up. Harkavy (2000) shows that military defeat, long-term domination, or colonial or lower racial status often produce humiliation that motivates international or intergroup vengeance, revolution, or withdrawal. French humiliation at their defeats in the Napoleonic Wars, together with their loss of Alsace-Lorraine in the Franco-Prussian War, contributed to World War I. German humiliation from their defeat and from being blamed for World War I was a major motivation for their instigating World War II. Arab shame and consequent vengeance motivation after the humiliating defeats of the Six-Day War in 1967 contributed to subsequent wars and terrorism. Defeat and revenge have been at the heart of the Hutu–Tutsi conflict and those of Northern Ireland, Kurdistan, the Caucasus, Afghanistan, and the former Yugoslavia (Harkavy 2000). These are cultures in which shame, honor, and vengeance are especially crucial, but these motivating emotions operate to a significant degree in all cultures.

Humiliation is humbling – disgrace and dishonor lower a nation's position. When threatened with loss of respect, nations fight to protect challenges to their relative status (Dolan, 2010). A nation cannot bargain over humiliating demands or violations of norms. Margaret Thatcher wrote about the Falklands War,

> What we were fighting for eight thousand miles away in the South Atlantic was not only the territory and the people of the Falklands, important though they were. We were defending our honour as a nation, and principles of fundamental importance to the whole world – above all, that aggressors should never succeed and that international law should prevail over the use of force.
> *(Thatcher, 1993: 173, cited in Dolan, 2010: 22–3)*

The British fought to hold their head high in the world. Eidelson and Eidelson (2003) propose that groups are most disposed to intergroup conflict when they believe that their group is cohesive, inherently superior, and entitled to a special role and a unique destiny; when they perceive that other groups have perpetrated humiliating injustices against them; when they see other groups as threatening to subjugate or annihilate them; and when they perceive outgroups as dishonest and untrustworthy (that is, disposed to violate social relationships); and when they perceive their own group as powerless, dependent, oppressed, and subjugated (that is, having an illegitimately low rank). In our terms, Eidelson and Eidelson are positing that conflict is over threats to AR entitlements among groups.

The moral motives discussed thus far are primarily about redressing illegitimately lowered status: in other words, about redressing and rectifying transgressions of AR hierarchy. But EM between kin groups, communities, or nations is also a significant motivator of violence. In many cultures when a member of one group injures or kills a member of a second group, members of the second group are morally obligated to retaliate in kind, matching the violence they received with violence they mete out, an eye for an eye, a tooth for a tooth, a hand for a hand, and a life for a life (Nivette, 2011). In this framework of moral vengeance, some communities are in a more or less continuous state of feud (e.g., Schieffelin, 2004; Waller, 1988). But even modern nations often retaliate in kind; consider, for example, the US bombing of Tripoli and Benghazi in 1986, said to be in retaliation for the bombing of a Berlin nightclub by Libyan agents; or the many counterstrikes by Israel and Palestinian organizations, which they say are responses to strikes by the other side.

Similarly, McCauley (2000) shows that President G. H. W. Bush mobilized public opinion in support of attacking Iraq by asserting that Iraq's invasion of Kuwait in 1990 was a moral violation. And, in fact, among politically unsophisticated respondents, when casualties are mentioned, moral punitiveness – retributiveness – predicts support for both Gulf Wars and for "punishing transgressor states," even after controlling for other values (Liberman, 2006, 2013, 2014). McCauley posits that competition for resources eventually translates into intergroup conflict, *but only when the in-group perceives the out-group as guilty of a moral transgression.* Indeed, most great-power decisions to go to war have been based more on issues of justice than on practical concerns about security (Welch, 1993). According to Welch (1993), "justice" was an especially strong factor in the Crimean War (especially for Russia but also Britain), a very strong factor in World War I (especially for Britain but also for Russia and Germany), a moderate factor in World War II (especially for Britain), and a conclusive factor in the Falklands/Malvinas War (for both Argentina and Britain).

Sometimes EM and AR motives converge to the point where they may be difficult to distinguish. Löwenheim and Heimann (2008) integrate a wide interdisciplinary literature and analyze the Second Lebanon War in 2006 to show that modern nations often wage war to take revenge, motivated by moral outrage. The more a nation feels humiliated by a moral violation against it, and the more the nation experiences the act as morally outrageous, the more it seeks vengeance. Löwenheim and Heimann argue that a vengeful retaliator aims for the satisfaction of making its enemy suffer for the wrong they did, with little or no regard for the material or human cost of doing so. Vengeance motivation "leads revengers to use excessive force, to harm innocents, and to employ far more violence than was used against them originally," hence tending to extend and expand the cycle of violence (pp. 686–7). Löwenheim and Heimann argue that "revenge is about suppression and disrespect of the opponent" (p. 692), "to enable and affirm position and status" (p. 694), and to reverse the harm-doer's declaration of superiority (p. 697) – in other words, vengeance aims to restore the avenger's legitimate AR standing by degrading the perpetrator nation. Humiliation lowers the victim nation's status and respect:

> It exposes the humiliated party as weak, unworthy, and inferior. The intent of revenge, in this sense, is to remove the harm-doer from the position of domination and thereby restore the dignity robbed from the victim.
>
> (Löwenheim and Heimann, 2008: 696)

Löwenheim and Heimann also analyze the metarelational model that embeds the antagonist nations in international relationships with other nations and international organizations. They show that the more strongly other states condemn the injury and express sympathy, solidarity, and identification (CS) with the injured nation, the less its loss of dignity and need for revenge. More generally, third-party moral assessments of the original injury and of the injured nation's response moderate that nation's response, as Löwenheim and Heimann show in Israel's attack on Hizbullah and Lebanon in retaliation for Hizbullah kidnappings of Israeli soldiers.

If the impetus to war is motivated by AR and EM, the *organization* of war between modern states is often motivated by MP.

> Proportionality should be a guideline in war. Killing 50 to 90
> percent of the people of 67 Japanese cities and then bombing them
> with two nuclear bombs is not proportional, in the minds of some
> people, to the objectives we were trying to achieve.
>
> *(Robert McNamara, speaking in an interview in* The Fog
> of War; *quoted in Blight and Lang, 2005: 114)*

Proportionality is the basis of utilitarian moral reasoning that consists of
computing what's right or wrong as a function of the costs and benefits,
probabilities and magnitudes, based on ratio value metrics of the fungible utilities of all consequences. In short, it is the basis for making
*ratio*nal moral decisions, where "rationality" does not mean selfish
individual maximization or materiality, but rather maximization of the
collective good and minimization of the harm to the evaluator's own
community. This kind of moral reasoning – and fundamental moral
motivation – is what modern civilizations demand of their leaders, expect
of their bureaucracies, and insist on as the fundamental strategic principle for their armies. It is the morality of doing the greatest good for the
greatest number at the least cost in lives and suffering.

In order to provide commanding generals with the basis for
making decisions about strategies for high-explosive and incendiary
bombing of Japan, Robert McNamara used data on air-crew loss rates
per sortie and the number of sorties per tour to calculate attrition rates
and project the manpower available for future bombing raids (Blight and
Lang, 2005: 120–2). When considering the plans for the initial invasion
of the Japanese home islands, Truman asked his chief of staff, Admiral
Leahy, "what the price in casualties for Kyushu [Japanese home island]
would be and whether or not that price could be paid" (Giangreco, 2003:
124). Minutes of the meeting report that "The President reiterated that
his main reason for this conference with the Chiefs of Staff was his desire
to know definitely how far we could afford to go in the Japanese
campaign" (Giangreco, 2003: 126). Initially, Truman had been told
that in the event of an invasion of Japan, "[T]he first 30 days in
Kyushu should not exceed the price we have paid for Luzon" [31,000
casualties] (Walker, 2004: 36). Later Truman was warned by former
President Hoover, and his top staff, that the invasion of Japan would
likely mean "the expenditure of 500,000 to 1,000,000 American lives"
(Giangreco, 2003: 109), based on the experience of battles such as that
on Saipan, where "it cost approximately one American killed and several

wounded to exterminate seven Japanese soldiers. On this basis it might cost us half a million American lives and many times that number wounded . . . in the home islands" (Giangreco, 2003: 100). This estimate was called "the sinister ratio" (p. 101), and was the basis for many discussions phrased in terms of the "cost" in human lives of war operations (Giangreco, 2003: 113, 128).

Later, justifying the decision to use atomic bombs against Hiroshima and Nagasaki, Truman said that "a quarter of a million of the flower of our young manhood was worth a couple of Japanese cities" (Alperovitz, 1996: 516). Truman wrote, "I asked General Marshall what it would cost in lives . . . [to invade Japan]. It was his opinion that such an invasion would cost at a minimum one quarter of a million casualties, and might cost as much as a million, on the American side alone, with an equal number of the enemy" (Alperovitz, 1996: 517; Giangreco, 2003: 129). Hence, the strategic moral decision to use atom bombs against the Japanese was motivated by MP proportionality – by a utilitarian moral calculation of the ratio of expected benefits to expected costs, denominated in lives and wounded. It was a matter of what the United States could "afford," what the alternative "costs" were, what would "economize" lives, what "price" the United States would pay in "lives and treasure," the number of young US soldiers the destruction of two Japanese cities was "worth," and "the sinister ratio."

Likewise in the Vietnam War, American "management did not care whether labor lived or died, only about producing a high enemy body count. United States lives were quite secondary to primary production of enemy deaths" (Gibson, 1986: 111). Draftees, especially, counted little in the "costs of production" (Gibson, 1986: 121). Officers evaluated their subordinates – awarding promotions, leaves, and even medals on the basis of their productivity – that is, the number of deaths they produced.

> Many high-level officers established "production quotas" for their units, and systems of "debit" and "credit" to calculate exactly how efficiently subordinate units and middle-management personnel performed. Different formulas were used, but the commitment to war as a rational production process was common to all.
>
> *(Gibson, 1986: 112)*

For example, in the 25th Infantry Division, the values were as follows: enemy killed (10 points), prisoner taken (1,000 points), supplies and weapons captured (10–200 points), and perfect CMMI inspection score (500 points); Americans killed in action (–500 points) and Americans wounded in action (–50 points) were deductions. In the 503rd Infantry Division, US casualties did not figure in the scores: it was enemy killed (200 points), prisoner taken (1,000 points), re-enlistment (100 points), AWOL (–3 points), delinquency report (–2 points), accident (–3 points), malaria (–5 points), narcotics (–5 points), Article 15 discipline (–1 point), Summary Court-Martial (–2 points), Specific Court-Martial (–3 points), and General Court-Martial (–15 points). Using this price system, each officer was "weighed according to his war production" (Gibson, 1986: 114).

This cost-benefit scoring resulted in the fabrication of body counts, either to justify casualties incurred or to reward officers (Gibson, 1986: 126ff.). Moreover, soldiers killed presumed civilians, women, and children, and prisoners in order to increase their unit's body count score; some ground units kept accounts with strings of ears or fingers.

The moral motives that move soldiers to go to war

Of course, the warrior morality of virtuous combat that we explored in the last chapter is a major motivator drawing men to join in warfare, but additional motives combine with it to move men to violence in organized, large-scale warfare. In chieftainships and feudal societies, when one's chief or lord goes to war, his followers or vassals must follow him; the AR relationship requires it. Indeed, feudal vassalage is fundamentally about allegiance in war: whether in medieval Europe or medieval Japan, the core of fealty is the commitment to follow one's lord into battle. This is the AR morality of loyalty and obedience. In contrast, in modern nation states, violent "service" in war is a patriotic duty to the mother-land. Patriotism is motivated by CS: *we must all join* in the fight to protect *our* nation, indivisible, because it *is our* "land," our collective heritage and traditions, the place where our ancestors are buried, the country for which our ancestors and brothers have sacrificed their sacred blood.

Among both feudal and modern soldiers, a secondary motiva-tion to go to war may be the EM equality motivation to match what one's peers are doing; a man doesn't want his peers to exceed him in virtue.

Moreover, evenly balanced EM conscription for warfare operates as a moral framework in modern societies, where, in many nations, either everyone (or every man) is required to serve for a fixed term, or there is a lottery to decide who is conscripted. Having been selected to fight by an EM mechanism morally binds the soldier to do his duty, killing when he must, because the equality of the obligation to serve legitimates the onus on the person serving.

In sum, whether primarily motivated by the morality of AR or CS, and to whatever extent co-motivated by EM, social relationships generate the moral motives to join in war.

Killing under orders

Once in war, AR is the RM fundamental to life in militaries whose function is to use violence to achieve whatever ends the armies are ordered to accomplish by political leaders. In his duty as admiral, Horatio Nelson repeatedly led his ships into battles with the intention of killing and wounding thousands of the enemy, in full knowledge that hundreds of his own men would die and hundreds more be horribly wounded. As a naval officer, he was motivated to kill the enemy to defeat them, or to punish those who resisted legitimate authority – and he felt great pride and satisfaction when he fulfilled his duty. In 1799, after completing a British mission to suppress a rebellion against the Sicilian king in the islands off Naples, Nelson wrote a fellow captain that "the hanging of thirteen Jacobins gave us great pleasure" (Nicolson, 2005: 233).

Soldiers are legally and morally bound to obey orders, including orders to kill or face certain death – this is the final AR moral imperative of every soldier in battle. That is, the foundational morality of organized armies throughout history and across cultures is simply, "Kill whoever you are ordered to kill whenever you are ordered to kill them, even if you must die trying." The *sine qua non* of military social relations is obedience to authority, where obedience means killing on command. Men of traditional military subcultures are deeply committed to absolute obedience, while ordinary conscripts must be verbally indoctrinated and simultaneously trained through incessant practice to kill, and to die if necessary, when commanded to do so. Soldiers must not make their own private moral decisions; they must follow orders. The duty to obey superiors *is* military morality. A soldier *must* obey orders to kill. In classical and medieval warfare, this duty encompassed killing civilians of defeated communities, including women and children. In modern times, duty has been similarly construed – for example, in World War II, strategic bombing and the widespread shooting and rape of civilians.

When the public and the judiciary determine that other moralities should take precedence over the military morality of obedience, people may doubt whether killers or torturers, especially killers of civilians, truly felt obligated to obey, regardless of other moral considerations. Such doubts notably arose over Lieutenant William Calley and his troops' murder of over 500 civilians in the My Lai massacre, the murders by Nazi officers of millions of Jews, and the torture performed by US guards at the Abu Ghraib prison in Afghanistan. To the extent that these people believed that they were not following orders, but rather engaging in their own brand of sadistic violence, their actions were immoral. But to the extent that they felt that they were legitimately following the orders and wishes of their superiors, they were morally motivated by AR hierarchy. Whatever the motives of these particular people in these particular instances, however, there is no doubt whatsoever regarding the absolute conviction of military personnel that they are obligated to kill when commanded. Killing on command is the function and *raison d'être* of the military; anyone who believes it is moral to have armies believes in that. Killing and willingly dying on command is the highest – and unquestioned – military virtue.

Killing for your comrades

There is also an important CS morality of mutual care and sacrifice, working together communally to achieve the mission, and putting the preservation of the unit and the accomplishment of the mission it was commanded to perform ahead of individual welfare or survival. This CS ethos is vital to military efficacy, and soldiers are often much more strongly morally motivated to fight to protect their comrades than they are by the duty of obedience. The intense CS emotion of devotion to one's fellow soldiers in the unit is what makes soldiers willing to kill, take enormous risks, suffer horribly, and die. American and German World War II soldiers and American soldiers in later wars consistently reported that they fought mostly because they couldn't bear the thought of "letting down" their buddies in the unit (Connole, 2008: 289–90; Shils and Janowitz, 1948; Stouffer, 1949; Wong *et al.*, 2003). Similarly, referring to his buddies in the unit, an American soldier coming out of combat in the Iraq war said

> That person means more to you than anybody. You will die if he dies. That is why I think that we protect each other in any situation. I know that if he dies and it was my fault, it would be worse than death to me.
>
> *(Wong* et al., *2003: 10)*

Another said of his buddies in the unit,

> You have got to trust them more than your mother, your father, your girlfriend, or your wife, or anybody. It becomes almost like your guardian angel.
>
> *(Wong* et al., *2003: 11)*

And they know that they can, they must, trust each other – while in turn others are trusting them with *their* lives.

> [W]hen the artillery started raining down and [stuff] started hitting the fan . . . everybody just did what we had to do. It was just looking out for one another. We weren't fighting for anybody else but ourselves. We weren't fighting for some higher-up who is somebody; we were just fighting for each other.
>
> *(Wong* et al., *2003: 12)*

What this means is that on the battlefield, soldiers are killing to protect each other – they feel intensely morally committed to do so, even if they die looking out for each other. Each "has the back" of everyone else. The success of military missions and the lives of soldiers and sailors depend on their fighting fiercely *for each other*, with absolute trust and confidence in each other. Hence, breaches of their CS solidarity may be severely punished, with the sanction of their officers. For example, a Roman soldier who stole from his fellows or a sentry who deserted his post was immediately tried by the tribunes, and, if convicted, his fellow soldiers beat and stoned him to death, a practice called *fustuarium* (Polybius (second century BCE): Book VI, 352, Phang, 2008).

Extremist violence and terrorism

It is not just wars between modern nations that are morally motivated; revolution, rebellion, and terrorism are, too. And make no mistake, it is a war that rebels and terrorists believe they are fighting, and it is against people they perceive as their enemies and oppressors. Reviewing the literature on political violence, Rule (1988: 220) writes that the best studies of aggressive political action, those by Muller (1979), found that "no aggressive behavior will occur unless people doubt the moral worth of the political regime as a whole – in other words, unless they come to view the entire system, as opposed to specific policies, leaders, or outputs, as illegitimate."

Jeremy Ginges and Scott Atran have pointed out that in spite of evidence for moral motives in decisions to go to war, most researchers have assumed that decisions to pursue war are driven by non-moral instrumental calculations of expected value, and this lens has been used to understand the minds of terrorists. That is, most researchers assume that people will engage in violent extremism if the act provides a great benefit at a relatively smaller cost. Supporters of these theories often point to the stories suicide bombers are told about how they will be rewarded in the next life for their sacrifice, suggesting that suicide bombers are somehow giving their lives out of self-interest. But in a series of brilliant studies designed to identify the motivations for war and terror in the context of the Israeli–Palestinian conflict (Ginges and Atran, 2009; Ginges et al., 2011), the authors demonstrated that support for violent acts of war and terrorism is typically driven by moral, rather than rationally instrumental, motives. In an initial survey, Ginges and his collaborators (Ginges et al., 2007) asked Jewish settlers on the West Bank to indicate their willingness to take actions against Palestinians if their settlements were threatened, including non-violent acts of protest, such as blocking roads and illegally occupying land, as well as violent acts of aggression. In addition, the settlers were asked to assess the effectiveness of the different strategies and the morality of the acts. Consistent with our theory of virtuous violence, Ginges and his collaborators found that although support for both non-violent and violent actions was predicted by the extent to which settlers viewed the actions as morally righteous, the perceived effectiveness of the actions only predicted support for non-violent actions. Thus, whether or not an action would be effective was inconsequential in determining whether a Jewish settler would be willing to support acts of violence toward Palestinians. *For violence, only the action's morality mattered*; settlers didn't care whether it was effective or not.

In other experiments, Ginges and his collaborators have demonstrated that failing to understand the moral motives underlying violent conflict and attempting to resolve them through rational means can backfire terribly (Ginges *et al.*, 2007). The authors asked Jewish settlers, Palestinian refugees, and Palestinian students to respond to possible peace deals. (Palestinian students associated with Hamas make up the majority of Palestinian suicide bombers, p. 7358.) Some of the deals they were asked to consider included material incentives for reaching a peace agreement. From a purely rational choice perspective, the addition of material incentives should have made the deals more appealing. Instead, the authors found that the addition of the material incentive led to *greater* support for war and acts of terror and *less* support for peace deals among people who saw the conflict in strongly moral terms. Indeed, a majority of Palestinian students reported that they would feel "joy" if they heard about a suicide bomb attack.

Could the material incentives have been perceived as an offensive bribe – an intolerable, evil, taboo trade-off (Fiske and Tetlock, 1997)? Atran (2010: 4; also see Ginges *et al.*, 2011) reports an exchange he had with a Muslim extremist in Indonesia:

Atran:	"What if a rich relative were to give a lot of money to the cause in return for you canceling or just postponing a martyrdom action?"
Extremist:	"Is that a joke? I would throw the money in his face."
Atran:	"Why?"
Extremist:	"Because only in fighting and dying for a cause is there nobility in life."

A great deal more could be written on the multitude of moral motivations for waging and fighting wars, but the research we have discussed is sufficient to show that AR is the principal motivating relationship, followed by CS and sometimes EM. The evidence of MP motivation and evaluative criteria in establishing US war-fighting strategies through kill ratios is also clear and unequivocal. The usual constitutive phase of waging and fighting wars is redressing what the perpetrators experience as wrongful reduction in their status. Humiliatingly lowered, the nation seeks to regain its rightful place high in the hierarchy. Indeed, national honor obligates leaders and citizens to attack those who have disrespected them – they must rise again. For extremists and terrorists, the moral motive for war is not an effort to raise rank within a legitimate system; rather, the system itself is seen as wholly illegitimate, and the violence is meant to completely transform or terminate the relationship with political powers that are seen as controlling them through illegitimate coercive force.

The impetus to war is not limited to the dyadic relationship between the enemies. As in warrior combat, nations and armed movements are concerned about their reputation – how others judge them. Ranking among nations and other groups is not merely dyadic: it is more or less linear and transitive. The rank of a nation depends not only on the power and prestige of that individual nation but also on the coalitions of mutual support that enable it to face down nations with fewer, weaker supporters. Moreover, in the international arena, nations have treaty commitments to allies, so that they are legally and morally bound to go to war against a nation that attacks an ally. To fail to come to the aid of an ally is not only a violation of their treaty; it threatens the credibility of all their other treaties: allies and foes will doubt their steadfastness. Coalitions and treaties are significant in international relations only to the extent that participants and third parties believe in the participants' moral commitments to the treaties. These metarelational moral configurations are additional major motives for nations to go to war.[1]

---

[1] In this chapter we have not explored motives for revolution and civil war, but we suspect that they are also moral and relationship-constitutive. Every American knows the EM moral motives, or at least the moral rhetoric, supporting the American Revolution, and the same EM motives evidently underlie most military struggles for independence against colonial powers. Rule (1988) and Petersen and Zukerman (2010) make that argument, theorizing that moral anger is the foundation for armed political violence. Likewise, research on riots has found that political grievances and oppression are important factors (Wilkinson, 2009), but there has been very little participant observation or interview research on riots that might identify the subjective motives of rioters.

8 VIOLENCE TO OBEY, HONOR, AND CONNECT WITH THE GODS

Some time later God tested Abraham. He said to him, "Abraham!"

"Here I am," he replied.

Then God said, "Take your son, your only son, whom you love – Isaac – and go to the region of Moriah. Sacrifice him there as a burnt offering on a mountain I will show you."

Early the next morning Abraham got up and loaded his donkey. He took with him two of his servants and his son Isaac. When he had cut enough wood for the burnt offering, he set out for the place God had told him about. On the third day Abraham looked up and saw the place in the distance. He said to his servants, "Stay here with the donkey while I and the boy go over there. We will worship and then we will come back to you."

Abraham took the wood for the burnt offering and placed it on his son Isaac, and he himself carried the fire and the knife. As the two of them went on together, Isaac spoke up and said to his father Abraham, "Father?"

"Yes, my son?" Abraham replied.

"The fire and wood are here," Isaac said, "but where is the lamb for the burnt offering?"

Abraham answered, "God himself will provide the lamb for the burnt offering, my son." And the two of them went on together.

When they reached the place God had told him about, Abraham built an altar there and arranged the wood on it. He bound his son Isaac and laid him on the altar, on top of the wood. Then he reached out his hand and took the knife to slay his son. But the angel of the Lord called out to him from heaven, "Abraham! Abraham!"

"Here I am," he replied.

"Do not lay a hand on the boy," he said. "Do not do anything to him. Now I know that you fear God, because you have not withheld from me your son, your only son."

Genesis 22:1–13; New International Version

For the great majority of people in nearly all cultures throughout history, morality has been inextricably intertwined with religion. Indeed, for many people in many cultures, morality *is* religion: the good is whatever the gods command, the prophets declare, the church leaders ordain, or the ancestors will. As the Israelites perceived their world, if God says "sacrifice your son," a faithful "God-fearing" person must do it without questioning; it is sufficient that God commands it. For a religious person, there is no morality that transcends God's will, and, indeed, morality precisely consists of obedience to God and communion with Him. Likewise, in many religions, what is right is what the ancestors ordain, or what the spirits of mountains demand.

In this chapter, we consider violence that is either relationally or metarelationally based on relationships with supernatural deities. In particular, we consider violence that is commanded by gods, human and animal sacrifice meant to honor or appease the gods, and self-sacrifice intended to create and enhance the relationship between the believer and the gods.

Gods command violence

Even in the total absence of any possibility of punishment for disobedience, most ordinary Westerners feel morally committed to obeying orders to harm others, or even kill them, though few are aware of their own or most others' disposition to obey such orders. In a famous set of experiments, Milgram (1974) demonstrated that a variety of normal people could be induced to commit violence if they were ordered to do so by an authority figure. In these studies, an experimenter told participants that as part of an experiment on learning they were to use a machine to administer electric shocks to a person in another room whenever that person responded incorrectly. The experimenter told them that after each error they should set the machine to administer a higher voltage shock when they pressed it to punish the next error. In reality, the person in the other room was an actor who was told to cry out in pain; then, as the shocks went up, to stress that he had a heart condition; then to plead for help and ask to stop the experiment; and eventually to go silent as the severity of the shocks increased. Although the participants became visibly upset at having to administer the shocks, Milgram (1974) found that even if they believed they were administering deadly electric shocks to another person, they would often continue to do so if the experimenter quietly told them they "must" go on.

We have argued previously (Rai and Fiske, 2011) that the people in these experiments were engaged in an AR relationship with the experimenter in which they were morally required to defer to the experimenter's legitimate authority, even if it meant inflicting severe and potentially mortal pain on a fellow human being. The authority of an "experimenter" is sufficient to make many people feel they really "must" inflict severe pain and possibly kill an entirely innocent person. And these were people in a so-called individualistic, extraordinarily egalitarian, and unusually anti-authoritarian culture: after all, the United States was founded on the principle of resistance to illegitimate authority, and that principle continues to be a vital core of the culture.

In the previous chapter, we examined obedience to the will of superior commanders as a moral motivation for violence in war. This violence is driven by metarelational moral motives that may have little or nothing to do with the dyadic relationship between the perpetrator and the victim. Rather, the perpetrators' motives are to sustain, enhance, or repair their AR relationships with a superior. They do violence against a third party because the superior commands it. Where morality consists of obedience to the will of a legitimate superior, if the superior wills a subordinate to harm or kill others, that violence is moral. In many cultures, the core of morality is obedience: the supreme will of a god, a prophet or religious authority, a divinely ordained king, a military commander, or a parent must be done: submission, fealty, discipline, and filial piety demand it. If a soldier's commanding officer says to bomb that village or shoot that child, the commander and the soldier may genuinely judge that it is the soldier's absolute duty to follow orders, whatever his other feelings about what he must do. Moral devotion to his duty to his superior impels him. He is obligated to do what he is commanded to do, regardless of what he feels about it, regardless of how difficult it is, regardless of anything but his sense of duty. For him, morality *is* obedience, nothing less, nothing more. To further investigate the metarelational models underlying violence in the name of obedience, in this chapter we will examine actions in obedience to God's will. (We will consider another example of this in Chapter 14, where we examine the metarelational moral motives of torturers.)

According to sacred texts, oral traditions, divination, and oracular pronouncements, the gods and ancestors often command violence. Men following these commands are morally motivated by their AR relationship with their god(s) or ancestors. The will of the gods or ancestors cannot be questioned, it must simply be obeyed. The Hebrew Bible and the Koran both enjoin believers to kill their unbelieving enemies, and God himself often destroys whole communities (Jenkins, 2010). In numerous passages God commands men to stone brides who are not virgins; torture, poison, and execute women who commit adultery; burn women if they become pregnant from fornication; kill female prisoners of war who are not virgins, along with male prisoners of war who refuse enslavement; and wipe out the entire populations of communities whose land His followers wish to occupy (Hartung, 2012).

In the Old Testament, Numbers 25 recounts the Lord's orders to kill the Israelites who have been sacrificing to the Moabite gods; the Lord then sends a plague, killing 24,000 Israelites. Phineas brings the plague to an end by running his spear through a miscegenous Hebrew man and his Midianite wife, for which God praises him and bestows priesthood on him and his descendants. God then commands Moses to kill all the Midianites. Numbers 31 recounts that after further battles in which the Hebrews kill all the Midianite men, the Hebrew soldiers return to camp with their plunder and captives. Moses is furious when he sees this:

> "Have you allowed all the women to live?" he asked them. "They were the ones who followed Balaam's advice and were the means of turning the Israelites away from the Lord in what happened at Peor, so that a plague struck the Lord's people. Now kill all the boys. And kill every woman who has slept with a man, but save for yourselves every girl who has never slept with a man."
>
> (Numbers 31:15–18)

God also commands, and the Hebrews obediently carry out, massacres of all Amalekite men, women, and children (1 Samuel); all the men and women, old and young, and all the animals of Jericho (Joshua 6); and every man, woman, and child subject of King Sihon and King Og of Bashan (Deuteronomy 2 and 3).

> By the rivers of Babylon we sat and wept
> when we remembered Zion...
> O Daughter of Babylon, doomed to destruction,
> happy is he who repays you for what you have done to us –
> he who seizes your infants
> and dashes them against the rocks.
>
> *(Psalm 137:1, 8–9, New International Version)*

Moses tells the Hebrews that they must annihilate the Canaanites, saying,

> I will take vengeance on my adversaries
> and repay those who hate me.
> I will make my arrows drunk with blood,
> while my sword devours flesh:
> the blood of the slain and the captives,
> the heads of the enemy leaders.
>
> *(Deuteronomy 32:41–42, New
> International Version)*

When Joshua defeated the armies of the five kings and captured the kings, he killed them and hung their corpses up on trees. He then overran Elgon, Hebron, Debit, and the entire region, killing everyone in the communities he defeated. "He left no survivors. He totally destroyed all who breathed, just as the Lord, the God of Israel, had commanded" (Joshua 10).

These AR injunctions to violence consist of religious texts and oral traditions that comprise prototypes for moral violence. These tales of exemplary violence of deities and heroes – paragons of virtue – are models for humans to emulate. These narratives *define* many violent practices as morally virtuous obligations, but do they actually *move* people to violence? It seems that they do.

> Medieval Christianity, with its judicial tortures, crusades,
> inquisitions, and witch-burnings, is not an aberration from the main
> patterns, but the pattern itself.
>
> *(Collins, 1974: 427)*

Moral motives based on the Bible were the foundation for the Crusades and the Inquisition. Beginning in Languedoc in 1233, European inquisitors imprisoned, tortured, and killed thousands for their purported heretical beliefs, while the Crusaders massacred thousands of Jews and Muslims (Eller, 2010: 177–9). Medieval Christian writers praised violence when it furthered the interests of the Church or political allies (Brown, 2011: 42–7). When violence was the fulfillment of God's will, it was admirable. Medieval clerics and others assumed that through bloody victories, God and his saints violently avenged wrongs against Himself and His followers, including revenge for injury or insult (Brown, 2011: 88–91, 156–9). In God's name, bishops commanded that miscreants be flayed or branded.

> Individuals or groups were entitled, and sometimes even required, to use violence to assert or protect their rights as they understood them and to avenge insult or injury... God and his saints did so as well.
>
> *(Brown, 2011: 189)*

> Christian bishops and monks were either violent themselves, or they celebrated violence carried out on their behalf by others. Christian saints both alive and dead used violence to defend themselves, their honor, and their followers, and to attack the enemies of God.
>
> *(Brown, 2011: 288)*

In short, medieval clerics and lords judged that violence was laudable, often required, and should be publicly displayed, enthusiastically observed, and widely celebrated. Similarly, drawing on violent biblical narratives as analogs, early modern and modern Europeans regarded themselves as equivalent to the Israelites and based their relations with other "races" on those that the Hebrew Bible prescribed. Thus, the verses quoted above from Numbers, Samuel, Joshua, Psalm 137, and Deuteronomy may have partially motivated and were certainly felt to justify a great many genocidal acts against native peoples around the world (Jenkins, 2010: 97–163).

Moral violence is basic to Abrahamic religions, but it is not unique to that religious tradition. Eller's (2010) comprehensive review of religiously motivated moral violence shows that it is widespread across history and creeds. Religions commonly assert that unquestionable supreme authorities ordain action against ultimate evils, in unqualified and unremitting pursuit of the ultimate good (p. 79). That action may include violence, particularly violence against those who did not accept the religion. In the *Bhagavad Gita*, the human prince Arjuna asks the supreme god Krishna for instructions.

> The Supreme Lord said: I am death, the mighty destroyer of the world, out to destroy. Even without your participation all the warriors standing arrayed in the opposing armies shall cease to exist.
>
> Therefore, get up and attain glory. Conquer your enemies and enjoy a prosperous kingdom. All these (warriors) have already been destroyed by Me. You are only an instrument, O Arjuna.
>
> Kill Drona, Bheeshma, Jayadratha, Karna, and other great warriors who are already killed by Me. Do not fear. You will certainly conquer the enemies in the battle, therefore, fight!
>
> *(11.32–4; translation by Ramanand Prasad at http://eawc.*
> *evansville.edu/anthology/gita.htm)*

In sum, people often do violence because they believe that gods or ancestors command it – a belief often supported by oracular consultations in which divine beings declare their will. Speaking on behalf of the deities, with the full authority of the gods, church authorities or prophets tell their congregations that they must kill the enemies of the gods, of the community, or of the nation. Furthermore, it is ultimately humans who perceive or attribute wrath to the gods. When a prophet declares that a god wills that we must kill, where does the prophet get that idea? Why does he imagine that a god must will violence? Why does anyone believe that the gods demand violence? The answer, of course, is that the human religious leaders and their followers are projecting their own social-relational emotions and moral motives onto the gods. Humans imagine the gods to have the same moral emotions they themselves experience. So every prophetic revelation or religious text ordaining violence is an expression of the human communicator's own moral motives.

Sacrificing animals and humans to the gods

In addition to engaging in violence at God's command, in a great many cultures people also experience violence as the primary way to *create and sustain* relationships with deities and spirits. In Africa, China, among the ancient Inca and Maya, in ancient Egypt, in early Mediterranean religions, and elsewhere, ancestors and deities are or were bloodthirsty – quite literally: they drink the blood of animals and humans sacrificed to them. In these cultures, feeding the gods is pivotal to the AR relationship between worshippers and their supernatural superiors. Depending on the ancestor or deity, to plead, placate, or connect, the people aiming to create, sustain, enhance, or redress their relationship with the supernatural being may find it morally necessary to offer up flowers or vegetable foods, or to kill animals or humans for the deity.

Offering up animals or humans by killing them is the core practice in many historical religions and some local contemporary religions. The religion of the Moose of Burkina Faso consists primarily of sacrificing chickens and, when possible, goats, by cutting their throats so that the blood flows over the "altar" (ApF, fieldwork). The sacrificer tosses bits of feather or flesh onto the altar, along with beer and flavored water. After boys butcher and roast the animal, the sacrificer tosses bits of cooked meat onto the altar. All the while, the sacrificer is addressing the ancestors by name in strict serial order, as well as invoking the Earth, the otiose god, and other beings, asking for protection from misfortune, and requesting good health and good crops. Then the assembled men of the lineage eat the meat of the sacrificed animals and drink the libation beer together. These sacrifices evidently feed the ancestors in a CS mode while they obeisantly propitiate them in an AR mode. Only the head of the lineage, its eldest male, may make sacrifices; everyone in the lineage depends on him to solicit the protective power of the ancestors and to intercede with the ancestors when they are ill or suffer misfortune. So these sacrifices enhance the lineage head's authority. At the same time the commensal consumption of the sacrificial meat and beer constitutes and reinvigorates the congregants' patrilineal CS relationship. Eating the sacrificial meat and drinking the offering beer together *makes* one a member of the lineage, and enhances the bonds and social identity that make them one with each other. Conversely, making these sacrifices is a moral obligation. It is the duty of the lineage head to revere and respect the lineage's ancestors, maintaining his own relationship to them. Moreover, he is morally required to protect, and speak up and intercede for everyone in the lineage: only he can address and feed the ancestors. So killing animals for the ancestors is both relationally and metarelationally virtuous. Indeed, it is morally mandatory: there is no other way to relate to the ancestors. Sacrifice *is* how a person relates. Revering the ancestors is the pivot of Moose religion and the crux of Moose morality, so sacrifice is the epitome of virtue.

These Moose practices closely resemble other sacrificial practices throughout West Africa, in ancient Greece and China, around the world, and throughout history. Of course, this is "violence" against animals, not humans, so it is on the margins of the subject of this book. However, informants indicate that the Moose formerly, though rarely, sacrificed humans, and it is well established that human sacrifice was frequent in West Africa (Law, 1985). The sacrifice of human victims has the same moral motives and sustains the same social relationships and metarelational configurations as animal sacrifice.

Likewise, "Animal and human sacrifice were central to early religious life" in late Shang (c. 1200–1045 BCE) and West Zhou (1045–771 BCE) China: the deities demanded 血食 xuèshí, "blood food" (ter Haar, 2011: 258; see also Lewis, 1990: 27ff.; Wilson, 2002).

> Religious activity in ancient China consisted primarily of the ritualized slaughter of animals (and sometimes humans), presentation of the victim to supernatural beings, and the eventual consumption of the meat by the living. Today, meat offerings, with or without a killing ritual, remain the dominant means by which the Chinese people interact with the sacred realm.
>
> *(Kleeman, 1994: 185)*

> Sacrifice remained the most important element of the religious program of the state up until 1911. Sacrifice was also the primary religious activity of the common man then as it is now. Three types of offering – those directed to gods, ancestors, and ghosts, as delineated by modern anthropologists – corresponded to a threefold division of Chinese society into officials, commoners, and outcastes. Each type involved blood-sacrifice.
>
> *(Kleeman, 1994: 188)*

As among the Moose and elsewhere, sacrifice in China was a combination of AR obeisance to superior supernatural beings and CS commensalism among the congregants, and between sacrificers and the beings they fed through sacrifice. In a discourse from 650 BCE, a duke reports, "I have heard it said, 'The gods do not partake of [the offerings of] those not of the same strain 類; the people do not sacrifice to those not of their clan 族'" (Kleeman, 1994: 191–2; bracketed clarification by Kleeman; note further that 類, *lei*, means "type," "kind," or "category" based on similarity – that is, CS equivalence). Indeed, the elite of ancient China forbade commoners to sacrifice to any deity with whom they had no kinship relation. Sacrifice in China in the Spring and Autumn Period (approximately 771 until probably 476 BCE) constituted the crucial bond uniting kin who sacrificed to a common ancestor, while sharing the blood of oath sacrifices was the only way to constitute covenants of binding trust between non-kin (Lewis, 1990: 9, 13, 15).

In ancient China, the higher one's rank, the higher the deities to whom one could legitimately sacrifice – and feudal lords personally performed the sacrifices, on the premise that ancestral spirits would only accept a sacrifice made by their eldest living male descendant (Lewin, 1990: 21; as indicated above, the Moose share this premise and practice). Sacrifice to the high gods was the prerogative of the nobility, metarelationally reinforcing and legitimating their authority *vis-à-vis* commoners (Kleeman, 1994; Lewis, 1990). At the pinnacle of the state, "the king was the sole legitimate link to his deceased, divinized forebears, who owed their divine position to their own previous service as chief officiants at state sacrifices" (Kleeman, 1994: 187). Thus, meta-relationally, authority among humans depended on superiors' sacrificial relationships with deities higher than those to whom their subordinates sacrificed. The subordinates of a sacrificer – in the limiting case, all of the subjects of the emperor – depended on the sacrificer to obtain the ancestors', ghosts', nature spirits', and gods' beneficent protection.[1] Two other forms of violence, warfare and hunting, also defined noble status (Lewis, 1990: 17). Indeed, sacrifice, hunting, and warfare were *the* activities proper to Chinese lords in Spring and Autumn Period China. They were closely integrated, for example, by the necessity to make sacrifices before initiating warfare, the conception that warfare, like sacrifice, was a form of religious service and sacrifice to the ancestors, and the motivation to win glory in war to maintain and enhance the glory of one's ancestors (Lewis, 1990: 22–6, 36).[2] Zhou period rulers sometimes

---

[1] The Old Testament also depicts struggles over the right to offer sacrifices, with all that this right implied for AR relationships among humans (Friedman, 1997).

[2] A moral framework for battle that resonates with nineteenth- and twentieth-century American motivational ideologies; cf. Marvin and Ingle, 1999.

sacrificed war captives; rebel leaders and assassins were cooked down into a meat sauce consumed by the court or army (Lewis, 1990: 27–8).

Furthermore, Chinese elites ranked themselves according to their precedence in the allocation of the meat sacrificed to the deities.

> During the Chou, sacrificial meats were regularly distributed among high members of the nobility and other officers of the state, who then would share them with subordinates and retainers. The mere display of such potent provender implied status.
>
> *(Kleeman, 1994: 190)*

Partaking in this meat crucially mediated the relationship between lord and master: Confucius resigned his office when the lord of Lu failed to give Confucius his share of the meat of the solstice sacrifice (Lewis, 1990: 30).

Animals were the victims of most traditional Chinese sacrifice. However, when a Shang ruler died, many retainers were killed to accompany him, and some elite members of the court seem to have killed themselves to join him (ter Haar, 2011: 259). When a Shang king built a new palace, he had whole army units buried in the foundation. Shang also sacrificed prisoners they captured, and indeed their wars were sanctified as hunts to obtain human sacrificial victims (Trigger, 2003: 242, 481, 579).

Other societies frequently sacrificed humans – sometimes in large numbers – to constitute the same sorts of social relationships and metarelationships that animal sacrifice constitutes. At the death of rulers and other elites, early Mesopotamian, Aztec, Maya, Yoruba, and Hawaiian priests and kings sacrificed many retainers or slaves (Trigger, 2003; Valeri, 1985). At the death of one's master in ancient Japan, followers might commit *junshi* suicide to accompany him (Tatai, 1983). Conversely, in premodern Japan, a master whose follower failed him could command or allow the follower to commit *hari-kari*, a form of ritual suicide, or the follower could take the initiative to do so himself. Likewise, when a First Dynasty Egyptian king died, Egyptians killed hundreds of servants and numerous artisans to go along with him (Trigger, 2003: 88). The Inca typically sacrificed 200 children for the enthronement of a king, and four children every time he became ill (Trigger, 2003: 80). The Inca sacrificed the most beautiful war captives and the most beautiful Inca children, including the children of subordinate rulers; the children were feasted for a period of time, then intoxicated, and then the sacrificers strangled them, cut their throats, ripped out their hearts, or buried them alive (Trigger, 2003: 480). Mayans especially prized the sacrifice of a conquered king or his close relatives; indeed, a new ruler could not take office until he had captured high-ranking enemies for sacrifice. Aztec and Yoruba nobles and rich merchants regularly sacrificed prisoners of war, criminals, strangers, and children to the gods – the Yoruba especially before setting off to war, the Aztec especially in celebrating victory with the sacrifice of royal captives and defeated soldiers (pp. 241, 476, 478). Aztecs preferred to offer up warriors and made war particularly to capture sacrificial victims, but between wars they made do with foreign slaves and inauspiciously born Aztec children. An Aztec young man had to wear his hair long until he captured enemy soldiers for sacrifice; to reach maturity with long hair was a perpetual humiliation (Trigger, 2003: 243). When not engaged in wars of conquest, Aztec and other highland Mexican states engaged in *xochiyaoyotl*, "flower wars," between friendly rival states, in order to provide both sides the opportunity to capture warriors to sacrifice (p. 244).

Hawaiian kings sacrificed humans at various life-cycle transitions (particularly funerals), healing, and purification ceremonies, to mark the stages of construction of canoes, houses, and temples, and as an integral part of warfare (Valeri, 1985). Most of the victims were people who had transgressed or rebelled against the king; chiefs were especially prized. In preparation for sacrifice, officiants often broke the victim's arms and legs, tore out one or both eyes, and, apparently, mutilated his penis (Valeri, 1985: 336, 402, note 259). Sacrifice was a triumphantly terrifying AR hierarchy display of royal authority. At the same time, sacrifice was a CS unity act of "renewed internal cohesion" in which "the incorporation of these victims into the god" who is "the synthesis of the land" ensured the integrity of the kingdom and the productive fertility of the land and of the kingdom's women (Valeri, 1985: 348).

The Viking gods also demanded blood offerings. "Sacrifices were made of male victims, including dogs, horses and men, to placate the gods, and their bodies, all mixed up together, were suspended from the trees in the sacred grove near the temple" (Batey *et al.*, 1994: 114). In the nineteenth century, Dahomeans and Ashanti sacrificed criminals and slaves to their gods (Bohannan, 1967b). Likewise, the ancient Greeks sacrificed humans to accompany their deceased husbands or masters, before going to war, on various other occasions, and in several cults (Hughes, 1991). In addition, there is textual and archeological evidence indicating that the Carthaginians sacrificed infants (Smith *et al.*, 2013; Xella *et al.*, 2013).

In sum, all or most of the great "civilizations" of the ancient world sacrificed humans, as did many other societies throughout history. Sacrificing animals to ancestors, spirits, and gods was even more present and continues today. AR relationships with these immaterial beings *consist* of killing a third being, human or animal. At the same time the blood or flesh fed to the immaterial beings and then consumed by the assembled congregants is what forms the CS bond among them all. But the social relationships are constituted not just by the offering and ingestion of these substances but also by the violence itself: the *killing* of the animal or human victim is necessary. It is by killing the victim at the altar that the sacrificer makes obeisance, asks for protection, and asserts a position just below the deity or ancestor and above the others on whose behalf he intercedes with the gods. The killing establishes a ranking with the supernatural being at the top, the sacrificer below, and the sacrificer's junior dependants at the bottom. In some cases, specific roles in the ritual or the temporal order of distribution of the meat constitute additional ranked status relationships.

Violent sacrifice is also fundamentally metarelational because, almost invariably, the congregants, dependants, or subjects are only able to relate to major ancestors, spirits, or deities through the sacrificer – he is the only one who can make the sacrifices that constitute everyone's relationship with the immaterial beings on whom everyone depends. Thus, every sacrifice operates metarelationally to mediate at least three social relationships: between the supernatural being and the sacrificer, between the sacrificer and his subordinate dependants, and, via those two relationships, between the dependants and the supernatural being. Among the Moose, for anyone but the head of the household to kill a chicken under any circumstances would be a major sin, because it would be treating the household head as if he were dead. Living in a Moose village in the late 1970s, whenever Fiske and his family wished to eat chicken, he personally had to kill it. Then (just as when sacrificing) anyone could pluck and butcher it.

Self-sacrifice to the gods

> Religious pain produces states of consciousness, and cognitive-emotional changes, that affect the identity of the individual subject

and her sense of belonging to a larger community or a more profound state of being. More succinctly, pain strengthens the religious person's bond with God and with other persons. Of course, since not all pain is voluntary or self-inflicted, one mystery of the religious life is how unwanted suffering can become transformed into sacred pain.

(Glucklich, 2001: 6)

In Chapter 1 we noted that medieval Europeans and people in contemporary Yap welcome their own suffering as an ideal, even an essential way to enhance social relationships with other humans or with God. Here, we consider another kind of religiously virtuous violence: practices of bloody or tortuous self-sacrifice meant to honor or appease the gods. Some Chinese, American Indians, Christians, Muslims, and others injure themselves severely in order to create and enhance relationships with spirits or deities. In these religious practices, violence is the medium for relating to supernatural beings: the relationship between humans and their deities *consists* of violence. To be moral is to be violent: amputating, piercing or tearing flesh, puncturing veins, or exposing oneself to extreme heat, cold, thirst, or hunger. This is what the gods demand; this is how a person relates to them.

In some Christian, Hindu, and Buddhist monastic traditions, the deepest religious devotion entails depriving oneself of comfort, food, sex, and sleep. For example, the Buddha is said to have gone through a period of extreme fasting and is sometimes represented as emaciated (e.g., Meisel and del Mastro, 1975). The Abrahamic religions, the Bahá'í faith, Hinduism, and Buddhism require fasting by all believers. In Jain religion, ideally true and total religiosity entails starving oneself to death (Dundas, 2002; Glasenapp, 1999). In medieval Christianity, lay devotion to God also took the form of self-starvation (Banks, 1996; Brown, 1988; Lester, 1995). Many other religions also enjoin fasting in various contexts (Westermarck, 1908 vol. I, pp. 292–308). Fasting generally enhances the CS between worshipper and God: the ascetic feels that to become one with God, she must abstain from most or all food, either in general or during certain calendrical intervals. In most of these traditions, abstaining from sexual intercourse is also involved and, conversely, in a great many religions, having sexual relations makes one unfit to relate to deities for an interval of time, or until one purifies oneself.

In many cultures, reverence, reaching out to, and demonstrating loyalty to the recently deceased, ancestors, spirits, or gods requires more than asceticism. One must endure terrible hardship, torture oneself, cut off one's own body parts to offer up, or make a sacrifice of one's own life. Such practices abound. Hindus traditionally praised self-sacrifice to the gods as an act of high devotion (Westermarck, 1908: vol. II, 244). Some religions, such as that of the Anatolian and Greek goddess Cybele, promoted castration (Hales, 2002; Ringrose, 2003; Stevenson, 1995). In ecstatic worship, followers of the north Syrian goddess Atargatis lashed themselves and each other, wounded themselves with knives, and castrated themselves (Lightfoot, 2002). Castrated eunuchs seem to have been prominent in early Christianity and monks of some monastic orders were also castrated (Stevenson, 2002). Here the purpose was to effect permanent celibacy, bringing the eunuch irrevocably and unfailingly close to God. In Russia from the late eighteenth century to the mid-twentieth century, male and female devotees of Skoptsky often had their genitalia cut off and female devotees were mastectomized (Engelstein, 1999).

China

In Chinese Buddhism there is a tradition of religious self-immolation (both burning and drowning) and also of amputating fingers and more (Benn, 2007). More broadly,

> The self-infliction of violence was an indispensable element in the construction of Chinese culture. It can be discovered in a variety of sources, including not only canonical literature and official history but also edicts, poetry, local gazetteers, novels, illustrations, drama, and even children's books. All of these sources demonstrate the pervasiveness of violence in how performers of these practices negotiated social relations, defined or redefined the nature of authority, and imagined human agency in relation to the cosmos.
>
> *(Yu, 2012a: 461)*

> Descriptions of state sacrifices, blood oaths, and the self-maiming practices of filial piety and female chastity are often imbued with a sympathetic understanding between the human world and cosmic agencies [such as gods, ancestors, ghosts, and geographically

identified spirits]. People expected gods (or Heaven) to intercede when they were in trouble, and by performing extreme forms of sacrifice they appealed for help.

(Yu, 2012a: 462)

From the tenth through the seventeenth century, it was relatively common in China for people to slice off a piece of their own flesh and boil it to make a broth to nourish and heal an ailing parent, uncle, or parent-in-law (*gegu*, "filial slicing"; Yu, 2012a, 2012b). "Nourishing the parents with [the flesh of the child] which came from them was a form of communion" (Yu, 2012a: 472). Local gazetteers report thousands of cases, highlighting the moral power of filial slicing devotion to evoke the sympathy of deities so they would heal the elder kinsperson. Sometimes literati highlighted metarelational implications of *gegu* to shame elites who, by contrast, were morally lax. Or, deploying another metarelational entailment, "local government officials legitimated their own mandate to govern their districts by rewarding performers of filial slicing, demonstrating how the virtue of performers directly reflected their own governance" (Yu, 2012a: 469).

In another example of self-harm to regulate relationships, Chinese eleventh- to seventeenth-century gazetteers eulogized girls who mutilated themselves to resist rape, and widows who mutilated themselves or committed suicide to resist remarriage (Yu, 2012a, 2012b). Such acts of *shouzie* consisted of "preserving moral fidelity" by branding one's face with a word or cutting off one's nose, ears, or fingers; such devotional self-mutilation was highly esteemed as an ideal of virtue. State-sponsored shrines and monumental arches commemorated such women's fierce preservation of their chastity.

Chinese rulers and high nobles were responsible for the welfare of their subjects, and they metarelationally depended on their relationships with deities, ghosts, and ancestors to maintain their power to rule over and protect their subjects. Rulers and nobles conducted their relationships with these beings through animal and human sacrifice, and, if necessary, self-sacrifice. In China since the Shang Dynasty (c. 1550–1045 BCE), to bring rain in a terrible drought, an official should expose himself to the sun until he died (ter Haar, 2012: 251, 259). Originally, the Shan Dynasty King Tang is said to have ended a great drought by attempting to self-immolate, but before he could set himself on fire, Heaven sent the rains. In other droughts, rulers and subsequently officials and Buddhist clerics exposed themselves naked to the sun for days on end or set themselves on fire to bring rain (Yu, 2012a, 2012b).

In this Chinese relational framework, Yu (2102a: 463) demonstrates that each of these acts of self-inflicted violence "reinforces traditional relationships and produces order" – moral order. Self-violence was admired, honored, and memorialized not just because of the devotion it evinced and the self-control required but essentially because of its transcendent intensification of social relationships with divine beings. Self-violence moved deities, ghosts, and ancestors to come to the aid of the self-sacrificer. Awed by the power of self-violence to elicit supportive divine intervention, humans revered the self-sacrificer. Thus, these Chinese self-harming practices morally created and enhanced dyadic relationships between human and supernatural beings, while also creating and enhancing triadic metarelational moral configurations.

American Indians

Olmecs, Mayans, and Aztecs frequently pierced their own tongues, penes, and earlobes to draw blood – often large quantities – to offer to the ancestors (Joyce et al., 1991; Trigger, 2003: 481). In aboriginal North America, self-violence was also widespread, and in some tribes an invariant rite of passage that raised the status of a youth, making him a man and a member of the community. This often consisted of excruciatingly painful, prolonged self-torture in order to form or revive an AR relationship with a guiding spirit who, as an AR superior, would bestow powers on the self-sacrificing follower, guide him, and support him. The first episode of self-torture was to discover or attract one's guardian spirit, whose nature and identity was unknown before the ordeal, but would appear in a vision after extensive suffering. So in many American Indian cultures, boys or youths frequently fasted or went without water in quest of visions of their personal spirit guardian (Benedict, 1922). To get in touch with their guardian spirits, men in many American Indian cultures of the Great Plains, in particular, fed the sun with bits of their bodies, using a blade to pry loose a disk of their own flesh as an offering (Benedict, 1922).

In order to envision their personal guardian spirit, Native American men of the northern Great Plains also inflicted extreme pain on themselves in the Sun Dance ritual, in which they had others insert sinews through the muscles of their back and later tore themselves loose by rupturing the muscles. The first time they did this was to identify and connect with a personal guardian spirit; subsequently, they did it to contact their guardian and receive a communication from him. Here is a Crow text exemplifying the social relationship between supplicant and the sun: "Medicine Crow fasted and prayed for four days. He cut off a finger joint and offered it to the Sun. 'Sun, look at me. I am poor. I wish to own horses. Make me wealthy. That is why I give you my little finger'" (Lowie, 1919: 117; see also Lowie, 1922: 342). Note that "poor" is not an MP situation; the horses would not be used to make money, nor sold; "poor" means lacking in status.

In answer to his self-sacrifice, Medicine Crow, like other Plains Indians, hoped for (and in this instance received) a vision that guided and instructed him, giving him special "powers": ritual knowledge and often (as in this case) authority to establish and lead a ritual society.

The Sun Dance was a focal ritual of Plains Indian cultures and remains so in modern times. Traditionally, a man vowed to stage a dance in connection with plans to avenge a death, lead a hunt or ask for abundant buffalo herds, seek shamanistic power, or heal others (Jorgensen, 1972). The performance of the Sun Dance benefited the entire community, and participants were greatly respected for dancing. They danced for three days and nights without water or food; when a dancer collapsed it was expected that he was likely to be receiving his vision.

In many tribes, men also performed solitary rituals with similar sociomoral aims. A Cheyenne man would go out early in the day with a helper to a lonely place on the prairie, where they would consecrate pins and a knife.

> He is then tied to the pole by means of wooden pins driven through
> the flesh. All day long, after he is left alone again, he must walk back
> and forth on the sunward side of the pole, praying constantly,
> and fixing his eyes on the sun, trying to tear the pins loose from the
> torn flesh. At night the helper returns, and pieces of the torn skin
> are held toward the sun and sky and the four directions and buried.
> That night he sleeps on the prairie and gets his power.
>
> *(Benedict, 1922: 5)*

Seeking guiding visions, the Dakota performed similar rituals, sometimes hanging by cords for days, or passing a knife through their body and waiting silently for the vision. The Dakota, Mandan-Hidatsa, Assiniboine, and Gross-Ventre also cut off finger joints and lacerated themselves for the same purpose.

In addition to simply establishing a relationship with a guardian spirit while proving themselves men, men of the Great Plains constituted, redressed, or regulated many other relationships through vision quest torture.

> Everywhere, even in those tribes where every man was expected to fast once in his life specifically for an individual guardian, the vision was sought also by the same means on continually recurring occasions – that is in mourning; as an instrument of revenge on one's enemies; on account of a vow made in sickness or danger for oneself or one's relative; on initiation into certain societies; and as a preliminary to a war party. On all these occasions, the seeker ordinarily received his power or commands directly, without specifically acquiring a guardian spirit.
>
> *(Benedict, 1922: 12)*

Interestingly, among the Blackfoot, it was important to own medicine bundles based on visions, but it mattered little whether one had these visions oneself, or purchased them from another:

> The visions themselves could be bought and sold. Every man went out at least once in his life seeking a vision on his own account. Many failed, so the Blackfoot repeatedly assert. But whether he met with success or failure, he must also buy other men's visions for his social prestige. They were the basis of the tribal economic system; the greater proportion of Blackfoot capital was invested in these readily salable commodities. Investment in them, as Dr. Wissler puts it, was equivalent to money in the savings-bank... In telling his story he makes absolutely no distinction in the use of the first person between those visions he has bought and those he has fasted for ... what he has really bought being the songs, the taboos, the "power," and the right of performing the ceremony that goes with it.
>
> *(Benedict, 1922: 17)*

To a lesser degree, the Crow, Arapaho, Hidatsa, and Winnebago also bought and sold "the blessings of the spirit," and in many tribes the vision or the medicine bundle based on the vision was inherited (p. 18).

Hence, as in other contexts in other cultures, MP relationships can be a means to establish or enhance AR relationships.

In these practices, like people in a number of other cultures, American Indians sacrificed their own bodies in order to establish an AR relationship with a deity whom they expected to guide and protect them all their lives. In the Sun Dance they simultaneously suffered for the welfare of the entire community, enhancing CS bonds.

Christian monastic asceticism

As the preaching of Jesus Christ spread in the first centuries after his death, men seeking to become one with God imposed on themselves an asceticism that was often agonizing. By around 200 BCE, a variety of hermits and ascetic communities had formed in the eastern Mediterranean region, particularly in Egypt and Syria (Hamman, 1977). Like modern monasteries, the ascetic communities, most of which were exclusively male, were cenobitic – members ate, slept, worked, and prayed together in a CS community. They characteristically were celibate and often abstained from meat and wine, or fasted (Rousseau, 1985). In Greek and Syriac (the language of the earliest Christian communities in Syria and Mesopotamia), the first texts that describe a person dedicated exclusively to the religious life (*monachos* in Greek and *îhîdâyâ* in Syriac) depict them as celibate ascetics (Guillaumont, 1979: 218–22). They modeled their cenobitism on the lives of the Apostles. Early Syriac ascetics were "single ones": they gave up their relations with their families, single-mindedly severed themselves from worldly interests, and committed themselves to Jesus. The concept and the practice were based on an idea of oneness or unity: undivided focus on God, in order to unite in CS communion with God. In particular, by the second century in Syria, baptism – which was closely associated with cenobitism – was seen as a means of becoming one with and *in* Christ (Winkler, 1982). Baptism dissolved the separations and distinctions among individuals, unifying and reintegrating persons into their original totality. Uniting with others in a cebobitic community was both a means and a result of this union with God. The sex and the food that these early monks gave up were not evils in themselves, but only relative to their single-minded dedication to God (Guillaumont, 1979: 222).

Consecrating oneself to Christ and entering the Covenant through baptism, converts were exhorted in a language of military struggle or athletic combat to prepare for conflict; they will be joined in Christ but separated from the rest of the world. These early ascetics sought union with Christ and often referred to themselves as bride-grooms of Christ. Many of the first Syrian ascetics were probably initially wanderers, without the architectural or institutionalized struc-tures of later monasteries. But their conception of themselves as communally united in Christ bound them together as strongly as in the more tangible monasteries. Writing in France early in the fifth century, Cassian reported on the Egyptian monastic tradition where he had studied: he wrote that "the ultimate end of monastic life is the Kingdom of God, that is, contemplative union with God in prayer" (paraphrased by Veilleux, 1986: 304). Augustine's (354–430 CE) pre-cept for the monastic community was that it must form a single heart, extending a common soul to God. This requires both celibacy and fasting; Chapter 5 of his *Rules* begins, "Subdue the flash by fasting and abstinence from food and drink as much as your health permits" (Augustine, 1961). This self-deprivation was often agonizing to sus-tain, but motivated by their religious devotion, many sought this ascetic life and many actually managed to sustain it.

Christian and Muslim self-flagellation

Christians and Muslims have sometimes gone beyond ascetic suffer-ing: some believers inflict pain and injury on themselves to connect in CS relationships in which their suffering makes them become one with their God (with sometimes also an element of AR devotion), while also bonding with others who suffer in the same manner – and perhaps gaining in AR status when other worshippers hold them in awe (Glucklich, 2001). As we noted in Chapter 1, religious mortifi-cation of the flesh was a central practice in medieval Christianity.

> Practically all the holy women of the later Middle Ages, nuns as well
> as Beguines and laywomen, practiced the self-infliction of pain and
> welcomed divinely inflicted suffering. Men were equally zealous,

with extreme cases such as Heinrich Suso, who carved a cross in his own flesh.

(Cohen, 2010: 27)

Self-destructive religious violence ... include[s] fasting or denying oneself particular foods, sleep deprivation, isolation or silence, enforced celibacy, hitting, cutting, scarring, piercing, burning, whipping, castration or amputation of body parts, holding awkward or painful poses, carrying weights, ingesting drugs or poisons, drawing the blood, and subjecting oneself to beating or torture and ultimately suicide or presenting oneself for execution.

(Eller, 2010: 118).

Such practices became institutionalized and routinized:

When religion becomes an important administrative and ceremonial adjunct to the state, as well as the basis for community organization, then the influence of ascetic cruelty becomes coercive. Not only is the ascetic individual rewarded with high status (and certain opportunities for power and wealth), but asceticism becomes a mark of membership in the community, and is enforced upon everyone by external authority.

(Collins, 1974: 435)

The icon of Christianity is the crucified Christ; many Christians wear a cross, the instrument of excruciatingly painful, slow execution. For Christians, the violence that Christ endured, his self-sacrifice, is considered the greatest act of virtue in all creation. His horrific pain is the crux of Christianity: God's sending his son to be sacrificed and Christ's redemption of humanity through his suffering on the cross define Christian virtue (for the history of this idea, see Fulton, 2002). To emulate Christ's suffering is to share it, and to partake in his virtue. So Christians have long celebrated the suffering of martyrs and saints, whose torture and execution make them paragons of virtue (Korsten, 2009). The greater their pain and suffering, the greater their virtue – and the more intense the CS relationship they create with Christ. In effect, Christians look up to saints because they nobly suffered for Christ: metarelationally, they are elevated in an AR relationship with other Christians by their extraordinary sacrifice to sustain their CS relationship with God while refusing to subordinate themselves in an AR relationship to the lay authorities who tortured them. For example, the very popular thirteenth-century English *South English Legendary* consists largely of narratives of beating, torture by molten metals or ovens, and death – for example, by decapitation (Crachiolo, 2004). The readers evidently revered and relished the extreme and prolonged pain, the gruesomely graphic depiction of which is the essence of such hagiography. This focus on the virtues of suffering continued for centuries; Gallonio's *Tortures and Torments of the Christian Martyrs*, first published in 1591 and subsequently very popular across Europe, was widely reprinted and translated. Furthermore, it is through the suffering of the martyrs and indeed all Christians that the Church wins its glorious victory not just in this historical world, but ultimately and transcendentally (Korsten, 2009). "The infliction of pain and the violation of life is not just the order of the day, but is needed in order to produce that world and propel it towards its end," salvation (Korsten, 2009: 400).

But self-sacrifice was not limited to saints. Early in the second millennium CE, monks in monastic orders such as the Franciscans and Dominicans began scourging themselves; this practice gradually spread to lay Christians (Eller, 2010: 126–9). Painful practices became integrated into everyday religiosity in the late Middle Ages. In early modern England, pain was "a form of *imitatio Christi*, a key ingredient of Christian identity, and a source of mystical insight and transformation" (van Dijkhuizen, 2009: 207). Even in nineteenth-century New Mexico, one extreme self-mortifying brotherhood used a great variety of self-torture; initiation into the Brothers of the Blood included having the emblem of the brotherhood carved into one's back (Eller, 2010: 127).

Worshipping through flagellating oneself is also prominent in Islam. During Muharram, Muslims fast for one or more days, and Shias in particular commemorate the death of Muhammad's grandson Husain ibn Ali in the succession battle at Karbala in 680 CE (Chelkowski, 2010; Pinault, 1992). Shias identify themselves with Hussain as the legitimate heir of the Prophet, while Sunnis identify themselves with the lineage of Yazid, the ruler who ordered the killing of Hussain and his followers. Shia men (especially in public processions or mosques) and women (in groups gathered out of sight in a household) share Hussain's suffering and exhibit their devotion to him and his people by *matam*, beating their chests in synchrony with each other, often to the point of causing significant bruising. In India, Pakistan, Afghanistan, Iran, Iraq, and

Bahrain, men also flagellate themselves by *zanier kea matam* with chains, some of which incorporate knives or razors. They experience and display the pain and bloodshed they inflict on themselves

> as a symbolic demonstration of love for Hussain with the purpose of earning rewards in Paradise; it indicates remorse at the community's inability to prevent Hussain's martyrdom and places men among those martyred with Hussain. *Zanjir ka matam* expresses at the collective level the courage to endure persecution and at the personal level the "desire to demonstrate physically the willingness to suffer the kind of wounds which they would have incurred had they fought at Karbala."
>
> *(Schubel, 1993: 93, quotation [corrected by ApF] in text by Abou Zahab, 2008: 108–9)*

Thus, this self-mortification is an act of CS empathy and compassion for Hussain and his followers and has also now become an act of making the flagellants all one together in CS by their shared pain, injury, and scars – marking Shia identity and at the same time marking Pakistani Punjabis and others who perform it as "true" Muslims, more Muslim than Arab Muslims (Chelkowski, 2010).

In sum, across many cultures people show their devotion to spirits or gods by causing themselves serious pain or harm. Self-torture and self-wounding are acts of devotion to deities or spirits, who are moved to care for humans who so sacrifice themselves. Secondarily, those who wound themselves together, or in the same way, become one with each other through the blood they shed in common and the common modifications and markings they make to or on their bodies. People conceive of and create CS relationships by consubstantiation: making their bodies alike (Fiske, 2004; Fiske and Schubert, 2012). Social selves are indexed in the physical bodies, so that when their bodies become the same, participants become bonded as one social person, each equivalent to all. The blood that people shed, the wounds and scars that people share, connect them to each other. In the Christian tradition, furthermore, the wounds that people inflict on themselves make their bodies resemble the crucified body of Christ, and hence indexically connect their selves to Him. In Muharram, Shias' wounding themselves make their bodies like the body of the martyred Hussain, thereby becoming one with him in pain and suffering. Other self-injurious and self-mortifying practices function like blood sacrifices of animals or humans: the pain and blood are offered up to deities and spirits, effecting experientially "direct" corporeal connections with them.

There is always a more or less instrumental facet of sacrifice: it is aimed at obtaining the worshipper's or others' good fortune and relief from suffering or danger. But sacrifice seeks welfare by constituting a social relationship between the sacrificer and the recipient of the sacrifice. Moreover, more fundamentally, regardless of the material or practical outcome, sacrifice is a pious duty. Subjectively, killing the animal or human victim or harming oneself are reverentially virtuous acts. The phenomenology of sacrifice is devotional – obeisant devotion to the supernatural being. The perpetrator is morally motivated and morally obligated to harm or kill because in many religious traditions sacrificial violence is the only way to constitute the most fundamental, essential, necessary, and sacred relationships between humans and their ancestors, spirits, and deities.

THEORETICAL ELABORATION

Bernard Shaw:	"Governor, If Kitty Dukakis were raped and murdered, would you favor an irrevocable death penalty for the killer?"
Michael Dukakis:	"No, I don't, Bernard, and I think you know that I've opposed the death penalty during all of my life. I don't see any evidence that it's a deterrent and I think there are better and more effective ways to deal with violent crime."
	(exchange between CNN's Bernard Shaw and Democratic candidate Michael Dukakis during the second presidential debate prior to the 1988 election)

When Dukakis unemotionally and without hesitation stated that he would be opposed to the death penalty even for a man who raped and killed his wife, his poll numbers plummeted overnight. On the one hand, this is just yet another example of support for morally motivated violence. Capital punishment's lack of deterrent effect is inconsequential to those who think that a killer deserves to be killed in retribution. On the other hand, Dukakis' response and the consequences that followed reveal important aspects of the nature of beliefs, theories, and claims. Perhaps Dukakis should have responded by saying that although he's committed to the moral principle that we should not kill anyone, no matter what, there are always going to be easy cases and difficult cases. Defending the thesis that killing criminals is wrong, no matter what their crime, is easier when the crime is robbing a bank, or even killing a stranger in the heat of an argument. It's much more difficult when the crime is violating and murdering the person in the world who is closest to you, the person you should have protected. Many people intuitively feel that the death penalty must be warranted when someone has killed a person they love. But for Dukakis, being opposed to the death penalty in all cases means being opposed to it in *all cases*, no matter how horrible or vile. Part of having a clearly defined position or theory means putting aside your intuitions and feelings sometimes, and committing yourself to a theory that captures not only the easy cases but also the difficult cases that have the same logical structure.

We have reached the midway point of the book, having characterized the moral motives and relationship-constitutive phases of defense, punishment, vengeance, fighting for respect and solidarity, violence ordered by and committed by authorities, honor violence, violence in war, and violent sacrifice. In presenting virtuous violence theory to colleagues, we have found that these are relatively easy cases to accept as morally motivated. In the second half of the book, we examine violent practices that were more difficult for our colleagues to accept as morally motivated, including torture, homicide, suicide, ethnic violence, intimate partner violence, rape, bodily mutilation, violence in mourning, and robbery. So before we move on to those topics, let us elaborate on virtuous violence theory to address questions and concerns that may be starting to come up in the reader's mind. In Chapter 9, we more fully explain our definition of moral psychology and what it includes, how people determine what is moral and what is immoral, and how people cognitively process moral motives for violence. In Chapter 10, we consider other approaches to explaining motives for violence, showing how virtuous violence theory complements and deepens these theories.

9 ON RELATIONAL MORALITY: WHAT ARE ITS BOUNDARIES, WHAT GUIDES IT, AND HOW IS IT COMPUTED?

Defining the moral space

Virtuous violence theory is based on a scientific model of moral psychology, and in the same sense that the scientific concept of mass is not identical to the folk concept of weight, virtuous violence theory does not encompass everything that is entailed by the Western folk model of "moral," nor is it limited to just what the everyday, folk concept denotes. Indeed, it could not do so because the folk model is different in every culture, and varies from person to person within any culture. In every culture that has a word that more or less translates as "moral," the term has a unique scope, unique presuppositions, and unique implications. And not every culture does have one word, or a set of synonyms, that neatly corresponds to the English *moral*. So to understand human "moral" psychology, we need to formulate a construct that aptly captures a natural kind in the world, even if no vernacular language does so precisely. However, virtuous violence theory is intended to capture much of what is meant in lay terms by the English "moral" and congruent terms in other languages, while still maintaining the advantages of a theoretically derived, deductively coherent enterprise. If virtuous violence theory encompasses a broad domain of important psychosocial phenomena that can be clearly and simply explained in terms of morally motivated relationship regulation, it is a good theory, regardless of whether the phenomena that it encompasses correspond precisely to the fuzzy and contentious folk domain of "moral" as any particular person in any particular culture uses that term, or something more or less corresponding to it. The scientific concept of *force* does not map exactly onto the (polysemic and fuzzy) folk concept of "force" in any culture, but it is nonetheless an invaluable concept – indeed, much better for describing and explaining physics than the folk concept. There are no vernacular terms at all for "Higgs boson," "carbon ring," "insular cortex," "sexual selection," "analog magnitude system," "Nash equilibrium," or "plate tectonics" – but science wouldn't get very far if it didn't construct valid technical terms for these important entities. To understand the world, we need technical terms that cut nature at its joints.

We have defined *morality* as the intentions, motivations, evaluations, and conjoined emotions that operate to realize ideal models of social relationships in a culturally meaningful manner. This definition seems to us to be a valid description of a natural kind in the world. But, of course, our definition doesn't precisely match the vernacular usage of the word "moral" in everyday English discourse, academic discourse, or research methods. Rather, we arrived at this understanding from a social-functional perspective and with reference to the theory of natural selection.

Homo sapiens engages in extraordinarily cooperative and complex social relationships (Fiske, 1991). These relationships permit humans to adapt to an exceptionally diverse range of ecosystems, and indeed to create whole new ecosystems. Unlike the great majority of mammals, people's fitness and psychological well-being are deeply dependent on the nature and quality of their social relationships. But sustaining these relationships is challenging because cooperation frequently requires the cooperators to exercise sufficient self-control to forgo immediate selfish satisfactions, make sometimes arduous efforts to contribute, and inhibit temptations to cheat (Fiske, 2002, 2010; Frank, 1988; Joyce, 2007). To sustain adaptive social relationships, the cooperator must consistently control hunger, thirst, pain, the need to regulate her temperature, exhaustion, sleepiness, sexual desires, and fear, while exerting herself to do what must be done for the sake of the relationship. The selfish benefits of defection (food, sex, rest, safety, and comfortable ambient temperature) are certain and immediately present, while the benefits of cooperation, though much greater, are often far in the future, distributed over long intervals, and uncertain. And the nonsocial selfish needs are experienced as very intense because they are deeply embedded in the basic mechanisms of the brain by hundreds of millions of years of years of natural selection on mostly solitary organisms. To counteract and overcome these basic asocial organic needs in order to enable people to sustain the adaptive social relationships that humans specifically need, human social-relational motives must often be even more intense than motives for individual well-being and survival (Fiske, 2002, 2010; Rai and Fiske, 2011). People subjectively experience these motives to constitute social relationships as sociomoral emotions such as love, belonging, awe, pride, the need for equality, or the desire for proportionality. Other sociomoral motives are experienced as anger, outrage, moral disgust, shame, guilt, social anxiety, and loneliness. The core thesis of virtuous violence theory is that any and all of these and other emotionally experienced moral motives sometimes impel people to regulate their social relationships violently.

The moral motives people experience depend on which of the RMs they employ and the local cultural preos that govern the implementation of the models. When people regulate their relationships through actions that accord with RMs and cultural preos, they are acting morally; when they regulate relationships through actions that violate RMs and cultural preos, they are acting immorally. Both types of acts regulate relationships, but whether the regulation is moral or immoral depends on the RMs and cultural preos that participants and observers are using.

Distinguishing between moral and immoral relationship regulation

Preos are the cultural prototypes, paragons, practices, precedents, para-digms, proscriptions, precepts, proverbs, and principles that guide people in implementing the universal, innate models. The structure of the RMs is abstract: it doesn't specify which model should be applied to coordinate any specific aspect of a particular interaction in a given situation with whom, how, when, where, and with respect to what entities. Use of the models differs across cultures and people use different models in different situations. Combining one of the four RMs with the culturally appropriate preos determines a complete RM to generate, interpret, evaluate, and coordinate some aspect of a social interaction. Hence, whether *any* behavior is moral, immoral, or non-moral depends on whether it regulates relationships according to the cultural preos people are using.

Suppose a guy loves a girl, and does everything to make her happy. He attentively figures out what pleases her, gives her thoughtful gifts, listens with concern, sensitively responds to her moods, cheers her up when she's down, takes care of her when she's ill, apologizes and makes amends when he offends her, and puts aside his work and other obligations when she needs him. He gently initiates sex, pleasing her, and she invites him to continue. In our terms, he regulates the relationship. Suppose her parents are fully aware of the relationship and they, too, consent to all this. It is all morally laudatory. He's 25 and she's 25. Or suppose she's 19. OK. Or she's 17 years and 364 days old – not quite legal in many US states, but legal in Canada and some US states. Hmm? If she's 11 and they're American, his actions are clearly immoral – the same actions, with the same relationship-regulatory intent, that would be morally commendable if she were 25. If she's 7, what he's doing is evil – in most cultures. But in some cultures men or boys marry very young girls, and it's pretty much up to the husband when and how he treats her sexually. The cutoff between virtuous and immoral ages, and the perceived rights of the man as a function of his relationship with the girl, vary greatly across history and culture. The age of consent in Asian nations varies from 13 to 21, in Europe from 13 to 18, and so forth – but in some jurisdictions it depends on how close in age the participants are, or whether they are of the same gender. Likewise, the kinship relations that separate moral from immoral sex or marriage vary greatly from culture to culture and across history in any one culture. In some cultures, the man's actions would be immoral if she were his father's brother's daughter – they'd be "siblings" – while in other cultures she would be the ideal bride to court. In a number of cultures, incestuous sexual relations that would be totally immoral under ordinary circumstances are expectable and tolerable, even laughable, when they occur on special occasions – such as a funeral. In some cultures, such as among traditional Hindu, sexual relationships with a widow are immoral, regardless of the participants' feelings. Yet, among the Moose of Burkina Faso, a widow *must* marry a brother of her late husband or one of his sons by another wife, while in other cultures marrying your late husband's son would be incest. In a monogamous culture, a person may marry and have sex with only one partner at a time, while in most cultures, either men or women hope to have multiple spouses at the same time, and have sex with any of them – and others esteem a man who has scores of spouses, like a West African chief. In some cultures at some points in history, men having sex with men was or is immoral, while in other cultures it's only morally degrading for the person who is penetrated – the penetrator is esteemed for his conquest.

It's not that sex is moral or immoral, *per se*: it's whether the cultural implementations of the basic RMs prescribe or proscribe sex between people in the specific type of relationship in question.

Even the most disinterested, reasonable, intelligent, well-trained people from the same segment of the same community in the same culture often disagree about how to apply the most carefully crafted, propositionally articulated laws to particular events or practices. Cultural preos are usually much less clear than laws: indeed, they are often quite ill-specified and ambiguous. Like laws, there are typically many different preos that could be applied to any given situation. Not everyone is reasonable and intelligent. People rarely have much, if any, *explicit training* in applying most preos. No one is ever really disinterested if he is participating in a relationship as perpetrator or victim, or engaged in any relationship with either. So there is always both latitude and ambiguity about how to apply preos to implement any RM. This means that morality consists of intentions, motives, emotions, and judgments about realizing RMs according to the cultural preos *as the perceiver interprets and applies the preos to the situation.*

The more cultural consensus there is about the preos for implementing a RM in a given situation, and the more closely the person's intentions correspond with that consensus, the more his or her actions will appear moral to observers. The difference between moral and immoral motives from the perpetrator's perspective is in whether the action is intended to realize a RM in a way that the perpetrator perceives to be congruent with the relevant cultural preos, or whether, on the contrary, the action is inconsistent with those preos. In the examples above, all of the romantic actions regulate the relationship, but whether they are perceived by participants and observers as wonderful or evil depends on whether the actions fit the operative cultural preos as construed by participants and observers.

In a number of African cultures, if a man wants to have sex with a women to whom he is not married, he should give her money. That's the morally correct, polite, and proper thing to do (Swidler and Watkins, 2007; ApF field notes). But in the West, paying someone for sex is immoral – if it's an explicit and direct *quid pro quo*. However, buying a woman an expensive bouquet, taking her to an elegant restaurant, getting ~d seats at a pricey show, and flattering her might do the trick (so to speak). Whether the man pays money directly, or to purchase things for the woman, or pays nothing at all but is simply nice to her without placing her in the awkward position of saying "no" after he's shown her such a good time, he's trying to regulate the relationship. What's moral to observers is either paying directly, paying indirectly, or just being nice, depending on the preos of the particular culture; and what's moral in the perpetrator's motives depends on his interpretation of the preos. There's nothing about the features of the act, as such, that gives the act its moral quality. It is moral in the eyes of an evaluator if she perceives it to be congruent with the cultural preos (regardless of whether the comparison is intuitive and unreflective, or explicitly analyzed and articulated).

Violence is morally motivated when the perpetrator intends the violence to regulate a relationship in a manner that is congruent with the cultural preos as the perpetrator perceives them. Suppose a child intentionally throws his father's watch off a boat. The father, who is holding a rod, regulates the relationship: he punishes the child by applying the rod he's holding to the child's posterior once with the force of 1 N, which is barely perceptible, and perhaps less than the force of the rod if it were merely resting on the child. Not worth mentioning; certainly the prerogative of the father in nearly any culture. What about striking the child's posterior four times with a force of 4 N: this makes a slight impression but is not exactly painful. Fathers ought to regulate their relationships with their sons: it's their moral duty. What about 16 blows with a force of 16 N each? In many cultures, perhaps in the low range of what a father or schoolmaster would be expected to do to correct a minor infraction, and would be esteemed and praised for doing – he's being the perfect father. Now 64 blows of 64 N each might be harsh but in some cultures, perhaps proper punishment for a boy destroying his father's good watch. But if the father strikes the delinquent boy with 256 blows of 256 N, or 1,024 blows of 1,024 N, the punishment has gone too far – it's cruel and unusual. It's all a matter of degree. And, of course, the morality of the punishment depends on whether the son is 14, 4, or 2 years old, or 6 months old. In each case the father is regulating the relationship. But at the low end of severity and the upper end of the boy's age, he's not seen as being sufficiently strict – a loving and responsible parent might be expected not to spare the rod and spoil the child. At the high end of severity and the low end of the boy's age, the father is committing child abuse, or murder. At any level of violence, however, he may be aiming to regulate the relationship, and in the mechanical form of the actions themselves there's no qualitative difference between the moral and the immoral levels of violence. Of course, the preos for parental discipline aren't specified in newtons, and don't specifically mention one's grandfather's rose-gold pocket watch inscribed with his personal motto. So how is a morally motivated father to know how hard to cane his child, especially if he forgot to bring along his force gauge?

Cultures differ in their approval of men having sex with young women or girls of a given age, depending on their kinship relation, and in their norms about whipping children. Every culture has standards for how old a girl should be before she has sex, and every culture has standards for the amount of force a parent may and should apply in punishing children for transgressions of varying severity. Informants from a culture feel that an act is moral when it's calibrated to the preos for the relationship; that is, when it's congruent with the cultural precedents, practices, prototypes, paradigms, precepts, principles, proscriptions, and prescriptions for implementing the relationship. The congruence of any act or practice with the preos of a given culture or subculture is always more or less ambiguous, especially at the margins. Within a community there is often a fair degree of consensus about the morality of particular acts, but not necessarily unanimity – differences in perception and perspective are ubiquitous.

What this means is that in any given instance in any given culture, any given person may feel that any given action to regulate a relationship is more or less moral, depending on the perceiver's perception of the degree of congruence between the action and those cultural preos that they perceived to be relevant. In a given culture, a father aiming to regulate his relationship with his son may strike him too lightly, too hard, or just right. When it's just right, it's perceived as moral. But it's all relationship regulation, whether it's too light, too hard, or just right.

To regulate a relationship with a deity, people in many cultures fast, as, for example, during Lent or Ramadan. In some cultures under certain circumstances, such as among mature Jain men, it is virtuous to abstain from all food, and consequently die. In most religions, that would not be the right moral choice, and, indeed, it would be improper to fast at all if it imperiled one's health. The precedents and prescriptions of each religion specify who should fast, how much, and when. But however much or little the devotee fasts, it's all aimed at regulating her relationship with a deity – even if she does it more, or less, than the preos of her culture specify, as she, or her sister, or experts variously interpret the preos.

What these examples demonstrate is that from an objective perspective independent of the culture or of the actor's intentions and perceptions, there is no qualitative, typological, categorical, or morphological difference between relationship regulation that is moral and relationship regulation that is immoral. The morality or immorality of the relationship-regulation motivation just depends on whether and how closely the actor intends her action to correspond to the preos she perceives to be relevant, in conjunction with the cultural validity of her perception of how the preos apply to the situation. As we show throughout this book, violent relationship-regulatory actions that in one culture or in one historical epoch are moral may be immoral in another culture or in another historical epoch. The acts are the same; what makes them moral or immoral are the cultural preos that people implement in order to compare the act with an ideal RM. At any point in any culture, whether relationship-regulatory violence is moral or immoral, and to what degree, depends on whether and how precisely the form and intensity of the violence is congruent with the preos people apply in evaluating it. Moral relationship-regulatory violence does not differ in kind from immoral relationship-regulatory violence: the same violent relationship-regulatory act may be moral in one culture and immoral in another, or even within one culture may be deemed moral or immoral depending on which preos people use when they evaluate the violence, how they weigh alternative preos, and how they apply them to particular circumstances and acts.

The social relationships that people want to constitute generally are the relationships that are culturally prescribed, ideally prototypical, or traditionally precedent – that is, the relationships that conform to the local cultural preos. When people try to constitute the social relationships that are culturally prescribed for them, in accordance with prevailing preos, their relationship-regulation motives are, by definition, moral. When they try to create relationships that are discordant with culturally prescribed relationships – that conflict with the preos for it – their relationship-regulation motives are immoral. So "moral motives" are motives to constitute culturally prescribed relationships in a culturally prescribed manner. When people try to regulate a culturally prescribed relationship through culturally prescribed violence, their motives for the violence are moral.

What are the cultural preos delimiting violence?

The fact that people sometimes are morally motivated to violently regulate their relationships does not imply that they believe that they are free to do *any* kind of violence to regulate any relationship. While violence regulates relationships, relationship preos also regulate violence. This "regulation" may consist of traditional practices, activities that people perform without complexly articulated "reasons" but nonetheless a strong sense of tradition. One feels that, according to tradition, one *must* do this just as it has always been done, that doing this is crucial to being a certain kind of person, and that it would be somehow terrible not to do it just so. In an intermediate form, this culturally informed social-relational "regulation" of violence may be articulated in discourse about the violence, its proper forms, and some reasons for doing violence and for certain people doing it in certain ways in certain circumstances. At the other pole of this dimension, violence may be fully rationalized, in the Weberian sense that there are legitimately established, propositionally formulated, written rules duly disseminated to the proper perpetrators, such as police and penal personnel. For instance, in South Sudan, the Nuer violently defended themselves against insult or theft, redressing any wrong by retaliating:

> The club and the spear are the sanctions of rights.

> Nuer are at once prepared to fight if they are wronged or insulted, unless kinship, or great disparity in age, restrains them.

> It is the knowledge that a Nuer is brave and will stand up against aggression and enforce his rights by club and spear that ensures respect for person and property.
>
> *(Evans-Pritchard, 1940: 169–71)*

The Nuer are very quick to regulate their relationships violently, but they don't employ just any random, impulsive violence to do so. When Nuer men of the same village or camp fight, they limit themselves to clubs (and stop before they kill). In contrast, men disputing with men from different Nuer villages, or raiding them, use spears, but do not spear women or children. However, fighting against foreigners, Nuer men do spear old women and children, or club them to death and throw their bodies on the burning huts (Evans-Pritchard, 1940: 128, 151–2). These rules regulating Nuer violence are not written, orally compiled, or systematically integrated – except by the ethnographers. Similarly, across cultures, most of the "rules" regulating the implementation of RMs are not explicitly articulated most of the time, and not even verbally taught to children – children learn them though observation, imitation, play, and incremental participation in community practices. Most preos are not propositionally formulated and many are not explicitly articulated.

Nevertheless, more explicit preos do exist, especially in modern literate cultures. For example, in just wars, when legitimately commanded to do so, soldiers are morally obligated to kill the enemy – but not with poison gas, and not after the enemy has surrendered. The 53-page NATO Rules of Engagement Manual MC 362–1 governs how much force and what kind of force may be used when and how and against whom under what circumstances. You're supposed to keep those rules in mind when deciding whether to pull the trigger. Similarly, US soldiers carry a Rules of Engagement Card that tells them what force they may use in what circumstances against whom. For example, in the 1991 Desert Storm operation, soldiers carried a card with text including the following:

A. Do not engage anyone who has surrendered, is out of battle due to sickness or wounds, is shipwrecked, or is an aircrew member descending by parachute from a disabled aircraft.
B. Avoid harming civilians unless necessary to save US lives. Do not fire into civilian populated areas or buildings which are not defended or being used for military purposes.
C. Hospitals, churches, shrines, schools, museums, national monuments, and other historical or cultural sites will not be engaged except in self defense.
D. Hospitals will be given special protection. Do not engage hospitals unless the enemy uses the hospital to commit acts harmful to US forces, and then only after giving a warning and allowing a reasonable time to expire before engaging, if the tactical situation permits.
E. Booby traps may be used to protect friendly positions or to impede the progress of enemy forces. They may not be used on civilian personal property. They will be recovered and destroyed when the military necessity for their use no longer exists.

In short, violence is moral when it's done right, but immoral and illegal when it violates the rules of engagement. Similarly, in American football, a linebacker is revered for decking the quarterback and even breaking his bones with a fair hit – but not with brass knuckles, and not after the whistle blows. To illustrate the precision with which violence is regulated, consider the core of the National Football League rules concerning player contact, which runs 5,366 words (www.nfl.com/rule book). It includes text such as the following:

Article 2: Illegal Crackback Block.

It is an Illegal Crackback Block if a defensive player is contacted below the waist within an area five yards on either side of the line of scrimmage, including within close-line play, by an offensive player who is moving toward the position from which the ball was snapped, and:

1) The offensive player was aligned more than two yards outside an offensive tackle (flexed) when the ball was snapped; or
2) The offensive player was in a backfield position when the ball was snapped and moved to a position more than two yards outside an offensive tackle.

Note 1: If there is a broken play, significantly changing the original direction, the crackback block is legal. When the change in direction is the result of a designed play (reverse), the restriction remains in effect.

Again, the quartermaster or bo's'n on a nineteenth-century military ship was legally obliged and morally motivated to enforce discipline by flogging a disobedient sailor – but he should inflict precisely the number of lashes the captain commanded, no more and no less. In initiation ceremonies in which boys achieve manhood and are admired for their stoic courage when their penes are cut while they remain imperturbable, the circumciser should cut quickly with a sharp blade – not saw slowly with a dull rusty one. Police may and must use force to apprehend and control a suspect – but not "excessive" force. Duelists win honor when they bravely face their opponents *in a fair contest*; so when one is supposed to be dueling with swords, it would be ruinously dishonorable to kill one's opponent with a shotgun. But in some feuding cultures, it's quite proper for a group of men to ambush and kill a lone, unarmed enemy. Regardless of the degree of articulate explication in these cases, the preos that guide legitimate violence are, indeed, *guidelines* that people rely on to specify when and how to implement morally motivated violence.

Going beyond the culturally prescribed limits to violence

People sometimes overdo violence. Morally motivated to violently regulate relationships, people may go too far, being excessively violent: they may do harm beyond what the cultural preos allow. A man discovering his lover having sex with another man might be culturally condoned for hitting him, but, in fact, he kills him. Or he might be culturally condoned for killing him on the spot, but instead he tortures him to death over two weeks. Sometimes violence is morally motivated but not quite justified with respect to local precedents, prototypes, precepts, or prescriptions. A boxer receives an illegal punch; he should wait and let the referee call a foul, but instead he strikes back with a retaliatory illegal punch. Fighter planes from hostile nations who are not at war nevertheless play chicken, threatening each other, testing the limits, and then one pilot overreacts, stretching the rules of engagement past what others would consider reasonable under the circumstances: he fires a missile shooting down the other plane. Here the motives are moral, the intent is to regulate a relationship, but an impartial hearing of the case would convict the perpetrator. We can describe such events with phrases such as "got too emotional," "was carried away by his emotions," "the strain was too much," "the situation got the better of him," "things got out of hand," "he used poor judgment," or "he lost his head." But whether we characterize the action as "loss of self-control," "impulsive," or "automatic," – or just say, as the distinguished personality psychologist Donald Fiske used to put it, "he was a damn fool" – however we characterize the action, the motives are the same ones we've been exploring throughout the book: moral, and aimed at regulating social relationships. These are just cases where moral motives were misimplemented: the action had the same motives and intentions as in all virtuous violence. The perpetrators experienced the motives as moral emotions and felt they *had* to do what they did, or they just did it without quite knowing how it happened, but by the consensual standards of their community they didn't get it quite right. Anglo-American jurisprudence often uses a legal fiction, "the reasonable person." A reasonable person gets the cultural preos right, doing just the right amount of the right kind of violence in the right circumstances. Real humans with moral motives don't always manage to get their violence right on the mark.

In short, there is good violence and bad violence. Violence of the "right" kind perpetrated in the "right" way in the "right" situations against the "right" people is morally good, legitimately regulating properly specified social relationships. The "wrong" kind of violence, or violence perpetrated in the "wrong" way, in the "wrong" situations, or against the "wrong" people not only fails to constitute those same relationships, but it also transgresses them. What is right or wrong violence depends on the cultural implementations of the RMs (Fiske, 2000; Rai and Fiske, 2011, 2012).

Is morally motivated violence rational and deliberative or emotional and impulsive?

Our core purpose in this book is to show that violence is morally motivated to make relationships right. That is, our theory concerns the impetus and aim of violence. We are less concerned with the complex and varied processes that lead from motivation to action. However, we do need to consider the basic parameters of these processes insofar as they affect whether and when people ultimately perpetrate violence, rather than regulating their relationships non-violently.

Humans have many relatively simple cognitive heuristics that evoke responses tuned to very specific aspects of immediate experience. Some of these impulsive heuristics are phylogenetically old cognitive systems whose function is to directly maximize survival and reproduction in the short run: flight from danger, grabbing food when hungry, copulating when the right opportunity arises with a promising partner, going to sleep when exhausted. But to make social relationships work, humans have also evolved relatively simple *social-relational* cognitive heuristics that evoke emotional responses tuned to very specific aspects of immediate experience of relationships. A crying baby evokes intense emotions that motivate kin caretaking, great prowess evokes awe, and a generous favor or gift evokes gratitude (Simão and Seibt, 2014). Likewise, an insulting blow evokes outrage that motivates vengeance. Thus, there are fast and simple heuristics for grabbing selfish, non-social benefits, for sustaining social relationships by benefiting others, and for regulating relationships by harming others. Receiving a kiss from an attractive person "automatically" makes you feel close, while observing the kiss "automatically" makes your partner jealous – and in some cultures, motivates him or her to respond violently.

These adaptive moral motives are typically generated by mental processes that the actor cannot access or analyze – people often experience adaptive motives as evaluative attitudes, moral sentiments, or pure, inarticulable emotions. On the other hand, sometimes people do use their explicit knowledge and general reasoning to work out what will keep them safe and will secure relational benefits for them. Particularly when people are facing moral conflicts based on competing relationships or ideologically contentious issues, some moral stances are privately or discursively deduced as more or less logically reasoned arguments. Moreover, it is crucial for us to recognize that even if moral motives – including those for violence – are experienced as emotions intrinsic to the apperceived situation, this emotional experience does not preclude self-control or planning how best to achieve the motivated goals. A person emotionally set on violently regulating a relationship may act on this intention immediately, or pursue it patiently, carefully, and methodically, with tactical wisdom and foresight. In short, emotions may generate immediate responses, or keep people focused on a goal that takes years of planning and preparation to achieve.

To a remarkable extent, moral emotions work rapidly, without conscious reflection, through processes that are inaccessible to introspection and hence can't be verbally articulated (Haidt, 2001). People often know what's right; they know what they must do, without necessarily knowing quite why. But without declarative knowledge of *why* something is right or morally necessary, without introspective awareness of *why* they are motivated to act morally, people often are able to reflect on and articulate the implications and consequences of their actions in a deliberative fashion. To think about *how to do* what is morally required, people do not need to know *why* they feel and know what they must do. And people often have multiple interacting and sometimes conflicting moral motives, together with many non-moral motives. So they often have to figure out how to balance, reconcile, or combine their motives. Some of the processes by which people do this involve conscious reflection, and some involve discussion with others.

The greater the retrospective and prospective temporal scope of people's thinking, the more social relationships they take into account, the more ways of regulating the relationship they incorporate in their thinking, and the more moral aspects they consider and integrate, the more *relationally reflective* it is. The other end of this dimension is *relationally impulsive* action. If a relationally reflective act defers, redirects, or overcomes competing, non-socially selfish impulses or social-relational impulsivity, we say that a person has taken the bigger social picture into account, and acted reflectively. Reflectivity is not the same as the construct of "rationality" in economic theory, however. Relational reflectivity has nothing directly to do with *material, economic, or practical benefits*; has nothing directly to do with *fitness*; and is not equivalent to a focus on *self-interest*. Reflectivity consists of decision-making, but it may be reflective without being based on explicit and stable preferences, it need not be logically or consequentially consistent with other action, and it need not maximize utility. Of course, social relationships have huge impacts on material, economic, and practical outcomes, and, of course, greatly affect survival and reproductive success, so our sociomoral emotions and motives have been shaped by fitness considerations. But the axiom of selfish instrumentalism operates at the ultimate level of natural selection, where human fitness depends on trusting, cooperative social relationships. We have evolved many adaptive psychological mechanisms for effectively constituting those essential social relationships. Some of these relational adaptations typically operate quickly and with little reflective articulation, but we are also capable of reasoning, careful planning, and strategic control to pursue the same relational ends.

The crucial point here is that both relationally impulsive and relationally reflective cognitive processes and the actions they generate are morally motivated; what differs is their social-relational scope. What this means is that morally motivated violence may be relationally impulsive, relationally reflective, or somewhere in between. So if you provocatively deny me my fair share of the game we hunted, provoking me to attack you, it's the unfairness that is the proximate motivation. I may attack you impulsively, attending only to your specific insult, or my decision to attack you may be relationally reflective, taking into account your long history of denying me and others our fair share, and fully considering how impressed others will be when I stand up to you. I may spear you immediately, or I may carefully consider how to redress the relationship; thinking it through, I may decide that I'd better ambush and kill you later, perhaps years later, at just the right opportunity, when you are not expecting it, are alone, or ill, or unarmed. Either way, the motivation is moral, intending to constitute one or more relationships.

Many situational, personality, and neurochemical factors may affect how impulsively or reflectively a person acts when he is morally motivated to regulate relationships. These factors have been extensively studied in many contexts, but we need not review them here because they are more or less orthogonal to the moral motives and relational aims of violence. However, focusing only on the immediate regulation of one relationship may make a person either more or less prone to violence than taking a long-run and relationally comprehensive perspective. A broad and deep perspective may strengthen the motivation for violence when a person considers all the relationships that will be created, enhanced, protected, rectified, terminated, or mourned, and how significantly they will be regulated. Or greater reflection may diminish a person's net motivation to regulate her relationships violently. Suppose that violence makes the immediately salient relationship right, right now, but has delayed deleterious effects on other linked relationships to which a person is not attending. For example, a person has been insulted by an interlocutor, so to restore his honor with that interlocutor and onlookers, he needs to retaliate violently – but violent retaliation is illegal. Under those conditions, anything that promotes reflectivity will deter violence, while anything that narrows a person's focus will promote violence. Take alcohol, for example. Alcohol doesn't "make" a person violent, and, indeed, in some cultures intoxicated people are exceptionally affectionate. But if the pharmacological effects of intoxication or the cultural scripts for drunken comportment focus a person's attention on the immediate relational present, then, when violence regulates *this* relationship *now*, alcohol may make people prone to violence – regardless of the long-term consequences for all of the perpetrator's other relationships, which he isn't regarding.

10 THE PREVAILING WISDOM

Virtuous violence theory posits that most violence is morally motivated, but that claim does not imply that people have no other motives pushing toward or against violence. People typically have many simultaneous motives pushing and pulling in divergent directions. In some cultures and some contexts where violence is highly restricted and rarely occurs, to perform a morally required killing may require the strengthening of moral and non-moral violence motives *and* the weakening of moral and non-moral peace motives. In this chapter, we will take a closer look at sadistic, rationalist, impulsive or self-regulatory, dehumanization, and moral-disengagement accounts of violence and how they complement virtuous violence theory, if at all.

Are most killers sadists and psychopaths?

In his book, *Evil: Inside Human Violence and Cruelty*, Roy Baumeister (1997) examines newspapers, myths, stories, movies, and the accounts of perpetrators and victims to detail what he refers to as "the myth of pure evil." According to Baumeister, most people have a folk theory of evil in which perpetrators are sadists who commit violence because they are biologically or dispositionally inclined to gain intrinsic pleasure from causing suffering through intentional harm to purely innocent victims, or, at the very least, they are psychopaths who have no sense of empathy toward those who suffer and feel no remorse for their actions as a result. Psychopathy is not the same as sadism, but it is the most relevant psychological disorder in regard to the belief that violence is perpetrated by "crazy" people. Psychopathy is defined largely in terms of the lack of social motives and moral emotions (Millon *et al.*, 1998; Patrick, 2005), so presumably the violence that psychopaths commit is not often morally motivated, and is truly immoral. So if most acts of violence are perpetrated by psychopaths, it would disprove our thesis that most violence is morally motivated.

Like all or nearly all personality disorders, psychopathy (antisocial personality disorder) is a continuous variable, not a discrete taxonomic category. Yet we have found no studies that correlate psychopathy as a continuous variable with the probability or frequency of perpetrating violence, criminal or non-criminal. Rather, studies of prison populations use conventional cutoffs on the standard scales; anyone scoring above this cutoff is assessed as a psychopath for the purposes of the study. All personality-disorder dimensions are difficult to measure, but psychopathy assessment is especially difficult. Data are based on interviews in which the interviewer asks the respondent questions about his or her life and scores the answers for presence or absence of characteristic behaviors. But prisoners may have many reasons to lie to researchers, and psychopaths are inveterate liars, so it is problematic to rely on their own accounts of their lives to diagnose them. With these caveats, we can consider the available evidence.

Psychopaths evidently commit only a small fraction of all criminal violence. In a sample of 125 Canadians convicted of homicide, 27% scored as psychopaths with the recommended cutoff on a standard scale (Woodworth and Porter, 2002; see also Haritos-Fatouros, 1995). However, in a broad stratified sample of 496 prisoners in England and Wales convicted of many offenses, violent and non-violent, Coid *et al.* (2009b) found that only 7.7% of men and 1.9% of women scored above the standard cutoff for psychopathy, and among all prisoners there was no correlation between psychopathy and any particular type of crime; psychopathy scores were not specifically associated with violent crimes. In a study of 416 German prisoners, 7% were categorized as psychopaths; just 8.8% of the 217 convicted of violent offenses were categorized as psychopaths (Ullrich *et al.*, 2003). In an Iranian stratified sample of 351 prisoners, just 12% of violent offenders met the usual criterion of psychopathy; percentages of psychopaths among those convicted of other types of crime were the same or higher (Assadi *et al.*, 2006). Given that the prevalence of psychopathy in the general population is estimated (with great uncertainty) at less than 1% (Coid *et al.*, 2009a), it is clear that psychopaths commit far more than their share of violent *crimes*, but most crimes are not committed by psychopaths, nor do psychopaths perpetrate most violence of other kinds. Two cohort studies confirm this. In Finland from 1984 to 1991, 97% of 1,037 homicides were "solved," and the court required a psychiatric evaluation by a neutral expert if it deemed that there was any possibility that the crime had been affected by a mental disorder, so 70% of the accused were examined. Men with antisocial personality disorder committed 11% of all homicides committed by men; women with antisocial personality disorder committed 13% of all homicides committed by women (Eronen *et al.*, 1996). Men and women with all personality disorders combined committed 34% and 36% of homicides, respectively; alcoholics committed a similar proportion. More generally, mental disorders of all kinds together account for only a small minority of crimes. In a national cohort of all Danes, the 2.2% of men who were ever hospitalized for a mental disorder committed 10% of all violent crimes by males for which convictions were registered; for the 2.6% of women ever hospitalized, it was 16% of all violent crimes (Brennan *et al.*, 2000).

Although Baumeister (1997) does not completely dismiss sadistic pleasure or psychopathy as a motive for violence, like us he notes that any evidence for it is quite rare, and that although it shows up quite commonly in victims' accounts of violence, it is almost always absent in perpetrators' accounts. Erasing this and other gaps between victim and perpetrator perceptions of violence is a key to reconciliation. According to Staub (2006), the first step toward reconciliation in the wake of the Rwandan genocide was to help victims recognize that their perpetrators were not motivated by incomprehensible evil, and to help victims understand the factors that led to the perpetrators' violence against them. Thus, although the belief that most violence can be attributed to sadism and psychopathy is widespread, it simply isn't the case, and may even hinder approaches to prevent and recover from violence.

Are killers rational?

When explaining why people are motivated to do violence, some scholars have focused on the instrumental value of violence purely as a means to amoral ends. Killing the other heir to the crown may be necessary in order to become king. Such rational-choice and realistic conflict models of violence assume that when the costs of engaging in violence are low and the benefits are high relative to other, non-violent, courses of action, people will be more likely to engage in violence (Felson, 1993, 2004). For example, it has been found that fighting is more likely to break out among siblings when the likelihood of parental intervention is *greater*, because younger, weaker siblings are more likely to fight with older siblings when there is a high likelihood of parents stopping the fight and punishing the older sibling. Essentially, when the costs of conflict are lowered by the potential for parental intervention, younger siblings are more willing to fight their older siblings (Felson, 1983; Felson and Russo, 1988).

Many rationalist models of violence, particularly those that are more economically oriented, are completely agnostic as to how the utilities are calculated or as to the specific sorts of values that underlie the utilities of different courses of action. At their most abstract limit, these theories are not even psychological, as they need only assume that actors pursue their preferences. In that sense, rationalist theories of violence are completely compatible with virtuous violence theory, and moral motives can be construed as simply one major kind of utility that informs moral action. But in order for rationalist theories to make any predictions or explain any data, they have had to make assumptions about what the relevant costs and benefits are and how they are calculated. That is, they have to identify people's "preferences." Historically, these models have limited their scope to material, quantifiable resources that can be monetized, and they have assumed that people must reflectively weigh costs, benefits, and probabilities in their decision-making. As a result, they can explain why violence increases as its material utility becomes more positive, but, as we saw in our discussion of the Israeli–Palestinian conflict and extremist violence, they fail to adequately explain why people engage in violence under conditions where, by any measure of practical or material individual benefit, its utility is clearly negative, and why people are unwilling to engage in rational trade-offs of material for moral goods. As Baumeister puts it,

> Only a minority of human violence can be understood as
> rational, instrumental behavior aimed at securing or protecting
> material rewards. The pragmatic futility of most violence has

been widely recognized. Wars harm both sides, most crimes yield little financial gain, terrorism and assassination almost never bring about the desired political changes, most rapes fail to bring sexual pleasure, torture rarely elicits accurate or useful information, and most murderers soon regret their actions as pointless and self-defeating.

(Baumeister et al., *1996: 5)*

Without an understanding of the moral motives that drive violence, rationalist models of violence are forced to assume that perpetrators of violence are motivated by the belief that their actions will result in material rewards. Yet, in fact, in most cases, it is obvious to all parties that there is no material utility to the perpetrator's actions. Rather, *the perpetrator is violent because he feels he must be.*

Are killers impulsive?

Imagine if instead of violence, this book was about sex, and in it we argued that people have a basic, biological urge to fornicate, and that the only reason they restrain themselves from having sex with anyone and everyone is because of their sense of self-control, which enables them to regulate their emotions. Imagine that we then supported our theory by citing evidence that when people are drunk, they have more sex because their sense of self-control, and specifically their ability to regulate their emotions, has been impaired. If this was our theory of sex – that it's a basic, incomprehensible urge, normally held in check by our sense of self-control, and that people engage in sex when their sense of self-control is compromised – wouldn't you feel that we had missed something crucial about the nature of sex? Wouldn't it seem odd that nowhere in our theory had we discussed "chemistry," desire, or love? That nowhere had we accounted for how sex grows out of social relationships, or why people don't want to have sex with their siblings or parents? Wouldn't it seem that, in fact, we hadn't provided a theory of the motives for sex at all; but, rather, we had provided a theory of the conditions under which competing motives *to abstain from sex* break down.

We think that this is exactly what has occurred in self-regulatory theories of violence. Self-regulatory theories of violence focus on the role that self-control plays in suppressing our violent impulses, and how violence occurs when those self-control mechanisms fail to control irrational flare-ups. A woman may feel that slapping her partner is morally wrong, but when she is stressed from work she loses her temper and takes it out on him. Self-regulatory models of violence posit that people commonly have violent impulses in response to aversive stimuli that impel them to engage in violence (Finkel, 2007), but most of the time people's moral sensibilities continually act to control and suppress these impulses to keep them from committing violence. When people are strongly stressed, threatened, distracted, or otherwise "depleted," their moral sense fails them and they give in to their violent impulses (Dollard *et al.*, 1939; Finkel *et al.*, 2009). For example, DeWall *et al.* (2007) asked participants to resist a temptation, such as eating an appetizing treat. Afterwards, participants who had to resist a temptation were more aggressive in their behavior and more likely to endorse retaliating with violence in a bar fight following an insult than participants who had not been asked to resist a temptation. The authors hypothesized that the effort involved in resisting the temptation weakened participants' self-control, and, thus, they were less able to resist temptations to respond with aggression to a provocation.

Thus, self-regulatory theories have reliably found that endorsement of violence goes up when self-control is weakened, but they take it for granted that it is endorsement of violence *in response to transgression*. People are not simply lashing out at *anyone* for *anything*. Just as in our sex example, self-regulatory theories provide little insight into why people wish to engage in violence in the first place. They are presented as theories of violence, but, actually, they are theories of the conditions under which peaceful, non-violent motives break down. This inability to capture the proximate motives for engaging in violence makes self-regulatory models inherently incomplete. In addition, whereas rationalist models that assume that people reflectively weigh costs and benefits prior to engaging in violence fail to explain impulsive acts of violence, self-regulatory models that assume violence is the result of impulsive urges to lash out fail to explain carefully planned, methodical violence that is pursued over months, years, and generations. As discussed in Chapter 9, virtuous violence theory can explain both relationally reflective and relationally impulsive forms of violence.

Are killers mistaken?

For moral psychologists who assume that a core feature of our moral psychology is a prohibition against intentional harm (Gray *et al.*, 2012; Hauser, 2006; Mikhail, 2007; Turiel, 1983), violence must be explained *away* as a mistake or error: it is incorrect moral reasoning. From this perspective, people engage in violence when they are "morally disengaged" or when they have "dehumanized" the victim of violence. In the case of moral disengagement, the perpetrator reframes the situation so that he no longer has to adhere to his moral obligations, and in the case of dehumanization, which is seen as one route to moral disengagement, violence is thought to increase when we perceive potential victims as non-human or less than fully human beings because they lack fully human mental capacities (Haslam, 2006). According to this approach, such a breakdown in social cognition reduces our compassion and empathy for victims, enabling us to be aggressive against them without remorse. It is less immoral to kick an animal than a fellow human being, and kicking a rock isn't even morally relevant (or violent) at all.

We do think that there are *some* conditions where people will be motivated to reframe a situation to enable them to act in ways that they would otherwise feel are immoral, or to deny the presence of *some* moral emotions or mental capacities in those they wish to punish, as suggested by Baumeister's (1997) findings that villains are perceived as intrinsically evil. But the difficulty is in how these constructs are realized in practice. Consider the following statements taken from Bandura *et al.*'s (1996) moral-disengagement scale, one of the most widely used scales on topics of disengagement and dehumanization.

> It's all right to fight to protect your friends.
> It's all right to fight when your group's honor is threatened.
> It's all right to fight when someone badmouths your family.
> It's all right to lie to keep your friends out of trouble.

Ask yourself: does being willing to lie or fight to protect and defend your friends, family, or group indicate that you are morally *disengaged* or morally *engaged*?

In fact, endorsing these items is scored as evidence for moral *dis*engagement. Aquino *et al.* (2007) used scores on these four items alone to argue that moral disengagement facilitates support for violence, as indexed by desires to violently attack the terrorists who orchestrated the 9/11 attacks. In other words, support for fighting to protect your friends predicted support for fighting terrorists who attacked America. But the authors drew the conclusion that it was a *lack* of moral motives that facilitated support for violence. From this perspective, "moral disengagement" refers specifically to a prescriptive morality of non-violence, and so any reasons for engaging in violence are immoral *by definition*. Thus, the evidence that disengagement researchers use to argue that violence is facilitated by the *absence* of genuine moral motives is evidence that, by our definition, actually demonstrates the *presence* of moral motives.

Waytz and Epley (2012) measured individual differences in dehumanization and found that when people dehumanized suspected terrorists they were more likely to endorse harming them. However, the dehumanization measure, also adapted from Bandura *et al.* (1996), appears to capture punitiveness more than the lack of human mental capacities. The four-item measure from the original scale includes the following: "Some people deserve to be treated like animals," "It's okay to treat badly someone who behaved like a 'worm,'" "Someone who is obnoxious does not deserve to be treated like a human being," and "Some people have to be treated roughly because they lack feelings that can be hurt." The last item captures what is intended by dehumanization, but the other three confound punitiveness with the use of animal and non-human terminology. In other words, expressing support for treating suspected terrorists badly predicted support for harsh torture techniques. Rather than evidence for dehumanization, this is evidence for moral motives to engage in punitive violence following transgression. Even more interesting from a relationship-regulation perspective, the authors found that punitiveness increased in the presence of a friend, suggesting that participants' social relationships reinforced their moral motives for violence.

One study that does seem to capture the construct of dehumanization with a valid measure is that by Leidner *et al.* (2013), who found that Palestinians who believed that Israelis lacked the capacity to feel compassion were more likely to agree that the only way to restore justice in the Israeli–Palestinian conflict was for Israelis to be punished and suffer. However, participants' judgments of Israeli capacities for compassion did not predict participants' support for suicide bombing attacks. In a second study, Israelis living in Jerusalem were asked what emotions Palestinians were capable of, including "disgust, shame, anger, pain, suffering, hope, admiration, fascination, and surprise" (p. 187), and similar results were found – perceiving that Palestinians lacked capacities for emotions predicted support for punishment and suffering abstractly, but not for concrete violent actions. More generally, in large surveys of Israeli settlers, Jeremy Ginges has found little correlation between perceptions of human qualities in the outgroup, such as capacities for self-awareness and moral emotions, and support for and willingness to participate in violence (Ginges, personal communication[1]).

We, the authors, would define moral disengagement as any effort to reframe a situation so that we no longer conceptualize our responsibilities and obligations in moral terms, and therefore cease to see ourselves as constrained by moral rules. We would define dehumanization as any case where we *remove* human mental capacities and emotions from people that we *previously* viewed as having those qualities in order to enable violence against them that is motivated by non-moral reasons. If violence is morally motivated, the violence is intended to regulate a relationship with a fully moral partner, against whom the perpetrator intends to inflict pain, injury, or death. There is no point in punishing or seeking revenge against a rock, tree, computer, automobile, snail, or turtle with no capacity for moral sentiments or reasoning, because they can't transgress relationships.

But this is not at all how moral disengagement and dehumanization are defined in the literature, where behaviors such as fighting and lying are categorized as immoral a priori. Disengagement frameworks

---

[1] Another prominent measure of dehumanization is Bastian and Haslam's (2010) scale, wherein rating a person as superficial, cold, unsophisticated, and lacking in self-restraint is scored as dehumanization, while rating the person as open-minded, warm, cultured, and rational is scored as humanization. In our view, this measure seems to capture general positive and negative appraisal as much as dehumanization *per se*. Although Bastian *et al.* (2013) attempt to control for this possibility, other studies do not (Greitemeyer and McLatchie, 2011). More broadly, dehumanization has been linked to alleviating guilt (Castano and Giner-Sorolla, 2006), reducing willingness to forgive (Tam *et al.*, 2007), and reduced willingness to help (Cuddy *et al.*, 2007), but we found only a few studies linking dehumanization to condoning violence by others, only one study linking dehumanization to endorsing hypothetical engagement in violence by participants themselves (Viki *et al.*, 2013), and no studies demonstrating that dehumanization leads people to actually engage in aggressive behavior.

presuppose that moral motives must be peaceful, while dehumanization is measured by willingness to punish. This makes no sense. In cases of retributive violence, where a person wants to see someone suffer for what he has done, imbuing the person with the ability to think or intend is often crucial for seeing him as guilty for what he has done (Leslie *et al.*, 2006), while imbuing the person with the capacity for experiencing pain and suffering may be crucially necessary in order for his punishment to have any moral meaning. In cases of retributive punishment, morally motivated perpetrators *want* their victim to feel pain, shame, humiliation, disgrace, or the fear and horror of dying precisely because the victim was capable of thinking, intending, and planning his actions. In these cases, perpetrators are not morally disengaged; they are morally *engaged*. Victims are not dehumanized; they are *humanized*.

Like self-regulatory theories, theories of moral disengagement and dehumanization are actually theories about the breakdown of peaceful, non-violent motives, rather than theories of the motives for violence, *per se*. They either implicitly or explicitly view violence as reflecting a breakdown or a mistake in correct moral functioning; these theorists never seem to consider that perpetrators could ever regard violence as morally necessary and legitimate. But as we have documented throughout the book, in many instances perpetrators of violence do not want to commit violence; rather, they feel they *must* engage in violence in order to do what is right and be good moral actors. In actuality, perpetrators often do see their victims as fully human beings deserving of moral consideration, and that is why those victims are deserving of violence.

Virtuous violence theory does not deny that people have moral motives to restrain from violence. Rather, it is precisely these powerful moral motives to restrain from violence that demonstrate that perpetrators of violence have even more powerful moral motives to engage in violence. Virtuous violence theory has the potential to refine theories of moral disengagement and dehumanization by considering cases where violence is morally motivated, and it may complement these theories by focusing on the moral motives for *engaging* in violence, rather than restricting consideration to the moral motives that *restrain* violence.

Western people (and people in many other cultures) tend to believe that only evil actors do violence, and that good people do not hurt others on

Table 10.1 *Explanations for committing and not committing violence*

	Moral mechanisms	Non-moral mechanisms
For not committing violence	Self-regulation: functioning conscience or internalization of norms Empathy, compassion	Rational weighing of costs and benefits Fear of punishment
For committing violence	Virtuous violence theory	Failure to self-regulate Psychopathology Dehumanization Moral disengagement Rational weighing of costs and benefits

The table represents the focus of each theory, showing that virtuous violence theory fills an otherwise empty cell.

purpose. This line of thinking has colored Western scientific theories of violence. We have shown that there are moral and non-moral motives for abstaining from violence, and there are many moral and sometimes also non-moral motives for engaging in violence. Most of the time, people have multiple motives, sometimes acting in concert and sometimes in competition, and in the medium- to long-term dynamics of social interaction, the motives that initially moved a person to initiate a course of action may be supplemented or supplanted by new motives that sustain, redirect, or block the original design. However, previous theories have focused only on rational, material motives to engage in or to abstain from violence, or moral motives to abstain from violence. They have not gotten to the heart of most violence, which is morally motivated in the eyes of the perpetrator; that is, it is aimed to constitute or regulate important social relationships, and is typically fully condoned by the perpetrator's primary group. As Table 10.1 indicates, virtuous violence theory is the only theory that posits moral mechanisms for committing violence.

More generally, we would argue that the ultimate, motivating aims of most rational or "instrumental" action are, in fact, social relational: except under the most extreme circumstances – and often even then – people's goals are mostly to constitute their social relationships. People seek money, land, material resources, and goods primarily to impress others in order to enhance their status in AR relationships, or to share in CS relationships, or to give in EM relationships, or to transact in MP relationships. Nearly always, under normal conditions, people optimally promote their long-term (and often short-term) individual self-interest by optimally regulating their social relationships – typically by mutualistic cooperation. Rationality is calculative reasoning about how best to *do something*, and what people are usually trying to do when they make rational calculations is to properly regulate their social relationships. Likewise, when people act impulsively, their most common and strongest impulses are to regulate their relationships. When people act emotionally, the most compelling emotions are usually relationship-regulating emotions: anger, shame, love, awe, and so forth. When people exercise self-control to regulate their actions, they almost always do so to preserve, protect, or enhance their social relationships (Fiske, 2002, 2010). Because social relationships are the adaptively most significant and the psychologically most compelling matters for human beings, self-interested, instrumental, rational, material, impulsive, emotional, reactive, or self-controlled behavior is generally all about *how people manage their social relationships*. They are about how people achieve social-relational ends. We cannot understand these relationship-regulating strategies until we recognize the social-relational motives that drive them and the relationship-regulating aims they seek to fulfill.

Approaches that focus on material costs and benefits, self-regulatory mechanisms, perceptions of humanness, or moral framing help us understand some factors that sometimes facilitate or inhibit morally motivated violence under restricted conditions. Virtuous violence theory does not immediately explain why young men are especially likely to engage in warrior violence, contact sports, rape, and torture, while women are equally or more likely to injure themselves in bereavement violence or engage in self-harm and suicide. Meanwhile, people are more likely to be perpetrators or victims of violence when they are drunk. As we mentioned earlier, intoxication almost certainly shortens potential perpetrators' temporal horizons and the scope of the social-relational repercussions that people take into account, reducing their consideration of the full breadth of the medium- to long-term social-relational consequences of violence. Finally, whereas virtuous violence theory aims to explain perpetrators' propensities to engage in violence, theories of dehumanization and disengagement may explain why third parties often turn a blind eye to violence committed against people who seem different or distant, or are simply anonymous, as in our tacit acceptance of sweatshops, mass violence, and starvation abroad. Our hope is that at a minimum virtuous violence theory complements existing theories by providing a valid new explanation of important motives that contribute to a great many kinds of violence across histories and cultures.

11 INTIMATE PARTNER VIOLENCE

> When you go to war against your enemies and the Lord your God
> delivers them into your hands and you take captives, if you notice
> among the captives a beautiful woman and are attracted to her, you
> may take her as your wife. Bring her into your home and have her shave
> her head, trim her nails and put aside the clothes she was wearing
> when captured. After she has lived in your house and mourned her
> father and mother for a full month, then you may go to her and be her
> husband and she shall be your wife. If you are not pleased with her,
> let her go wherever she wishes. You must not sell her or treat her as a
> slave, since you have dishonored her.
>
> *Deuteronomy 21:10–14; New International Version*

In a great many historical societies, including classical Greece, a person
taken captive by force may be obliged to become a dependent subordinate in an AR relationship with his or her captor; everyone in the culture
construed this relationship as entirely legitimate, and it had full moral
and legal validity. In many historical cultures, many women captured in
warfare or raids were married by their captors, with more or less full
status as wives (except that they had no kin to support them in conflicts
with their husband, or to return to if they had to leave their marriage;
e.g., for Africa, see Kopytoff and Miers, 1977; Robertson and Klein,
1983). In many such societies, the predominant form of marriage was
that lineage elders gave their daughter to a husband chosen by the elders,
who typically did not consult the bride about her preferences, so marriage did not involve the bride's choice in any case. (In some cultures, the

groom was not necessarily consulted, either.) In social systems where everyone was a subordinate dependant of someone who exercised control and ownership over them but also looked out for and protected them, the AR relationships between master or husband and wife, concubine, or slave were similar in many respects (Kopytoff, 1988). Likewise, in many historical African, Asian, and other societies, male dependants, whether born into the family, purchased, adopted, or captured, related to their elders and chiefs in similar ways, although in general slaves had lower status and were stigmatized.

Even in the great many societies that do not employ violence to obtain brides and do not have legal slavery, violence is one of the mechanisms that spouses use to regulate their relationships with each other. Intimacy entails exposure, trust, and commitment – which means great vulnerability. Deep CS relationships entail intense moral emotions: rapturous love when the partners are one, but ferocious rage when one partner threatens to end or betray the relationship. Likewise, strong AR relationships entail total loyalty. So whether bound by CS or AR, spouses and lovers are often intensely committed and deeply dependent on each other – and often violently regulate their relationship. When a person discovers his or her partner has a sexual relationship with another person, or shows indications of intending to engage in such a relationship, the cuckolded person may kill his partner or her lover. From the point of view of the killer, and in many traditional cultures and a few modern ones, this is what the unfaithful partner deserves (Black, 1998: 36). When a subordinate spouse fails to perform her duties properly, her master may feel that he is fully entitled to beat her, and that, indeed, the future of the relationship depends on his meting out proper punishment. In a number of cultures, men's honor depends on their control of and dominance over "their" women, so men are entitled and expected to use violence to control and dominate (Vandello and Cohen, 2003, 2008). In these cultural and relational frameworks, violence redresses relational transgressions, while preserving third parties' respect for the perpetrator (or victim).

The more intimate, multifaceted, and prolonged the relationship, the greater the chances and the more frequent the occasions that the partners will intentionally or even quite inadvertently betray the other's trust. To love is to depend on the other. To love is to be vulnerable. To love is to idealize. Humans, being the imperfect, sometimes inadequately empathic creatures they are, very often failing to adequately appreciate the other's perspective, sometimes fail each other. They offend each other. Offended, they retaliate – verbally, materially, or violently. They curse, they throw plates, they poke, punch, burn, beat, stab, or shoot. This violence cannot be explained by the personalities of the individual perpetrators; on the contrary, the data "suggest that the roots of the violent behavior lie with the couples' 'relationship' rather than in individuals" (Goodyear-Smith and Laidlaw, 1999: 293–4).

Intimate partner violence is widespread

Some men are known to ethnographers to beat their wives in 84% of the world's cultures; in 19% of societies, virtually all men beat their wives (Levinson, 1989: 31). In 47% of cultures, some men sometimes beat their wives so severely as to permanently injure or kill them. In a sample of 32 non-state societies, 90% of ethnographies reported the moral acceptance and presence of wife beating (Rosenfeld and Messner, 1991; for a brief review and some examples, see Black, 1998: 29). It isn't only men who start attacks: Western husbands and wives both initiate violence against each other, though their motives are not always the same (Goodyear-Smith and Laidlaw, 1999). Domestic violence is often immediately reciprocated and escalates, sometimes ending in homicide. Many Americans in the 1970s regarded violence as a normal part of marriage (Goodyear-Smith and Laidlaw, 1999; Straus et al., 1980). It was just part of what it meant to be married, or, indeed, to be a romantic couple. And in many traditional and modern cultures throughout history, to be married naturally means that when your partner "hurts" you, you *hurt* them back. A 1990s New Zealand questionnaire study of 21-year-olds in partnerships found that 37% of women and 21% of men reported perpetrating physical violence on their partner in the previous year; 19% of women and 6% of men reported kicking, hitting, biting, hitting with a weapon, or using or threatening to use a knife or gun (reviewed in Goodyear-Smith and Laidlaw, 1999). Correspondingly, 34% of men and 27% of women in the study reported being victims of partner physical abuse in the past year. Replicating these results, interviews in another New Zealand study found that nearly half of men and a quarter of women reported that a partner had physically assaulted them, or attempted or threatened violence in the past year (reviewed in Goodyear-Smith and Laidlaw, 1999). One-third to one-half of women in lesbian relationships reported receiving physical abuse in the past year (reviewed in Goodyear-Smith and Laidlaw, 1999). Violence is common in marriage, domesticity, and romance because for many people violence isn't detached from or inconsistent with intimacy – it is *intrinsic* to the everyday regulation of the relationship.

Intimate partner violence is morally motivated to regulate relationships

Reviewing the literature on intimate partner violence, Flynn and Graham (2010) found the following reported motivations: the perpetrator's partner had cheated on the perpetrator or was suspected of doing so (in different studies, 7–46% of instances), the partner didn't care about the perpetrator, the perpetrators were afraid their partner was going to leave them, or the partner did attempt to leave. Other motives included lack of full commitment and, conversely, objecting to a mistress. Less common motives included "general provocation, starting an argument, lying, disrespect and insensitivity, and sexual refusal" (Flynn and Graham, 2010: 244). In some studies perpetrators reported being violent to punish for an infraction, or, notably, to prove their love or show affection!

The partners in a relationship are likely to develop a joint moral framework, so that when the perpetrator feels that his or her partner deserves a beating for a perceived transgression, the victim often more or less concurs. Peers and family may see it the same way, too. When intimate partners are violent, both the perpetrators and the recipients of the abuse often feel that the partner who is punished had it coming. In an anonymous internet survey of people who had formerly been in abusive relationships, half of both abused men and abused women indicated that a reason for remaining with their abusive partner was that "I thought the abuse was my fault" (Eckstein, 2011). Two-fifths of both men and women felt that "It was not his/her fault he/she hurt me." Three-fourths of both men and women felt "I would have been a failure if I left the relationship," and three-fifths stayed because they "did not want to appear weak." These are the factors that survivors of abuse reported *using in their own decisions* – their *explanations to others* usually differed.

Physical abuse is profoundly, fundamentally morally wrong – to us. So it's hard to conceive of the perpetrators feeling morally motivated to do such violence. Yet, the evidence indicates that many abusers *are* morally motivated: they feel entitled, even obligated, to do violence to redress wrongs that they perceive themselves to have suffered, and to sustain what seems to them to be the right kind of relationship.

In other cases, violence is a mutually agreed-upon way to relate. Some couples consensually engage in sexual practices in which at least one partner hurts the other, often when the victim is bound or restrained with special-purpose apparatus. BDSM – bondage and dominance or sadomasochism – is not rare or aberrant (Richters *et al.*, 2008; Weinberg, 1995). The evidence suggests that such practices are not pathological *per se* but are a way of conducting mutually meaningful, mutually rewarding AR relationships, sometimes with an element of EM, if the participants *switch* (the term for role turn-taking in these relationships), and perhaps sometimes the bondage enhances CS bonding. When both parties freely choose to engage in BDSM, it certainly meets the criterion of virtuous violence intended to constitute a relationship.

12 RAPE

In this chapter we consider moral motives for rape. We must emphasize again that our focus is on the perpetrator's motives, not the victim's experience or perception of the act, and not our own moral values. From the victim's perspective (and the reader's, and our own), the rapist is the epitome of evil – it seems that his actions could not possibly be morally motivated. But as we have already learned, perpetrators do not see themselves the way that victims do, and, as we will demonstrate in this chapter, by our definition, many rapists' actions are morally motivated to regulate relationships.

It might seem obvious that most rapes are primarily instrumental acts in which the perpetrator just uses the victim like an object for simple sexual satisfaction, and this is sometimes more or less how the perpetrator perceives his action. But more often, forcing someone to be a sex partner against her will is unequivocally meant as the enforcement of AR hierarchy. The rapist controls the victim, making her obey his will, in order to assert his superior AR position, especially when he feels his superiority has been challenged. A man may rape because he feels entitled to demand sex from his partner. He may rape because he feels that his victim has demeaned herself by her "provocative" dress, behavior, or unaccompanied presence in an inappropriate locale – so, since she's "asking for it," he's entitled to give it. Likewise, a man may rape because his attitude is that women in general are "whores" and "sluts" who are "asking for it" and deserve what their immoral status evokes. Other men rape to avenge either the victim's affront to the rapist's dignity, or to collectively avenge offenses committed by women, where women are all equivalent. These men feel that they have been humiliated by a woman or women, and avenge their humiliation by degrading the humiliator or any other woman who serves as a substitute. Gang rapes are often motivated by the metarelational desire – the "need" – to belong: raping together is an act of consubstantial assimilation, connecting the rapists in a CS relationship through their body fluids like blood brothers (on consubstantial assimilation, see Fiske, 2004; Fiske and Schubert, 2012).

There are important individual differences in whether men find sexual aggression arousing and appealing, and in whether men perceive sexual relations as fundamentally about AR. It is not clear whether these differences reflect genetic and unsystematic, environmental-experiential variation as such, or subcultural and social-class differences in norms. Sexually aggressive men have a comparatively high explicit need for power and more strongly tend to explicitly associate the concept of power with the concept of sex (Chapleau and Oswald, 2010). Using statistical analyses of mediation, Chapleau and Oswald found that explicit belief that sex is a means of asserting dominance[1] leads to acceptance of norms that rape is morally legitimate. This then leads to the participants' stating that they would likely rape an acquaintance, and this, in turn, was highly correlated with self-report of having been sexually coercive in the past. In short, the more men think of sex as constituting a superior position in AR, the more likely they are to believe that sexual coercion is morally legitimate, and hence the more they rape.

Among New York City male college students, subliminally priming power activates associations with words indirectly linked to sex – but only among men who score high on a scale measuring how attracted and aroused they are by the idea of rape and forcing a woman to do something sexual she does not want to do, and how likely they rate themselves to do such things (Bargh et al., 1995).[2] Men who did not report being attracted to sexual force did not associate power with sexuality. In a second sample, among men scoring high on the same

[1] Measured by endorsement of items stating that sex involves "control," "power," "being in charge," "submitting to the will of another," "persuading," one person "should be dominant" and one person "should be submissive," and "sex means gaining possession of someone else's body."

[2] This was true whether priming authority power stimuli with words such as "authority, executive, boss, influence, rich, and control," or priming physical power with words such as "mighty, strong, tough, macho, muscular, and boxer."

Attractiveness of Sexual Aggression scale, men who were primed with power words by completing anagrams reported that they found a female confederate more "attractive" than those primed with neutral words. (It is not clear whether the items on the attractiveness scale were explicitly sexual.) This study did not investigate whether men whose thoughts about power led to thinking about sex felt morally entitled to force women, such as subordinates, to have sex. But it suggests that for sexually aggressive men, thinking about power aroused sexual thoughts.

Rape is usually embedded in and grows out of the vicissitudes of a relationship. People committing assault or rape usually have a prior relationship with the victim (Vera Institute, 1977). Most such rapists rape to redress a relationship that they perceive the victim to have transgressed by refusing to defer to their wishes – wishes that must be granted, because women are subordinates who should obey. If a man perceives that women are chattels who must do his bidding, and in particular that in a romantic relationship or marriage, men have the right to sex whenever they want it, then it simply doesn't matter what the woman's wishes are. In many countries and many US states until recently, the law did not recognize the possibility that a man could "rape" his wife because it was her duty to have sex with him whenever he demanded it; if he had to use violence when she illegitimately refused or resisted, so be it (Clinton-Sherrod and Walters, 2011; Hasday, 2000). Moreover, people often construe AR relationships as coming down to *will*. When one is dominant, one's will prevails, and to assert one's will over another is to dominate them, to be superior. If so, then a man may perceive that a woman's refusal to have sex is an assertion of her will over the man's will, challenging the man's dominance. In a contest of wills, he feels that for him to give in and allow the other's will to triumph is to accept humiliating subordination. He – and his peers – think that a man who "allows" "his" woman to refuse him is "pussywhipped". According to their culturally shaped morality, he must impose his will on women or else he's less than a man; he's "henpecked" – reduced to a position below women in the pecking order.

Many studies have shown that rapists are angry at women for perceived transgressions and that rapists are motivated by a "need" to assert power over women (Lisak and Roth, 1988). A study of southeastern US college men found that men who reported that they had sexually assaulted, raped, or attempted to rape a woman

> perceive themselves as having been more often hurt by women, as
> having been deceived, betrayed, and manipulated. They appear to be
> more attuned to power dynamics between men and women; more
> often feel put down, belittled, ridiculed, and mothered by women;
> and more often feel the need to assert themselves because of this.
>
> *(Lisak and Roth, 1988: 800)*

In this study, feelings of anger resulting from perceptions that women
had "hurt" them – that is, done something morally wrong against the
man – predicted self-reported sexual aggression. In other words, men
sexually assault women to punish them – to get revenge for other
women's transgressions against them. These perceived transgressions
consist primarily of violations of what the perpetrator perceives of as
his rightful position of superiority over women.

In interviews with 114 men convicted of rape or attempted rape
in Virginia, many rapists reported that they raped for revenge or to
punish, typically treating all women as collectively responsible for one
or more specific woman's alleged transgressions against the rapist (Scully
and Marolla, 1985). Revenge rapists were angry at women for violating
the rapist's moral code; they raped the "transgressor" or any other
woman to "get even" (Scully and Marolla, 1985; see also Hale, 1997).
Some men were metarelationally motivated: they had raped a woman to
"get even" with the woman's *partner* for a perceived transgression
against the rapist, or as redirected "punishment" against an unrelated
third party (Scully and Marolla, 1985). One man raped and murdered
five strangers; he explained,

> I wanted to take my anger and frustration out on a stranger, to be in
> control, to do what I wanted to do. I wanted to use and abuse
> someone as I felt used and abused. I was killing my girlfriend. During
> the rapes and murders, I would think about my girlfriend. I hated the
> victims because they probably messed men over. I hated women
> because they were deceitful and I was getting revenge for what
> happened to me.
>
> *(Scully and Marolla, 1985: 257)*

Other rapists whom Scully and Marolla interviewed reported the perception that a woman at a bar, hitchhiking, or walking alone at night is
offering herself up for sex, so if she subsequently refuses to have sex,

forcible sex is justified. Many rapes – perhaps most – were acts of domination "to put women in their place."

> For example, one multiple rapist believed his actions were related to the feeling that women thought they were better than he was.
> [The rapist said] 'Rape was a feeling of total dominance. Before the rapes, I would always get a feeling of power and anger. I would degrade women so I could feel there was a person of less worth than me'.
>
> *(Scully and Marolla, 1985: 256)*

In other words, "I may be treated as if I'm at the bottom of the heap, but I can show them – I'm pushing women down below me!" For one such man, "With rape, I felt totally in charge. I'm bashful, timid. When a woman wanted to give in normal sex, I was intimidated. In the rapes, I was totally in command, she totally submissive" (Scully and Marolla, 1985: 259).

Questionnaire responses of 132 incarcerated rapists in the US Deep South indicated that their primary motives for rape, in order of the frequency of respondents' first choices, were revenge/punishment, control/power, and anger (where anger may express a response to perceived violation; Hale, 1997). In interviews with 15 southeastern US college men who reported 22 events in which they had used force to have sex with women against the woman's will, hardly any reported doubts or remorse (Lisak and Roth, 1988). Consistent with a number of earlier studies, compared to controls, on the Anger-Hurt scale these rapists exhibited more feelings of anger toward women, reporting that they felt betrayed, deceived, or manipulated by women. On an Underlying Power scale, compared to controls, these college rapists reported higher perceptions that women put them down, belittled them, and made them feel "inadequate," while, on a Dominance in Sex scale, they indicated that dominance is a greater motive in sexual relations.

A large survey with careful representative sampling of regions in seven Asian countries found that 24% of men aged 18–49 reported having raped a partner or non-partner at least once (Jewkes *et al.*, 2013). Responding on a 4-point Likert scale with ratings of agreement or disagreement to items indicating their reasons for rape, the great majority reported that they felt they were entitled to rape the non-partner woman they had most recently raped: Bangladesh 82%, Cambodia 41%, China

91%, Indonesia 77%, Papua New Guinea 73%, and Sri Lanka 78%. The percentages of those who reported feeling guilty for any rape they had committed were as follows: Bangladesh 34%, Cambodia 50%, China 50%, Indonesia 76%, Papua New Guinea 57%, and Sri Lanka 33%. In most of the samples a high percentage of men indicated "anger and punishment" as a reason for their most recent rape of a non-partner: Bangladesh 29%, Cambodia 40%, China 52%, Indonesia 30%, Papua New Guinea 51%, and Sri Lanka 16%. It's not clear what proportion of these rape victims were close associates of the rapists, but the percentages of men who were ever "punished by friends or family" for any rape they had committed are generally lower than the felt guilty rates: Bangladesh 8%, Cambodia 38%, China 35%, Indonesia 34%, Papua New Guinea 64%, and Sri Lanka 7%. These rates of "punished by friends or family" are similar to the percentages arrested in each sample.

Clearly, many Asian men are willing to report their own rapes; many of them don't feel guilty about it and weren't sanctioned by their family or friends; and many feel that the rapes they committed were morally permissible. A great many Asian rapists indicate they were angry (at a perceived transgression against them) and raped to punish (apparently the questionnaire did not distinguish between intending to punish the victim, a category of women, or women in general). Similar proportions of South African men report feeling entitled to rape women and "punish" women who "deserve" to be raped (Jewkes *et al.*, 2011). These survey data by themselves are consistent with moral motivations and social-relational functions of rape, although they aren't proof. But on the basis of their extensive studies of rape, Jewkes *et al.* (2013) conclude that in many Asian cultures and in South Africa, rape results from cultural prescriptions for male dominance demonstrated and expressed through sexual coercion. In other words, in these cultures, to be a man, you must have your way with women – and a woman's resistance is merely an opportunity to prove your manhood.

In short, the literature is overwhelmingly clear that rapists in everyday life are often motivated by their perception that they are redressing women's moral transgressions against them by putting women down – rape asserts the rapists' "rightful" dominance, restoring women to their proper place below the rapist. In the minds of rapists, rape is punishment for women's violation of the authority of the rapist.

Rape in war

In warfare, rape is a common means of establishing or enhancing AR relationships – between men and women, among soldiers, but especially between the victors and the foes they defeat.

> Ex-combatants reported that those who participated in rape in Sierra Leone were seen to be more courageous, valiant and brave than their peers. Those who committed rape were respected by their peers as "big men" – strong and virile warriors.
>
> *(Cohen, 2013b: 26)*

Raping enemy women demeans and degrades them while, metarelationally, it humiliates the defeated men who should have protected them. Soldiers in many cultures through the ages have perceived enemy women to be a prize of war: "to the victor go the spoils." In other words, to rape is to vaunt one's victory and display superiority.

In addition, victorious military leaders sometimes order their troops to rape, so, subject to the military code and military honor, soldiers must do so (Beevor, 2002; Fogel, 2000; Naimark, 1995). In some cultures, an aspect of this is the idea that the victorious commanders should have their pick of the women; the relative beauty of the victims marks relative status among the rapists. For example, eastern Congolese Mai Mai militia commanders often commanded rape; militiamen sometimes obeyed out of respect for commanders, sometimes in fear of serious beating – apparently perceived as legitimate – if they refused, and sometimes from both sentiments.

> Women were given as a reward; soldiers were ordered to abduct women, and these women were then "given" to soldiers, with higher ranking officers given precedence. As one man said, "[The commander] will have his [girl] brought first before he can ask me to bring mine. In that case, if you refuse, it becomes an open conflict."
> The interviewer pressed the soldier saying:
> Q: Do you really bring her?
> R: That is exactly what I must do. You say: "Great chief, here is the girl you asked me to bring to you."
>
> *(Kelly, 2010: 8)*

Other Mai Mai militiamen were adamant that it is evil to rape, and that when any soldier in their militia raped, the civilian population would hold them all responsible. Many expressed horror at rape with objects, rape of young girls, or foreign militias raping Congolese women. Nevertheless, Mai Mai militiamen reported that the magic they use to win their battles *requires* that they have sex – it doesn't work without sex – so that rape is necessary for their victory over their enemies and the protection of the Congo (Jackson, 2008). In this normative framework of warfare, perpetrators perceived that rape, like killing, serves a higher moral good.

Gang rape

Much of the rape in warfare is gang rape, which is often more or less explicitly intended to create or enhance group cohesion – that is, CS unity (Cohen, 2013a). Combatants in the Sierra Leone civil war who were abducted into insurgent armies, and, hence, initially felt frightened and isolated among hostile strangers, developed loyalty and trust through public gang rapes. "Interviews with fighters provide abundant detail that rape fostered cohesion" – cohesion among former strangers that endured long after the fighting (Cohen, 2013a: 474). Cohen found that in Sierra Leone and across societies and settings, "rape – especially gang rape – enables groups with forcibly recruited fighters to create bonds of loyalty and esteem from initial circumstances of fear and mistrust" (Cohen, 2013a: 461). Among fighters in Sierra Leone, "rape served a bonding function. Ex-combatants reported experiencing feelings of belonging in the aftermath of gang rape" (Cohen, 2013: 404). Furthermore, rape was not simply a CS-constitutive act; it was a culturally admired way of raising the rapist's position in AR relationships:

> Interviews provide ample evidence that rape was a cohesive
> activity... Ex-combatants reported admiration, not disgust, for
> those who had perpetrated many rapes. In interviews, they described
> a culture in which those who had raped many women achieved a
> legendary status among their peers – one interviewee spoke with awe
> about a fellow combatant who had raped more than 200 women.
>
> *(Cohen, 2103b: 405)*

Several studies have found that men engaging in gang rape are primarily motivated by the desire to bond with each other as "brothers," and to enhance status in the eyes of others in the group by humiliating the victim (reviewed in Cohen, 2013a). In particular, fraternity gang rape

> operates to glue the male group as a unified entity; it establishes
> fraternal bonding and helps boys to make the transition to their
> vision of a powerful manhood – in unity against women ... a little
> like bonding in organized-crime circles, generating a sense of family
> and establishing mutual aid connections that will last a lifetime.
>
> *(Sanday, 2007: 7–8)*

Male bonding is also the motivation for gang rape by street gangs. A judge who tried many cases writes of the similarities between fraternity and street-gang rape:

> Both groups frequently engage in sexual behavior that others call
> gang rape. Both call it "playing train" or "pulling train" (one man
> follows after another). Both groups consider it a form of male
> bonding in which the female is merely an available instrument. Both
> may prepare themselves for this test of manhood by ingesting
> quantities of alcohol and fortifying themselves with drugs
> [commensally reinforcing the CS among them]. Both consider this
> acceptable, indeed normal, conduct. Both are amazed to learn that
> such actions could be crimes.
>
> *(Lois G. Forer, in Foreword to Sanday, 2007: 23)*

When there is danger involved, civilian gang rape may also be an exciting adventure in "male camaraderie engendered by participating collectively in a dangerous activity" (Scully and Marolla, 1985: 259).

As in individual rape, there is also an AR component in gang rape:

> I suggest that "pulling train" is a form of sexual expression that is
> defined as normal and natural (hence normative) by some men and
> women... The sexual act is not concerned with sexual gratification
> but with the deployment of the penis as a concrete symbol of
> masculine social power and dominance. The male sexual bonding
> evident in "pulling train" is a sexual expression and display of the

power of the brotherhood to control and dominate women. The discourse associated with acts of "pulling train" defines this form of control and domination as part of normal male sexual expression ... that sanctions the deployment of male power in sexual aggression.

(Sanday, 2007: 40)

However, whereas the AR component of superiority of men over women, and the focus on the woman as an object of retribution, appears to be primary in individual rape, it appears to be a secondary motivation in gang rapes, which are motivated primarily to create CS cohesion among the rapists. Whereas in individual rape the woman represents a relational partner to be retaliated against and subordinated, Sanday (2007) argues that gang rapists typically perceive their victims as mere objects to be used. As such, dehumanization and moral disengagement may play a greater role in the relationships between perpetrators and victims in gang rape than in individual rape.

Rape is repugnant to us, the authors, to you, the readers, and to those who have been victims of rape or who care about them. But *our* moral judgment of it should not blind any of us to *the perpetrators'* moral motivations. Yes, to label the motivation to rape "moral" seems horrific and bizarre, but that's what it truly is, both subjectively and in the objective technical sense. Phenomenologically, many rapists feel that they are entitled to demand sex and get it from women in general, from the partner they apperceive as belonging to them (in a subordinate, possessive sense), or from women who go to places, wear clothes, or act in ways that – in the rapists' interpretation of their subculture – signify that the women are "asking for it" and, indeed, are morally degraded to the point where they "ought" to get what's coming to them. In the relational and metarelational psychologies of the perpetrators (and often their reference groups), the rape is intended to enhance or restore an AR hierarchy. The perpetrator feels that raping a woman makes him dominant over her, and perhaps over women like her, or reasserts men's legitimate dominance over women. Or a group of men sequentially rape a woman to create or enhance a CS relationship among the men: mixing semen in the woman's body makes their essence one, connecting them in a communal bond. For these men, rape is much like sacrificing an animal and eating it commensally, or making blood brotherhood by mixing the bond partners' blood in a shared cup of beer that they both imbibe.

In prisons and some other environments, men often rape men. We were not able to locate sources that clearly indicate the motives or relational intentions of the perpetrators, but we imagine that when the victim is male, too, rape may often be intended to humiliate and subordinate the victim, establishing or reinforcing the perpetrator's dominance in an AR relationship. However, while we aren't aware of extensive evidence about the motives of adults who rape young children (family members or others), we doubt that many child molesters are morally motivated. We don't know whether those who sexually abuse children ever do so to regulate their social relationships with the child or others. While inherently coercive, sexual abuse of children generally may not be specifically intended to *hurt* them; if and when it is not intended to physically harm the victim, sexual abuse would be outside the scope of action we intend virtuous violence theory to explain.

Rape is often morally motivated to regulate CS and AR relationships, or to enhance a metarelational model. However, most men today do not perceive sex as an AR relationship. CS and AR relationships among men or between caring men and women often motivate men *not* to rape, and many metarelational moral frameworks forbid rape (Wood, 2009). Social relationships cut both ways, generating violence but also motivating participants to treat each other humanely. As we will discuss in Chapter 21, we need to understand why, how, and when social relationships motivate people to hurt others; then we can figure out how to cultivate motives for mutual respect, care, and compassion.

13 MAKING THEM ONE WITH US: INITIATION, CLITORIDECTOMY, INFIBULATION, CIRCUMCISION, AND CASTRATION

If you love your children and want them to become just like you; if you deeply identify with kin or age-mates and they deeply want to become one with you; if you meet someone you want to incorporate into your group, bond with, and become able to trust with your life; in short, if you want and need to create the most intense and enduring CS relationships with someone for the rest of your life, then in many cultures you must cause them excruciating pain by cutting their genitals, terrify them and inflict degrading suffering, or beat them horribly. That is, you must circumcise a boy, excise a girl, initiate them, "jump them in" to the gang, or haze them into the fraternity. Severe initiation creates life-long CS bonds of unconditional altruism and total identity with the other initiates, with the initiators, and with others whose bodies are marked like theirs. So in communities whose existence totally depends on absolute, selfless loyalty, people violently initiate their sons and daughters, brothers and sisters, nephews and nieces, grandsons and granddaughters. Love, identification, and the moral obligation to forge unbreakable commitment to CS bonds – they are what motivates cutting genitals, horrific initiations, and other kinds of group-incorporation violence. The pain itself is crucial to the formation of the CS identity with the initiating group; indeed, the pain may be experienced as the sacrifice of an aspect of the self for the group as a whole (Morinis, 1985).

Initiation rites

> A child becomes an adult, or an outsider becomes an insider when
> ritually controlled pain weakens the subject's sense of empirical
> identity and strengthens his or her sense of attachment to a highly
> valued new center of identification.
>
> *(Glucklich, 2001: 7)*

In a representative world sample of 182 cultures, Schlegel and Barry
(1979) found that 46% of the societies reportedly performed initiation
rites for girls and 36% for boys. Among girls' initiation rites, 8%
involved a genital operation, 25% inflicted only non-genital pain such
as "beating, tatooing, tooth extraction, or eating of obnoxious substances," and none inflicted both. Among boys' initiation rites, 21% involved
a genital operation, 32% inflicted only non-genital pain, and 11%
inflicted both. In initiation rites, fraternity hazing, boot camp, and similar practices, people willingly inflict pain, fear, deprivation, and loath-
some experiences on others – who often choose and willingly endure the
violence. Severe initiation rites (a term we will use here to encompass all
of these painful bonding practices) form intense CS relationships that
motivate participants to risk or sacrifice their lives for each other (for two
examples of such practices, see Herdt, 1987; Ricks, 1997). Initiates may
be whipped, beaten, stung with nettles, burned, subjected to extreme
cold, doused or immersed in very cold water, forced to ingest toxic
substances or unpleasant psychoactive drugs, scarified, pierced, tat-
tooed, have teeth extracted, or be whipped, circumcised, subincised, or
excised (Dulaney and Fiske, 1994; Levinson, 1989: 30; Young, 1985).
Many initiation rites incorporate long periods of social deprivation, sleep
deprivation, severe food restrictions, or forced ingestion of disgusting
substances.

Initiations are often designed to be terrifying before and during
the experience. The initiates may be afraid of what they have to endure,
but they are typically proud to have reached the status of prospective
inductees, and may boast of their courage. Usually, they go willingly to
be initiated, or even eagerly request it. The initiators may be eager to
perform the initiation or may have "gut" qualms about subjecting
the initiates to the fear, pain, deprivation, and degradation. But both
prospective victims and perpetrators know it has to be done, should be

done, is natural and right to do. Typically, it is the immediate superiors, parents, uncles and aunts, or other close kin who administer these rites, thereby reinforcing their AR relationships as well. But the principal effect and collective function of initiation is to create intense and enduring CS bonds. The cruelties of initiations are constitutive of solidarity. The more important in-group loyalty is for the community, the more severe the initiations (Collins, 1974: 436; Young, 1985). The violence, fear, pain, degradation, and stressful isolation "produc[e] an exceptionally strong bond among the initiates" and between them and their initiators (Cohen, 1964; see also Bloch, 1986). Often the initiate's status as a fully adult male and his reputation depend on bravely facing the fear of pain of circumcision or other initiation procedures, and, above all, stoically enduring the pain without flinching, grimacing, or crying out (e.g., Heald, 1986). The initiate's father and other kinsmen are proud and often gain honor when he displays unflinching courage, or are shamed along with him if his courage fails. Those who have been initiated are very proud that they went through it, and they soon initiate the next cohort, inflicting the same horrible experiences on them. For participants and their proud kin and friends, initiation is a feat of virtue and a moral triumph.

Initiators may inflict terrific pain. Among the Bimin-Kuskusmin of Papua New Guinea, the initiates' nasal septums are "pierce[d] ... from the right side with a cassowary-bone dagger ... with blood cascading down their bodies ... [and] hot marsupial fat and dew water are applied to the boys' inner forearm ... [while they] struggle and shriek as large blisters form" (Poole, 1982: 127). Many Australian Aboriginal initiations include incisions cut so as to make permanent scars, removing an incisor, piercing the septum, and circumcision followed by repeated subincision of the penis at higher-stage initiations (Eller, 2010: 120–1).

Initiation violence is by no means limited to traditional cultures. In St. Louis, as in other US cities, joining a gang typically entails "beating in," wherein existing members severely beat the initiate for a few minutes; he may fight back (Decker, 1996a). Those who are not beaten in have the alternative of wearing the gang colors while walking into the turf of an enemy gang, inevitably resulting in violent conflict. If the initiate survives, he's in. Brazilian military police hit recruits with paddles and weight belts and make them compete in races dragging cars (Linhares de Albuquerque and Paes-Machado, 2004). American university fraternities terrify, humiliate, and inflict pain on initiates in order to forge the CS bonds that incorporate them into the fraternal body, and, at the same time, to display the initiators' superiority over the pledges they initiate (Sanday, 2007: 165–79). High-school sports teams sometimes paddle or duct-tape those joining the team or kick them while they sleep; initiates earn the respect from the initiators by enduring the violence, which at the same time reinforces the superiority of the initiators (Kirby and Wintrup, 2002; Waldron *et al.*, 2011).

> By taking hazing it made me tough; it made me part of the team, and because I knew if I took it as a freshman, I was gonna be able to give it back when I was a senior... I think hazing is a way of finding status between those who are inferior and those who are superior... The people that did the hazing were the hot shots of the team ... and since they don't really know you as a freshman, once you get hazed, then you could hang out with them... After being hazed, then they're your friends.
>
> *(Waldron et al., 2011: 117–18)*

For the previously hazed athletes, initiating someone else into the team is a way to raise their own status on the team: "[Y]ou do it to somebody so it brings them down in order to let yourself up" (Waldron *et al.*, 2011: 118; see also Kirby and Wintrup, 2002: 57). For all team members, the act of initiation through violence elevates them above the non-initiated. As one person commented on a blog:

> The claim to belonging to a superior "elite" must have some justification, and hazing forms part of that. It separates those who have undergone it from the larger groups of people around them, a separation that the former initiates of hazing see as lifting them over those less, unhazed people.
>
> *("jb," posted in response to Blow, 2011; see also*
> *other comments posted there)*

Many initiation rites are long-standing traditions, but new rites immediately emerge with the formation of new groups where everyone's life depends on everyone else's totally loyalty. Young men inducted into Mai Mai militias in the eastern Congo were scarified to mark their membership, and then beaten in.

Q: If someone wishes to join you, what can he do?

R: That civilian must be spilt in the dust, be beaten black and blue so that he might leave his civilian thoughts.

Q: Beat him first? How is this helpful?

R: The civilian will come out of him. You must spill him in the mud, to beat him black and blue before he is taken care of and given his uniform as well as a gun.

Q: Will he not be trained?

R: He will be trained after receiving a uniform and a gun. You will be shown the field and explained things as they are. Since you have already dropped civilian thoughts because of the flogging, you will start saying, "Ahhhh! So it is like this!" Then you will be practicing what you have learned.

Another soldier described his first beating, saying new recruits were taken to the river, stripped naked, and flogged. After the beating they were "anointed" with the river mud.

The soldier described himself as being "molded in the mud" and went on to say, "All those sticks that you were beaten with put into you another ideology."

(Kelly, 2010: 7)

Nearly all of the research on truly painful initiation is ethnographic, but one questionnaire study of a religious ritual in Mauritius found that compared to participation in painless ritual, participation in rituals that entail extreme and prolonged pain is associated with high levels of generosity and with wider, more inclusive identification immediately after the experience (Xygalatas *et al.*, 2013). Experimental studies have also shown that the prospect of experiencing moderate pain increases people's generosity. In one experiment, participants who expected pain were more willing to donate to charity. In a second experiment using real money, participants contributed more to a joint pool of money rather than keeping money to themselves if they had to place their hands in freezing water for 60 seconds *in order to contribute* (immersing one's hands in ice water is quite painful). Follow-up studies suggested that participants were more likely to donate under these conditions because they derived a stronger sense of meaning from charities that involved pain (Olivola and Shafir, 2013). These studies suggest that in addition to creating bonds among initiates, it's certainly conceivable that suffering and observing suffering actually intensify CS unity bonds with others who are not participating in the ritual.

Circumcision and excision

Arnold Van Gennep was one of the first ethnologists to analyze initiation rites.

> Cutting off the foreskin [among Jews] is exactly equivalent to pulling out a tooth (in Australia, etc.), to cutting off the little finger above the last joint (in South Africa), or cutting off the ear lobe or perforating the ear lobe or the septum, or to tattooing, scarifying, or cutting the hair in a particular fashion. The mutilated individual is removed from the common mass of humanity by a rite of separation (this is the idea behind cutting, piercing, etc.) which automatically incorporates him into a defined group; since the operation leaves ineradicable traces, the incorporation is permanent.
>
> *(Van Gennep, 1960/1909: 71–2)*

Simple circumcision is outside the boundary of "violence" as we define it in this book, insofar as inflicting pain or suffering as such is not the intent. As we have just seen, however, in many male initiation rites a key intent of the circumcisers *is* precisely to terrify the initiate and inflict excruciating pain.

In female genital excision, while the operations are excruciatingly painful, evidently inflicting pain during or immediately after the surgery is *not* usually the explicit aim, although in some cultures, as with male circumcision, the stoic courage of the initiate enhances her status and her solidarity with other women in the community (Shweder, 2002). However, clitoral excision and infibulation *are* often intended to reduce sexual pleasure, so they are "violent" if we consider deprivation of pleasure to be suffering, which seems like a fair assessment (though there is little or no solid evidence about which, if any, forms of such surgery actually *do* reduce sexual pleasure (Shweder, 2002)). Moreover, generally the goal – and the result – is to make sexual intercourse uncomfortable or actually painful. Parents and elders in a number of African and other cultures have operations performed on girls to cut or remove the clitoris, remove some or all of the labia, or stitch the labia together. For the mother and other family members, it is an act of responsible love, ensuring their daughter a bright and honorable future. Traditionally and to a great extent today, all concerned regard this as morally necessary and highly virtuous (Abusharaf, 2001; Ahlberg *et al.*, 2000). Above all, it helps ensure female chastity, which is *the* core moral value in these societies, most of which emphasize honor and shame (McKenna and Howarth, 2009). Sometimes girls themselves take the initiative to have the surgery performed. In most of the cultures where it is practiced, the crux of morality is virginity before marriage and fidelity after marriage; female genital surgery is thought to be an essential foundation for such chastity (Slack, 1988). The surgery makes it difficult to have intercourse, but, more fundamentally, it is intended to prevent any experience of pleasure in sex and indeed to make sex painful, so that excised or infibulated women no longer desire and may actively avoid sex, minimizing shameful fornication. Violence of this sort serves the constitutive phase of terminating immoral relationships before they have the chance to begin, so that the woman can create other, proper, and necessary relationships instead. Moreover, the surgery constitutes the identity of the girl as a pure and true woman, and not as a person with genitalia that would grow to be like those of a man (Abusharaf, 2001: 123; Atiya, 1982: 11). As one Sudanese mother of Douroshab township put it, "circumcision is what makes one a woman" (Abusharaf, 2001: 123). Another mother said that she recognized the pain and danger, but she was glad to have the operation when she had it because "I wanted to be like everybody else in my family and my neighborhood" (Abusharaf, 2001: 134).

This surgery also raises a woman's status, explained another woman, telling why she had the operation done on her daughters:

> I chose pharaonic circumcision for my two daughters. I thought of
> their future. The woman who is circumcised behaves in a way that
> forces people around her to respect her. But a woman who is not
> circumcised cannot enjoy the same status. Men respect women who
> have self-respect and who do not get involved in sexual relations. We
> know that when a woman gets married, this background is
> important... Pharaonic circumcision ensures the woman's strong
> place in the family. She is very trustworthy because she does not
> allow men to take advantage of her. She is her own person, even for
> the man she is married to. This is a source of respect and I think it is

more important than how painful it is. The wound heals, but the relationships remain strong. By preserving her reputation, a woman will become powerful and respected by members of the community.

(Abusharaf, 2001: 131–2)

Furthermore, a person whose genitalia are not properly modified is a disgusting, horrific freak: her bodily oddity separates her from the broadest and most fundamental CS relationships (Shweder, 2002). When I (ApF) was doing fieldwork in a Moose village, my daughter was a toddler, widely loved and cared for by our friends and neighbors. They unanimously and insistently urged us to have her clitoris excised; for them, it was obvious, natural, and necessary. As they emphasized, a woman with an intact clitoris would have no prospects for marriage and no one would want her as a lover (Moose traditionally have long-term lovers outside their marriages). She would be reviled and excluded. Our friends and neighbors repeatedly urged us to do the right thing for her. Nevertheless, we refused.

Female genital excision is intrinsically metarelational. The intent of excision is to prevent the woman's seeking or engaging in sexual relations that are culturally inconsistent with other crucial social relationships. It is also metarelational because the genital surgery ordained by parents is usually performed by someone else, so the metarelational model is a composite of at least five dyadic relationships: parent–victim, operator–victim, (obstructed) sexual partner–victim, (obstructed) sexual partner–desired husband, and desired husband–victim. In addition, more extended genital-excision metarelational models link the relationships between the parents and the woman's prospective and then actual husband. And the excision metarelational model often incorporates the desire to protect the honor of the family, which depends on the female victim's chastity: excision has moral implications for the woman's siblings, children, aunts, uncles, and grandparents. Moreover, the parents and the person circumcised or excised are often motivated to have the surgery done because it is God's will. Many believe that it is a religious duty to obey what they believe to be the Prophet's command to circumcise women (El Dareer, 1983). Likewise, for Jews, circumcision was, and for many still is, the crucial index constituting the covenant between God and the Jews. More generally, as traditional practices linked to Abrahamic religions, male and female genital excision are acts of obedience to God, necessary to the AR relationship between the parent and

God, and between the victim and God (Gruenbaum, 2001). Hence, in all of these religious traditions, excision is deeply and essentially moral. To fail to do what has been ordained would be to disobey God, and also to risk ostracism from the congregation and isolation from the community.

Eunuch opportunities

Powerful rulers cannot trust men who are tempted to seduce the ruler's wives and concubines. Furthermore, paternal love and the desire to be succeeded by one's son and perhaps to establish a dynasty may compete with other loyalties; men who cannot have children do not have family ties competing with their commitment to their masters. So, to improve their sons' prospects of becoming trusted courtiers and administrators, in some societies parents have had their sons castrated. This was an expression of the parents' love and aspirations for their sons, and it was felt to be morally valid because it was in the sons' own interest – it opened important career opportunities. It also made it more likely that the mature son would provide amply for his parents as they grew old. Like female excision and infibulation, castration forestalls and inhibits sexual relationships that compete with or threaten more important relationships, allowing these other relationships to be created and sustained. Usually, the pain of castration was incidental, and was not the aim, but because castration was meant in part to deprive men of sexual pleasure or desire, it seems that it, too, should be regarded as a form of violence, like clitoral excision.

Assyrian, Byzantine, and Sung and Ming Chinese rulers and nobles prized, purchased, and made gifts of castrated eunuchs. Eunuchs were servants, administrators, and military leaders, sometimes becoming trusted confidants and attaining the very highest social positions and powers (Metamura, 1970; Ringrose, 2003; Stevenson, 1995; Tougher, 1997, 2008; Tsai, 1996). In these cultures, foreign men captured in warfare or raiding were often castrated and sold. In the eighteenth and early nineteenth centuries, slavers in the Sudan brought their captives through Upper Egypt, where Coptic monks castrated many of the boys, with the approval of the governor, to whom the slavers paid a tax (Meinardus, 1969). The slavers then sold these eunuchs in Constantinople, where they fetched a much higher price than intact males. Sometimes citizens of these empires were castrated for crimes. In the Sung dynasty, the military provided a castration service for volunteers who wished to join the palace service (Metamura, 1970: 66–7). Moreover, many poor Byzantine and Ming families castrated young boys, and a few men castrated themselves in adulthood, in order to become eligible to serve in royal or aristocratic courts. Self-castration was legally prohibited by Ming law, but continued at a high rate nonetheless (Metamura, 1970; Ringrose, 2003; Tougher, 1997; Tsai, 1996). At any point in time in each of these empires, thousands of eunuchs were serving in these royal courts and noble palaces. Some of them were missing only their testicles, while others also had amputated penes.

In Byzantium, "castration of one's children could be seen as a positive Christian act" (Tougher, 2008: 129), and the opportunities for eunuchs eventually became so great that

> Castrated eunuchs of the twelfth century often were the offspring of well-established families. They were highly educated and dedicated to a life of perfect, loyal service within the aristocratic family, at court, or in the church.
>
> *(Ringrose, 2003: 127)*

Ringrose (2003: 3) notes that eunuchism would not have prevailed as a central feature of the political center of Byzantine society for so long if it had not been culturally condoned. The perceived merits of castration in late Byzantium transcended the pragmatic employment and political opportunities it enabled; it greatly facilitated – though it did not ensure – chastity, purity, and avoidance of sin (Ringrose, 2003: 197ff.).

> Established families had become accustomed to the idea of castrating sons for careers that would support the family trajectory in the imperial city. They had also come to accept the socially constructed gender assigned to eunuchs. This, in turn, meant that they believed not only in the limitations imposed on eunuchs by society but also in the special talents and spiritual potential that eunuchs were perceived to possess.
>
> *(Ringrose, 2003: 193)*

In sum, castrators and often the eunuchs themselves intend castration to prevent eunuchs from engaging in sexual relationships, in order to foster other, more valued social relationships. Men without sexual desire or genital capacity are more trustworthy followers because they cannot be sexually tempted to betray their masters. Relationships involving sex, as well as paternal–child relationships, interfere with or directly conflict with other relationships, so by greatly reducing the disposition to relate sexually and eliminating the primary medium of male sexuality, castration opened up the possibilities for the relationships people sought to create.

There is little ethnological evidence from these cultures that castration created identity, solidarity, loyalty, or affection among castrated men. Although it seems as though it might have had that effect, so far as we are aware, no evidence has come to light that it did. Perhaps the lack of CS bonding from castration results from the fact that castration was rarely ritualized. However, in one culture, castration does constitute significant CS relationships. *Hijras* have a very highly marked CS gender identity that makes them quite distinctive in South Asia, based on being born male but not being sexually male adults. In South Asia for centuries *hijras* have castrated boys whom they abducted or who willingly join the caste and its social, ritual, and religious practices (Nanda, 1998; Sharma, 1989). Apparently castration is not essential to being *hijra*, but it seems to facilitate this identity, and some *hijra* communities perform ritual initiations whose focus is the removal of the penis, scrotum, and testicles.[1]

The initiatory violence, circumcision, excision, and castration practices described in this chapter are each morally motivated to create important social relationships, while forestalling or terminating other relationships. In the case of initiatory violence, initiates are elevated into a new CS relationship with other group members through their pain, while their relationship with outsiders lower in status is terminated. For female

---

[1] Boys were castrated in middle childhood to preserve and enhance their singing in sixteenth- to nineteenth-century Europe, ancient Greece, the Roman and Byzantine Empires, Ottoman Turkey, the Near East, China, and probably classical India (Witt, 2002). This practice enhanced the family's social relationships with the Church and their social standing more generally, and castration was seen as a worthwhile sacrifice in the service of singing more glorious hymns to God. However, whereas castration is fundamental to eunuch opportunities (i.e., the eunuch must have reduced sexual pleasures and desires), the deleterious effects on sexual desire and pleasure are only incidental when it is in the service of improving singing. Hence, castration to preserve or enhance singing does not meet our definition of violence.

circumcision especially, the violence elevates a woman's status in the group, without which she would have no respect. In addition, the violence pre-emptively terminates any relationships she might have had with other men by reducing her sexual pleasure, thus maintaining her chastity and worthiness as a wife. Likewise, for men castrated in order to become eunuch servants and administrators, the genital violence creates relationships with elites and nobles by pre-emptively terminating any relationships they might otherwise have had with their rulers' wives and concubines, and pre-emptively ends the eunuchs' capacity to father sons to whom the eunuch might be more committed than to his master.

14 TORTURE

In Plato's *Gorgias*, Polus describes the punishment for a usurper's unjust attempt to make himself a tyrant: the failed usurper is racked, mutilated, and, after having had all sorts of further injuries inflicted on him, must watch the same done to his wife and children before he has his eyes burned out and is impaled or tarred and burned alive (Benjamin Jowett translation). Sophocles took for granted the justice of this way of executing the man. To Plato, such torture evidently seemed perfectly moral and perfectly natural. That was 2,400 years ago. Now, a survey of Amnesty International's research files from 1997 to mid 2000 found reports of torture or ill-treatment by agents of the state in over 150 countries (Amnesty International, 2003). In more than 70 countries, the victims included political prisoners, but ordinary criminals and criminal suspects had reportedly been victims of torture or ill-treatment in over 130 countries. People had reportedly died as a result of torture in over 80 countries. In 2011, there were plausible reports of state-inflicted torture in 101 nations (Amnesty International, 2012). In sum, throughout modern history up to the present day and across cultures, innumerable societies have practiced and condoned torture to enforce state authority (Conroy, 2000; Lazreg, 2008; Otterman, 2007; Peters, 1985). Many people have devoted a great deal of careful thought and technical ingenuity to designing procedures and tools to make torture as painful as possible (Donnelly and Diehl, 2011).

Motives of leaders who order torture

Leaders order torture when they perceive that the people to be tortured are resisting and threatening the leaders' legitimate authority. Authorities are entitled to answers from those beneath them, so they feel justified in torturing if the answers are not forthcoming. Authorities are entitled to deference and loyalty, so they feel justified in torturing traitors. Indeed, Collins (1974) posits that the aim of torture is "to enforce submission. The cruelty is not incidental; it is the main purpose" (Collins, 1974: 420). Likewise, Collins argues that authorities order amputation, gouging out of eyes, castration, and other mutilations expressly to humiliate. Historically, in the exceptionally stratified conquest societies that practiced torture and mutilation, "these cruelties are not only deliberate, they are ceremonially recurrent defenses of the structure of group domination" (Collins, 1974: 421).

> "Making them talk" implies more than just making them talk about something in particular. "Making them talk" is also about power, about imposing one's will on another. One party is absolutely powerful, the other, coerced party, is totally powerless and defenseless.
>
> *(Crelinsten, 1995: 37)*

Motives of torturers

While it is tempting to assume that torturers are psychologically disordered, torturers do not exhibit antisocial personality characteristics. However, training for torture often involves extensive hazing, isolation from outsiders, shared fear, and other features of initiation such as "repetitive drills and meaningless tasks performed in unison," which create CS bonds with the torturer's military unit (Crelinsten, 1995: 47; see also Haritos-Fatouros, 2003; Huggins *et al.*, 2002). Conversely, the torturers often place their victims as enemy outsiders beyond the pale of CS moral obligations or compassion: "The exclusion of torture victims from the torturer's moral community goes back to the early history of torture" (Kelman, 1995: 31).

Moreover, torturers perceive their actions as moral because they perceive their victims as evil.

> A central assumption in the contemporary practice of torture ... is that the victims are guilty. The question of whether or not they are guilty never arises... Thus, torture is designed only to punish the guilty, to warn their accomplices, and most importantly to elicit the truth from them.
>
> *(Kelman, 1995: 32)*

Excellence in torture can be a path to advancement. In many recent South American "security" organizations, at least, potential torturers are recruited among boys from the lowest social classes; if they perform well, they are selected into prestigious elite units, acquiring a superior status they could not hope to obtain in any other way (Haritos-Fatouros, 1995: 143). Torturers also often come from religious families that emphasize obedience to authority, and during training, they are often brutally beaten in ways that instill a strong sense of group solidarity and camaraderie among torture recruits (Moio, 2007). Torturers may even develop a sense of competitiveness with each other, such that they do not wish to let someone else succeed in "breaking" the suspect after they have tried (Fanon, 1965).

When torture is conceived of as a "rational" MP bureaucratic practice, it is justified on the grounds that it is speedy and efficient. Trainees are taught that the pain they must inflict is proportional to the culpability of the victim or the social value of the information they reveal. At the same time, promotion is rationally based on results: a torturer's rise through the ranks depends on his efficacy. A Uruguayan army lieutenant and ex-torturer explains:

> I think advancement was linked to the efficiency and general performance of the officer in different branches and details of his military career. However, this capacity and efficiency in repressive methods, among which I include torture, definitely demonstrates his military capacity, and it is just this capacity which is rewarded by the authorities either in promotion or assignment.
>
> *(Plate and Darvi, 1981: 141)*

When police or security forces are overwhelmed by the number of criminals or terrorists they have to process, and when they need information quickly so as to pursue accomplices who will soon flee, torture is "rational" (Huggins *et al.*, 2002: 101–18). A Brazilian police torturer explains that the necessity for torture comes down to "proportionality" between police resources and crimes. And, when the policeman is a "professional," torture is moral when he "does his job" in what we would call a utilitarian framework:

> Speaking like an institutional functionary, Márcio explains that scientific rationality should guide torture: the rational torturer has "a view of the common good" and believes that "torturing will gather more evidence so there are greater possibilities of indemnifying the victim {of the crime the person tortured is accused of committing}, as well as convicting the thief or murderer..." Márcio believes that moral and rational police who only use torture to discover evidence, are "apparently normal [and] controlled in their torture [because they] have limits..." The policeman needs to make sure that torture causes just the right amount of suffering to achieve the most optimal ends.
> (Huggins et al., 2002: 103–4; *square brackets in original; braces added by the present authors*)

Motives of the public that approves of the use of torture

Support for torture may also be driven in large part by a desire for retribution against a perceived transgressor (Janoff-Bulman, 2007). In an EM framework of getting even, people are motivated to reciprocate violence with violence, regardless of the potential information they may receive through torture. In a telling experiment, Carlsmith and Sood (2009) presented participants with a fictional vignette describing "Ahmad Farid," an Afghani man who had been captured by the US military. Participants were led to believe either that Farid likely had little useful information to divulge about potential terrorist operations, or that he likely had a lot of information to reveal. In addition, some participants were told that Farid had been an active member in a terrorist group that had participated in several roadside bombings, and had been involved in an attack that resulted in the deaths of four soldiers. All participants were told that Farid was to be interrogated, and they were asked to rate how severely he should be interrogated on a scale that ranged from simply asking questions, all the way to techniques that would be "aversive, degrading, painful, and in some cases cause permanent physical or psychological scars" (p. 193). The experimenters were interested in whether the participants' choice of torture levels would be swayed more by information about the likelihood of Farid having information than by his past terrorism. The experimenters found that although Americans tend to *justify* torture on utilitarian grounds, they *prescribed* more severe interrogation techniques both when Farid was likely to provide useful information *and* when Farid had a previous history of terrorist acts. In fact, Farid's previous history of terrorist acts was a slightly better predictor of support for torture than the likelihood of his providing useful information. The experimenters found that they could even predict whether participants would support torture based on a single question about Farid's moral character. If participants thought Farid was an evil man, they were more likely to support torturing him, even if they were explicitly told that it was highly unlikely that he had useful information. Like support for other forms of violent redress, such as corporal punishment or the death penalty (Carlsmith, 2008; Carlsmith *et al.*, 2002, 2007), this experimental evidence shows that support for torture among the public is driven by retributive motives, not merely the instrumental value of the information to be gained by torture, or its deterrent effects.

In short, authorities order torture to sustain or restore their AR relationship with the victims. The torturers themselves are typically motivated by hierarchy: the desire to sustain and enhance AR relationships with the torturer's superiors, or competitive AR relationships with peers. Torturers see torture victims as enemies existing outside the CS group, and they are motivated by MP proportionality to acquire information for the common good, using the most efficient means possible, particularly when time and resources are scarce. Public approval of torture is often driven by EM sentiments of vengeance, making the victim suffer as punishment for the evil he is thought to have done.

15 HOMICIDE: HE HAD IT COMING

Tio: When I was fourteen years old, this guy beat me down in the streets. And my stepfather took his life right in front of me. And I felt, good about it, really.

From the documentary The Interrupters *(James, 2011)*

"I could kill him!" people say – and sometimes do. More dryly put, sometimes people are disposed to violently enforce relationships, and often they are *supposed* to do so. The provoking injury may be limited to the social self, but the retaliatory attack is often directed at the offender through his or her body. That is, when people perceive that they themselves, their CS partners, or their AR dependants have been morally "injured," they may be disposed to inflict bodily injuries on the offending party – or on others whom they treat as collectively responsible for the offense. Often they want to get even in an EM framework, avenging the wrong done to them, an eye for an eye. This disposition is moral in every sense: the injured parties feel themselves to be victims of a transgression that *demands* punishment. Subjectively, the affront morally "requires" a violent response, and, indeed, the offender may have intended her provocations to incite a fight. The phenomenological experience of the offended person is that they "had to" strike back to preserve their moral integrity.

Peers and reference groups may condone these forceful responses to insults or infringements of social-relational rights; in nearly every culture there are intolerable transgressions to which an offended person *must* strike back violently, whatever the practical or material consequences. More distant outside observers, especially modern edu-cated Westerners (including ourselves), may deplore violent retaliation, condemning what we judge to be horrific, cruel, callous, or uncivilized cruelty. We may fail to see the perpetrator's perspective, incorrectly attributing the violence to the perpetrator's having lost self-control, being amorally impulsive, or failing to understand that he was making the victim suffer. Socially dominant moralities, expert philosophical doctrines, sanctified and institutionalized religious precepts, or official legal frameworks may prohibit violent retaliation, and punish it. But none of that implies that the retaliator's violence was not morally motivated. To defend vital relationships, to redress grievous wrongs, or to terminate intolerable relationships, people may feel morally impelled to homicide. In the eyes of the perpetrator, pain, maiming, or death is just what the victim deserves – it is justice.

How many homicides are morally motivated?

Only a minority of murders are asocially instrumental: it is rare for murder to be merely an expedient means to an asocial material end. Rather, most murders are embedded in and morally motivated by social relationships.

For example, homicides and gun violence in Boston in 1995 were described as follows:

> Most of the violence was personal – respect, boy/girl, Hatfield-and-McCoy vendetta – rather than about the drug business.
>
> *(Kennedy, 2009: 2)*

> The killing was overwhelmingly not about money, drugs, markets, or anything economic. Over and over and over, it was about "beefs" – standing vendettas between groups.
>
> *(Kennedy, 2011: 42)*

The same was true of Baltimore (Kennedy, 2011: 108). Maxfield's (1989) statistical analysis of 195,543 homicides in 15 large US cities between 1976 and 1985 showed that 51% of homicides whose circum-stances were known grew out of arguments or other social conflicts, and 77% of killers knew their victims. In other urbanized industrial societies, around 90% of homicides are between people with pre-existing social ties, and in smaller-scale societies, the proportion is even higher (Gould, 2003: 67–9). The prevalence of violence and homicide varies enormously depending on the type of relationship. Examining case records of all 121 homicides in Victoria, Australia, in 1985 and 1986, Polk (1993) found that 51% occurred in sexual, family, or friendship relationships; another 22% resulted from male–male confrontations over honor.

These social conflicts are quintessentially moral. In a sample of 138 New York City arson cases, 53% were motivated by revenge (Pisani, 1982; see also Black, 1998: 34). In Los Angeles throughout the twentieth century, a substantial proportion of homicides resulted from "arguments over gambling debts, girlfriends, rip-offs in drug transactions, and verbal insults about one's masculinity, race and family background" (Miethe and Regoeczi, 2004: 118). The proportion of such homicides increased from 40% in the first decade of the twentieth century to 65% in 1960–77 (p. 125). Other Los Angeles homicides occurred when someone intervened on behalf of a family member or friend, especially when the ultimate victim then disrespects the person who is intervening (Miethe and Regoeczi, 2004: 120–1).

Daly and Wilson (1988) showed that homicides in American and other cultures are typically retaliation for verbal or physical abuse, "escalated show-off contests" in which honor or social rank are at stake, male conflicts over women, jealous men's punishments of their partners for actual or imputed infidelity or for their partner's leaving the relationship, and business conflicts and debts.

Furthermore, the possession and use of guns increases the status of men in certain American communities and subcultures. "Manhood now it's like gunhood. If you got a gun you the man (laughing). Ain't no more manhood it's gunhood" (Wilkinson and Fagan, 1996: 81). Having a gun "boosts up" an adolescent's reputation as "bad."

People confront others and threaten violence to gain AR status, and respond with violence to maintain or gain status. What is at stake is not just the AR relationship between the participants but also status in the eyes of their audience and reference group – violence contests are about "face" (Felson, 1982; Luckenbill, 1977). Sometimes a person simply makes a request, politely or not, and the respondent perceives that to comply would be to show deference, which they are not willing to give; then the defiance escalates to violence. One might imagine that drug-related homicides, at least, are purely instrumental, but, in fact, many occur when one party "disses" the other (Miethe and Regoeczi, 2004: 124). Lundsgaarde (1977) compiled evidence on 237 Houston homicides in 1969, finding that virtually all were triggered by moral transgression, including many cases of dominance confrontations where one party insulted or threatened an associate or stranger, such that their status in the AR relationship was determined by who backed down, or, failing that, who killed whom. Most of the homicides in Luckenbill's (1977) California sample and Decker's (1996a) St. Louis sample were similarly motivated – people killed to demonstrate that they were not someone whom people should "mess with." Kubrin and Weitzer (2003) found that 19% of St. Louis homicides in 1985–95 were explicit retaliations for insults or offenses against the killer or against a friend, girlfriend, or relative of the killer. Analysis of 185 assaults recorded in Las Vegas police files for 1998 found that two-thirds arose from "character contests" about "social face," especially "relative social power and prestige" (Deibert and Miethe, 2010). In the neighborhoods and subcultures where such homicides are most prevalent, any sort of disrespect or challenge is sufficient to motivate killing, and these character contests are not limited to men or to young people.

> The offender, victim, and two neighbors were sitting in the living room drinking wine. The victim started calling the offender, his wife, abusive names. The offender told him to 'shut up.' Nevertheless, he continued. Finally, she shouted, 'I said shut up. If you don't shut up and stop it, I'm going to kill you and I mean it.' Whereupon he didn't and she did.
>
> *(Luckenbill, 1977: 182)*

Others in the community may approve of killing someone who consistently violates social relationships.

> Neighbors who have no relation to those involved in a dispute may not only tolerate but also actively support the use of retaliatory violence... In several cases residents were quite vehement in saying the person killed was a legitimate victim, so disliked in the neighborhood that his passing was regarded as a good riddance, and

for this reason they would not cooperate with the police. Familial support for retaliatory violence is also evident in our data. In several instances, the killer proudly tells family members about a planned or completed killing.

(Kubrin and Weitzer, 2003: 176)

Katz (1988) interprets nearly all American and British violence as moral, finding that

> Central to all these experiences in deviance is a member of the family of moral emotions: humiliation, righteousness, arrogance, ridicule, cynicism, defilement, and vengeance. In each, the attraction that proves to be most fundamentally compelling is that of overcoming a personal challenge to moral – not to material – existence. For the impassioned killer, the challenge is to escape a situation that has come to seem otherwise inexorably humiliating. Unable to sense how he or she can move with self-respect from the current situation, now, to any mundane-time relationship that might be reengaged, then, the world-be killer leaps at the possibility of embodying, though the practice of "righteous" slaughter, some eternal, universal form of the Good.
>
> *(Katz, 1988: 9; see also pp. 312–13)*

In other words, the moral aim of many homicides is termination of an intolerable relationship that the killer cannot evade or escape. Or else an intolerable relationship is so tightly linked to other essential relationships through metarelational models that withdrawing from the focal relationship would cause irreparable harm to those other essential relationships. Such homicides result from moral rage when the victim has attacked the killer's moral character or standing, so the humiliated killer perceives that "the situation requires a last stand in defense of his basic worth" (Katz, 1988: 19). Katz analyzes these situations as challenges to AR status, in particular:

> Both humiliation and rage are experienced on a vertical dimension. . . Humiliation drives you down; in humiliation, you feel suddenly made small, so small that everyone seems to look down on you. . . In contrast, rage proceeds in an upward direction . . . angry people "rise up."
>
> *(Katz, 1988: 27)*

> Rage is often coherent, disciplined action, cunning in its moral
> structure. Would-be killers create their homicidal rage only through
> a precisely articulated leap to righteousness.
>
> *(Katz, 1988: 30)*

As recently as 40 years ago in the United States, police, prosecutors, grand juries, trial juries, and judges often agreed that killers were morally justified in killing to preserve familial relationships: many such killers were not convicted, or were convicted but put on probation or given minimal sentences (Lundsgaarde, 1977; Vera Institute, 1977). Family homicides and other homicides among acquaintances were especially unlikely to result in prosecution or time served (Lundsgaarde, 1977; Vera Institute, 1977). These official third parties' metarelational stance was to condone or at least tolerate murder motivated by the intense moral emotions of the closest relationships. Still today, people who kill close CS partners are often treated very leniently compared to those who kill strangers (Cooney, 2009: 156–83, 189).

Most of the data on motives for homicide are from the modern West, but the moral motives for homicides in a number of African societies that have been studied are generally similar to those identified in the West, though, of course, the specific social relationships and hence the precise moral provocations leading to homicide are different (Bohannan, 1967a). Additionally, in most traditional societies, people also experience many kinds of suffering as punishable moral transgressions. People attribute many deaths, illnesses, injuries, setbacks, and misfortunes to witchcraft or sorcery, even when human agency has not been directly observed, but has been inferred from divination, oracles, or spirit mediums. In most cultures people know that witchcraft operates more or less "directly" though the medium of the emotions, attitudes, or motives of the witch without her taking palpable actions in the material world. Indeed, in some cultures, some witches are thought to be unaware of their witchcraft. In some cultures it is the prerogative of the chief or king to execute witches and sorcerers, but the bereaved family may also avenge themselves, or mobs of community members may kill women accused of witchcraft or men accused of sorcery. However, in many cultures, people aren't able to identify the witch or sorcerer who killed a family member, so they use magic to avenge themselves against whoever did it (e.g., Evans-Pritchard, 1937; Overing, 1986). Eventually, someone in the vicinity dies whom the oracles then identify as the guilty party. In the many cultures where people fear witches or sorcerers, it is also common for people to deploy protective magic against them; the magic is supposed to kill anyone who supernaturally attacks the possessor of the magic. In order to prevent the targets of magic from deploying effective countermagic, people using magic almost always keep secret the nature of their magic, and typically also conceal the fact that they are using magic at all. In these instances, people confidently experience themselves as using violence to regulate their social relationships, morally motivated by their right to self-protection and vengeance. Magic used in these ways is somewhat like carrying a concealed gun.

In many cultures people also use magic to enhance their relationships and pursue social goals such as attracting a lover, being appointed chief, supporting victory in war, gaining customers, or facilitating success in other ventures. Often it is implicitly understood – though hardly ever stated – that the magic may work by harming rivals. Such magic is motivated to regulate social relationships. It is nearly always kept secret to prevent others from countering it effectively, but above all it must be concealed because any harm it does, however justifiable it may feel from the perpetrator's egoistic perspective, is likely to be judged illegitimate by the victims and their supporters, and perhaps by the traditional or modern authorities (Evans-Pritchard, 1937; Fiske, field notes; Knauft, 1985; Schieffelin, 2004).

Mass murder

Mass murder, in particular, seems pathological, yet even if it is, the perpetrators' motives are often moral. In a study of mass murders committed by adolescents, the most common precipitant was rejection by a real girlfriend – or by someone who hardly recognized the killer (Meloy et al., 2001: 726). "Unfair" treatment by others, including one's family, was the second most common perceived insult. Examining newspaper reports of 106 incidents of mass murders in public places committed by 137 perpetrators, Petee et al. (1997) found that more than half of the mass murders were morally motivated relationship regulation. They found that 32% were motivated by revenge directed at persons, institutions, or more defuse targets. In an additional 5% of incidents, the motives derived from domestic or romantic relationships; 4% were due to "direct interpersonal conflict"; 6% were motivated by gang relationships; and 10% were politically motivated (terrorism).

Research consistently shows that mass murders are typically motivated by redressive sentiments; let's briefly consider the evidence. Based on all the data available for the cases they examined, Levin and Fox (1996) found that the majority of mass murders were motivated by revenge, sometimes carried out against proxies for the persons who were perceived to have wronged the killer, or to get even with a whole social category (e.g., the Post Office, feminists). Levin and Fox found that some family murders were motivated by "love" where the perpetrator killed his children to keep them from an intolerable relationship, such as the custody of an estranged wife. In another study of documentary evidence on adolescent, male mass murderers in the United States between 1958 and 1999, 59% of the perpetrators appeared to have been motivated by relationship issues:

> Such events included the loss of a real or fantasized relation with a female, a family dispute, suspension from school, insults by peers, termination from a job, anger over involuntary hospitalization, a physical injury that hampered athleticism, and denial of entry into the military. These triggering events usually occurred within hours or days of the mass murder.
>
> *(Meloy et al., 2001: 722)*

> "They never treated me like a son – they treated me like an outsider all the time. I mean – I don't think they cared." 19 year-old male who killed his father, stepmother, and stepbrothers.
>
> *(Meloy et al., 2001: 723)*

The US Secret Service and Department of Education's study of 37 incidents of school shootings and other mass violence from 1974 to 2000, involving 41 attackers, found that 71% "of individual attackers had experienced bullying and harassment that was long-standing and severe. In some of these cases the experience of being bullied seemed to have a significant impact on the attacker and appeared to have been a factor in his decision to mount an attack at the school" (Vossekuil *et al.*, 2002: 21).[1] While the

---

[1] For comparison, a large nationally representative survey by the US National Institute of Child Health and Human Development found that 4.8% of male 10th graders (ages 15–16) reported being bullied at least once a week during the current term (Nansel, 2001).

community is horrified at the evil of these murders, in the minds of the perpetrators they are necessary and right; the perpetrators feel obligated or entitled to act to rectify their most vital social relationships – and often expressly intend to terminate all of their bad relationships by dying at the end of their killing spree.

Homicides committed by the mentally ill

Moral motives to constitute social relationships are culturally informed such that any individual's motives are generally more or less congruent with those of other people in the same roles in the same culture. This congruence is a matter of degree, however. In a culture of honor, some men may be too meek or gentle to kill people who insult them or dishonor their daughters. Conversely, an individual in a Quaker, an Amish, or a Mennonite community may respond with violence to an insult when they should turn the other cheek and walk away. Moreover, many psychological disorders affect the intensity of moral emotions and social motives, or affect perceptions of the state of social relationships and the significance of others' social actions. Hence, a person afflicted with a psychological disorder may commit violence that is morally motivated, yet excessive or bizarre by community standards. A paranoid man may retaliate against people he believes have caused him harm, or plan to do so – so, in his mind, he is acting virtuously. Likewise, a depressed woman may believe that she has failed her family, and kill herself to punish herself and terminate the relationships that feel intolerable to her. A schizophrenic person may perceive that God is ordering him to kill the devil, who is disguised as Santa Claus. These or other disorders can facilitate a man's belief that he is justified in killing the boss who fired him, along with the coworkers who conspired against and humiliated him. Just because a person is crazy doesn't mean her motives are not moral, even when those motives result in violence.

Among all 6th through 10th graders of both sexes, 8.4% reported being bullied weekly. Among males, 17.8% of those bullied reported being hit, slapped, or pushed at least once a week; the rest reported bullying that was verbal or gestural. For females the percentage being physically bullied at least once a week was 11.1.

Metarelational motives for homicide

Alongside moral sentiments generated by dyadic relationships, there are commonly metarelational moral considerations. In the contexts of cultural concerns with honor, especially, failure to stand up for one's dignity is a moral failure that weakens or jeopardizes the offended person's social relations with many others. Indeed, an offended person's family, friends, and neighbors may egg him on, and mock him as weak and cowardly if he doesn't strike back. And, especially in non-state and non-modern societies or in ghettos where the police are not likely to enforce the law effectively, CS relationships are constituted by collective moral responsibility for violence. If a person is injured or killed, the victim's kin group or age set or gang is collectively responsible for vengeance, which may be carried out against any member of the perpetrator's group. Both as victims and as perpetrators, the essence of the primary group is its corporate liability, its corporate accountability. The primary group is a unit in which all are equivalent as perpetrators and as retaliators – EM vengeance is served regardless of who in the victim's group kills whom in the perpetrator's group (the famous example is the Nuer; see Evans-Pritchard, 1940; Gough, 1972).

In short, when people kill, they usually do so because they feel that a crucial relationship is being threatened or has been violated, that their position in a crucial relationship is as stake, or that the relationship has reached an intolerable state and cannot be rectified, yet they cannot simply withdraw from it by ceasing to interact.

16 ETHNIC VIOLENCE AND GENOCIDE

Historically, CS unity and AR hierarchy moral motives may become connected to caste systems, in which the moral order is crucially constituted by preserving the CS essence of a high caste from degrading pollution by the substance of a lower caste. In some caste systems, the high caste is polluted if they eat or drink or share comestibles with low-caste persons, or eat food prepared by low-caste persons. In South Asia, the American South, and other caste systems, the collective corporeal purity of the high caste is perceived to be fundamentally polluted if a high-caste woman has sexual relations with a low-caste man. In these moral systems, "miscegenation" is a grave threat to the CS integrity of the high caste and at the same time a violation of its superior social status. This CS unity morality may motivate lynching of low-caste men, and, at its most extreme, it can generate mass killing and genocide.

Violence against African-Americans in the US South

In the US South, "Negro" disrespect to any white person, or, far worse, dishonoring the purity of a white woman, justified immediate lynching (Black, 1998: 152–3). Most whites regarded "Negroes" as a degraded kind who had to be kept in their place, and the sexual potency of Negro men was a particular threat to the purity of white women and hence to the honor of white men (Graves, 1906). Negro men accused of violence against any white, or of even the slightest sexually tinged communication with a white woman, were typically lynched, and this might involve burning alive or otherwise torturing to death (Clark, 1998; Godshalk, 2000). Often a large, appreciative, and encouraging audience of respectable citizens assembled to enjoy the show and then to vie for souvenir body pieces. For example, in 1899, after being accused of killing his employer and sexually assaulting the man's wife, Sam Hose was chained to a stake, his ears and fingers were sliced off and tossed to the audience, his tongue was removed with pliers, and he was then doused in coal oil and set on fire. White men then butchered his charred corpse and sold pieces as souvenirs to the audience of 2,000 who had arrived by special excursion train. The Georgia Congressman James M. Griggs made a public statement about the lynching:

> I appeal to you, gentlemen – you fathers, you husbands; to all men, white or black, north or south, east or west – do you blame these people for that burst of human fury? God forbid there should be any man on this continent who would! Thank God there is not a man in Georgia who does.
>
> *(Grem, 2006: 36)*

Even a scuffle between boys could lead to mob violence against a whole community (Ginzburg, 1962). In race-based AR, Negroes were severely punished for any lapse in servility to whites:

> For generations, young black men learned early in their lives that they could at any time be grabbed by a white mob – whether for murder, looking at a white woman the wrong way, or merely being "smart" – and dragged into the woods or a public street to be tortured, burned, mutilated.
>
> *(Ayers, 1995: 110)*

From the point of view of the perpetrators in the American South or elsewhere, lynching of insolent caste inferiors defends the moral order (Thurston, 2011). "Collective violence, then, is commonly a moralistic response to deviant behavior. And, aptly enough, it is sometimes described as "popular justice" (Senechal de la Roche, 1996: 98).

In general, lynching in the US South redressed and sustained AR relationships between whites and blacks, but also CS bonds of purity among whites. For some recent immigrant participants, lynching simultaneously enhanced their otherwise tenuous CS bonds with established white people and ensured their AR position above local blacks.

> By the turn of the century, when they were arriving in Brazos County [Texas] in droves, the county's foreign-born immigrants began claiming whiteness with a vengeance. They did so by taking advantage of, even participating in, the South's most brutal form of racial domination: the lynching of black men. For each of the immigrant groups caught up in the violence – Italians, Irish, and Bohemians – the deaths of black men helped to resolve the immigrants' ambiguous racial identity and to bestow the privileges of whiteness.
>
> *(Nevels, 2007: 6–7)*

Genocide

> Whatever its origin, group conflict does not produce violence without a consensus among the in-group, or at least its leaders, that another group has done something wrong and harmful, something dangerous to the in-group.
>
> But what motivates those who carry out these deeds is also solidarity and identification with their own group, which, they feel, benefits from such actions. Thus the obverse of genocide is identification with a loved group – friends, family, village, clan, tribe, class, nation, or religion on whose behalf the massacres are carried out.
>
> *(Chirot and McCauley, 2006: 71, 75–6)*

When people kill, rape, or drive out a whole category of persons, the perpetrators' motives are usually moral. State-run programs of the Soviet Union, China, North Korea, and the Congo Free State, and the Armenian genocide killed approximately 89 million people during the twentieth century (Leitenberg, 2006). From the sixteenth through the nineteenth century, invaders and settlers from Europe killed many millions of indigenous people in the Americas. In every country, jingoistic or racist sentiments generated, drove, and justified the killing, as can be seen in this excerpt from the Hutu ten commandments, a piece of propaganda used to spur anti-Tutsi sentiment prior to the Rwandan genocide:

The Hutu, wherever they are, must have unity and solidarity and be concerned with the fate of their Hutu brothers. The Hutu inside and outside Rwanda must constantly look for friends and allies for the Hutu cause, starting with their Hutu brothers. They must constantly counteract Tutsi propaganda. The Hutu must be firm and vigilant against their common Tutsi enemy.

(Berry and Berry, 1999)

A people who feel that another people's presence or intermarriage pollutes their CS-defining collective essence may wipe them out to purify and cleanse this endangered essence. "The Nazis executed up to six million Jews who were ideologically portrayed as a 'disease,' as 'bacilli,' and as 'parasites' that threatened to poison the German national body and contaminate the purity of German blood" (Hinton, 2002: 14). Staub (1989) has argued that this exclusion of the out-group as something separate from the in-group leads to a transformation of indifference to the out-group into a moral obligation to kill them.

But this moral motivation to wipe out entire kinds of people is not a modern invention. Sixteenth-century French Catholics killed and mutilated Protestants and burned their villages to purify themselves of the Protestant heresy (Chirot and McCauley, 2006). In the Great Mutiny of 1857, Indians cleansed their community of the British Kafir infidels. The Old Testament Israelite genocides of the Midianites and Amalekites, and the massacres of Jews by Crusaders, were simultaneous unity-motivated acts of purification and hierarchy-motivated obedience to God's will (Chirot and McCauley, 2006). The perpetrators essentialized both their own group and the polluting out-group as CS equivalence categories, setting the stage for a moral outcry to decontaminate the in-group polluted by the out-group. This was the moral motivation at the core of the Holocaust, the Cambodian genocide, the purges by Stalin and Mao, the Catholic extermination of Huguenots, and the Hutu massacres of Tutsis.

The result of this double essentializing is a battle of good and evil, or two incomparable essences in which love of the good means necessarily hate for the threatening out-group. This is what lies at the heart of the most extreme genocidal cases, where the fear of pollution can lead to what would otherwise seem to be incomprehensible mass murder. The out-group's essence must be

kept from contaminating the in-group's essence ... that is
endangered by contact or infection.

(Chirot and McCauley, 2006: 86)

Based on his comprehensive review of the history of genocide, Kiernan
(2007) concludes that "fetishes of purity and contamination" have
aggravated the violence of many intergroup conflicts. Kiernan reports
that in 1580 the British commander in Ireland, Lord Grey, referred to
Catholicism as a disease and a canker. In 1641, the English commander Sir
Charles Coote ordered his soldiers to kill Irish women and children
because "Kill the nits [eggs of the body louse] and you will have no
lice," and Scottish soldiers shouted this slogan in 1642 as they massacred
thousands of Irish Catholic civilians: men, women, and children. The nit
slogan reappeared in the American West and the Australian outback as a
call to eliminate indigenous populations, in Nazi declarations about Jews,
and Al-Qaeda statements about Shi'a communities (Kiernan, 2007: 606).
Hitler was obsessed by concerns about racial purity and the defiling Jewish
"disease" or "virus"; Pol Pot was obsessed by the necessity to eliminate
all traces of polluting Vietnamese blood from the Khmer essence
(Chirot and McCauley, 2006; also see Hinton, 2002). This is not simply
dehumanization: it constitutes the derogated group as a filthy infestation
that defiles the CS purity of the in-group. Again, from the Hutu ten
commandments, the first three commandments are explicitly focused on
preventing Hutu men from having sexual intercourse with Tutsi women
because it contaminates the purity of the Hutu people.

1. Every Hutu should know that a Tutsi woman, whoever she is,
   works for the interest of her Tutsi ethnic group. As a result, we
   shall consider a traitor any Hutu who
   - marries a Tutsi woman
   - befriends a Tutsi woman
   - employs a Tutsi woman as a secretary or a concubine.
2. Every Hutu should know that our Hutu daughters are more
   suitable and conscientious in their role as woman, wife and
   mother of the family. Are they not beautiful, good secretaries and
   more honest?
3. Hutu women, be vigilant and try to bring your husbands,
   brothers and sons back to reason.

In conjunction with CS unity motives to cleanse the in-group of the
impurities of the derogated out-group, genocide is also motivated by

AR hierarchy in which the in-group has the right and the requirement to put the derogated out-group in its place as a subordinate race. The Nazis claimed that Aryans are a race superior to all others, the pinnacle of evolutionary progress, and hence destined to rule the world: it was natural, right, and necessary that they do so, eliminating any entities that stood in their way. Similar judgments motivated the massacres and displacement of the indigenous populations of the Americas.

> The indigenous populations were stigmatized as savages who ought to make way for civilization. In his book *The Winning of the West*, for example, Theodore Roosevelt justified the treatment meted out to the Indians of the United States in the following terms: "The settler and pioneer have at bottom had justice on their side; this great continent could not have been kept as nothing but a game preserve for squalid savages" (Roosevelt, 1889: 90). General Roca, the minister for war in Argentina at the end of the nineteenth century, put it even more bluntly when he stated the case for clearing the pampas of their Indian inhabitants. Speaking to his fellow countrymen he argued that "our self-respect as a virile people obliges us to put down as soon as possible, by reason or by force, this handful of savages who destroy our wealth and prevent us from definitively occupying, in the name of law, progress and our own security, the richest and most fertile lands of the Republic" (Serres Güiraldes, 1979: 377–8). Roca then proceeded to lead a campaign, known in Argentine history as the Conquest of the Desert, whose express purpose was to clear the pampas of Indians.
>
> *(Maybury-Lewis, 2002: 45)*

Everywhere, imperialist genocide "was often inspired furthermore by the rulers' determination to show who was master and who was, if not slave, then at least obedient subject; and it was often put into effect as deliberate policy where the masters felt that their subjects had to be taught a lesson. Acts of resistance or rebellion were often punished by genocidal killings" (Maybury-Lewis, 2002: 47–8). Caesar annihilated the Eburones, Genghis Khan eliminated the inhabitants of Herat, and the German general von Trotha massacred the Herero people, in each case because they refused to submit to imperial authority (Chirot and McCauley, 2006). In short, imperial and colonial genocide was the morally motivated redress and enforcement of AR relationships deemed legitimate by the imperial killers.

In some cases, mass killing and genocide take the form of vengeance or revolution against what is perceived as an illegitimate authority. In the case of the Rwandan genocide, the minority Tutsis were given control of the country over the majority Hutus when the Belgian government ruled the colony. Hutus refer to this period as a time of slavery. In the late 1950 and early 1960s, the Hutus rebelled against Tutsi and Belgian rule, resulting in the deaths of over 50,000 Tutsis. Over the next three decades, the Hutus engaged in violence and discrimination against Tutsis. In 1990, Tutsi fighters known as the Rwandese Patriotic Army (RPA) invaded Rwanda from Uganda. The RPA comprised primarily the children of Tutsis who had been forced out of Rwanda by the decades of severe discrimination and the violence. Hutus responded by arguing for the need to purify the in-group against the Tutsis and eventually attempted to wipe out all of the Tutsis in Rwanda (Staub, 2006).

Null attitudes and dehumanization in the perpetuation of mass violence

Although the Holocaust was ultimately motivated by a desire to purify Germany and protect Aryans from polluting vermin, Bauman (2001) cogently underlines that once Hitler had determined the objective, the proximate mechanisms of extermination were motivated by an MP proportionality desire for rational efficiency: the most extermination at the least possible cost.

> The department in the SS headquarters in charge of the destruction
> of European Jews was officially designated as the Section of
> Administration and Economy... To a degree much too high for
> comfort, the designation faithfully reflected the organizational
> meaning of activity. Except for the moral repulsiveness of its goal
> (or, to be precise, the gigantic scale of the moral odium), the activity
> did not differ in any formal sense (the only sense that can be
> expressed in the language of bureaucracy) from all other organized
> activities designed, monitored and supervised by "ordinary"
> administrative and economic sections. Like all other activities
> amenable to bureaucratic rationalization, it fits well the sober
> description of modern administration offered by Max Weber.
>
> *(Bauman, 2001: 14)*

Nazi experts, including engineers and scientists, carefully designed the most rational procedures, chose the optimal technologies, and carefully, economically salvaged all the labor and material value they could extract from the people they exterminated. So the motivation for the operational procedures for carrying out the Holocaust were as rationally calculative as those of any modern bureaucracy.

> The most shattering of lessons deriving from the analysis of the 'twisted road to Auschwitz' is that – in the last resort – *the choice of physical extermination as the right means to the task of* Entfernung [removal] *was a product of routine bureaucratic procedures:* means-ends calculus, budget balancing, universal rule application. To make the point sharper still – the choice was an effect of the earnest effort to find rational solutions to successive 'problems', as they arose in the changing circumstances.
>
> *(Bauman, 2001: 17; italics in original)*

> At no point of its long and tortuous execution did the Holocaust come in conflict with the principles of rationality. The 'Final Solution' did not clash at any stage with the rational pursuit of efficient, optimal goal implementation. On the contrary, *it arose out of a genuinely rational concern, and it was generated by bureaucracy true to its form and purpose.*
>
> *(Bauman, 2001: 18; italics in original)*

But this proportionality-motivated MP rationality requires the perpetrators to treat human lives and suffering as entirely fungible with all other commodities or utilities. How can we make sense of this apparent commodification of the lives of victims of mass violence that allows morally motivated actors to engage in MP proportionality or asocial means–end calculus in the extermination of their victims? RMT posits that there are just four morally motivated universal schemas for social coordination. But RMT also recognizes that the mere co-presence of two or more persons does not imply moral social coordination. People can simply ignore each other, but they can also treat other *Homo sapiens* as if they were mere organisms or objects. In this case, where a person takes account of another human merely as an object or animate agent, the person has a *null relationship* with the other human. People intending to make a farm can clear a field of rocks or trees, and they can also shoot the deer who eat their crops or the wolves who may eat their sheep. Ordinarily, there is no moral social relationship between the farmer and the rocks, trees, deer, or wolves. In human history, farmers have sometimes driven off or killed indigenous *Homo sapiens* who were competitors for the land, and who might eat their crops or their livestock (Maybury-Lewis, 2002). In such a case, the farmers have a null "relationship" with – or perhaps more aptly characterized, null *attitude* toward – the *Homo sapiens* they kill: the farmers are treating their victims just like rocks, trees, or deer – as mere animate objects. Of course, the farmer is likely to be morally motivated by his love for his family to remove the rocks or the indigeni; he has a responsibility to feed and protect his spouse and children. But he has no moral motivations with regard to the rocks, trees, deer, wolves, or indigeni, because moral motives are concomitants of social *relationships*, and the farmer has no social relationships with the objects and agents he needs to eliminate.

If the farmer originally did have a social relationship with the indigeni, and then that relationship transformed into a null attitude, we could term the process "dehumanization." But "dehumanization" implies an original state of social relatedness, although, in fact, in many circumstances there never was a relationship in the first place. The concept of "moral disengagement" likewise falsely assumes that moral engagement is the original and default attitude. If the farmer does engage in social relationships with the indigeni, and hence humanizes and morally engages with them, he doesn't treat them like rocks or wolves. Of course, if some indigeni killed other settlers like him, EM might morally motivate him to seek vengeance against other indigeni, whom he would likely treat as all equivalent for revenge, regarding them as a collectively responsible CS group. In contrast, if he has no social relationship with them in the first place, then, driven by his moral motives regarding his family, he is likely to engage in traditional practices of clearing his fields and protecting his livestock without much reflection; these practices may involve killing predators or indigeni. If and when the farmer stops to reflect, his decisions are likely to involve a purely dispassionate rational calculation of the most efficient and effective way to remove the rocks or eliminate the indigeni.

Such configurations of moral social relationships linked to amoral null attitudes operated in slave trading, colonial rubber plantations, and warfare. Harry Truman and Robert McNamara must have been genuinely morally motivated by their AR responsibilities and their CS patriotism to use MP to calculate how to minimize the price to be paid in American casualty rates to achieve eventual victory. But Truman and McNamara dehumanized, respectively, the Japanese and North Vietnamese, allowing themselves to make rational strategic decisions. European slave traders and colonial rubber-plantation managers killed tens of millions in the course of their enterprises. "During the slave trade, in King Leopold's Congo and in the Peruvian rubber-gathering regime, genocide was quite simply a business expense, the human cost of capturing and coercing unwilling laborers to produce for the international export trade" (Maybury-Lewis, 2002: 47). Slave traders, slave owners, and rubber-plantation managers were morally motivated by their AR and EM relationships with their employers and bosses, their CS desires to provide for their families, and no doubt their AR ambitions. But their cruelty was literally inhumane because they perceived no morally motivating social relationship with their victims. Contemporary managers of international corporations who contract with Third World sweatshops where children work in dangerous and unhealthy conditions are operating within a similar configuration of morally motivated responsibilities toward their CEOs, stockholders, and customers, joined with distant and indirect rational links through subcontractors that allow them to disregard, disengage, and dehumanize the laborers who produce their products.

17 SELF-HARM AND SUICIDE

> To be, or not to be – that is the question:
> Whether 'tis nobler in the mind to suffer
> The slings and arrows of outrageous fortune
> Or to take arms against a sea of troubles,
> And by opposing end them. . .
> For who would bear the whips and scorns of time,
> Th' oppressor's wrong, the proud man's contumely,
> The pangs of despis'd love, the law's delay,
> The insolence of office, and the spurns
> That patient merit of th' unworthy takes,
> When he himself might his quietus make
> With a bare bodkin? Who would these fardels bear,
> To grunt and sweat under a weary life,
> But that the dread of something after death –
> The undiscover'd country, from whose bourn
> No traveller returns – puzzles the will,
> And makes us rather bear those ills we have
> Than fly to others that we know not of?
>
> *Shakespeare*, Hamlet, *Act III, scene i*

A person may redress a wrong by harming the transgressor, or by harming someone with whom the transgressor has a vital CS relationship. Suicide and self-harm take both forms, sometimes simultaneously. Thus, Annie may kill herself because she has violated a relationship that only her self-punishment can redeem, or she may kill herself to punish Bill who has transgressed against her, but who loves her and will suffer when she kills herself. In either case there are often important metarelational motives at work. Hurting or killing oneself may restore the collective honor of one's primary CS group, such as family or military unit. Suicide and self-harm may also show that one accepts full individual responsibility for failure, so third parties should not blame anyone else. In other metarelational processes, Annie's suicide to punish Bill's transgression against Annie may make George, who loves Annie, hate Bill, or at the very least shame Bill by drawing George's and others' attention to the gravity of Bill's transgression against Annie. Similarly, like Lucretia's suicide after being raped by Sextus, it may spur others to avenge a grave transgression. More recently, Tibetan monks' suicide by setting themselves on fire to protest Chinese rule over Tibet and repression of Buddhism have put great moral pressure on China, and in 2010 Mohammed Bouazizi's suicide by fire in Tunisia brought out masses of protestors who overthrew the government. All of these moral motivations for suicide and self-harm are aimed at redressing and rectifying transgressions of one or more relationships.

Non-suicidal self-injury

Non-suicidal self-injury (NSSI), including cutting, burning, and injurious blows, often functions like suicide, to morally regulate relationships. Flett *et al.* (2012) found that NSSI is often self-punitive: among women university students, NSSI is associated with shame, self-reported parental criticism, socially prescribed perfectionism (e.g., "I find it difficult to meet others' expectations of me"), and over-generalization of self-evaluation (e.g., "How I feel about myself overall is easily influenced by a single mistake"). Reviewing 18 studies of NSSI, Klonsky (2007) found widespread evidence for its self-punishment function. Nock (2009) reviews several studies showing that NSSI is often self-punishment, or is social signaling when less intense forms of communication have proven ineffective. In a survey of western Canadian urban adolescents, Laye-Gindhu and Schonert-Reichel (2005) found that, among a sample of 64 who reported self-harming, their motivations included the following: "I wanted to punish myself," 27%; "I was angry at my parent(s)/guardian(s)," 39%; "I was angry at myself," 63%; "I was angry at someone (friend or other)", 39%; "I wanted to get back at someone," 21%; and "I felt like I was a failure," 64%. In a university student sample in which 183 participants reported NSSI, 40% of participants indicated that their reason for initiating self-injury was anger at themselves, while 22% started NSSI because they were angry at someone else, 11% wanted someone to notice them or their injuries, 6% wanted to fit in with others, and 5% wanted to shock or hurt someone (Muehlenkamp et al., 2013). Reasons for continuing to self-injure had mostly to do with "regulating emotions," but also included dealing with anger, 27%; self-punishment, 15%; self-hatred, 11%; shocking or hurting someone, 7%; "because my friends do it," 4%; and "to be part of a group," 2%. In an online study of 162 mostly English-speaking women who reported NSSI, 100% endorsed some self-punishment functions, while 85% endorsed some interpersonal communication functions (e.g., "to communicate or let others know how desperate I am"), and 51% endorsed some interpersonal influence functions (e.g., "to get back at or hurt someone" (Turner et al., 2012).

Suicide

Durkheim (1951/1897) posited that when social integration is very strong, people may perceive a normative duty to commit suicide under certain circumstances; he called this "obligatory altruistic suicide." Dutiful suicide includes Indian suttee (*sati*), in which a widow throws herself on her husband's funeral pyre, and the suicide of attendants and followers of a chief when he dies among the Gauls, Hawaiians, and Ashanti (Durkheim, 1951/1897: 219). When a person has a duty to commit suicide, people disrespect the person who fails to do so, and often believe that the defaulter will suffer in the afterlife. Suicide is required, Durkheim observes, when the wife or followers are strictly subordinated to the deceased such that they must follow him even into death: they cannot live independently. That is, the dependant exists only as a dependant, without any other social role, so her intention is to sustain her relationship with her deceased partner in the realm of the dead (Hawley, 1994). Conversely, in ancient northeastern Europe and India, when an old man was unable to perform his duties as a leader and protector, he must honorably kill himself rather than ignobly succumbing to death in bed (Durkheim, 1951/1897: 217–18). In other words, the AR relationship between superior and inferior is their only possible life; without it – or rather, to maintain it – they must die. In addition, Durkheim cites East Asian, American Indian, and Polynesian norms that valorize suicide when a person has violated an important social relationship, or someone has violated a relationship with the person, as well as suicide performed to demonstrate superiority and gain prestige (p. 222). Durkheim also ascribes high rates of suicide among military officers, in particular, to the experience of "a refusal of leave, a reprimand, an unjust punishment, a delay in promotion, a question of honor, a flush of momentary jealousy" – in other words, to someone violating a social relationship with the officer (p. 239). As he puts it, "the profession of a soldier develops a moral constitution powerfully predisposing man to make away with himself," a moral constitution of CS solidarity.

People occasionally kill themselves to be with God, in close, secure, peaceful rest; they may also kill a spouse, lover, or child first to bring the victim along or have the victim all to themselves (Douglas, 1967: 297–300). The ultimate Hindu, Buddhist, and Jain renunciation is suicide that, in RMT terms, is necessary to attain CS union with ultimate oneness (Durkheim, 1951/1897: 223–4). Durkheim mentions East Asian suicides of self-sacrifices to Shiva, Amida Buddha, and other gods. In short, Durkheim's thesis is that obligatory altruistic suicide is suicide to sustain or redress a crucial social relationship.

Manning (2012) cogently reviews the subsequent literature across cultures to show that suicide is "moralistic" – in sociological terms, it is "social control" of "deviance." In the language of sociology, suicide as vengeance, punishment, atonement, avoidance, political protest, or appeal to a third party is "conflict management" (see also Black, 1998). A person may execute himself as atonement for harming or doing wrong to others (Douglas, 1967: 302). Indeed, in Britain and the United States in the twentieth century, apparently more people executed *themselves* for homicide than were executed by the state (Bohannan, 1967b).

A person may commit suicide as self-punishment for failing in his duty to a superior (Westermarck, 1908: vol. II, 240), or, conversely, as a way of sanctioning a superior who has violated the AR relationship with him. People may commit suicide to evoke love, sympathy, and regret – and to make others acknowledge responsibility and feel guilty for their suffering (Douglas, 1967: 309–19). In some cultures and circumstances, people may carry out a suicide in such a way as to magnify the impact of the suicide on others, making the others feel guilty, shaming them, or exposing them to sanctions (Manning, 2012). Following Black's (1998) paradigm, Manning presents ethnologic evidence that suicide is most likely when the transgressed relationship is between people who are socially close (intimates who share a culture) and functionally interdependent. A person is most likely to commit suicide when they are in a distinctly subordinate position in the violated AR relationship, and when they have little effective social support from others.

In Japan, Taiwan, Singapore, Sri Lanka, India, Iran, Pakistan, Syria, Jordan, and Egypt, suicide is very often motivated or provoked by quarrels within the family or disputes with neighbors or associates; occupational or educational failures; romantic rejection, jealousy, or blockage by third parties; desertion, dissolution of relationships, bereavement, or social isolation; disgrace, dishonor, shame, or the person's own transgressions (Headley, 1983). In Japan, China, and some other cultures in various historical periods, suicide has been especially virtuous when performed for the welfare or honor of the group, or as an apology and atonement for failing in one's duties or committing a major transgression (Iga, 1986; Westermarck, 1908: vol. II, 241). Similar motives and events provoke suicide among the Soga, Gisu, and other African societies where suicide has been studied; men often commit suicide due to circumstances that drastically reduce their status (Bohannan, 1967a, 1967b; Fallers and Fallers, 1967; La Fontaine, 1967).

Interviews with 50 suicide-attempter patients in a Midwestern US suburban psychiatric facility diagnosed with major depressive disorder (MDD) and data on 50 suicide completers retrospectively diagnosed with MDD found that the major precipitants were interpersonal conflicts; divorce or relationship breakup; and, especially among the completers, job stress and financial stress (DeJong et al., 2010). Responding to questionnaires, 35 New York City adolescents who seriously considered killing themselves and 32 who attempted to commit suicide identified the precipitating situation; 43% and 56%, respectively, reported that fighting with a parent was a precipitant; 31% and 37% indicated fighting with others was a precipitant; 14% and 22% indicated school problems (respondents could indicate more than one precipitating situation; Negron et al., 1997). Describing their emotions at the time, 64% and 69% reported they were angry; 43% and 81% felt isolated.

Among 254 adolescents who were seen in a hospital for attempted suicide in a suburb of Oslo, Norway, between 1984 and 2006, clinical interviews found that a relational conflict was the most common trigger (50%), and a dysfunctional family (conflicts within the family) was the most common underlying reason (44%) (Dieserud et al., 2010). Other studies have found that the major suicide-attempt triggers for adolescents and young adults are relationship conflicts; relationship breakups; and economic, school, and work difficulties (reviewed in Dieserud et al., 2010). Among 104 Australian suicidal adolescents seen between 1994 and 1998, clinical interviews found that they were "perfectionistic, were overly conscientious and experienced enormous inappropriate guilt"; in addition, their parents described them as unable to accept being wrong and overly sensitive to perceived criticism (Haliburn, 2000). In 56 suicide notes from completed adult suicides in the United States and 262 in Australia, love or marital problems were very common for both men and women; other motives arose from problems with achievement, school, or work (Canetto and Lester, 2002; Lester et al., 2004). The most common reason for suicide in Russia, and among the Apache and Navaho, is an interpersonal conflict or relationship problem, particularly in marriage, romantic relationships, and the family; grief over the death of a loved one also provokes some suicides in some cultures (Ambrumova and Postovalova, 2010; Everett, 1975; Wyman and Thorne, 1945).

> Among White Mountain Apache [suicide] is aggressive, retaliation
> for a real or supposed offense committed by an antagonist who is
> either a spouse or close kinsman.
>
> *(Everett, 1975: 278)*

The aim to redress a social-relational transgression against a person, and sometimes other moral motives, may lead to either suicide or homicide, depending on the circumstances. For example, Elwin (1950) describes major causes of both suicide and homicide among the indigenous Maria of Maharashtra, India: avenging a transgression or an insult, family quarrels, love affairs gone wrong, other disputes, and fear of – or self-defense against – the assaults of witches or sorcerers. However, the loss of an essential relationship partner, or the prospect of social isolation, such as the ostracism of lepers or those shamed by their own egregious misdeeds, leads specifically to suicide. Depending on the circumstances, suicide may be aimed at punishing oneself for a relationship transgression, punishing relationship partners for their transgression, terminating a relationship, or preserving a relationship in death.

All of these studied cases converge on the conclusion that non-suicidal self-injury and suicide are intended to constitute relationships, especially to rectify or terminate relationships, but sometimes to sustain a crucial relationship by staying with a partner who has died. The subjective phenomenology of injuring or killing oneself is moral as well: it is motivated by shame, guilt, moral outrage, loyalty, love, or the need to evoke love, guilt, or shame. Violence against the self has a lot in common with violence against others, both emotionally and with respect to its regulative functions.

18 VIOLENT BEREAVEMENT

"Alas, my royal lord Achilles ... Patroclus has been killed..."

When Achilles heard this he sank deep into the black depths of despair.
He picked up the dark dust in both his hands and poured it on his
head. He soiled his comely face with it, and filthy ashes settled on his
scented tunic. He cast himself down on the earth and lay their like a
fallen giant, fouling his hair and tearing it out with his own hands. The
maidservants whom he and Patroclus had captured caught the alarm
and all ran screaming out of doors. They beat their breasts with their
hands and sank to the ground beside their royal master. On the other
side, Antilochus shedding tears of misery held the hands of Achilles as
he sobbed out his noble heart, for fear that he might take a knife and cut
his throat.

Homer, Iliad, Book XVIII, *18–34*

Briseis came back, beautiful as golden Aphrodite. But when she saw
Patroclus lying there, mangled by the sharp bronze, she gave a piercing
scream, threw herself on his body and tore her breast and tender neck
and her fair cheeks with her hands.

Homer, Iliad, Book XIX, *310–15*

The phases of relationship constitution begin with the creation of the
relationship, and variously proceed in no particular sequence though
conduct and enhancement, protection, and redress and rectification.
Eventually, a relationship "terminates" through one or both parties'
choice, their involuntary separation, or death. Yet the loss of one's

partner, even his death, doesn't actually end the relationship. Just as a person can sustain a social relationship with a deity, spirit, or other supernatural being, a person can continue to relate to someone who leaves even if that person never directly or materially communicates with the person left behind. Similarly, you can relate in every psychological sense through e-mail, or text, or telephone – even if your interlocutor doesn't actually receive the message when there is a technical glitch, or the person has died without your knowing it. If you are talking to someone in the next room, you are relating, although it might turn out that she's *not* really in the next room, after all; she's gone out of earshot.

But it is typically quite distressing to know that the other person has intended to break off the relationship, or can't receive ordinary communications from you or can't communicate with you as he previously did, or can no longer be touched or fed or kissed or seen. This distress often makes the isolated partner angry, makes him suffer in many ways, or evokes a feeling of burdensome sorrow. Any of these emotions may lead to violence against others, or the self. This is especially pronounced when a partner dies. As Homer recounts, ancient Greek women mourners, for example, lacerated their cheeks, beat their breasts so as to cause wounds, and tore their hair out to such a degree that eventually laws were promulgated prohibiting mourners from lacerating their flesh (Garland, 2001: 29, 121; Graves, 1891: 36–8; Toohey, 2010).

> There can be no doubt that in normal mourning anger expressed
> towards one target or another is the rule... Furthermore, there are
> good grounds for believing that even in healthy mourning a person's
> anger is often directed toward the person lost, though it may equally
> often be directed towards other persons, including the self. Among
> the many problems requiring study, therefore, are the causes of these
> various expressions of anger, the functions they may serve (if any),
> the targets towards which they may be directed, and the vicissitudes,
> many of them pathological, that angry impulses may undergo.
>
> *(Bowlby, 1989: 29)*

There are few if any quantitative data on the incidence of anger, let alone violence, following the death of a partner (or loss due to choice or separation), but anger is certainly a common component of bereavement (Bonanno and Kaltman, 2001; Bowlby, 1973: 245–57, 1989; Rosenblatt *et al.*, 1976: 29). In Western cultures such as that of the UK, some bereaved just feel generally irritable and diffusely angry (Parkes, 1996: 81–4). But as we have seen in diverse cultures, when a person's crucial relationship partner betrays the relationship or terminates it, the aggrieved person sometimes harms or kills himself, sometimes attacks or kills the partner, and sometimes does both. Bereavement anger and its violent expression can be entirely normative: in quite a few cultures, people deal with death by harming themselves or other mourners (Stroebe and Stroebe, 1987: 40–1). In a diverse though perhaps not perfectly representative sample of 78 cultures examined by Rosenblatt et al. (1976: 19), the bereaved were angry or aggressive in 76% of the societies where this variable could be rated. In 67% of the cultures, some mourners – often those in culturally specified relationships with the deceased – normally injured themselves (females in 45% of cultures, males in 40%; p. 142). Notably, out-group persons were "institutionalized targets" of attack in 22% of the sample, while the presumed killer was the "institutionalized target" in just 17%. In 17% of the sample, raters found evidence that "spontaneous aggression after sudden death" was typical, but the authors do not explain how they coded this (Rosenblatt et al., 1976). These percentages are lower than the true proportions, since the ethnographer's not mentioning a practice does not imply the absence of that practice in that culture. Evidently, many cultures prescribe bereavement injury to the self or others, probably in part as a strong signal of the bereaved's attachment, sorrow, or determination to avenge the death. And even in cultures in which deliberate self-harm is not culturally prescribed in bereavement, some individuals nevertheless harm themselves (Haw and Hawton, 2008).

Psychoanalytic theory would explain anger, guilt, or shame after loss as displacement or another hydraulic "defense" mechanism in which anger at the dead person for leaving/ending the relationship is displaced onto others. Bowlby (1989: 68) writes, "To direct anger away from the person who elicited it and towards some more or less irrelevant person is so well known that little need be said about it." But there is little or no empirical evidence for such displacement mechanisms. So, while it is empirically well established that bereavement and loss by separation often evoke anger or guilt, it is unclear whether that anger always, or even commonly, arises from blaming the deceased. In any event, particularly when the circumstances of a close partner's death are terrifying or horrific, the surviving partner's resulting rage may endure indefinitely. As the definition of PTSD makes clear, the experience of an associate's "death, threatened death, actual or threatened serious injury, or actual or threatened sexual violence" often results in "anger" and "irritable or aggressive behavior, self-destructive or reckless behavior" (American Psychiatric Association, 2013). In the United States, people with PTSD are more likely to be "aggressive" and, in particular, violent against their intimate partners (Bell and Orcutt, 2009). And, of course, people often hurt or kill someone they blame for their partner's departure or death. But it's not entirely clear whether or how mourning and PTSD emotions are linked to these punitive, retaliatory, and vengeful emotions that are probably universal.

Subjectively, sometimes the mourners simply "can't take it any longer," so they attack or kill others more or less indiscriminately – and this is precisely what they are culturally expected to do. Anything less would be a failure to honor the relationships with the deceased, would be offensive, and would be widely criticized. Among the northern Australian Aboriginal Unmatjera (Anmatyerre) and Kaitish (Kaytej, or Kaititja), when a man dies, the *gammona* ("mother's brothers," – that is, men who have married women of the deceased's clan) cut themselves on the shoulder. In a subsequent funerary ceremony, the widow "and other relatives cut themselves, both to show their sorrow and to indicate to the dead man's spirit that he has been sufficiently mourned for, and that now he must return to his Alcheringa camping-place and leave them in peace" (the Alcheringa is the Dreamtime, the era when the totemic spirits created the world) (Spencer and Gillen, 1904: 508). The *gammona* shave off the deceased man's hair and make it into a band to girdle the waist; wearing this "is supposed to make the inward parts of the man hot and savage, and it is then his duty to avenge the death of his *ikuntera*" ("sister's son," or "daughter's husband" – that is, a man of the clan into which women of his clan have married) (p. 510).

> Amongst these tribes there is a curious custom according to which the *gammona* who secures the hair of a dead man is obliged to go and first of all fight with some other *gammona*. Along with a party of men whom he has summoned for the purpose, he goes to a distant part of the tribe and there challenges another *gammona* man belonging to that locality to fight. The challenge cannot be refused, and, when they have fought and cut one another about on the thighs and shoulders, the challenger hands over the dead man's hair to his opponent, who will later on challenge another *gammona*, and so

the quarrel, if such it may be called, passes on from group to group. Not seldom a distant *gammona* will hear that some special individual, belonging to another local group of the tribe, has his dead *ikuntera*'s hair-girdle, and will come up armed with that of another dead *ikuntera*. This necessitates another fight, and, when it is over, the two men pull their hair-girdles off, rub them in their own blood, and then exchange them. Young *gammonas* will often have arm-bands presented to them which have been worn by the dead man. In the event of this, when the fight between the older men is over, these younger ones will fight and cut one another, after which the fur-bands are rubbed in their own blood and exchanged.

In addition to all that has been described above, it not infrequently happens that, with the assistance of the medicine men, the *gammona* learns who was really the cause of his *ikuntera*'s death, and then it is his further duty to organise an avenging party and kill the guilty person.

(Spencer and Gillen, 1904: 510–11)

The Arunta (Aranda, or Arrente), a nearby Australian tribe, engage in similar mortuary violence.

In the Arunta, unless the *gammona* cuts himself when an *ikuntera* dies, then any one of the men who stands in the same relationship to the deceased may take away his wife and present her to some more dutiful son-in-law; but the attempt to actually kill, or at least seriously injure, a *gammona* seems to be an extreme expression of this feeling. It is not even suggested that the gammona who suffers has actually had anything whatever to do with the man's death; in fact, not seldom another man, who is suspected of being the real culprit, is also killed at a later time.

(Spencer and Gillen, 1904: 514–15)

Among the nearby Warramunga, when someone dies, there is a kind of violent pandemonium in which people cut, burn, and injure themselves and others in prescribed ways (and the bereaved women then cease to speak for years, restricting their communication to signing) (Kendon, 1988: 70, 85–93; Sansom, 1982; Spencer and Gillen, 1904).[1] Spencer

---

[1] Durkheim's (2008/1912) theory presented in *The Elementary Forms of the Religious Life* drew extensively on Spencer and Gillen's ethnographies; see pp. 391–2 for Durkheim's discussion of self-injury in Warramunga mourning.

and Gillen (1904) describe the scene they observed as a Warramunga man died, with men and women of the camp wailing and women cutting the crowns of their heads. People tore the dying man's dwelling to pieces and then men rushed to the scene and piled themselves all together on top of the dying man. Then a man

> rushed on to the ground yelling and brandishing a stone knife. Reaching the camp, he suddenly gashed both thighs deeply, cutting right across the muscles, and, unable to stand, fell down into the middle of the group from which he was dragged out after a time by three or four female relatives – his mother, wife, and sisters – who immediately applied their mouths to the gaping wounds while he lay exhausted on the ground. Then another man of the same class came rushing up, prancing about, and to all appearances intent upon gashing his thighs, but, watching him, we saw that in his case it was merely a pretence. Each time that he pretended to cut he merely drew the flat side of his knife across his thigh, and so inflicted nothing more serious than a few slight scratches. Gradually the struggling mass of dark bodies began to loosen, and then we could see that the unfortunate man was not actually dead, though the terribly rough treatment to which he had been subjected had sealed his fate. The weeping and wailing still continued, and the sun went down leaving the camp in darkness. Later on in the evening, when the man actually died, the same scene was re-enacted, only this time the wailing was still louder, and men and women, apparently frantic with grief, were rushing about cutting themselves with knives and sharp-pointed sticks, the women battering one another's heads with fighting clubs, no one attempting to ward off either cuts or blows. Then, without more than an hour's delay, a small torchlight procession started off across the plain to a belt of timber a mile away, and there the body was left on a platform built of boughs in a low gum-tree.

> Next morning there was not a sign of any habitation to be seen on the side of the creek on which the dead man's camp had formerly been placed. The only trace left was a small mound of earth called *kakiti*, piled up on the actual spot on which the man had died, and around this the ground was carefully smoothed down for a few feet in every direction. Every camp was removed to a considerable distance from the scene, as no one was anxious to meet with the spirit – the *ungwulan* – of the dead man, which would be hovering about the spot, or with that of the man who had brought about the

death by evil magic, as it would probably come to visit the place in the form of an animal. It must be remembered that, though the man was declared by the old doctors to have died because he had violated tribal custom, yet at the same time he had of course been killed by some one, though by whom they could not yet exactly determine.

The next day was a busy one in camp, because, according to etiquette, there were certain mourning ceremonies which had to be performed, the omission of which would indicate a want of respect for and be very displeasing to the spirit of the dead man. Different men belonging to the Thungalla, Tjupila, Thakomara, and Thapungarti classes were lying hors de combat with gashed thighs. They had done their duty, and henceforth, in token of this, would be marked with deep scars [a photograph shows one such man with deep wounds]. On one such man we counted the traces of no less than twenty-three wounds which had been inflicted at different times. Of course everything is hedged around with very definite rules, and when a man of any particular class dies it is always men who stand in a special relationship to him who have to cut themselves. On this occasion it was a Tjunguri man who had died, and the men who gashed their thighs – an operation called *kulungara* – stood to him in one or other of the following relationships: – Grandfather on the mother's side, mother's brother (the same as son-in-law), brother of the mother of the dead man's wife, and brother of the last. In addition to this the Tjupila, Thungalla, and Thakomara men had cut their hair off closely, burnt it, and smeared their scalps with pipe-clay, whilst the Tjapeltjeri – the tribal fathers – had cut their whiskers off. Groups of men and women were sitting about embracing each other and weeping. The leg of the Thapungarti man who had most deeply gashed himself was held by his father, a Panunga man, who at the same time was embraced from behind by an aged Thungalla, as if to support him in his grief. Then a tribal brother of the dead man came up and embraced the Thapungarti, both of them howling loudly. The Tjunguri man then sat down and was embraced from behind by an old Tjapeltjeri man who was his tribal father, and who in turn was embraced by other Tjapeltjeri, Tjupila, Tjunguri, and Thapungarti men, all of them alternately howling and moaning... [Soon] the women set to work wailing and cutting their scalps. When this had gone on for some time they once more got up and approached the lubras' [women's] camp, where forty or fifty women were assembled. The latter came out in small bands of perhaps six or eight at a time, every individual carrying a yam-stick [a fire-hardened stick for digging tubers] (Fig. 138). After a series of sham fights they all sat down in groups with their arms round one another, weeping and wailing frantically (Fig. 139), while the actual and tribal wives, mothers, wives' mothers, daughters, sisters, mothers' mothers, sisters' husbands' mothers, and grand daughters, according to custom, once more cut their scalps open with yam-sticks. In addition to all this the actual widows afterwards scared [sic] the scalp wound with a red-hot fire-stick. The men apparently took no notice whatever of what the women were doing, though of course they were well aware of what was taking place; in fact if a woman does not do her duty in this respect she is liable to be severely chastised, or even killed, by her brother.

(Spencer and Gillen, 1904: 517–22)

In the following days, Warramunga men looked carefully over the spot where the deceased had died, and around the tree in which his body had been placed in a nest of branches, and then examined the flow of liquids from the decomposing body, looking for signs to indicate what sorcerer killed him. During the same period they performed a set of magical and ascetic acts to kill the unidentified sorcerer responsible. Quite some time later the community retrieved the deceased's bones and performed an elaborate series of rituals with them, over the course of months, culminating in the killing of the sorcerer blamed for the death. Toward the end of their ritual preparations before they set off to kill the sorcerer,

all of the men stood up, opened veins in their penes by means of sharp flakes or pointed sticks, and, standing opposite to one another, allowed the blood to spurtle out over each other's thighs. This gruesome ceremony is supposed both to mutually strengthen those who take part in it, and at the same time to bind them still more closely together and to make anything like treachery quite impossible.

(Spencer and Gillen, 1904: 560, 562)

Among Australian Aboriginal cultures, mortuary wounding of the self and others was evidently rather widespread, but the specific practices varied. The mortuary rituals of the Lardil of Mornington Island, Australia, always included a "square up." This consisted of a controlled battle between two *ad hoc* groups.

Spears and boomerangs were thrown at will in an unorganized fashion, and then the two groups rushed at each other. Needless to say, people did their best not to hurt close relatives on the opposing side. Normally, as soon as someone was seriously injured or killed the battle would stop. Ideally, in the evening the two groups danced together, thus indicating that hostilities had ceased.

(McKnight, 1986: 146)

Violence is also intrinsic to bereavement in other cultures. Tahitians have long been noted for their placidity and gentleness, but in the eighteenth century when a person died, for two or three days the bereaved women would strike the crown of their heads repeatedly with sharks' teeth, making themselves bleed extensively (Levy, 1973: 289–91). (Women also struck their heads with a shark's tooth when reunited with someone they loved after a long separation; it seems to have been an expression of being deeply moved by transitions in close CS relationships.) Then late at night and early in the morning the men ran about seeking anyone they could strike with clubs set with shark's teeth. But the marauding men were preceded by boys who warned anyone they saw to hide, so apparently they typically found few if any victims. Interestingly, when Levy (1973) intensively studied contemporary Tahitians' emotional lives, the Tahitians showed remarkable composure and avoided displays – or experience – of strong emotions; they minimized the seriousness of death, quickly moving on with their lives.

Violent mourning may be coupled with beautifully elaborated visual and poetic esthetics. In Papua New Guinea, Kaluli villages host groups of men from other villages, who come into their longhouses at night in magnificent feathered garb. The feathered visitors dance and sing of places imbued with the memories of their hosts' deceased relatives and friends (Schieffelin, 2004). Through these songs, the singers aim to evoke great sadness in their hosts by making them feel the loss of those they loved. If the singers are successful in evoking their hosts' painfully sad memories of lost loved ones, their hosts, enraged to feel such sorrow, grab burning brands from the fire and burn the dancers, often severely. In the morning, the dancers have to pay compensation to their hosts for making them feel so sad. Burning the dancers is entirely normative: they deserve to be burned for making their hosts feel so hopelessly sad. Yet, on another occasion, their hosts, in turn, will compose touching songs of places that remind *their* hosts of lost loved ones, create elaborate feather garments, and ceremonially visit their former guests or others, where they will perform their songs to make hosts so sad these men in turn burn them for evoking such painful memories.

In another culture area, the Philippines, the central virtue for the Ilongot is *liget*: fierce, energetic, restless "anger" (M. Rosaldo, 1980). *Liget* motivates people, especially young men, to take the risks to perform dangerous acts such as climbing out on limbs of the giant trees that shade their gardens to cut back the branches and let sunlight in. More generally, *liget* moves people to overcome lethargy, laziness, fear, or other barriers to action, provoking them to make the effort to *do something*. A rough analogy, albeit not at the same level of intensity, would be the fierce spirit that an American football coach might try to inspire among his players to come from behind and beat their rivals in the championship game. *Liget* is a moral emotion, motivating Ilongot to do what they must do to meet their responsibilities and realize the full potential of crucial relational affordances. It is the core virtue of the culture: it is admirable and morally necessary for a man, especially, to be *liget*. When an Ilongot dies, the bereaved feel an unbearable burden that weighs on them and, perhaps, like depression, makes them not want to make any effort to do anything. Young Ilongot men seek a catharsis that will rid them of this paralyzing weight of grief. They want to transform the weight of grief into the fierce assertion of *liget*. So they seek one or more elder men to lead them on an expedition through the forest. The first person they encounter – whoever it is, it doesn't matter – they spear and decapitate. The first young man to grab the head and toss it to the ground is a hero. Relieved of the burden of death, the euphoric head-tosser and his peers returns home to be feted. The head-tosser, in particular, is admired by all and envied by his peers who have not yet tossed a head. Tossing a head is the epitome of male virtue (M. Rosaldo, 1980; R. Rosaldo, 1980, 1984).[2]

On yet another continent we again see men raging against death. Among the Nyakyusa of southern Tanzania, at funerals the young men commonly danced a war dance, which often led to spear fights (Wilson, 1951: 151, 1957: 24–30, 35). The motivating moral emotion, *ilyojo*, is

---

[2] When grievous rage motivates a killing, this death may provoke further killing, in a potentially endless chain. As far as we can make out from the ethnographies, such chains do occur, resulting in very high rates of death in some societies at some points in history. But in some cases it seems that the victim's kin may lack the cultural moral motivation or aggressive capacity to retaliate, or be too terrified to strike back. Many other factors may intervene, including the state. For an investigation of such factors, see Renato Rosaldo's (1980) historical analysis of how Ilongot headhunting waxed and waned.

somewhat similar to *liget*. The war dance at a Nyakyusa funeral was impressive:

> It is led by young men dressed in a special costume of ankle-bells and cloth skirts and, traditionally, bedaubed with red and white clay. All hold spears and leap wildly about, stamping down the soft earth of the grave as they dance. There is little common movement, each dances alone as if fighting a single combat. Among the men some of the women move about, singly or in twos and threes, calling the war-cry and swinging their hips in a kind of rhythmical walk. Under a tropical sun in a damp heat, with the thermometer often over 90°F. in the shade, they dance for hours. In the dust and excitement there are no very apparent signs of grief; and yet if you ask the onlookers what it is all about they reply: 'They are mourning the dead.'
>
> This burial dance is traditionally a dance of war; now, as also in former times, it provides those men most affected by grief and fear with a violent and passionate means of expression, in which their feelings are assuaged by the touch of life; for the others it was, in the old days, an assertion of their own and their dead neighbor's warlike quality, and this significance is still vividly present to their minds...
>
> 'This war-dance (*ukukina*)', said an old man, 'is mourning, we are mourning the dead man. We dance because there is war in our hearts. A passion of grief and fear exasperates us (*ilyojo likutusila*)'... *Ilyojo* means a passion of grief, anger, or fear; *ukusila* means to annoy or exasperate beyond endurance. 'A kinsman, when he dances, assuages his passionate grief (*ilyojo*); he goes into the house to weep and then he comes out and dances the war-dance; his passionate grief is made tolerable in the dance (lit. he is able to endure it there in the dance), it bound his heart and the dance assuages it'...
>
> 'We used not actually to fight at burials so much as to dance and become conscious of our strength for future wars against other chiefdoms, when, on another day, we would go to raid their cows.'
>
> But although an actual fight was not a necessary part of the funeral it frequently occurred; and burials are still one of the most usual occasions of spearing. 'In the old days, before the country was at peace [under colonial administration], we men often fought at burials; we ran in front spearing one another, while our wives ran behind calling the war-cry and watching the prowess of their husbands'...

> 'At burials there was often war. If the men of two chiefdoms were
> there together at a burial they would often quarrel and fight.'
>
> *(Wilson, 1957: 23–5)*

In indigenous North America, mourning was also quite violent. In the
Western Plains of Native North America, bereavement took the form of

> a violent expression of loss and upheaval. Abandon took the form of
> self-mutilation, especially for women. They gashed their heads, the
> calves, they cut off fingers. Long lines of women marched through
> camp after the death of an important person, their legs bare and
> bleeding. The blood on their heads and legs they let cake and did not
> remove... At the grave the man's favorite horses were killed and
> both men and women wailed for the dead.
>
> *(Grinnell, 1923: vol. II, 162)*

In mourning, the Blackfoot and the Crow cut off a finger joint, while
Omaha and Pawnee cut their arms and legs (Benedict, 1922). On the
death of children these actions were especially intense, and bereaved
parents sometimes committed suicide. Among the Assiniboine

> should anyone offend the father during this time his death would
> most certainly follow, as the man, being in profound sorrow, seeks
> something on which to wreak his revenge, and he soon after goes to
> war, to kill or be killed, either being immaterial to him in that state.
>
> *(Denig, 2000 46: 573)*

Diffusely directed violence was characteristic of Plains Indian mourning
(Benedict, 1932: 7–8), similar to mourning in other cultures of indigenous North America. But the Kwakiutl of the Northwest coast went
further. The Kwakiutl, famous for their potlatches, were extremely
competitive; pride based on besting others was everything, while anything but success was humiliating – so much so that men not infrequently
committed suicide when shamed (Benedict, 1959).[3] Nothing was more
humiliating for a man than the death of someone close to him.

---

[3] In her analyses of the fieldwork reports of her mentor, Franz Boas (the founder of
American anthropology), Benedict doesn't say whether women were similarly competitive, felt deeply shamed by death, or reacted violently to it.

Death was the paramount affront they recognized, and it was met as they met any major accident, by distribution and destruction of property [to reassert superiority], by head-hunting, and by suicide. They took recognized means, that is, to wipe out the shame. When a chief's near relative died, he gave away his house ... it was potlatching... It was called 'craziness strikes on account of the death of a loved one,' and by means of it the Kwakiutl handled mourning by the same procedures that they used at marriage, at the attainment of supernatural powers, or in a quarrel.

There was a more extreme way of meeting the affront of death. This was by head-hunting. It was in no sense retaliation upon the group which had killed the dead man. The dead relative might equally have died in bed of disease or by the hand of an enemy. The head-hunting was called 'killing to wipe one's eyes,' and it was a means of getting even by making another household mourn instead.

(Benedict, 1959: 216)

When the chief Neqapenkem's sister and her daughter did not come back from Victoria either, people said, because their boat capsized or they drank bad whiskey, he called together the warriors. "Now I ask you tribes, who shall wail? Shall I do it or shall another?" The foremost responded, "Not you, Chief, let some other of the tribes." They set up the war pole, and the others came forward saying, "We came here to ask you to go to war that someone else may wail on account of our deceased sister." So they started out with full war rites to "pull under" the Sanetch [a neighboring tribe] for the chief's dead relatives. They found seven men and two children asleep and killed all except one girl whom they took captive.

Again, the chief Qaselas' son died, and he and his brother and uncle set out to wipe out the stain. They were entertained by Nengemalis at their first stop. After they had eaten, "Now I will tell you the news, Chief," Qaselas said. "My prince died today and you will go with him." So they killed their host and his wife. "Then Qaselas and his crew felt good when they arrived at Sebaa in the evening... It is not called war, but 'to die with those that are dead.'"

(Benedict, 1932: 21, citing Franz Boas, Ethnology of the Kwakiutl (Washington, DC: Bureau of American Ethnology (BAE-R), vol. 35: pp. 1363, 1385)

Another informant relates his experience when a chief's daughter died. The grieving, humiliated chief sent a war party of sixty men to kill another chief, his cousin; they beheaded him in his canoe in front of his young son and brought his head home for the grieving chief (Benedict, 1959: 217–18). The choice of the person to kill was based purely on the rank of the person who died: to balance the humiliating blow of death, to maintain his position, the mourner needed to kill someone whose rank was equivalent to the person who had died. Otherwise it didn't matter who the victim was.

In Amazonian Ecuador the Waorani are resolutely, fiercely independent, believing that each person should be self-reliant, fully capable of getting what they want for themselves (Robarchek and Robarchek, 2005). They are passionately egalitarian: each feels that it is wrong for anyone to have more than he or she has. Their most central moral concern is that no one should tell anyone else what to do, or in any way attempt to control or interfere with anyone else. Everyone has an absolute right to control his own destiny, free of any interference. The expected and legitimate response to other humans "deliberately" infringing one's autonomy or interfering in one's life is *piinti*, homicidal rage. It is not frustration of pragmatic goals that evoke this rage – it is the sense that someone has violated one's fundamental right to control one's own life. In this unbearable state of *piinti*, killing someone – anyone – reasserts one's sense of autonomous efficacy. Killing re-establishes control – regardless of who is killed. The death of a loved one is the quintessential affront to one's autonomy, because all deaths are murders.

> One's child is bitten by a snake and dies; a sibling contracts polio and is dead in a few days; a man's wife is stung by a scorpion, goes into shock, and dies in hours. In all of these cases, the almost immediate reaction on the part of surviving kin was homicidal rage. In situations such as these, the relationship between culture and emotion enters into the processes of definition and evaluation in at least two ways. First, all of these situations were *culturally defined* as the consequences of the actions of other persons, as acts of sorcery. Thus each was defined and perceived by surviving kin as a human attack on their autonomy...
>
> Second, all of these situations violated the assumptions of the autonomous and effective self that has the capacity to control its experience; they generated the subjective experience of powerlessness. The emotion that is culturally appropriate to that experience is, for Waorani, rage, and it was in terms of rage that the

survivors defined their feelings. The emotional response, in all of these cases, was rage, and the behavioral response was homicide...

Curiously (to us), however, the rage and violence elicited in these kinds of situations are not necessarily directed at the perceived "guilty" party. As the Rosaldos described for the Ilongot, an innocent person may serve just as well as a target. Returning from a raid in which a sibling has been killed by *kowudï* [foreigners/ outsiders], a Waorani youth sees his elderly grandmother lying in her hammock, and drives a spear through her where she lies...

In the Waorani psychological map, the natural reaction to such rage, one that restores a sense of autonomy and control, is homicide. As with the Ilongot, the identity of the victim is largely irrelevant.

(Robarchek and Robarchek, 2005: 214–15)

Emotions more or less similar to these may be widespread in some people in many cultures. Waorani, however, are morally licensed to experience this rage and to act on it. They feel that a person is entitled to reassert control, and judge that killing is the ideal way to do that.

Ilongot, Nyakyusa, Waorani, Kwakiutl, Coast Salish, Blackfoot, Crow, Omaha, Pawnee, Assiniboine, Tahitians, Arunta, Warramunga, Unmatjera, Kaitish, Lardil, and people in many other cultures evidently experience emotions at the death of a close relationship partner that seem to be something like what would provoke a contemporary American to scream, "I can't take it anymore!" It is an unendurable vexation or exasperation amplified into rage. Death deprives the survivors of the control they are morally entitled to – it is a moral affront. Kwakiutl, Coast Salish, Waorani, Ilongot and other men are not just morally *entitled* to kill anyone to escape, or rather to transcend, the paralyzing despair of loss, to reassert themselves against the terrible defeat that death is – rather, this is what everyone judges that men *should do, what they must do.* Tahitians, Warramunga, and Kaluli ordinarily don't kill anyone in these mourning practices, but they wound themselves and others painfully. Doing so testifies to the love and loss they feel, while acting out the rage that would otherwise be paralyzing. In each culture the bereaved or offended people just want to hurt someone, anyone – and it feels right, it feels like they are morally entitled to do it, and "the world" deserves the mayhem. In all of these cultures, peers, family, and community reference groups unanimously approve of this exasperated rage and the violence that ensues: it is virtuous violence. Good people do it and it is good to do.

As we have reviewed in previous chapters, there are numerous historical and archeological records of cultures in which, when an elite person died, the mourners killed family members or retainers to inter with and perhaps continue to serve the deceased. In some instances, close kin or retainers may have killed themselves to accompany the deceased. In India to the present day, people sometimes perform *sati*, the voluntary or forced immolation of a wife on the funeral pyre of her husband (Hawley, 1994). In some of these cultures and others, the mourners sacrificed captive enemies, slaves, or others to the deceased in the mortuary or subsequent commemorative rites. Taken together, these self-injurious, other-harming, and homicidal practices are normative in a substantial proportion of the world's cultures, and in these and many other cultures, grief at the death of a loved child or partner can be so unbearable that a bereaved person may kill herself. If we add all of these practices together, violent mourning is relatively common.

Why are people sometimes enraged by death?

Note that in the practices described in this chapter, the mourners are not especially angry *at anyone in particular*. In the mourning practices as such, focused blame does not seem to be what gives rise to the rage – in this context, the mourners are not primarily motivated to hold any specific person accountable – they're simply *outraged at their loss*. Of course, nearly every society has a history of killing persons deemed responsible for murder: vengeance homicides and capital punishment are widespread. In the societies in which diffuse anger and randomly directed violence are normative mourning practices, if the deceased is thought to have been murdered, people *also* are angry at the killer and seek to avenge the death by killing him, or someone equivalent to him. If there is no manifest killer – when the deceased died of an illness, injury, drowning, lightning, or snakebite – in most of these cultures people do divination or consult an oracle to determine who is specifically responsible. If people died because they themselves did something wrong and the ancestors or deities punished them, then in many cultures the mourners make appropriate propitiatory sacrifices: they kill animals as offerings to the aggrieved ancestors or deities. (Note that they don't kill the animals angrily.) But as we discuss elsewhere in the book, in many cultures throughout history, including some in Africa today, a great many deaths are attributed to witchcraft or sorcery; occasionally, women identified as the witches or men identified as the sorcerers responsible for a death, or for an illness or any misfortune, may be stoned or killed. This is done in angry retaliation, to punish the witch or sorcerer.

In short, diffuse, generalized angry violence occurs alongside retaliatory, vengeful, punitive violence; they are distinct aspects of response to death. They may have the same source and they may have the same orientation, or they may not. In any case they evidently differ enough so that the two sorts of violent anger, or the dimension on which they are poles, should be analytically distinguished.

So, then, why do people get diffusely angry, even go into a rage, when an important relationship partner dies (or ends their relationship while still alive), when that anger is not directed at anyone whom the mourners blame for the death? Beyond just anger, why is it that in some cultural practices the bereaved are self-injuriously or homicidally *violent* – toward just about anyone? Why do they hurt themselves? The adaptive, psychological, and social functions of bereavement rage or violence are not obvious. Violence directed at whoever happens to be present or whomever the raiding party comes across doesn't seem to do anything to regulate a relationship. What's the use of killing some random stranger, let alone attacking a family member, neighbor, or ally – or injuring oneself?

Clearly, in the cultures we considered in this chapter, bereavement violence is expected, condoned, or even admired as the most seemly expression of the bereaved's affection for the deceased. Violence shows – it means – that the mourners *cared*, that their loss is great, and that they are virtuously engaged in mourning. And it shows they will not give in and let themselves be defeated by death. Violence is a way to fiercely, defiantly, and cathartically assert oneself when one could easily become overwhelmed and inert. But in what way is bereavement violence constitutive of any social relationship? Does it have any intended or unintended social-relational functions? Specifically, does it regulate relationships?

The loss of a crucial relationship partner typically means that a new relationship must be forged to replace the lost relationship. While the original relationship endured and could be relied on, third parties' evaluations of the perpetrator were less important. But when the perpetrator needs to attract a new partner, he needs to establish that he is a worthy, attractive, motivated candidate – and that he will be a committed and trustworthy partner in new relationships. In the societies in which bereavement entails virtuous violence, it seems that mourners committing violence raise their rank in the AR status hierarchy of the community, or restore the balance in EM relationships threatened by the death. By killing someone or injuring himself, the perpetrator demonstrates that he is courageous and that he cares deeply about his lost relationship – making him a more appealing potential partner with whom attractive others might want to form a relationship to take the place of the one that death has ended. The homicide and severe self-injury are very costly, reliable, honest, unfakable signals of meritorious courage and determination, along with the capacity for commitment; so this signal may increase the perpetrator's chances of forming a good, new relationship with a desirable partner. It seems possible that this is an evolutionary foundation for psychological responsiveness to cultural affordances to bereavement violence. Violence proves that despite the mourner's loss, he is still a formidable force to be reckoned with.

Note the crucial fact, however, that this proclivity is only adaptive when violence *actually does* raise rank or restore EM balance. So if there is an evolved foundation for the proclivity, it must be highly sensitive to that sociocultural contingency. In most societies, killing random persons drastically *reduces* the perpetrator's chances to form new fitness-enhancing relationships to replace the lost one, and substantially undermines existing relationships. So an "adaptation" consisting of a fixed violent response to bereavement that ignored these crucial local social-relational consequences could not evolve. Indeed, while we described these practices in the conventional ethnographic present, the historical record is that in every one of these cultures diffusely violent and homicidal responses to bereavement disappeared as soon as the consequences of violence became maladaptive. Being imprisoned or executed is quite detrimental to fitness (not to mention psychosocial well-being). Once people were reliably imprisoned or executed for homicide or random assault, it became foolish to do it, people ceased to admire what was now seen as reckless and pointless violence, and bereavement violence consequently ceased.

There may be another contributing adaptive benefit to generalized bereavement anger under some social conditions. The bereaved may not know for sure whether someone killed his partner, or conspired in or indirectly contributed to her death. The circumstances may be ambiguous, and the causes of death are not always clear-cut without autopsy and extensive detective work. Generalized violence may not hit the culpable target, even if there are culpable parties, but it is a dramatic warning to anyone who might wish the bereaved ill. It screams, "If I ever found out that someone killed her, I'll get the son of a bitch if it's the last thing I do!" If someone *did* kill his partner, or is thinking of killing another or future partner of his, or the mourner himself, they clearly see that "they'd better watch out!" As Frank (1988) theorizes, a reputation for irrational violent rage will dissuade potential aggressors or defectors from preying on a person whom it would otherwise be rational to attack or betray. Moreover, when a person has suffered the loss of a crucial partner, the loss of the ally weakens him and makes him vulnerable. He needs to make it clear that despite his loss of the deceased partner he is *not* an easy mark. To demonstrate convincingly how fierce and formidable an adversary he is, what better way is there than killing someone, or, to show how brave and determined he is, willfully injuring himself?

This sort of ferocious random violence may be adaptive when it is actually fairly likely that others *will* attempt to kill, abduct, or seduce a person's partners, and likely that others *will* prey on a person when they have an advantage over him. However, when there is an effective chief or a powerful state that enforces laws against assault and homicide, randomly directed violence is disastrous to one's fitness. And, indeed, it is not a common cultural practice in states or chiefdoms that enforce laws; in such societies, the bereaved may be generally, indiscriminately angry, but most mourners in most cultures don't hurt anyone, because they would be severely punished for doing so. The societies in which mourners killed random outsiders are societies in which there was no state and virtually no laws, as such. When these societies were incorporated into states with effective police, judges, and penal systems, mourning violence ceased. That's exactly what we expect of an adaptive psychology – discriminating responsiveness to adaptive conditions, constraints, and opportunities. Bereavement violence is senseless when powerful third parties provide protection, when people rarely use force to pursue their social objectives, and where there is little risk that isolated people with few allies will be forcibly exploited.

We admit that until someone systematically investigates the conditions under which people react to a partner's death with indiscriminate violence, this is just another "Just So Story." We will examine this signaling aspect of violence in greater detail in Chapter 21, but regardless of the validity of this tentative theory of bereavement violence, the clear fact is that the loss of a significant partner does tend to make people angry. People often feel diffusely irritable or enraged even if they don't see anyone to blame, or can't legitimately assign blame: the bereaved often feel a generalized anger that is not based on any attribution of responsibility. Although they are not essentially angry at anyone in particular, they may take it out on random associates – whoever crosses their path. Or there may be cultural prescriptions about whom to injure. They may injure themselves. Furthermore, social practices, conflicts, and animosities, in conjunction with cultural beliefs and personal attributions, may orient what starts out as diffuse anger, focusing it on a particular person or social being who is eventually held culpable and "should" be punished. "Someone should pay for this!" So, "naturally," mourners are often angry at people whom they blame for the loss or death of their partner: tangible murderers, intangible witches or sorcerers, negligent professionals or corporations, evil governments, hidden conspiracies, malevolent ancestors, or callous deities. Not infrequently, people blame themselves for the loss or death of a partner: they feel guilty. This process leads to violence against the "culpable" person or beings, corporations, or nations. But we should not ignore the fact that in many cultures bereaved, angry perpetrators simply lash out at any or all associates or onlookers, or harm themselves, without being motivated by blame – they hurt or kill people whom they don't think are in any way responsible for their loss. In some cultures, bereavement anger evolves into morally expected practices of violence or homicide that entail killing just about anyone. The death of a partner feels unfair; it's wrong, it shouldn't be, it's an injury, insult, and offense. It's humiliating. It's outrageous and it enrages. It's the ultimate affront to the need to control one's world. So the end of a relationship sometimes makes people angry enough to hurt or kill someone, and feel entitled to do so. The culture may require it, so that good, loving mourners must do so. In sum, the final phase of the constitution of social relationships is loss by death, and like every other phase of constituting relationships, loss can be violently enacted.

19 NON-BODILY VIOLENCE: ROBBERY

What was the motive behind it? What made it worthwhile to me? I strongly wanted to get even with society for the wrong which I felt it had done me. This spirit of revenge, instilled into me by the years of suffering and ill-treatment behind prison walls, pervaded my whole nature ... I left prison with a feeling of bitterness and of hatred in my heart... Almost every man with whom I came in contact while in prison expressed that same feeling... He was "going to get even" and "make somebody pay" for his punishment and suffering.

(Davis, 1922: 148–9)

There was an almost magical transformation in my relationship with the rest of the world when I drew that gun on folks. I always marveled at how the toughest cats on those street corners whimpered and begged for their lives when I stuck the barrel of a sawed-off shotgun into their faces. Adults who ordinarily would have commanded my respect were forced to follow my orders like obedient kids.

(McCall, 1995: 101)

Western popular culture and social science have tended to conflate material goods with selfish individualism. But except under the most desperate circumstances – and sometimes even then – the principal meaning and function of goods and money are to constitute social relationships. This has been most cogently demonstrated by studies of "gifts," but also by research on eating, raiding, marriage, ritual, and political economy (e.g., Komter, 2004; Lévi-Strauss, 1961/1949;

Malinowski, 1922; Mauss, 1925; Polanyi, 2001; Sahlins, 1965; Veblen, 2007/1899). People want and use money and goods primarily to share, give, exchange, flaunt, conspicuously consume, or measure success and achievement. Material goods mediate relationships. Research on the social-relational meaning of goods and money has focused primarily on giving and sharing initiated by the giver, exploring the moral motives and social-relational aims of giving. But the motives and aims of the taker are similarly moral and relationship-constitutive, even when the taker takes violently.

Our primary focus in this book has been on corporeal, bodily harm. But, as we stated at the beginning, we think that virtuous violence theory can ultimately explain non-corporeal forms of violence. In this chapter, we examine the motives that underlie acts of robbery. What we find on the whole is that most robberies are not principally motivated by the material gains of the robbery *per se*. Instead, two distinct moral motivations appear. The first is a redressive EM equality motive intended to enact vengeance in response to a perceived violation on the part of the victim. The second is an AR hierarchy motive directed toward elevating the robber over his victims and winning him legitimate status in the eyes of his peers.

Robbery for equality-matching vengeance

Robbery and burglary are irrational courses of action from a purely material point of view; they don't pay off economically, given the risks of being hurt, killed, or imprisoned. But property crimes may make sense morally. Robbers steal to get revenge on someone or some category of persons who, they feel, has transgressed against them. A career burglar sums it up for us, explaining why he took the risks and pursued breaking and entering:

> For me, the loot which was secured constituted a small factor in the question. What I wanted was to take something away from society in retaliation for what I felt it had taken away from me.
>
> *(Davis, 1922: 151)*

> In those days, I could not see or comprehend anything but the jungle law of "an eye for an eye, a tooth for a tooth."
>
> *(Davis, 1922: 159)*

In a sample of St. Louis robbers, EM "payback" was a common framing of drug-dealing transgressions; dealers responded to a violation with a symmetrical retaliation:

> A direct, tit-for-tat response to a business-related dispute is the stereotypical use of robbery as retaliation in the street criminal underworld. Somebody robs you and you rob them back. It also fits the commonsense understanding of what retribution and just deserts are all about: The punishment, at least theoretically, matches the type and general seriousness of the wrongdoing [originally perpetrated against the robber] and is calibrated with both of these objectives in mind.
>
> (Jacobs and Wright, 2008: 515)

Sometimes, like rape, robbery is revenge redirected from an unavailable perceived transgressor onto a substitute regarded as equivalent in some fundamental respect, thereby getting even indirectly (Jacobs and Wright, 2008: 517–18).

Robbery for authority-ranking status

Like many others before and since, Greek warriors went to battle seeking booty, especially the armor and the women of the warriors they defeated. Medieval and early modern soldiers were similarly motivated to fight to acquire booty (Brown, 2011; Whitman, 2012). But this was not only, and usually not primarily, because of the asocial individual subsistence value of the booty. The spoils of battle constituted the relationships not only between the victor and the vanquished but also among the victors. As we noted, the *Iliad* revolves around Achilles' wounded honor when, after the Achaeans had awarded the beautiful captive Briseis to Achilles to honor his prowess in the battles, Agamemnon takes Briseis from him. At the beginning of the epic, Achilles angrily rebukes Agamemnon for his dishonorable greed.

> Achilles scowled at him and answered, "You are steeped in insolence and lust of gain. With what heart can any of the Achaeans do your bidding, either on foray or in open fighting? I came not warring here for any ill the Trojans had done me. I have no quarrel with them.

They have not raided my cattle nor my horses, nor cut down my harvests on the rich plains of Phthia; for between me and them there is a great space, both mountain and sounding sea. We have followed you, Sir Insolence! for your pleasure, not ours – to gain satisfaction from the Trojans for your shameless self and for Menelaus. You forget this, and threaten to rob me of the prize for which I have toiled, and which the sons of the Achaeans have given me. Never when the Achaeans sack any rich city of the Trojans do I receive so good a prize as you do, though it is my hands that do the better part of the fighting. When the sharing comes, your share is far the largest, and I, forsooth, must go back to my ships, take what I can get and be thankful, when my labour of fighting is done. Now, therefore, I shall go back to Phthia; it will be much better for me to return home with my ships, for I will not stay here dishonoured to gather gold and substance for you."

(Homer, Iliad, *Book I (Trans. Samuel Butler))*

As with traditional leaders and warriors in innumerable other cultures, for Achilles the value of goods is their potential to constitute AR and CS relationships when they are shared, given away, and ultimately consumed by *others* who are thereby bonded to the giver (Boas and Codere, 1966; Polanyi, 2001; Rappaport, 1967). And simultaneously, the violent acquisition and ostentatious display of booty asserts AR status over those defeated, and those who won less booty. Achilles rebukes Agamemnon for failing to respect an AR-based distribution of booty, including the women captured. Similarly, cattle raiders in Crete and East Africa take cattle for the glory of success and possession (Herzfeld, 1985; Spencer, 1965). The possession, display, or gifting of the spoils of violence simultaneously demonstrate moral AR superiority over those whom the victor vanquished, superiority over those who won less, and CS solidarity with those with whom the victor freely shares his spoils. As we saw in the previous section, taking or displaying booty may also be EM retaliation for the victim's previous victory over or affront to the taker.

   Although their cultural reference group does not extend to the entire society in which they operate, modern robbers commonly have moral motives and relationship-constitutive aims very similar to those of traditional warriors and raiders. Armed robbers are often proud of their status and look down on other criminals, as well as the pitiful people who have to *work* long hours to support themselves (Katz, 1988; Wright and

Decker, 1997: 16, 47–9). Some American robbers and gangsters were heroes in their own day and became legends: Billy the Kid (William Henry McCarty), Jesse James, John Dillinger, and Al Capone. Evidence that their ethos resonates with dominant cultural values is the popularity of movies such as *Bonnie and Clyde*, *Thelma and Louise*, *Butch Cassidy and the Sundance Kid*, *Reservoir Dogs*, *Heat*, *The Usual Suspects*, and *The Fast and the Furious* – whose audiences identify with the robbers. Likewise, the fastest selling entertainment product of all time (with a billion dollars in sales over its first three days of release) was the video game *Grand Theft Auto V*, in which the player controls a crew of criminals that wreak destruction throughout a fantasy version of the greater Los Angeles area. As these movies and video games illustrate, the shared risk, adventure, and collective responsibility for robbery is an added relational motive – a moral motive, because the partners or gang members are morally committed to looking out for each other, even sacrificing their lives for each other. Most robbers are less charismatic, less chivalrous, less loyal, and less cool than their depictions in legends or movies, but their motives apparently are often similarly moral and the culturally informed relationships they seek to constitute are often the same.

Many mundane real-world robberies redress violations that diminish the robber's status. Addicts may rob a dealer who explicitly and excessively degrades the addict. An addict who chose the pseudonym "Low Down" described his response to a dealer telling him he looked bad, evidently because he was on drugs. Low Down says he thought, "Why do you look down on me when you probably doing things wrong? ... I just sit down and think about, OK, so he got all this [money] and then he gonna talk down on me like that? ... I was like, I'm gonna get this dude" (Jacobs and Wright, 2008: 521).

Robbing a violator "puts the violator in a submissive position and enjoins him to think about the humiliation long after the offense has passed" (Jacobs and Wright, 2008: 523).

> Taking violators' valuables deals a financial blow to them that likely will be felt for some time. Using or threatening force against people who have crossed you establishes you as a so-called "badass" who should not be messed with. Seizing [the original] violator's assets brings the violator down and the aggrieved party up.
>
> *(Jacobs and Wright, 2008: 512)*

Stolen money and valuables enable the robber to ostentatiously display and dispense (Honaker and Shover, 1992; Katz, 1988: 232, 315; Wright and Decker, 1997: 40–2).

> We'd pimp into school the next day, clean as hell, profiling in clothes we'd stolen off somebody's back the night before... Our sharp clothes and hip style boosted our popularity in school. I saw girls and dudes, especially young underclassmen, gazing admiringly at [my accomplice] Shell Shock and me the same way I had admired Scobie-D, Kennie Banks, and other old-heads not very many years before.
>
> *(McCall, 1995: 101)*

Ostentatious display of luxury – "flossing" – is a claim to superiority, and those who resent the flosser's claim to superiority are motivated to relieve the claimant of his glitter (Wright and Decker, 1997: 37). Brazen cruising in a car decked out with expensive wheel rims, myriad speakers booming and subwoofers thumping, is a provocation to any onlooker who rejects being put down by this ostentatious display, not uncommonly provoking a carjacking (Jacobs and Wright, 2008: 522). Auto thieves sometimes steal a car specifically so that *they* may drive it around "flossing," to take parts to upgrade their own car, or to sell it for money to buy parts to make their own car flashier (Copes, 2003). This gives the thief prestige (Shover, 1996: 103–4). When the money from the last robbery runs out, thieves become envious of those with resources and ashamed of their loss of capacity to party and their all-around stigmatization. "It just makes me upset, angry, mad, jealous ... cause I ain't got the stuff that [others] got" (Wright and Decker, 1997: 36). Having ample funds from robbery raises the robber's AR position, and enables him (or her) to generously share food, drink, and drugs in commensal CS events; running out of money makes the impoverished robber feel humiliated and envy those who have funds.

Moreover, the bravado of armed robbery is an act of domination relished by the robber, an assertion of superiority through the domineering declaration, "This is a robbery – don't make it a murder" (Katz, 1988). In *other* contexts the robber's identity is degraded, but in the act of robbery, it is the victim who is humiliated by the triumphant robber. From analysis of 437 Chicago robberies in 1982–3, Katz concludes, "In virtually all robberies, the offender discovers, fantasizes or manufactures *an angle of moral superiority* over the intended victim" that justifies the robber's appropriation of the victim's property, while creating a satisfying dominance relationship (Katz, 1988: 169).

Armed robbers enjoy the domination, power, and control over their victims, and the terror they project. They take pride in giving orders and getting their way. To bring off a robbery successfully, he must "succeed in having the authority to control people" (Wright and Decker, 1997: 56). The weapon is not sufficient: armed robbery succeeds only if the robber can establish dominance over the victim (Wright and Decker, 1997: 103). In a Nietzschean way of thinking, "outlaws" are proud of their power identity. Motivated by AR hierarchy, "inevitably they prey on the weak who, they believe, are destined and even *deserve* to be victims. Since it is their refusal or inability to employ violence that invites victimization, victims have no one to blame but themselves" (Shover, 1996: 87). "Victims who resist are thought stupid and deserving of whatever countermeasures they necessitate" (Shover, 1996: 64). Note that especially in commercial robberies or where there are multiple victims, robbers often make the victims lie down. This is not just an instrumental act to reduce the danger of resistance or flight, it iconically constitutes social superiority: the robbers "put down" the victims, who can't "stand up" to them.

Robbery is sometimes an EM moral retaliation for a transgression against the robber, but at other times it is a way of proclaiming or reclaiming a high position in AR relationships. The fact that material goods and money are the medium of regulating the robber's social relationships should not blind us to the fact that the robber's violence is morally motivated: he aims to enhance his culturally ideal relationships through the culturally legitimated means of robbing foolish people who have more than they deserve. All social action is intentional – it is meant to *do* something, and hence is a means to some end – but construing robbery or any other action as "instrumental" doesn't illuminate its relational motives or relational aims. Within these cultural subgroups, the robbers' violence is exalted, praised, and admired. In the eyes of their peers, their violence is virtuous. The robbers' motives are moral to the extent that they subjectively believe that their position in the hierarchy is legitimately contestable and that they deserve a higher position, or they believe that someone has transgressed against them, and that robbery is a legitimate means either to demonstrate their deservingness or to rectify the original transgression. If robbers felt that they had not been transgressed against or that they deserved to be subordinate, and that robbery was not a legitimate means within their subculture of either rectifying a wrong or elevating status, then their robberies would not be morally motivated. (We have not located evidence to suggest that robbers acknowledge and embrace the responsibilities of authority in addition to its material entitlements, but we predict that they do feel these moral responsibilities of superior AR status.)

Ironically, a core motivation – sometimes *the* core motivation – for "property crimes" is not to secure the property for its material use value. Robbers often take property to get revenge for a previous transgression against them, to establish their dominance over their victims, to elevate their status within a group, to show it off ostentatiously, to treat their associates to drinks and drugs, or to share it with family. Thus, the main motive for forcefully taking material things is quite often moral, and the main function of taking, like giving, is to constitute social relationships.

20 THE SPECIFIC FORM OF VIOLENCE FOR CONSTITUTING EACH RELATIONAL MODEL

People violently constitute relationships though circumcision and excision, brutal initiations, killing rivals to the throne, proving loyalty to a superior by killing someone who threatens him, and human sacrifice. People enhance their own relationships with their deities by extreme asceticism, flagellation, or amputating a digit as an offering; others facilitate a vision of their personal companion spirit by hanging themselves by hooks through their chest muscles. The conduct or performance of many relationships consists of organized, socially instituted violence such as boxing and mixed martial arts, ice-hockey checking and football tackling, or combat among warriors who fight for glory. Redressive and terminative violence in response to transgressions of social relationships includes all sorts of corporal and capital punishment: burning witches, killing adulterers, eye-for-an-eye vengeance and feuding, killing men who insult one's honor, and honor suicide by those who have failed to do their duty. Redressive violence is ubiquitous, ranging from dueling to resolve a dishonor, judicial combat to determine guilt, lynching those perceived as disrespectful, beating wives perceived as having failed to be sufficiently dutiful, attacking husbands who are disrespectful jerks, terrorist bombing, and targeted killing by drones. Sometimes violence is intended to enforce a relationship by forestalling transgression – for example, by terrorizing subjects or slaves into submission. Torturing heretics and enemies falls somewhere in between redress and enforcement, as do violent self-defense and killing intruders. In honor cultures, killing a dishonored sister, daughter, or cousin terminates an intolerable relationship, cleansing the stain and thereby restoring the family honor. Innumerable cultures conduct, or used to conduct, trial by ordeal – for example, adjudicating witchcraft guilt by submerging the accused to see if she drowns, making her hold a hot iron to see if it burns her, or giving her poison to see if she dies. The atomic bombing of Hiroshima and Nagasaki was morally motivated violence on a mass scale, motivated by MP proportionality cost and benefit computations aimed to reduce American casualties in the most efficient way. The most massive moral violence practices in history were twentieth-century ethnic cleansings, acts of "purifying the race" or the nation, where the removal or killing of persons construed to "pollute" the shared essence of a "people" was motivated by the feeling that "mixture" or "mongrelization" is evil, unnatural, disgusting, dishonorable, and dangerous.

Violence is morally motivated to regulate relationships. That much is clear. But why do people hurt and kill in specific ways? There are innumerable ways to inflict pain; to maim; to cause suffering, fear, or distress; and to kill. Violence can be characterized by the actions involved, or by the manner in which it causes distress or death. In either respect, are those forms of violence that people tend to use for constituting one RM less likely to be used for constituting other RMs? Do people experience and perceive some forms of violence as *more apt, more natural, more intuitively "right"* for certain relationships than for other relationships? Are some forms of violence *more effective* for regulating some types of social relationships than others? While we can't offer a confident or definitive answer to these questions about the RM-specific morphology of violence, we think we do see some patterns that are consistent with the available accounts of violence.

Conformation systems theory (Fiske, 1991, 2004; Fiske and Schubert, 2012) posits that people employ a semiotically distinct medium – the conformation system (ConSyst) – for constituting each RM. That is, there is a natural, intuitive, especially evocative, especially binding conformation system through which people constitute each RM. The ConSyst of a RM is the primary way in which people regulate that RM; and it is the primary way that people represent the RM in interpersonal communication and in intrapersonal cognition. Children innately expect each RM to operate in its own distinctive ConSyst; seek, attend to, and are uniquely responsive to the ConSyst of a RM when constituting it; and intuitively initiate each kind of RM, using its particular ConSyst. The ConSyst of a RM arouses especially intense motives to sustain the RM, evokes especially strong moral commitments to it, and invokes especially effective normative enforcement of the RM by participants and others.

Communal-sharing violence: indexical consubstantial assimilation

The ConSyst of CS models is *consubstantial assimilation*: by making their bodies equivalent, people make themselves socially equivalent. Thus, consubstantial assimilation is semiotically indexical, with the correspondence in substance, surface, or motion of people's bodies indexing the correspondence of the social persons so embodied. Prototypical examples are caressing and kissing, intimate sex, giving birth, nursing, feeding, and commensal consumption of food, drink, tobacco, or other comestibles or drugs. To form a CS group, people may make their body surfaces equivalent by tattooing, scarification, circumcision, and excision, along with hair arrangements, body coloring, insignia, uniforms, and other clothing. Rhythmic synchronous movement such as military drill, tai chi or calisthenics, and ritual and recreational dance also have strong bonding effects because participants experience their congruently moving bodies as merging into one.

Conformation systems theory predicts that violence to constitute CS relationships should be focused on the bodily essence of the victim in relation to the bodily essence of the person with whom the relationship is being constituted: violence to create CS should join bodies, make them alike, or conversely, to rectify or terminate CS, should separate or purify the bodies. Indeed, as we have seen in our overview of genital modification, where violence is intended to create, reinforce, or restore the CS relationship, it aims to make the victim's body the same as the perpetrator's. In initiation and identify marking, people bleed together or modify the body to make it the same as others, thereby making the embodied person one with those similarly marked or who bled together. When a person is wounded, the blood that flows on the ground, along with viscera or brain matter, is not just the substance of the body; it is the social person and the substance of his CS relationships. Disrupting the integrity of the body, especially when weapons or rape pierces the body envelope, desecrates the body and hence defiles the embodied social person. So when people want to attack the social essence of a person, the most fundamental way to do this is to penetrate or pierce their body, shed his blood, and mutilate his body. In genocide, where the aim is to restore the perpetrator's purity by severing the relationship, the violence separates the polluting victim from the perpetrator, and may consist of desecrating, destroying, or eliminating the body of the victim, removing all traces of the "polluting" persons. In contrast, in some cases, perpetrators may take body parts as souvenirs and trophies that index the destruction and removal of the victim from the community. The wholesale killing of women and children to eliminate a "race" is also characteristic of CS violence.

Authority-ranking violence: iconic physics of magnitudes and dimensions

The ConSyst of AR is the *physics of magnitudes and dimensions*, in which relative magnitude or order along the dimension corresponds to social rank. This is iconic because the spatiotemporal relations map onto social relations: the linear ordering of persons on a physical dimension is congruent with their linear social ranks. People think, communicate, and constitute AR according to the dimensions of

> above – below
> bigger – smaller
> many – singular
> in front – behind,
> stronger – weaker
> preceding – following
> brighter – dimmer
> louder – quieter.

That is, "superiors" are "great" and "powerful," "lead" their "backers" and "followers," and are often addressed or represented as plural. Those who are "senior" go first, and are often dressed or represented as luminous. Trumpets, drums, bells, gongs, or cannon salutes may mark their appearances or their worship.

Hence, when it constitutes an AR relationship, violence generally should make the victim lower or below the perpetrator, make them smaller, behind, or quieter; or the violence should prove that the perpetrator is "stronger," "more forceful." Dungeons, of course, are the lowest part of a castle, iconically constituting the status of the miscreant below the lord who imprisons him. When a vertically construed AR relationship is at stake, flattening an opponent and standing above him is an iconically powerful act of "superiority." That is, the violence consists of the perpetrator "putting down" the victim and "belittling" him. In battle, combat, and contact sports, the aim is to bring the opponent down, so the victor stands above the defeated opponent, raising his arms in triumph. Likewise, for all kinds of infractions, drill sergeants and coaches often order painfully prolonged series of pushups, putting the miscreants' faces against the ground, while the sergeant or coach stands tall above them. Nineteenth-century and earlier parents, schoolmasters, and naval officers punished insolent or disobedient children and youths by making them bend over to receive a whipping – often with pants lowered to bare their buttocks. For treason or any other offense against the overarching state, offenders may be hanged by dropping them from a platform, or they may kneel and bend low as if bowing on the block, and then be decapitated so that their head rolls down while their body falls to the ground.

Equality-matching violence: concrete ostensive operations

The ConSyst of EM is *concrete ostensive operations* that establish one-to-one correspondence: turn-taking, fair lotteries, even shares counted out one-for-one, starting and stopping an activity simultaneously, counting-out rhymes, casting ballots, in-kind balanced reciprocity, and eye-for-an-eye vengeance. These concrete operations are operational definitions of evenness among the participants: if the procedure is correctly followed, the participants are matched and balanced.

Thus, violence to create or sustain EM relationships should consist of concrete operations of one-to-one correspondence: each of us must jump into the freezing water, or run across the same red-hot coals. Violence to rectify an EM relationship should concretely, ostensively match a corresponding violent act that the victim did to the perpetrator: it should be a practical demonstration that balance is restored. The harm should be evenly matched: "life for life, eye for eye, tooth for tooth, hand for hand, foot for foot, burn for burn, wound for wound, stripe for stripe" (Exodus 21:23–5). EM violence should usually adopt natural bodily units of this sort (an eye) or units of action (a spear thrust, a burn) that readily afford one-to-one correspondence. That is, the violence will be perceived and construed in terms of manifestly matching chunks or acts. Furthermore, as far as feasible, EM-redressive violence will comprise a one-to-one correspondence-matching operation, performed in the same way, following the same procedure, that the victim previously carried out against the perpetrator. In baseball, it's throwing a pitch at a batter in retaliation for the other team's pitcher hitting our batter. In homicide, it's a life for a life. In warfare, it's a bombing for a bombing, or nuclear annihilation in reciprocity for nuclear annihilation. In the case of an assault that resulted in paralysis of the victim, a Saudi Arabian judge even inquired whether the perpetrator could have his spinal cord medically severed at the exact same place as the victim's, as the victim requested (Jamjoom and Ahmen, 2010).

Market-pricing violence: arbitrary conventional symbolism

The ConSyst of MP is *arbitrary conventional symbolism*, in which the signs have constitutive meaning and effect purely by virtue of their conventional use in a particular culture. The prototype is money: pieces of metal or paper, "signed" documents, or strings of digits whose value totally depends on people's use, understanding, and acceptance of the signs, along with their expectation that everyone in the system will continue to use, understand, and accept them in the same manner. Other examples are numerals that people use to calculate and communicate prices, taxes, fines, penal sentences, efficiency, or cost-benefit utilities.

MP violence is proportionally computed as "the price you pay" for something, or "the cost of doing business." The violence is metered by a conception of how the quantity of harm inflicted is fungible with the relational acts, events, or states that the violence regulates. For example, "rationalized" violence includes computations of penalties meted out as strokes of a cane or whip, or the infliction of a number of days of a specified degree of suffering. Moreover, MP violence is rationally planned and administered according to abstract rules and formal regulations, such as "rules of engagement" and sentencing guidelines. It is impersonally carried out in a bureaucratic manner by trained technicians and professionals working according to manuals based on criteria logically designed to maximize efficiency and expected utility, impersonally assessed in terms of such abstractions as "casualties" and "collateral damage." Perpetrators will often keep careful records to facilitate rational review to improve the efficiency of violence, maximizing the "return" while minimizing the "cost" and "risk."

Perhaps the most notable aspect of MP violence is that it is indifferent to the manner of harming or killing except insofar as that is relevant to the desired results. Different sorts of pain or harm or different periods of suffering are fungible, in that people construe them all as interchangeable ways of "paying" the "same" "price." In the abstract, formal, rational calculus of MP violence, the body is merely a biological mechanism in which all forms of pain and suffering and all means to death are comparable on some conventional metric of efficacy. The only question is which is cheaper and more cost-effective: destroying their crops so as to starve them, killing them with machine guns, incinerating them with napalm, or vaporizing and incinerating them with atomic bombs. The violence in MP is morally motivated to regulate social relationships in the most efficient, cost-effective, utility-maximizing, *ratio*nal manner. MP is social coordination oriented to proportionally valued costs and benefits – where harm and death may be fungible with every other value, so that the right thing to do is to compute the course of action that brings the greatest good to the greatest number with the minimal costs, even when the costs include morbidity and mortality.

Many dyads and groups with multifaceted relationships use different RMs to coordinate different aspects or phases of their relationship. If a violent act or practice performs multiple constitutive roles with respect to aspects or phases coordinated by different RMs, conformation systems theory would predict that the form of the act or practice is likely to have features of the conformation systems of each model that the perpetrator is regulating. This may make it difficult to discern and discriminate the component conformation systems that shape the violence, but that's simply because human action is often multiply motivated.

Overall, conformation systems theory promises to extend virtuous violence theory by illuminating the distinct morphologies of violence that people are apt to perpetrate to constitute the respective RMs. The forms of violence that regulate the respective RMs seem to differ, but the available evidence is insufficient, so it would be productive to focus more research on the forms of violence, asking precisely *how* people harm, hurt, or kill to constitute each of the elementary types of social relationships. In each respective RM, a distinctive kind of violence should be intuitively expected, should feel natural, should most readily evoke relationship-appropriate emotions, and should be especially "satisfying."

21 WHY DO PEOPLE USE *VIOLENCE* TO CONSTITUTE THEIR SOCIAL RELATIONSHIPS, RATHER THAN USING SOME OTHER MEDIUM?

Violence is not the usual way to constitute relationships; people usually constitute relationships non-violently. So while we have explained the motivation for violence, this explanation raises a new question: why and when do people use violence to constitute their social relationships, rather than using other means? Sometimes people shoot a person who runs over their dog, but much more often the driver apologizes and the dog owner accepts the apology, or the driver offers compensation, or the dog owner brings a law suit. Other options are to complain, or exit: when do people merely walk away from an unsatisfactory interaction, or gossip about it? Sometimes people connect and become one with each other by cutting their bodies the same way or scourging their bodies together, but much more often people connect and become one by feasting commensally, dancing together, hugging, and kissing. What determines which course people follow?

Of course, the incidence of violence is greatly influenced by social-structural, technical, and biological factors, such as the lack of a reliable third-party state police force, the nature and availability of weapons, or the hormones that drive young males. But in terms of the *motives* to engage in violence, we suggest that the major factor that determines whether people constitute a relationship violently, and, if so, with what kind of violence, is the set of cultural preos that guide the implementation of the relationship. From the observer's point of view, the best predictor of violent regulation of a relationship is the cultural context. From the actor's point of view, whether violence is natural or unnatural, inevitable or evitable, depends on his cultural psychology. For eighteenth-century Europeans and American fathers, it was natural and inevitable that they should whip their sons for disobedience, disrespect, or lack of diligence. In this cultural-historical context, fathers made tactical decisions about precisely when and how much to whip, but they didn't strategize about *whether* to whip their sons; they didn't analyze alternative child-rearing strategies or in any meaningful sense "choose" to whip. That was simply what good fathers did when a son was bad. In turn, those sons learned that whipping was right and necessary from their fathers, and reproduced the practice when punishing their own children.

Certainly, every father had to interpret the precedents and prescriptions for whipping, applying them to decide whether a particular infraction merited whipping. Presumably, the latitude built into the ambiguity of any preo and the multiplicity of potentially relevant preos resulted in some difficult decisions, and variation between families. In the long run, these decisions and variations must have been involved in the historical decline in whipping. So, while keeping clearly in mind that the cultural preos for paternal responsibility were the overwhelming determinants at any given point in time, we should consider the psychosocial factors that must have gradually contributed to the decline, disregard, disapproval, and ultimate criminalization of whipping. Given that in many cultures in which parents and schoolmasters formerly felt morally obliged to whip disobedient children they now feel morally obliged not to do so, the question is why these judgments changed when they did – in some cultures, but not others. More generally, what kinds of social psychological, social ecological, political, and other historical factors operate in the long run to transform and replace cultural preos toward or away from violently regulating relationships? Sometimes argued and political, sometimes imperceptible and practical, cultural historical changes in the preos for violence (or anything else) must be mediated by social psychological processes. The ultimate factors may be environmental, technological, communicative, and demographic, but the effects of these factors on cultural preos and hence motives for violence are proximately mediated by social psychological processes.

Not much is known about this. Few theorists and fewer empirical researchers have addressed this question in these general terms, so if virtuous violence theory contributes nothing else, at least it should direct attention to the issue. However, thanks to Steven Pinker (2011), we know that people use violence much less now than they ever have in history or prehistory. Pinker shows that rates of violence have dramatically declined over recent decades, over the past few centuries, and over the last several millennia. Relying on existing theories of violence, he attributes the decline in part to culturally and ontogenetically cultivated self-control and empathy. He also theorizes that CS and AR are intrinsically most likely to motivate violence, so that violence diminishes as CS and AR relationships are displaced by more dispassionate MP, along with the super-rationality of impersonal perspective-taking that MP leads to. This thesis echoes Durkheim's (1997/1893, 1973/1899–1900) theory that transgressions of organic solidarity evoke retributive sanctions, while transgressions of mechanical solidarity evoke restitutive sanctions. These are helpful observations about the changing incidence of violence, but they don't answer our question. However, they provide a crucial historical framework for it: whatever the factors are that promote violent regulation of relationships, they must have greatly declined over the last several millennia, over the last few centuries, and over the last few decades.

Criticality

Our thesis is that people constitute their social relationships violently when

- it is necessary to attract participants' and others' attention to a constitutive transformation of the relationship;
- it is necessary to raise the stakes in the relationship because the relationship is crucial;
- they are constituting the relationship, rather than merely conducting (performing) it;
- there is a great deal at stake;
- people are responding to transgression through redress or protection rather than regulating relationships in other ways;
- people are acting according to CS and AR relational models rather than more dispassionate EM and MP relational models;
- people have no good alternative ways to regulate the relationship, nor do they have alternative relationships, so they cannot simply leave this relationship and start a new one;

- the violence will enhance the metarelational models within which the perpetrator–victim relationship is embedded or enhance the constituent relationships that comprise those metarelational models.

More informally, virtuous violence theory posits that people use violence to grab others' attention and impress them by demonstrating that the relational stakes are high – so long as the violence is consistent with the web of social relationships comprising the metarelational models in which the action is embedded. Milder, weaker, gentler, less salient ways of regulating relationships are adequate for most everyday purposes, often require less effort, and are usually safer.

These conditions for violence are highly correlated and interdependent: they do not act separately and their violence-fostering effects combine in a mutually reinforcing manner that is more than additive. Sometimes these attentional, stakes, and metarelational model issues shape behavior intuitively without people being aware of them, and sometimes they are explicit strategic considerations. Since they are typically intertwined, we will discuss these factors together and refer to the violence-triggering level of this constellation of highly interactive, violence-fostering factors as the *criticality* of the relationship. This term evokes the apt analogy of the self-sustaining state of a nuclear chain reaction that results when sufficient fissionable material is in sufficiently close proximity without too much impeding material absorbing the radiation. Criticality is the condition where the participants get very hot very fast and are likely to explode. We address here the first seven components of criticality, focusing on metarelational factors in the following chapter.

Attention to violence

People are intensely interested in violence: they want to hear all about it, and they often go to see it. From Plato to Edmund Burke to Baudelaire, commentators have noted the magnetic attraction to viewing, hearing, or reading about injury and death – especially when the injury or death is inflicted by humans (Sontag, 2003: 97–107). People are consistently drawn to art and photographs depicting pain and death (Sontag, 2003). For example, stories and images of humans and gods inflicting pain and death are widespread in classical antiquity: consider the detailed descriptions of wounds and death in the *Iliad*, and in Christian iconography the Crucifixion and the torture and deaths of the martyrs (Sontag, 2003: 41, 74). Images of Christ on the cross and martyrs suffering and dying have long been popular, as well as stories about their torture and death (Crachiolo, 2004). The readers evidently revered and relished the extreme and prolonged pain, the depiction of which is the essence of such hagiography. Similarly, Gallonio's *Tortures and Torments of the Christian Martyrs*, first published in 1591, and very popular across Europe, was widely reprinted and translated. Huge Roman audiences came to see animals kill criminals and watch gladiators fight. Today, there is a huge audience for American football, ice hockey, rugby, boxing, and mixed martial arts. British and American public executions often drew thousands of spectators (Goldberg, 1998). In the mid 1800s, throngs visited Madame Tussaud's Chamber of Horrors, which depicted the executions during the French Revolution and excruciating executions of criminals (Goldberg, 1998). In Britain and its North American colonies, the popular press of the mid-eighteenth century prominently displayed gruesome images of murders and war casualties (Goldberg, 1998).

Today, the whole highway slows to a crawl as drivers peer at a gruesome traffic accident, but what draws the most avid attention is a human who kills.

> The sufferings most often deemed worthy of representation are those understood to be the product of wrath, divine or human. (Suffering from natural causes, such as illness or childbirth, is scantily represented in the history of art; that caused by accident, virtually not at all – as if there were no such thing as suffering by inadvertence or misadventure.)
>
> *(Sontag, 2003: 40)*

Moreover, research on cinema violence suggests that people experience an almost euphoric feeling of elation when an extremely violent, evil character suffers and dies, getting what he deserves (Zillmann, 1998).

The evidence of the attention-grabbing power of violence is all around us, and always has been. Violence is ubiquitous in news media, movies, video games, and, throughout human history, mythology and storytelling – ubiquitous because people want to see and hear about it (Scott *et al.*, 2013). In one sample of 220 freshman and sophomore students from a Midwestern high school, 95% reported that they like and regularly view "slasher" films that involve graphic killing (Johnston, 1995). Asked to explain why they go to such movies, many respondents responded, "I watch because I'm interested in the ways people die," "I like to see blood and guts," and "I like to see the victims get what they deserve" (Johnston, 1995: 527). Even fourth and fifth graders (ages 9–11) in the United States play very violent video games and watch violent movies (Funk *et al.*, 2004). American children watch hours of violent television every week; even very young children watch cartoons that consist of extremely violent interactions of the sort that would be horribly painful or fatal to real animals or humans (Cantor, 1998). The most popular video games today involve very graphic, realistic images of killing (e.g., *Call of Duty*, *Halo*). It is not merely the "action" that attracts players: in 1993 when Sega sold a version of *Mortal Kombat* graphically depicting violence such as bloody decapitations, while Nintendo sold a much less graphic version in which the violence was toned down, the graphic Sega version outsold the milder Nintendo version 7 to 1, despite there being more Nintendo systems in US homes (Goldstein, 1998). "Superviolent" movies attract huge audiences everywhere in the world where they are shown (Zillmann, 1998). But, of course, children loved war and cowboy and Indian killing games long before such "entertainment" was digitalized. And for centuries adults have told stories to (or written stories for) children recounting gruesome mortal consequences of moral transgression (Tatar, 1998).

Pain and fear are the most attention-grabbing of all stimuli, dominating other modes of perception. Furthermore, the motives evoked by intense fear or pain are very strong: they usually get people to act with great immediacy and effort. Under extreme danger and stress, one's own pain sensations are muted, and sometimes fear as well. But what was not felt in the height of battle is nonetheless unforgettable later: pain and fear are extraordinarily memorable. Memories of great pain or terrifying fear of death or severe injury, one's own or others', typically last a lifetime, are easily re-evoked, and leave enduring effects. PTSD is the extreme syndrome, but violence is always unforgettable.

For perpetrators, this all means that their violence will be noticed by a wide audience, and then quickly and vividly communicated to many others. Violence is so dramatic, so enthralling, that people will know what the perpetrator did and not soon forget it. Because people pay so much attention to their own and others' pain and danger, and to others' death, and remember the experiences so vividly, inflicting or threatening harm are powerful means to regulate social relationships, while killing is incomparable. No one will miss the message, no one who gets the message will ignore it, and no one will ever forget it. In sum, violence grabs people's attention: people perceive, note, and remember what happened. So the salience of violence is a major component of criticality.

Sometimes criticality evokes violence without any conscious reflection, so that people are not aware of explicitly making a decision to be violent. At other times, perpetrators are more or less aware of the dramatic impact of violence, and use it accordingly. Studies of intimate partner violence in some cultures also show that quite often the perpetrator's stated reason for violence was to get a partner's attention, as, for example, when the partner wasn't listening (Flynn and Graham, 2010: 245).

Pain and fear of injury or death, hearing of killing or observing it, don't simply grab people's attention, and stay in their memory – they also get people to act, or refrain from action. For perpetrators, this all means that the motivational impact of violence and credible threat of violence is virtually unmatched – violence is an extraordinarily effective way to influence others to accommodate the perpetrator's social-relational goals. Threatening or carrying out violence is a very risky strategy that may sometimes jeopardize the relationship which it aims to regulate, not to mention the life and functioning of the relational partner and of the perpetrator. But when the stakes are high and safer strategies are ineffective, it may be adaptive.

High stakes

> The physical death of the sacrificial victim, the martyr, or the war
> dead charges an action with a seriousness or a compelling power
> it would otherwise lack; the bodies of the dead give a tangible form
> to an abstract commitment or belief. In the latter the belief that life
> is precious leads men to use killing or dying as a measure for value;
> what men die for is supremely important.
>
> *(Lewis, 1990: 3)*

Harming oneself or loved ones, as by taking a hard hit from an opponent to protect a teammate or circumcising one's son, are sacrifices that demonstrate great commitment to one's team or community. Killing a female relative who has shamed the family declares the family's total commitment to honor – it shows that the family will give up what they love most to adhere to the fundamental morality of the honor code. Aztecs risked their lives and the lives of their comrades and subordinates in raids to secure sacrificial victims, and then cut out the victims' beating hearts on the altar of their gods. This practice terrorized their enemies, their vassal states, and their subjects because it demonstrated that resistance to royal authority meant a horrible death. A modern mundane example is the defensive end who blindsides the quarterback, leaving him dazed or writhing in pain. By doing so, the defensive end has changed the relationship between the offense and defense: now the quarterback is not only diminished as a passer and scrambler, he is humiliated and afraid. The quarterback now knows that the longer he waits before passing, the more he risks being hammered again. Harming an opponent, inflicting pain on recruits in boot camp, or killing a man who insults your daughter enforces a relationship by imposing a huge cost. Braving pain and suffering, the agent demonstrates that he can be counted on to do his part, even at great cost to himself. The person who inflicts violence is a relational partner to be reckoned with – others cannot take lightly the creation, maintenance, regulation, or redress of relationships with him.

In general, virtuous violence demonstrates to the violent agent's partners, and to observers, that a great deal is at stake in their relational performance. Violence immediately gets people's attention, and then "forcefully" warns them that the violent agent is committed to enforcing the relationship, even at great risk or cost to himself or his partners. Hence, virtuous violence motivates the violent agent's partners to perform their parts energetically and scrupulously, however difficult it may be for them to do what the relationship requires. It is analogous to raising the ante: it increases the stakes in the relationship, like placing a big bet or making a big raise. When you raise the stakes in poker, you are impressively signaling that you expect to win the hand, you are committing yourself to a big loss if you don't, and you are giving the other players a choice: fold, conceding the pot, or risk the amount of the raise to stay in and contest the hand. Violence works in a similar way, except that often there are no cards: whoever imposes sufficient harm to make the other concede, wins. In other words, if a player is willing and able to bet more than the other players' stakes – more than the others are willing to put into play and risk losing – he wins. Hence, if it is *essential* to create a relationship, if an essential relationship *must* be sustained, if an essential relationship is going badly or there is a risk that it will, violence may be an adaptive strategy to protect or to transform the relationship to ensure that the perpetrator gets what he feels he's "entitled to" in relational terms. In this sense, violence can be analyzed as a *chicken game* (Rapoport and Chammah, 1966) or *hawk–dove game* (Maynard Smith, 1979) or as a *deterrence strategy* (Frank, 1988; Kavka, 1986, 1987), with the added factor of interdependence.

As Frank and Kavka show, in order to win it isn't always necessary to actually impose any harm: it is sufficient that your opponent be convinced that in order to win, you are committed to imposing more harm than they are willing or able to endure. But how does your opponent know you will actually impose such terrible harm? Given that it may be emotionally difficult and very dangerous to be violent, why should your opponent believe that you actually will be, if they contest the relationship? Frank (1988) argues that the only way to persuasively demonstrate that you *will* be violent is to consistently *be* violent. That is, you must have a consistent track record of violence in similar circumstances in this relationship or similar relationships. In small communities, people learn by observation and gossip who actually will be violent if they are crossed. And occasional, arbitrary pre-emptive violence will keep uppermost in everyone's mind the prospect of violence if they contest a relationship with you.

Is the constitution of the relationship at stake, or merely its conduct?

This brings us to an even more fundamental aspect of relationship-regulating violence. Relational acts differ in their constitutivity: some actions are fundamental to the creation and existence of a relationship, while other less constitutive acts are more peripheral. To simplify somewhat, we can distinguish those acts that make or break a relationship from those acts that are merely the performance or conduct of the relationship. So, a wedding makes a marriage, while depositing money to a joint checking account or taking joint responsibility for household chores merely follows from the relationship that the wedding ceremony created. Likewise, sexual faithfulness is crucially constitutive, while doing the dishes together is not. People are more motivated to violence by unfaithfulness than failure to deposit money or wash dishes. An officer may shoot a soldier for blatantly refusing to obey an order, but not for running too slowly to perform it. In short, actions that are crucially constitutive, that make or break a relationship, are more likely to consist of or provoke violence than actions that simply comprise the routine conduct of the relationship.

What is the constitutive phase of the violence?

People are more frequently violent when responding to transgressions, either through redress or protection, than when creating, conducting, terminating, or mourning relationships. As we have seen, all these constitutive processes sometimes motivate violence, even homicide, but punishment and defense are the most frequent motives. It's not clear why.

What type of relationship is being constituted?

When a relationship doesn't matter very much, people are unlikely to escalate to violence. Pinker (2011) suggests that people generally aren't as invested in MP relationships as they are in CS and AR relationships, so that the historically increasing prevalence of MP relationships (progressively replacing CS and AR) is an important cause of the huge historical decline in violence. This seems plausible, and finer grained analyses might show that within each RM, the incidence of violence also depends on the importance of the relationship. Any type of relationship, whether consisting of CS, AR, EM, or MP, can vary in its emotional intensity, motivational impetus, and moral obligatoriness. CS varies from merely casual friendship to true love, from merely being American to being ready to die for your fellow soldiers in the platoon. The stronger the relationship, the more the participants are prone to violently regulate it.

Does the perpetrator have alternative means to regulate the relationship or alternative relationships to join?

In addition, violence only makes sense when alternative, less risky, and less costly means of regulating relationships are not readily available. This may mean that the more verbally articulate and persuasive people are, the more "attractive" they are in various respects, or the greater the material inducements and extrinsic social resources they can bestow, the less violent they are likely to be. That is, if someone can effectively influence their partners in other ways, they don't need violence. Alternatively, there may be meta-relational means for regulating relationships non-violently, such as the presence of third-party governing bodies to enforce rules. None of this may involve reflectively weighing or even consciously considering these factors, much less making choices through a rational calculus that the perpetrator can articulate. But natural and cultural evolution along with individual experience will tend to support violence in some circumstances and inhibit violence under other conditions.

When it is feasible to abandon a bad relationship and replace it with another, violence may be maladaptive. That is, where there is relational mobility, such that old relationships are easily abandoned and new relationships are easily formed, it may not be worthwhile to use violence to sustain a relationship that is in jeopardy (cf. Cooney, 1998: 115–22; on some other ways that relational mobility affects relationships, see Yuki and Schug, 2012). Don't like this relationship? Leave it and find a better one. But if there are few or no alternatives to an existing relationship, then people may resort to violence to make it work – because *this* relationship *must* work. In addition, if relational-mobility opportunities are few, the victim of the violence may not be able to leave the relationship, diminishing the perpetrator's risk that her violence will lead to her partner's exit. Thus, violence may be prevalent in small, closed communities in which it is ecologically, economically, or socially difficult to leave unsatisfactory relationships, and there are few new alternative relationships available. Where kinship ties are not crucial for survival or well-being, where it's easy to leave almost any unsatisfactory relationship and find a better substitute, why regulate any relationship violently?

In short, violence impresses the victim, the audience, and the many others who quickly and reliably learn of it through gossip (or, today, the media). People notice violence, remember it, and are highly motivated by it. As a result, doing violence or effectively threatening violence can be a very effective way to regulate relationships. But the risks of engaging in violence are high, and so it should only be used when the social-relational stakes are high, and less costly, non-violent means are unavailable. We suggest that where violence has declined, it has done so when the socioecological conditions have effectively lowered the social-relational stakes and provided alternative, less costly, non-violent means to regulate relationships.

22 METARELATIONAL MODELS THAT INHIBIT OR PROVIDE ALTERNATIVES TO VIOLENCE

As we have seen throughout the book, perpetrators may inflict violence on one person to constitute relationships with others. For example, a soldier may kill an enemy in obedience to an officer, or an initiate may kill a member of a rival gang. A perpetrator may kill one member of another group in retaliation for some other member of that group's killing a member of the perpetrator's group. A man may kill his wife's lover to regulate his relationship with his wife, or, in an honor culture, kill his niece's lover, and his niece, in order to regulate his relationships with his family and with everyone in the community. As we saw, the Trojan War was all about men fighting men to constitute relationships with *other* men, or with the gods. In all these and many other cases we have considered in this book, the motive to constitute one or more of the component relationships of a metarelational model morally requires violence in another of the relationships that compose the metarelational model. In general, relationships have moral implications for other relationships with which they are metarelationally linked.

But these moral links often work the other way around. As we mentioned briefly in Chapter 2, metarelational models may inhibit violence. If a soldier is ordered to kill a family member or his village chief, he may refuse. The gang initiate may avoid killing his sister's boyfriend. In a feud, potential perpetrators may refrain from violence if the opposing group includes in-laws, co-members of an age set or secret society, blood brothers, or compadres. Conflict-restraining relationships such as these are "cross-cutting ties" that limit violence in many societies, including ones where there are no effective police, judiciaries, or chiefs

(Colson, 1953; Cooney, 1998: 90–6; Evans-Pritchard, 1939; Gluckman, 1954, 1963; LeVine, 1961; Nader, 1990; Rae and Taylor, 1970; Ross, 1993). Such metarelational cross-cutting ties operate in all societies, including modern ones. For example, Varshney (2003) found that violence between Hindus and Muslims was less likely to occur following an instigating act of violence elsewhere in the country in cities where Hindus and Muslims were already working together on joint civic projects.

Inhabitants of modern states have powerful cross-cutting ties with the state. Indeed, the definition of a state is something like "a political power that claims legitimate authority to use force to regulate relationships between itself and its subjects, along with many relationships among its subjects or citizens, and between its subjects and citizens and outsiders." So, if I rob a store or beat up someone, armed police will intervene, and they will exercise their mandate to use force if I resist. Then the courts may forcibly incarcerate me. This is the operation of metarelational models in which the state is obligated to use violence to regulate relationships among citizens. More generally, where there is an effective Hobbesian Leviathan – a powerful chief, or an executive with police and a penal system – the Leviathan is the ultimate third party in metarelationships regulating all of the social relationships among its subjects or citizens (Hobbes, 2010/1651; Kavka, 1986; Schneider, 1971).

Figure 22.1 schematically graphs some violence-inhibiting effects of metarelational models. In the simplest case, diagramed in Figure 22.1a (identical to Figure 2.3b), the potential perpetrator, P, is morally motivated toward violence against the victim, V, but also morally motivated to sustain a relationship with another person, O, who in turn wants to sustain a relationship with the victim, and hence cares about the victim, or is obligated to protect her. Because O cares about V, any harm P does to V threatens P's relationship with O – and, indeed, O may sanction P for harming V. For example, if the perpetrator catches a man stealing his money, the perpetrator may restrain himself or limit his violence if the thief is his wife's brother or his daughter's husband. Even when there is a chain of three (or more) relationships linking the P with V, as in Figure 22.1b, P may mitigate or avoid violence in order to sustain his relationship with O. Consider here the case of a warlord disposed to punish an insubordinate soldier, but checking his rage because the soldier is his mother's brother's child, or his age-mate's blood brother's son.

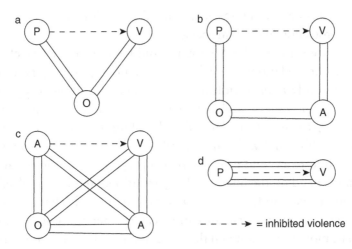

Figure 22.1: Violence-reducing metarelational models

Figure 22.1c illustrates the obvious fact that there may be as many as six linked relationships among four persons, all of which may be linked in a metarelational model to all of the others. So a suicide bomber may hesitate to detonate his bomb if one of his victims will be a man who is his closest friend's guru *and* his teacher's guest, where the guru and the guest are also brothers. Likewise, you will be less inclined to hang a cattle rustler if you discover that the rustler is the son of your sister, especially if your sister's husband, the rustler's father, is your close friend. The more such ties that the perpetrator is directly or indirectly concerned to preserve, and the stronger they are, the greater the inhibition of his violence.

Figure 22.1d displays the simplest inhibitory metarelational model, if we can call it that. This is the case when two persons have multiple relationships with each other. Suppose a man buys a horse, but discovers that the seller cheated him: the horse is lame. He might be inclined to violently rectify the wrong he has suffered. But if the seller is also the buyer's pastor, and his oldest friend, the buyer may find a way to rectify the wrong without violence. If the man who insults you, offending your honor, is your brother or a fellow soldier in the same platoon, you may let him off with an angry warning, rather than stab him. In short, when two parties have multiple relationships, the parallel relationships may inhibit violence morally motivated by one of those relationships. Here, and in the multiparty metarelational models, moral motives based on different social relationships conflict. To act on moral motives impelling toward violence against someone may be to violate moral motives toward compassion, care, or protection of the same person.

As we analyzed in Chapter 2 and have seen in every chapter, however, metarelational models often potentiate, morally permit. or, indeed, morally *require* violence. Some metarelation models promote violence, while others inhibit it. A warrior may be motivated by his relationship to his girlfriend to kill, if she admires valor, or not to kill, if she hates killing and will end their relationship if he kills anyone. The severity, frequency, and probability of a perpetrator's violence against a victim depend on the number of metarelational models involved and their importance, and, of course, *how* they are linked. That is, violence in one relationship may enhance or threaten other relationships linked to it. The more important and the more numerous these metarelational models, the greater is their total effect on the severity, frequency, and probability of A's violence against V. A Quaker who commits violence against anyone diminishes or jeopardizes his relationships with all other Quakers. But a traditional Greek shepherd who fights a man who insults him thereby gains the respect and admiration of everyone else, except the victim's kin: his violence enhances his honor with many people.

Whether or not violence occurs depends on the balance of moral motives, which in turn depends on the number of component relationships of the combined metarelational models, the importance of each of those relationships, and how strongly the violence constitutes each of the morally linked relationships in the metarelational model. Thus, we can qualitatively summarize the variable effects of metarelational models in three tenets:

1. The more important and the more numerous the other relationships that are linked through metarelational models to the focal relationship, the greater their potential effects (facilitating or inhibiting) on the frequency, intensity, and lethality of the violence in the focal relationship.

2. The greater the imbalance between the number and importance of linked relationships that are enhanced by violence in the focal relationship, compared to the lower number and importance of linked relationships that are jeopardized by violence in the focal relationship, the greater the frequency, intensity, and lethality of the violence in the focal relationship. And vice versa.

3. In general, the more metarelational models in which a relationship is embedded, the less violence will occur in it (less frequent, less injurious, less lethal). This is because, more often than not, violence in one relationship undermines or jeopardizes most other relationships linked to the focal relationship, and most relationships are mostly peaceful. That is, most people don't want most of their associates to be harmed. People typically sanction or avoid people who are violent in other relationships – for their own safety, and because the harm to the victim is objectionable to most of the people who relate to the victim. That is, most of the time most relationships inhibit violence in most of the other relationships in the metarelational models that they are enmeshed in. So, on the whole, the more metarelational models a relationship belongs to, the less violence will tend to occur in it. But, as we have seen, there are many exceptions, the most dramatic of which are cultures of honor and shame.

This last principle may seem to be inconsistent with the long-term decline of violence (Pinker, 2011). However, as communications improve, and as people come to depend on wider and wider MP and other networks, anything a person does in any relationship comes to have wider and wider ramifications. A person's conviction for murder is in the public record, preventing him from ever being hired by most employers or being trusted by just about anyone. A person convicted of rape is listed on an online database of sex offenders.

Our representation of metarelational models potentiating and constraining violence represents the links among relationships synchronically and depicts persons as mere points at the intersection of relationships. But relationships are dynamic, their moral motivational implications for each other evolve, and people are not the passive circles these graphs connote. *People actively manage their relationships and metarelational models.* When there is conflict or threat of conflict between two persons with whom a person is relating, she often intervenes to *mediate* the conflict between her partners (Black, 1998; Cooney, 1998). That is, she seeks solutions for the conflict between her relationship partners and pushes them to find a way out of the conflict, sometimes implicitly or explicitly putting her relationship with either or both on the line. The prototype is the parent interceding in conflicts between her children. She makes it clear to her children that the status of their respective relationships with her depend to some degree on their moderating or ending their conflict or avoiding violence. For the potential perpetrators, this often provides a face-saving way out of the conflict: the opponents can step back, making it clear that they do so out of respect or affection for the mediator. Legal anthropologists and political scientists have studied these mediational rituals and practices extensively (e.g., Lienhardt, 1961; Middleton and Tait, 1954), while political and legal historians have illuminated the development of police, courts, and the whole apparatus of the state as third-party guarantor and regulator of social relationships. The business of civil courts – and professional mediators – is to mediate relationships, which reduces recourse to violence. And disputants know that the criminal justice system will intervene if there is violence, a fact that gives them both motivations and excuses for avoiding violence. In short, people intercede to regulate each other's relationships – sometimes interceding violently, but more often mediating to forestall, moderate, or end each other's violence.

A great mystery of violence is that the perpetrators are often very ordinary people who are good neighbors, good friends, good siblings, and good parents. But bewilderment about this results from an assumption that violence can be attributed to some trait or state of the individual perpetrator. Within this individualistic worldview, the natural question is, "What is it about this person that made him violent?" But perhaps traits or states of the individual person *can't* account for violence – because violence isn't a product of an isolated individual. Virtuous violence theory offers an alternative paradigm: that violence is emergent from social relationships. If you ask, "What is it about oxygen that makes it explosive?" or "What is it about hydrogen that makes it explosive?" there's no answer to either question, because there isn't anything specific to oxygen, as such, or hydrogen, as such, that makes it likely to explode. In isolation, neither one will ever explode. But when combined, the tiniest spark will set off a blast. Put the oxygen together with the nitrogen (making laughing gas) *before* bringing them together with the hydrogen and despite endless sparks there will never be an explosion. Put the oxygen and hydrogen together in a polymer exchange membrane fuel cell and instead of an explosion you have a nice, controllable source of clean energy for your car, releasing water. If virtuous violence theory is correct, then it is often fruitless to seek purely individualistic explanations of violence – because separate individuals as such don't produce violence. Of course, traits of persons make some prone to violence in social-relational circumstances that others would simply shrug off. But even the most violent people are not violent in most of their interactions, and when they *are* violent, their violence is motivated by the perception that violence is necessary to constitute a particular, crucial social relationship that cannot readily be regulated more easily, safely, or gently. Furthermore, many sets of dyads (or groups) that would be peaceful and gentle by themselves are nevertheless components of metarelational models whose configurational moral implications motivate violence.

23 HOW DO WE END VIOLENCE?

Empirically, as we have seen in chapter after chapter, the objective fact is that people are sometimes morally motivated to harm or kill. Sometimes people feel that to be good, to be just, to be honorable, to do their duty, they have to hurt someone. Morality consists of regulating social relationships (Rai and Fiske, 2011, 2012), and the inductively assembled evidence shows that sometimes moral motives impel people to regulate critical relationships violently. This reveals how profoundly important social relationships are: people will sometimes kill or die to make their relationships right. People's relationships sometimes are more important to them than their bodies or their very lives, and sometimes to make their relationships right, people sacrifice the bodies or the lives of their spouses, children, friends, neighbors, or others.

Thus, the essential message of virtuous violence theory is that we cannot attribute most violence to the "breakdown" of morals, or to individualistic rational actors amorally maximizing their personal asocial utility functions. The obverse message is that we cannot equate morality with just gentleness, compassion, caring, or harm-avoidance: there are moralities that impel to violence. Meritorious performance of one's moral duty may consist of kindness or killing.

From these facts there are three conclusions that we cannot draw. These facts do *not* imply that a person *cannot help* but constitute relationships violently. These facts do *not* imply that human society will *inevitably be* violent. These facts do *not* imply that we *ought* to constitute relationships violently. Consider the analogy with procreation. All animals maximize their reproductive success, and nearly all human populations have done so throughout history, limited only by their ecological constraints. But today most people use contraception; some people abstain from sex; birthrates in most modern societies have dropped to replacement levels and in some cases below that; and there is no moral obligation to have as many children as possible. The same conclusions apply to violence. So to end violence, what should we do?

One thing is clear: the better we understand the moral motivations for violence, the better we will be able to reduce it. If virtuous violence theory is valid, then to reduce violence we will have to do more than provide economic or material incentives, and we will have to do more than impose punishment. It will not be enough to minimize frustration, foster self-control, humanize victims, or reinforce moral reasoning. To reduce violence, people must develop other ways to constitute and regulate their social relationships. Violence will be reduced when potential perpetrators can implement critical relationships non-violently. Violence will be avoided when potential victims can freely and safely leave relationships in which they are subject to violence – and form new, violence-free relationships. Violence will be reduced as metarelational models emerge that make violence in one relationship incompatible with many other important, meaningful, rewarding relationships linked to the potentially violent relationship. When violence in *any* relationship is an intolerable violation of *all* of the perpetrators' relationships, most violence will be eliminated.

In his work on preventing additional outbreaks of violence following the Rwandan genocide and other intergroup conflicts through efforts at reconciliation, Ervin Staub (2006) argues for the importance of helping victims understand that the perpetrators were not motivated by pure evil, in order to rebuild relationships between the two groups in the conflict, and to encourage bystanders to violence to take active steps to stop it. Mapping these recommendations onto virtuous violence theory, we would argue that key elements of violence reduction and prevention must involve understanding that perpetrators feel morally motivated in their actions; that the key to preventing violence lies in constituting supportive, non-violent relationships among the participants, particularly CS relationships that elicit a shared group identity; and that the meta-relationships within which relationships are embedded will be crucial in forcing potential perpetrators to understand the impacts that their violence has on all of their relationships and the relationships of everyone they relate with. Let us consider two approaches to this, the first based outside existing political structures, and the second within them.

Civil disobedience and hunger strikes

One of the rarest but most virtuous forms of morally motivated violence is that which non-violent protestors intentionally provoke against themselves, or foresee and accept, when they deliberately, publicly, and flagrantly resist illegitimate authority or unjust laws (Roberts and Ach, 2011). By blatantly violating illegitimate power, then accepting and nobly enduring the violent sanctions their civil disobedience likely evokes, those who civilly disobey shame the perpetrators of that violence and those who support or tolerate it. Similarly, the self-imposed suffering of hunger strikers shames those who would violently oppress them. Resisters' non-violent response to violence may make some perpetrators question the morality of their own violence; at a minimum, it disavows violent regulation of the relationship. However, these forms of non-violent resistance are metarelational, because their aim is not primarily to make the police or military perpetrators themselves feel guilty, but to shame those who command the enforcers to be violent, and especially to shame the supporters of those commanders, moving them to withdraw their support for the violent enforcement and, ultimately, for the authority and rules being enforced. Furthermore, by risking or even seeking violent punishment but not responding to violence with violence, the resisters demonstrate commitment to their cause and moral superiority over those who inflict the violence. Refusing to adopt violent means to resist the authority, even when they suffer violent retribution for their transgressions, the resisters delegitimate all violence, and hence delegitimate the policies and practices that can only be enforced with violence. Perhaps this is what Jesus intended when he preached that "If someone slaps you on one cheek, turn to them the other also" (New International Version, Luke 6:29, corresponding to Matthew 5:39).

The civil rights movement in the American South was based on the movement's use of Southern authorities' violence against them. Consider some of the events of the early 1960s:

> In some Southern counties, almost no African-Americans in the
> twentieth century had ever even attempted to register, so there
> were few cases to litigate. One goal of voter-registration drives was
> to build up the inventory of litigable cases.

The primary goal, though, was to provoke official reaction
sufficiently violent to compel the White House to produce a
voting-rights bill with enforcement bite. The provocation part
proved amazingly easy. All that the protesters had to do was to walk
to the courthouse and ask to register. There was nothing covert
about the strategy – "We are going to bring a voting bill into being in
the streets of Selma," King proclaimed from the pulpit of Selma's
Brown Chapel – yet Southern police, troopers, sheriffs, and deputies
clubbed, sicced police dogs on, blasted fire hoses at, teargassed,
and shocked with cattle prods nonviolent demonstrators, many of
them clergymen and children, with an indifference to national
and international opinion that was almost blithe. Their tactics
were encouraged, defended, and sometimes ordered by Southern
city halls and statehouses.

But in Birmingham, when the Commissioner of Public Safety,
Eugene (Bull) Connor, brought out the police dogs and fire
hoses, and in Selma, when Sheriff Jim Clark socked a black
minister, C. T. Vivian, in the face, reporters and cameramen
were right there. Many white Americans who saw or read
about the violence blamed the demonstrators, but the world
blamed the American government. That got the attention of the
White House.

Southern mayors and governors were playing to their
electoral bases. But American Presidents were trying to run a Cold
War. They could live with Jim Crow when it was an invisible
regional peculiarity, but once conditions were broadcast around the
world they experienced an urgent need to make the problem go
away.

The pressure of world opinion was crucial to the speed with which
civil-rights gains were made after 1954. It forced American
Presidents to do something...

Kennedy finally took the moral high ground and gave a
nationally televised speech on civil rights. A week later he delivered
a civil-rights bill to Congress... Less than three months later,
Kennedy was dead. Lyndon Johnson was known to civil-rights
leaders as the man who, when he was Senate Majority Leader, had
carefully emasculated Eisenhower's Civil Rights Bill in order to
secure enough Southern votes for passage. But, as President,
Johnson unexpectedly assumed the mantle of a crusader for racial
justice, and he pushed the 1964 Civil Rights Bill through the
longest filibuster in Senate history.

(Menand, 2013: 82–4)

As this illustrates, civil disobedience does not work unless a pivotal audience has common knowledge – everyone knows, knows that everyone knows, and knows that everyone knows that everyone knows, etc. – of the violence inflicted on the resisters. Nor does it work unless that audience morally condemns the punitive violence and reflects on the validity of inflicting it to regulate the existing relationships, and has the capacity to transform the social relationships that the resisters are disobeying. If the entire audience feels that the resisters deserve violent punishment for their disobedience, as many of the white American southerners at the time felt, civil disobedience fails. If the audience is indifferent to the suffering of the hunger strikers, or regards the relationships they are resisting as valid, self-starvation fails. So, ironically, for passive resistance to work, the audience, or at least an influential part of it, must form a relationship with the resisters in which violence is immoral. That relationship may be compassionate CS unity, protective AR hierarchy, fair EM quality, or utilitarian MP proportionality, so long as the audience implements the relationship such that the enforcers' violence against the resisters implicates the audience metarelationally. The audience must be horrified and ashamed, feel incriminated, and take indirect yet significant responsibility for the violence against the resisters. If they don't see the violence as illegitimate, the peaceful resistance fails. In the case of the civil rights movement, the global audience condemned the acts of southern forces, while national leaders and northerners felt implicated and ashamed by what was going on in their country.

The decision to use non-violent resistance to transform a political regime may be based on either moral or pragmatic foundations (Roberts and Ash, 2011). Empirically, non-violent resistance has sometimes been accompanied or followed by violent action by the resisters, or their predecessors, allies, or successors. The success of non-violent strategies may depend on support from nations or groups prepared to use violence to protect the resisters or advance their cause. However, it is striking that an analysis of 323 violent and non-violent resistance campaigns in the last century found that only 26% of the violent campaigns "succeeded," while 53% of the non-violent ones succeeded (Chenoweth and Stephan, 2011; Stephan and Chenoweth, 2008).

> There are two reasons for this success. First, a campaign's commitment to nonviolent methods enhances its domestic and

international legitimacy and encourages more broad-based participation in the resistance, which translates into increased pressure being brought to bear on the target. Recognition of the challenge group's grievances can translate into greater internal and external support for that group and alienation of the target regime, undermining the regime's main sources of political, economic, and even military power.

Second, whereas governments easily justify violent counterattacks against armed insurgents, regime violence against nonviolent movements is more likely to backfire against the regime. Potentially sympathetic publics perceive violent militants as having maximalist or extremist goals beyond accommodation, but they perceive nonviolent resistance groups as less extreme, thereby enhancing their appeal and facilitating the extraction of concessions through bargaining.

(Stephan and Chenoweth, 2008: 8–9)

We suggest that non-violent campaigns are also more likely to succeed than violent ones when and because the number of people willing to engage in non-violent resistance – even at great risk or certain harm to themselves – is orders of magnitude greater than the numbers willing to use violence against others. Of course, when social movements do succeed in transforming or replacing violent regimes, there is a danger that the successful leaders may themselves become violently oppressive. However, in addition to being more likely to succeed in their objectives, compared to violent insurrection, non-violent campaigns against repressive regimes are more likely to result in transitions to liberal democracies (Karatnycky, 2005). As Gandhi argued, the means are inseparable from the ends (Gandhi, 1998).

Since the metarelational impact of non-violent resistance depends on common knowledge, it is enormously potentiated by mass communication, and especially by mass exposure to images and videos of violent suppression of non-violent resistance. Furthermore, non-violent campaigns are inspired by and learn strategy and tactics from previously successful ones when people can readily learn about them through modern decentralized communications (Roberts and Ash, 2011; Stephan and Chenoweth, 2008). This presumably is a major factor in the extraordinarily rapid acceleration of the deployment of and participation in non-violent campaigns over the past century.

Urban gang homicide

> It is a world with its own rules, its own standards, its own
> misunderstandings. It *is* a community, make no mistake; it is a
> community were men will kill for their [gang] brothers, die for their
> brothers, where being a thug is a good and honorable thing, were
> *thug love* means having your brothers' backs, no matter what the
> cost... As long as the community of the streets sees itself as righteous
> and justified, the killing will continue. As long as the community of
> the streets sees its own neighborhoods as approving, it will continue.
> As long as the streets see the police as racist and hateful, it will
> continue.
>
> *(Kennedy, 2011: 20–1)*

In some cases, it is not enough that the larger society or world condemns
and punishes violence, because violence is a function of the moral
motives of the perpetrators and potential perpetrators themselves.
"Their own ideas about right and wrong matter most; the ideas of
those they care about and respect matter more" (Kennedy, 2009: 182).

To control violence associated with gangs and drug-dealing, for
many decades police forces in every city in the United States and many
other nations have used violence, often extreme violence, and mass
incarceration. It hasn't worked. However, with his colleagues and
associates, David M. Kennedy (2002, 2009, 2011) developed remark-
ably effective non-violent interventions to reduce gang- and drug-related,
urban American homicide. Essentially, Kennedy and his collaborators
found that when perpetrators get the message that violence against anyone violates the perpetrators' relationships with everyone, violence
diminishes. The core of the program consists of meetings in which
influential local leaders, speaking for the community, publicly tell the
principal perpetrators that killing is intolerable, and victims and
bereaved families confront the killers with the social consequences of
killing (Kennedy, 2002, 2009, 2011). Swift and certain legal sanctions
are used alongside these meetings, but are insufficient by themselves:
family members and respected community leaders must clearly and
forcefully state that violence is *wrong*. "People care about what other
people think. Social-bonding theory suggests that those with strong ties
to others, and with "investments" in those ties, will be less likely to risk
those ties and those investments by offending" (Kennedy, 2009: 32).

The "Cure Violence" program in Chicago, previously known as CeaseFire Chicago, enacted similar strategies and had similar success, reducing gun violence by 40–70% in all of the areas in which the program operated (Hartnett *et al.*, 2008). "Cure Violence" was built on the assumption that violence spreads like an infectious disease, and so violence must be stopped at the source of the outbreak. In our terms, violence is embedded in metarelational models where any single act of violence can lead to violence being morally required in the connecting relations. "Cure Violence" employs "interrupters" to reach out and stop potential perpetrators from engaging in violence, especially when someone is considering retaliation in response to an attack on their loved ones. The documentary *The Interrupters* (James, 2011) depicts this process, as in this exchange between a community member referred to as Flammo and the interrupter Cobe.

Flammo: Fuck a problem. Fuck a solution. You ain't just crossed me, you cross my fuckin' mama. For my mama nigger I come in your crib and kill every motherfuckin' body.

Cobe: Two of your brothers gone. If you be gone that ain't gonna do nothin' but hurt your mama.

Oftentimes, the interrupters use the potential perpetrators' relationships as a starting point for engaging in discussions about non-violence, such as when the interrupter Tio is talking to two brothers, Kenneth and Bud, who are affiliated with rival gangs.

Tio: I ain't putting you on the spot, but if they came at your brother, would you stop them?

Kenneth: Yeah.

Tio: You would. Okay. (To Bud) The clique you in, if they came at your brother, would you stop them?

Bud: Of course.

Crucially, the interrupters must be respected members of the community, which in these communities often means being a former gang member themselves.

Tio: Most of the violence interrupters come from the hierarchy in some of these gangs. Because can't no anybody come in and tell a guy to put his gun down.

When potential perpetrators respect and are socially connected to the person telling them to refrain from violence, and when interrupters convey to the potential perpetrator that violence is not the answer and that it will carry immense consequences for all of their relationships and the relationships of all of their loved ones, perpetrators do restrain themselves from killing. In our terms, interrupters make clear to potential perpetrators the metarelationships within which their actions are embedded, thus convincing them that violence is not the optimal way to regulate their relationships.

> Cobe: But shit you look like you doin' great.
> Flammo: Tryin' to do stuff positive and seein' how it workin'. And
>   I ain't been to jail, I ain't been arguin' and fightin'. I ain't
>   been havin' to shoot nobody.
> Cobe: Man I just so happy for you. I promise you boy, I'm so
>   happy for you man.
> Flammo: I hope you do feel good about yourself. Cuz, to keep it
>   real with you man, I had like three, four people lined up.
>   And I was really plottin' on how to get them. But you was
>   just in my ear, you know what I'm sayin'?

While the deterrence strategies used by these programs are designed specifically to target criminal violence committed by young men in gangs or networks, many of the basic principles of their interventions can be generalized to point to ways of reducing other kinds of culturally condoned violence. Retheorized and expanded in terms of virtuous violence theory, de-emphasizing the forms of deterrence whose relevance is limited to crime, and with a few additions, steps to reduce any kind of violence might consist of:

1. Generate precedents, prototypes, and precepts for non-violent relationship regulation.
2. Generate precedents, prototypes, and precepts that prohibit violent relationship regulation.
3. Generate metarelational models that make important and desirable social relationships follow from and contingent on non-violent relationship regulation. Thus, make peaceful relationship regulation reliably foster other good relationships.
4. Conversely, make violent regulation of any relationship irreconcilable with positive relationships with the perpetrator of violence.

Publicly demonstrate to perpetrators that their violence hurts good people whom they should care about, and whom the people they care about care about. Shame, shun, and ostracize those who are violent to anyone.

5. Make these preos and metarelational models definite and clear, so there is no latitude or ambiguity about the unacceptability of violent relationship regulation.

6. Develop near-unanimous consensus among the primary groups, reference groups, and respected leaders of potential perpetrators, ensuring that nearly everyone adopts the peaceful preos and the metarelational models that ensure them.

7. Ensure that these preos and metarelational models are universal common knowledge: everyone knows them, everyone knows that everyone else knows them, and everyone knows that everyone else knows that everyone else knows them.

To enact these prescriptions will always be a challenge, but they can be enacted, and often have been. For, ultimately, these steps characterize what cultural change consists of: consensual transformation of preos and metarelational models.

If we fail to take these steps – if we fail to change the cultures of violence – people will continue to hurt and kill each other to regulate their relationships. Taking these steps to change our cultures is the only way to reduce morally motivated violence. We can do it and we must. People hurt and kill because they feel that they should; if their own primary reference groups make them feel they *shouldn't* be violent, they won't be. If violence is immoral, people generally won't do it.

We are not moral philosophers, and as scientists we are skeptical about whether any objective foundation can be established for prescriptive ethics. We doubt that moral prescriptions can ever be logically derived from empirical facts or analytic principles. Nevertheless, as humans, we have to make moral choices and judgments. Even though we cannot ground our actions in purely logical reasoning from irrefutably true premises, the foundation for our choices and judgments ought to be as coherently articulated as possible, so as to guide us as clearly as possible in difficult circumstances. We all want to live in a world where we don't have to hurt others, we don't have to fear being hurt, and we don't get hurt. To do so, we must cultivate a morality of non-violence. Violence is not the only way to constitute social relationships, it's not the predominant way to constitute relationships, and it's not necessary for constituting good relationships. We *can* motivate ourselves to constitute our relationships gently. That is what we must do.

Morality is culturally informed relationship regulation, so just what is moral depends on the cultural preos for the relationships we form. And we are perfectly capable of forming tolerant, forgiving, caring, compassionate relationships – they are just as natural, indeed, evidently more natural, than violent relationships. The huge preponderance of relationship regulation is non-violent: we all regulate all sorts of relationships day after day without any violence. And all of the constitutive phases of all sorts of relationships that in earlier millennia, previous centuries, and past decades most people often regulated violently, nearly everyone now regulates peacefully (Pinker, 2011). So violence *is not necessary* to regulate relationships.

There is a clear and simple implication of the thesis that most violence is morally motivated to regulate relationships in accord with cultural implementations of the four fundamental RMs: *to reduce violence we must make it immoral.* And we *can* make violence immoral. People have many competing moral motives; our disposition to violently constitute our relationships is only one among many, many dispositions, all just as natural as our disposition to violence. We can cultivate, combine, and call upon these non-violent moral dispositions to block the disposition to violence. If it is common knowledge that everyone unequivocally condemns violence, and there are clear and respectable cultural guidelines for regulating relationships non-violently, people will regulate their relationships non-violently. Preos in some cultures at some points in history guide people to violently perform some of the constitutive phases of some relationships. But other cultural preos guide people to perform those same constitutive phases in other, non-violent ways – and these preos are progressively replacing the preos that orient people to regulate their relationships violently (Pinker, 2011). The same moral motives to regulate relationships may generate violent or non-violent relationship regulation, depending on the culture. So it's the culture we must change.

24 EVOLUTIONARY, PHILOSOPHICAL, LEGAL, PSYCHOLOGICAL, AND RESEARCH IMPLICATIONS

Evolution

Virtuous violence theory is an explanation for *human* violence, but naturally one would like to know whether it is "natural" for violence to be morally motivated. Has *Homo sapiens* been morally violent since the species emerged? Do other primates shape their social relationships violently? How early in life do moral motives for violence emerge?

In fact, *Homo sapiens* is not the only species that uses violence to constitute social relationships. In non-human animals, violence is not simply a way of gaining access to resources: it is about regulating relationships. And in certain circumstances, it may be evolutionarily adaptive to violently regulate social relationships. As de Waal (1992: 43) points out, "aggressive behavior is not by definition antisocial or maladaptive." As in humans, much of the aggression observed in non-human primates and other mammals enforces social coordination and indirectly promotes cohesion, or organizes dominance relations that are adaptively beneficial for all participants. For example, in captive chimpanzees and other primates, reconciliation after conflict results in increased proximity after fights, compared to other times. De Waal (1992: 45) also observed that in captive chimpanzees, stinginess in food sharing is "sanctioned" by aggression. In cercopithecine monkeys (vervets, baboons, etc.), "older relatives (e.g., mothers) use aggressive behavior to punish and inhibit 'unacceptable' behavior patterns in young monkeys" (p. 46). De Waal interprets this aggression as "teaching" and "active socialization" (p. 49). Although one might argue that he uses these terms in an overly broad and anthropomorphic sense, the violence he describes and analyzes is certainly constitutive of relationships, and evidently intended to do so.

As in humans, non-human relationship-constitutive violence is often organized by metarelational models. There is ample evidence in non-human primates and many other animals of male violence and threat of violence to keep their mates from consorting or mating with other males. Moreover, in many primate species and a number of other mammals and birds, a third party may intervene in ways that tend to halt conflicts between two animals, either by threatening or attacking one or both combatants or by making affiliative gestures toward either or both (e.g., Petit and Thierry, 1994; see Fiske, 2011). For example, silverback gorillas frequently intervene in conflicts between females and in conflicts involving immature members of their troop, usually supporting the younger of the immature opponents (Boehm, 1999: 155; Robbins, 2007). Social mammals are often organized into matrilines or coalitions in which violence by a member of one group against a member of a second group evokes "retaliatory" violence by *another* member of the second group against *any* member of the first group. Captive juvenile rooks (*Corvus frugilegus*, in the crow family) form partnerships both across and within sex. Compared with control periods, after a fight between two birds that belong to different partnerships, the victim's partner is more likely to attack the aggressor, the victim is more likely to attack the aggressor's partner, and the victim's partner is more likely to attack the aggressor's partner (Emery *et al.*, 2007). Similarly, in baboons, rhesus macaques, Japanese macaques, vervet monkeys, and spotted hyenas, when animals from different matrilineal kin groups fight, members of the matrilines who were not involved in the original conflict are more likely to attack members of the other matriline in the ensuing hours (Cheney and Seyfarth, 1992, 2007: 96–103; Engh *et al.*, 2005). This tit-for-tat retaliation regulates the social relationships between groups.

It appears that even human babies are naturally predisposed toward virtuous violence before they have had much, if any, opportunities for relevant social learning. In a series of studies, Hamlin and colleagues (Hamlin *et al.*, 2007, 2011) found that infants as young as 3 months preferred "helper" blocks that aid a "struggling" block up an incline, compared to "hinderer" blocks that push the struggling block down. Hamlin also found that infants as young as 8 months preferred a puppet who helped a previously helpful puppet to one who hindered a previously helpful puppet. Critically for virtuous violence theory, Hamlin found that infants preferred a puppet that "punished" a previously antisocial puppet to a puppet that helped a previously antisocial puppet (Hamlin *et al.*, 2011). In other words, infants are predisposed toward what appears to be moralistic third-party punishment. These findings indicate that young infants do not have a simple aversion to harmful behavior that blocks another's intentions, but actually think through metarelational moralistic models that motivate their affiliative choices.

Philosophy

Our objective in this book is primarily descriptive and explanatory, not prescriptive. When we write that violence is morally motivated, we are not justifying violence; we are simply describing the motives, emotions, and judgments of perpetrators. As we stated in the previous chapter, a natural disposition to constitute social relationships violently does not legitimate doing so. Ubiquity is not license. The fact that violence *is* widely used to constitute relationships, and the fact that human perpetrators feel and judge that their violence is moral, does not imply that everyone must make the same judgment. To infer *ought* from *is* would be to commit the naturalistic fallacy (Moore, 1903). *The validity of the description* of the perpetrator's state of mind and the cultural morality in which it is embedded *does not imply the prescription* that anyone else is ethically required to make the same judgment, or feel the same way about the violence.

But our sense of right and wrong has to come from somewhere. When the scientist claims that in spite of a natural predisposition toward violence we should continue to work toward non-violence, the scientist is ignoring the fact that her own belief in non-violence is itself based in natural predispositions instantiated in the particular cultural conditions to which the scientist is attuned. The scientist is implicitly stating that *we as a society* have determined what is morally right and wrong without reflecting on *why* her particular society has deemed some actions right and other actions wrong.

Ethical naturalism refers to the position that any prescriptive ethics must be based on the needs, desires, and goods that people are naturally predisposed toward. From this perspective, prescriptive ethics should be geared toward facilitating human welfare, or human flourishing, by prescribing how best to achieve the basic goods that people are naturally predisposed toward. Ethical naturalism denies the validity of any prescriptive ethics based either on supernatural beliefs or on "moral realist" approaches that rely on rules of logic independent of human experience, such as Kant's categorical imperative (1989/1785). Regarding deontic moral prescriptions based on pure logic, Flanagan et al. (2008) write, "[S]uch theories affirm a metaphysical thesis which naturalists deny – namely, the existence of irreducible and non-natural moral facts or properties" (p. 5). For ethical naturalists, empirical science plays a crucial role in any prescriptive ethics because it has the power to identify the basic human goods that people are naturally predisposed toward, as well as the conditions that support those goods. As Flanagan et al. (pp. 15–16) put it, "the ends of creatures constrain what is good for them," "morality cannot seek to instantiate behavior that no human beings have a propensity to seek," and "there are a limited number of goods that human beings seek given their nature and potentialities."

We agree wholeheartedly with the naturalist approach, and in this book and elsewhere (Rai and Fiske, 2011, 2012), we have argued that among the goods essential to human flourishing are in fact social-relational goods potentiated and constrained by the four RMs. At the same time, we believe that the insight that violence is morally motivated to regulate relationships according to the four RMs raises a difficult set of challenges for ethical naturalism. First, there are multiple ways to achieve what people perceive as moral goods, some of which include violence. In this sense, violence may be gratifying, and under certain conditions can contribute to human welfare. As we have seen throughout the book, initiatory violence creates long-lasting CS relationships that bind groups together; some violence is intrinsic to the conduct of certain relationships, without which they would cease to exist; protective and redressive violence keeps people from violating their relational obligations; and so forth. Second – and this problem is not unique to violence – some social-relational goods, particularly those related to AR, are at complete odds with the prescriptive ethics favored by Western liberals, which is strictly antiauthority and favors equality of all. How do we satisfy needs and desires to achieve status and to rank ourselves within a hierarchy, to follow inspiring leaders, and to wisely guide and protect loyal followers if we are also motivated by an EM ethics to make everyone equal? Finally, many of the problems related to violence are exacerbated at the level of groups, as they fight to satisfy AR hierarchy and CS unity motives. If these are the goods that humans seek, what does a naturalized ethics prescribe?

We don't know the answers to these questions. We suspect that part of the answer will require acknowledging that some sorts of AR are actually conducive to human welfare when well implemented: parents, teachers, officers, chairpersons, CEOs, mayors, and presidents can lead in good ways that benefit their followers, so it can often be good to follow legitimate leaders loyally. Another part of the answer will require faith that if and when people *can* constitute the social relationships that make life meaningful through non-violent means, they will.

Knowing that our violence is naturally predisposed, and knowing that in many times and cultures, violence has been widely condoned, should make us keenly aware that any current, culturally particular beliefs in the moral superiority of non-violence are empirically tied to the socioecological conditions within which non-violence is adaptive. Prescriptively, in order to maintain and enhance moral motives for non-violence, we must descriptively understand the socioecological conditions that give rise to it, including the shifts from primarily CS and AR relationships to EM and MP relationships, the greater relational mobility to leave unsatisfying relationships, and the embedding of social relationships in the cross-cutting ties of metarelationships.

Some people may see the use of empirical science as a means to inform our prescriptive ethics as inherently wrong. They may object to the entire enterprise. Indeed, we have seen many instances in recent years and throughout modern history of scientists attempting to justify the superiority of their own particular Western, liberal, secular beliefs by invoking scientific findings that either presuppose the goods that people should pursue or that identify universal human goods on the basis of studies of their own particular culture. But it is precisely because science has failed on so many occasions that we cannot give up on its potential to guide prescriptive ethics. Everyone is using *some* framework to figure out how to lead a good life – the issue is simply whether they've reflected deeply about the framework they're using or not, and whether they are aware of the cultural and historical dimensions of moral motives. In other words, anyone's intuitive sense of right and wrong must come from somewhere. We need cultural psychology and psychological anthropology to discover where our moral intuitions come from, to identify the social-relational goods that we are trying to satisfy, and to delineate the conditions that will be most conducive to achieving those goods and facilitating human welfare through non-violent means. No doubt we will make mistakes in this process, but that's true of any theory that people use to guide their actions, implicit or explicit, scientific or non-scientific.

Law

The quandary comes down to this. We are morally opposed to violence, yet we know that perpetrators of violence are morally motivated – and that perhaps we ourselves could experience or even act on similar motives under certain circumstances. Perhaps we, or you, have already committed morally motivated violence on the football field, or when punishing a child, or in a fight, or in a jury vote to condemn a defendant. So we are facing two conflicting moral frameworks. The perpetrator (perhaps ourselves) says her violence is right, good, and obligatory, while another person (perhaps ourselves, as perpetrator at a later point in time, as observer, or as victim) says that the violence is wrong – that all violence is wrong.

So while we are not legal scholars, let alone jurists, it seems to us that virtuous violence theory has potentially far-reaching implications for the criminal justice system, and for law itself. First, virtuous violence theory suggests that the deterrent effect of criminal punishment will be limited if perpetrators feel and judge that they are morally obligated to do violence, and that merely pragmatic consequences of the action are less important. Penal "rehabilitation" will be most effective if it changes perpetrators' moral frameworks such that they no longer feel or believe that their violence is right. Virtuous violence theory also appears to be relevant to sentencing for crimes. If sincere expression of remorse is to be a mitigating factor in sentencing, does this imply that sincerely moral motivations for violence must be punished more severely than amoral motives, because the sincerely moral perpetrator cannot honestly feel remorse unless he has changed his moral framework? One cannot expect the perpetrator to feel entirely remorseful if she did what she felt was right, and still thinks so.

Even more fundamentally, virtuous violence theory bears on the adjudication of legal responsibility. Under the M'Naghten rules, a defendant cannot be judged guilty if he "did not know he was doing what was wrong" due to "a disease of the mind." There is considerable ambiguity as to whether the defendant must know that what he was doing was legally wrong or morally wrong, but US courts have tended to interpret this insanity defense in terms of knowledge that an act was morally wrong (Packer, 2009: 36–8). Among US jurisdictions that apply the moral standard, there are differences in whether the defendant must have the capacity to know that her act is "objectively" wrong by "societal" standards, or whether a defendant should be allowed to plead that, while she recognized that her act was wrong by societal standards, it was nevertheless morally justified by her own "subjective" standards (Packer, 2009: 38–42). From the evidence we have collected, it certainly appears that most perpetrators feel that their acts are morally justified with reference to the moral code they share with their reference group, local community, and subculture. Under another standard that prevails in many jurisdictions, the American Law Institute (ALI)'s Model Penal Code (1985, Sec. 4.01), "a person is not responsible for criminal conduct if at the time of such conduct as a result of mental disease or defect he lacks substantial capacity to either appreciate the criminality of his conduct or to conform his conduct to the requirements of the law" (this is sometimes known as the Brawner rule). Of course, a moral framework that motivates and legitimates violence is not a disease of the mind or a mental defect, but the M'Naghten and Brawner rules seem to implicitly assume that there is no other possible cause for a defendant not knowing that he was doing what was wrong. The American Law Institute's Model Penal Code also allows for reduction of a murder charge to manslaughter if the homicide was

> Committed under the influence of extreme mental or emotional
> disturbance for which there is a reasonable explanation or excuse.
> The reasonableness of such explanation or excuse shall be
> determined from the viewpoint of a person in the actor's situation
> under the circumstances as he believes them to be.
> *(ALI, 1985, Section 210.3[1][b], quoted by Packer, 2009: 19–20)*

The evidence we have collected in this book suggests that from perfectly sane perpetrators' viewpoints many homicides – and other forms of violence – are morally "reasonable" within their reference group and local community under the culturally constituted circumstances perceived by the perpetrator.

These rules all function within the broader scope of the Anglo-Saxon doctrine of *mens rea*, which boils down to the concept that a person's guilt or liability for a penal sentence depends not only on what they did but also on the mental state that led to the action. The concept of *mens rea* grew out of a judgment that people are guilty only if they intended to do wrong:

> The first and historically original concept embodied an explicitly normative requirement that the offender not only intentionally commit a criminal act, but also do so out of evil motivation. The second and currently more predominant tradition adopts an essentially nonnormative approach that finds sufficient ground for liability in the presence of particular states of mind without evaluating or even appealing to the motives underlying the offender's actions. As will be shown, however, the "evil motive" tradition has not been totally abandoned.
>
> *(Gardner, 1993: 640)*

In practice, contemporary jurisprudence still makes guilt highly contingent on the perpetrator's having "the evil motive essential for moral blame"; for most crimes, the defendant is typically guilty only if her intent is wicked – that is, if she meant to be immoral (Gardner, 1993: 693; see also 695–750).

Mens rea doctrines have generally been concerned with the intent to cause the effects (e.g., death), or at least the intent to do harm of some sort, or reckless disregard of the risk that doing the intended harm could have further harmful consequences. Jurists and legal scholars have usually taken for granted that everyone knows that it is wrong to do harm. In the rare instances where legal theorists have recognized that defendants might think it right to do harm, the theorists have argued that it is impractical to allow exculpation based on sincerely virtuous motivations embedded in moral systems other than the one that forms the basis for the state's criminal code (Gardner, 1993: 687). "Furthermore, if a subjective criterion of malice were adopted, it would seriously challenge the authority of criminal law by allowing [each individual] to set his own standards rather than conform to a general code of conduct applicable to all citizens" (p. 715).

Thus, the fundamental Anglo-Saxon legal idea represented by the term *mens rea* seems to be that a person is guilty and should be punished if he thought "this is wrong, but I'm going to do it anyway," and then acted to cause harm. But as we've seen, this is not at all what's going through the minds of most people doing violence. So this leaves us asking both the moral and the legal questions, "if a mentally healthy person honestly and firmly believed that it was right to do violence – indeed, that he had a moral obligation to be violent in this way – should that be exculpatory?" More fundamentally, what is the moral meaning or legal purpose of punishing people for doing what they sincerely believed they ought to do? Does it make sense to punish people for acting on their moral convictions? The answer, we suppose, depends on the purpose of punishment (is the aim deterrence or retribution?), whether one believes that the perpetrator is embedded within a metarelational model of the state and therefore must always act within that web of interrelations, and perhaps, ultimately, on whether punishment ever makes sense.

Psychology

In many cultures, parents and schoolteachers hit or whip children for misconduct, and everyone feels sure that children who misbehave *should* be beaten. Is the fear, the experience, or the memory of being *legitimately and properly* beaten traumatic? That is, if the victim knows that the perpetrator was truly morally motivated, is violence traumatic? In cultures where parents are *supposed* to beat misbehaving children, parents have regularly beaten billions of children – without apparently traumatic effects. Does this suggest that the perception that the violence was evil is necessary for the fear, experience, or memory of it to be traumatic? (Of course, it's conceivable that many or all children who've been beaten actually have suffered traumatic effects that have simply been taken for granted as normal aspects of personality in these many cultures.)

What are the short- and long-term effects on the victim if the victim understands that the perpetrator was morally motivated, but the victim herself feels that the harm was undeserved, and indeed wrong?

What about the effects on the perpetrators of their own moral motives and judgments? Is it more traumatic for the perpetrator if she kills or injures someone accidentally than if she does it with moral motives? What are the effects on the perpetrator of doing violence that she perceived as immoral, but was selfishly motivated to do? Or suppose a father beats his son because everyone in the community, including his wife, the boy's mother, is certain that beatings are essential to raising a God-fearing, conscientious child – but the father personally thinks it's wrong. Is it traumatic for the father to do violence that he felt was wrong, but was socially pressured to do, and was well regarded for doing? If men and women believe that a husband is entitled to have sex with his wife whenever he wishes, and may justifiably use force against her if she resists – and if they both know that men often do use force to overcome their wives' resistance – is the violence less traumatic in its immediate and long-term effects than a husband's rape of his wife in a culture in which such force is understood to be immoral and illegal? That is, is it the violence as such that is psychologically harmful, or does the harm largely or partly result from experiencing the violence as *transgressive*?

There is a temporal dimension to these questions, because what perpetrators or victims perceive to be moral at the moment they may later perceive to be wrong. Does the retrospective judgment or feeling that it was evil make the pain or suffering more traumatic, even if at the time it felt right? If a victim of incest or child sexual abuse didn't know at the time that it was wrong, but later discovers that it was, does this subsequent discovery cause additional psychological harm? Conversely, what if a person perpetrates or experiences what he perceives at the time to be selfish, immorally motivated violence but later comes to unequivocally believe that it was, after all, in fact, fully justified and morally necessary? Does that make the experience less traumatic later? People may attempt to alleviate their guilt through self-punishment (Nielssen and Zeelenberg, 2009). So perhaps if victims feel that they deserve punishment for a transgression they committed, they might feel *more* pain, compared to the pain from harm they experience as unjustified.

Finally, there is some suggestion that when the violence is perceived to be morally wrong, the perpetrator's apology, punishment, or payment of compensation is a relief to both the perpetrator and the victim. How do such redressive, rectificatory actions assuage the trauma? Do truth and reconciliation reduce the traumatic effects of violence experienced as evil? How does their effect on trauma compare with the effects of punishment, or compensation?

Virtually all research on trauma conflates pain with evil, but if we appreciate that inflicting pain may be morally motivated and may be experienced as morally necessary, we have to ask whether that which is traumatic is the fear or memory of pain as such, or is it the experience of suffering evil that traumatizes?

Research

To understand *Homo sapiens*, it is crucial to begin with a comprehensive, thorough knowledge of the natural history of the beast in its natural setting. Until we know how humans act and interact in the wild (that is, outside the scientific laboratory) *across the full spectrum of cultures and into the depths of time*, we cannot understand their action or interaction. We can't understand people by only studying what they are doing in just one setting at one time in one culture – with those blinders narrowly focusing our investigation, we can't understand what they are doing *even in that one setting, time, and culture*. We need to appreciate the full range of human behavior in order to understand behavior in any specific instance, whether that instance is a particular natural practice or a response to a contemporary psychological laboratory experiment.

Most previous theories of violence and most previous descriptive theories of morality have been derived from the explicit or implicit folk theories of the theorist's specific culture, together with the theorist's experiences in his or her own culture. Most theorists have had very limited knowledge and less understanding of other cultures, and none have systematically explored their ideas across the wide range of cultures and times. Hence, in this book we have made every effort to collect observations from around the world and across history. Of course, our search was far from exhaustive, and existing sources are not in any way statistically representative of the species. Nor could we randomly sample existing sources, given that we needed detailed, deep ethnographic accounts of perpetrators' subjective perspective. But in a wide selection of research on a great variety of violent practices in diverse cultures, we found that perpetrators' motives are so consistently moral that we are confident about our conclusions. Since these conclusions contrast rather dramatically with the conclusions of most other theories of violence (except those of Pinker and Black), what are the implications of our findings for methodology in the social and behavioral sciences? We believe that, instead of deductively formulating theory starting with philosophical conceptions or armchair speculation, psychologists and other social scientists would often do better to begin by observing natural behavior, making comparisons of human actions across the widest spectrum of settings and cultures, and from these wide-ranging collections of real-world behavior, searching for patterns and deriving theory inductively.

Sometimes Western philosophy – in this case, Western folk and moral philosophy – is a poor guide to psychology, human or even merely Western. Armchair reasoning based on folk theory and intuition, explored though experimentation that isolates responses to artificially constructed stimuli, often leads away from the real world. This is especially true when the researchers are contemporary Westerners, because in most respects contemporary Western society and culture are unlike most other contemporary or historical human societies or cultures, and hence are poor foundations for understanding the sociality of *Homo sapiens* (Human Relations Area Files; Murdock, 1967). Likewise, the psychology of Western, educated, industrial, rich, democratic (WEIRD) populations is quite atypical of the psychology of the human species (Henrich *et al.*, 2010). Even if our goal were so limited that we only wished to understand WEIRD humans, we must situate their psychology and sociality in the entire spectrum of humanity, because we need to understand why their psychology and sociality are so weird.

When we first started this project, I (TsR) was hesitant because although I felt the thesis had merit, I could not imagine how to investigate it experimentally. Only now, after deeply thinking through these issues and consulting the ethnographic and historical evidence, have the experimental directions become clear, and in fact, obvious. For the experimental psychologist interested in running laboratory studies of violence, there are several empirical research avenues that follow from the ethnological finding that across cultures and throughout history, most violence is morally motivated.

1. At the most basic level, any controlled studies of first-person accounts of violence among either criminal or civilian populations should reveal the presence of moral motives, and these motives will be more prevalent than evidence of self-regulatory failure, instrumental gain, moral disengagement, dehumanization, or sadistic pleasure and psychopathy.
2. Meanwhile, if some violence is seen as *obligatory*, then doing violence requires increased self-regulatory control. A parent who hates to see his child in pain but knows that a good spanking is what the child

needs will be less likely to be able to carry out the punishment when he is tired or his self-control is otherwise diminished. We predict that support for some forms of costly punishment, the kind of punishment that the actor believes is right and obligatory but that requires self-control, will be reduced under conditions of depletion, challenging the view that self-regulatory failure always increases the likelihood of violence.

3. Regarding rationalist approaches to violence, we have already discussed Jeremy Ginges and Scott Atran's work (Ginges *et al.*, 2007; Ginges and Atran, 2009, 2011) demonstrating that the addition of material incentives for peace can actually increase support for violence. We propose that in the same way that the addition of material incentives often weakens intrinsic motivation (Deci *et al.*, 1999; Heyman and Ariely, 2004), providing material incentives to engage in violent action may lead participants to consider the violence in instrumental rather than moral terms. Hence, adding material incentives when none are currently present may *reduce* the propensity to engage in violence if the material benefits are small and the potential costs are great.

4. To the extent that dehumanization does facilitate violence, we should expect *selective dehumanization* of victims to occur, depending on the moral motives of the perpetrators, such that different kinds of violence may be tied to different kinds of dehumanization when it actually occurs. Thus, there is no reason to expect victims of retributive punishment or revenge to be deprived of mental capacities related to feeling pain, as this is necessary for the violence to have its intended effect, nor should the victim be deprived of capacities for reason or intention, as they are what make the victim deserving of punishment. Victims may, however, be deprived of certain moral emotions, such as compassion or empathy. But, of course, victims of initiation rites such as genital excision or violent hazing are often beloved members of the community, so they should be seen as capable of having moral emotions, and to the extent that their stoic endurance of pain is a crucial aspect of the initiation, they should be seen as capable of feeling pain as well. Only under conditions where perpetrators harm someone they are not morally motivated to harm (i.e., the motivation is non-moral) or where they are a passive third-party to harm, do we expect perpetrators to fail to perceive their victims as experiencing pain.

5. If violence is morally motivated to satisfy relational aims, then support for specific forms of violence will depend on the RM and corresponding moral motive people are using. For example, collateral damage, wherein some innocents are sacrificed in order to bring about a greater benefit, should be seen as more morally right when people are relating according to MP, but should be seen as more morally reprehensible when people are relating according to CS, wherein we are all in this together and anyone's pain is my own pain. Similarly, when relating according to EM, people will feel that a person is required by equality to respond to violence with the same violence in return, but when relating according to AR, people will feel that violence may be committed only by superiors toward subordinates, not vice versa.

These are just a few of the research directions that emerge only after careful consideration of the ethnological literature on motives for violence. We have also considered the possibility that propensities to engage in violence may depend on the relational mobility and metarelational ties of the partners, and in the previous section we asked whether it might be possible that pain that the victim perceives as moral, legitimate, and deserved may actually *feel* different than pain the victim perceives as immorally suffered. Let's find out.

THE DÉNOUEMENT

What do we mean by "most" violence?

Reviewing a multitude of literatures, we've been impressed by how much violence seems to be morally motivated. But given the available data, there is no way to quantify the proportion of violence, or the proportion of specific forms of violence, such as homicide, that are morally motivated to regulate social relationships. Some violence is just coercive force instrumentally used in pursuit of non-social aims. As we've discussed, psychopaths commit a significant proportion of the violence that is not morally motivated, though there are few data to indicate what that proportion is. However, we can greatly advance our understanding of violence without waiting for an answer. Newton didn't show what proportion of the motion of objects his laws explained, and a general answer isn't very meaningful, in any case. To describe and predict the motion of objects, we know that friction has to be taken into account in certain cases, but in many cases can be ignored for all practical purposes. Newton's laws are poor descriptions of motions at relativistic velocities or on quantum dimensions, they make the false, simplifying assumption that objects are points in space, and they can't provide exact analytic solutions for the motions of three or more bodies. Still, Newton's three laws of motion are extremely general and useful, elegantly describing a huge range of dynamic systems. Likewise, virtuous violence theory makes simplifying assumptions and may not explain violence under the most extreme conditions. But we believe that our theory parsimoniously and clearly describes most violence under most ordinary conditions in all cultures throughout history and prehistory. There are other, non-moral motives for violence. But until we account for the major mechanism, we can't identify the minor ones, can't understand the conditions under which each source operates, and can't figure out how different sources of violence interact. Until Darwin described natural selection, it wasn't possible to identify or delineate sexual selection, genetic drift, population-isolation factors, and other mechanisms of evolution. Likewise, without acknowledging that the prevalent forms of violence are morally motivated and culturally legitimated, we will never adequately understand differences in propensities for violence across cultures, among individuals, across the life span, or between genders.

Marx didn't tell us how much of social organization was explained by the organization of the economy, Durkheim didn't address the question of what proportion of social solidarity results from religious ritual, and Weber didn't say to what extent power relies on legitimation. We still don't know. But when we want to understand social systems, solidarity, or power, we know where to focus our attention – we know where to start looking. When we see violence, we should start by asking whether and how it was morally motivated, which social relationships it might have been aimed to regulate, and how it regulated them.

The need for general explanations

Our theory is simple, but we ourselves are not so simple-minded as to believe that our theory *fully* accounts for the violence of any particular act, any historical event, any individual, or any cultural practice or social institution. No theory can reveal with any certainty the causes of any particular event – that's not what theory does. In the real world, there are always myriad, complexly interacting influences on anything that happens. Particular cases are always mysterious and unpredictable, and ultimately not fully explicable. But it is not the aim or task of science to explain individual cases. The goal is to explain what would otherwise be disparate, perplexing particularities by providing elegantly parsimonious accounts for the aggregate patterns and consistencies that obtain in a population of observations. To theorize is to discern and describe the patterns, to characterize the regularities of an infinitely complex world as precisely, concisely, and validly as possible. Science is simplification.

Many anthropologists and humanists are skeptical about general accounts and instead aim to understand particular persons, particular events, or particular cultural practices in particular communities at particular points in history. Many contemporary anthropologists believe that actions are so embedded in unique contextual webs of context that no general theories are possible or plausible. From this perspective, the best account of an event or practice is an elaboration of the complexity of its roots and the subtle nuances of the interactions among the contributing factors. Yet a crucial aspect of describing human action, let alone understanding it, is providing an account of the motivational, emotional, normative, phenomenological, and intentional bases for action. Understanding of this sort has to build on *some* foundation and to frame and explain action with respect to *some* framework: in this case, foundations and framework comprising axioms about what moves people, what constrains people, what sorts of intentions people have. Thus, to make sense, even the most particularistic accounts must be based on assumptions regarding the bases of human action. In practice, these assumptions are quite often implicit, unexamined assumptions unreflectively borrowed from the interpreter's culturally and historically shaped folk theories. We suggest that accounts of particular violent persons, events, and cultural practices will be more valid, more profound, more insightful, and more illuminating if the accounts are based on the realization that most violence is morally motivated to regulate social relationships.

In this book we aimed to show that moral motives to regulate social relationships are the major factor generating most violence, but not the only factor, and not all violence; moral motivation is not a completely exhaustive explanation for any violence. But it's usually fundamental. And, of course, it is not the "truth" about violence in any final or ultimate sense. It is just the best we can do at this point in the history of science; it will surely be superseded sooner or later by theories with greater scope, greater precision, or more elegant parsimony.

We acknowledge all of the complexities and uncertainties, and we look forward to their resolution. But a good theory should be elegantly parsimonious, capturing the most important patterns in the simplest possible characterization. And a good book should not aim to emulate an encyclopedia. So virtuous violence theory intentionally ignores the messiness of violence in order to characterize its principal patterns as elegantly as possible. The idea that most violence is morally motivated to regulate crucial relationships is parsimonious and captures the crux of the matter. That idea provides something else that a theory should provide: new and fruitful questions to ask. When we encounter violence, we can ask,

> Is it morally motivated?
> Which RM is the person constituting?
> Which constitutive phases is the violence intended to realize?
> What are the metarelationships that facilitate or inhibit the violence?
> What led the perpetrator to use violence to regulate the relationship, rather than alternative means?

Let's ask these questions and see what we discover.

REFERENCES

Abou Zahab, M. (2008). 'Yeh Matam kayse ruk jae?' ('How Could This *Matam* Ever Cease?'): Muharram Processions in Pakistani Punjab. In K. A. Jacobsen, Ed., *South Asian Religious Display: Religious Processions in South Asia and the Diaspora* (pp. 104–14). Oxford: Routledge.

Abu-Lughod, L. (1986). *Veiled Sentiments: Honor and Poetry in a Bedouin Society*. American University in Cairo Press.

Abusharaf, R. M. (2001). Virtuous Cuts: Female Genital Circumcision in an African Ontology. *Differences*, 12: 112–40.

Ahlberg, B. M., Njau, W., Kiiru, K., and Krantz, I. (2000). Gender Masked or Self-Inflicted Pain: Female Circumcision, Eradication and Persistence in Central Kenya. *African Sociological Review*, 4: 35–54.

Alperovitz, G. (1996). *The Decision to Use the Atomic Bomb*. New York: Vintage.

Ambrumova, A. G., and Postovalova, L. I. (2010/1989). The Motives for Suicide. *Russian Social Science Review*, 30: 77–89. Trans. M. Vale.

American Law Institute (1985). Model Penal Code and Commentaries (Official Draft and Revised Comments). Philadelphia: American Law Institute.

American Psychiatric Association (2013). *Diagnostic and Statistical Manual of Mental Disorders*, 5th edn. (DSM-5). Arlington, VA: American Psychiatric Association.

Amnesty International (2003). *Combating Torture – A Manual for Action*. London: Amnesty International Publications.

  (2012). *Facts and Figures* (http://files.amnesty.org/air12/fnf_air_2012_en.pdf).

Antoun, R. T. (1968). On the Modesty of Women in Arab Muslim Villages: A Study in the Accommodation of Traditions. *American Anthropologist*, 70: 671–97 (see also comments by N. M. Abu-Zahra and Antoun's reply, 72: 1079–92)

Aquino, K., Reed, A., II, Thau, S., and Freeman, D. (2007). A Grotesque and Dark Beauty: How Moral Identity and Mechanisms of Moral Disengagement Influence Cognitive and Emotional Reactions to War. *Journal of Experimental Social Psychology*, 43(3): 385–92.

Arlachi, P. (1983). *Mafia, Peasants and Great Estates: Society in Traditional Calabria*, Trans. J. Steinberg. Cambridge University Press.

Armstrong, A. MacC. (1950). Trial by Combat Among the Greeks. *Greece and Rome*, 19(56): 73–9.

Assadi, S. M., Noroozian, M., Pakravannejad, M., Yahyazadeh, O., Aghayan, S., and Shariat, S. V. (2006). Psychiatric Morbidity Among Sentenced Prisoners: Prevalence Study in Iran. *British Journal of Psychiatry*, 188: 159–64.

Atiya, N. (1982). *Khul-khaal, Five Egyptian Women Tell Their Stories*. Syracuse, NY: Syracuse University Press.

Atran, S. (2010). *Talking to the Enemy: Faith, Brotherhood, and the (Un) Making of Terrorists*. New York: HarperCollins.

Attili, G., and Hinde, R. A. (1986). Categories of Aggression and Their Motivational Heterogeneity. *Ethology and Sociobiology*, 7: 17–27.

Augustine, Saint, Bishop of Hippo (1961) [c. 397 CE]. *The Rule of Saint Augustine*, Trans. J. C. Resch. De Pere, WI: Saint Norbert Abbey.

Austin, J. L. (1956). A Plea for Excuses: The Presidential Address. *Proceedings of the Aristotelian Society*, 57: 1–30.

Ayers, E. L. (1995). *Southern Crossing: A History of the American South, 1877–1906*. Oxford University Press.

Baaz, M. E. (2009). Why Do Soldiers Rape? Masculinity, Violence, and Sexuality in the Armed Forces in the Congo (DRC). *International Studies Quarterly*, 53: 495–518.

Baker, M. (1985). *Cops: Their Lives in Their Own Words*. New York: Simon and Schuster.

Bandura, A. (1999). Moral Disengagement in the Perpetuation of Inhumanities. *Personality and Social Psychology Review*, 3: 193–209.

Bandura, A., Barbaranelli, C., Caprara, G. V., and Pastorelli, C. (1996). Mechanisms of Moral Disengagement in the Exercise of Moral Agency. *Journal of Personality and Social Psychology*, 74(2), 364–71.

Banks, C. G. (1996). "There Is No Fat in Heaven": Religious Asceticism and the Meaning of Anorexia Nervosa. *Ethos*, 24: 107–35.

Barbier, P. (1996). *The World of the Castrati: The History of an Extraordinary Operatic Phenomenon*, Trans. M. Crosland. London: Souvenir Press.

Bargh, J. A., Raymond, P., Pryor, J. B., and Strack, F. (1995). Attractiveness of the Underling: An Automatic Power → Sex Association and Its Consequences for Sexual Harassment and Aggression. *Journal of Personality and Social Psychology*, 68: 768–81.

Barlett, C. P., and Anderson, C. A. (2012). Direct and Indirect Relations Between the Big 5 Personality Traits and Aggressive and Violent Behavior. *Personality and Individual Differences*, 52: 870–5.

Barrett, H. C., and Behne, T. (2005). Children's Understanding of Death as the Cessation of Agency: A Test Using Sleep Versus Death. *Cognition*, 96: 93–108.

Barth, F. (1965). *Political Leadership Among Swat Pathans*. London School of Economics Monographs on Social Anthropology, No. 19. New York: Humanities Press; London: Athlone Press.

Bartlett, R. (1986). *Trial by Fire and Water: The Medieval Judicial Ordeal*. New York: Oxford University Press.

Bastian, B., Denson, T. F., and Haslam, N. (2013). The Roles of Dehumanization and Moral Outrage in Retributive Justice. *PLoS ONE*, 8(4): e61842.

Bastian, B., and Haslam, N. (2010). Excluded from Humanity: The Dehumanizing Effects of Social Ostracism. *Journal of Experimental Social Psychology*, 46(1): 107–13.

Bates, D. G., and Rassam, A. (1983). *Peoples and Cultures of the Middle East*. Englewood Cliffs, NJ: Prentice-Hall.

Batey, C. E., Clarke, H. E., Page, R. I., and Price, N. S. (1994). *Cultural Atlas of the Viking World*. Abingdon: Andromeda Oxford.

Bauman, Z. (2001). *Modernity and the Holocaust*. Ithaca, NY: Cornell University Press.

Baumeister, R. F. (1996). Self-Regulation and Ego Threat: Motivated Cognition, Self-Deception, and Destruction in Goal Setting. In P. M. Gollwitzer and J. A. Bargh, Eds., *The Psychology of Action: Linking Cognition and Motivation to Behavior* (pp. 27–47). New York: Guilford Press.

(1997). *Evil: Inside Human Cruelty and Violence*. New York: Freeman.

Baumeister, R. F., Smart, L., and Boden, J. M. (1996). Relation of Threatened Egotism to Violence and Aggression: The Dark Side of High Self-Esteem. *Psychological Review*, 103(1): 5–33.

Baumeister, R. F., and Vohs, K. D. (2004). Four Roots of Evil. In A. G. Miller, Ed., *The Social Psychology of Good and Evil* (pp. 85–101). New York: Guilford.

Becker, G. S. (1968). Crime and Punishment: An Economic Approach. *Journal of Political Economy*, 76: 169–217.

Beevor, A. (2002). *Berlin: The Downfall 1945*. New York: Penguin.

Bell, K. M., and Orcutt, H. K. (2009). Posttraumatic Stress Disorder and Male-Perpetrated Intimate Partner Violence. *Journal of the American Medical Association*, 302: 562–4.

Benedict, R. (1922). The Vision in Plains Culture. *American Anthropologist* (New Series), 24: 1–23.

(1932). Configurations of Culture in North America. *American Anthropologist* (New Series), 34: 1–27.

(1959/1934). *Patterns of Culture,* 2nd edn. Cambridge, MA: Riverside Press.

Benn, J. A. (2007). *Burning for the Buddha: Self-Immolation in Chinese Buddhism.* Kuroda Institute Studies in East Asian Buddhism, vol. 19. Honolulu, HI: University of Hawaii Press.

Berkowitz, L. (1989). Frustration-Aggression Hypothesis: Examination and Reformulation. *Psychological Bulletin,* 106: 59–73.

Bernstein, R. (2006). *The Code: The Unwritten Rules of Fighting and Retaliation in the NHL.* Chicago: Triumph.

(2008). *The Code: Baseball's Unwritten Rules and Its Ignore-at-Your-Own-Risk Code of Conduct.* Chicago: Triumph.

Berry, J., and Berry, C. (1999). *Genocide in Rwanda: A Collective Memory.* Washington, DC: Howard University Press.

Besse, S. K. (1989). Crimes of Passion: The Campaign Against Wife Killing in Brazil, 1910–1940. *Journal of Social History,* 22: 653–66.

Betz, J. (1977). Violence: Garver's Definition and a Deweyan Correction. *Ethics,* 87(4): 339–51.

Bissinger, B. (2011). NFL Playoffs: Why Football Needs Violence. *Daily Beast,* January 17. Web, May 6, 2012 (www.thedailybeast.com/articles/2011/01/18/nfl-playoffs-buzz-bissinger-on-why-football-needs-violence.html).

Black, D. (1998). *The Social Structure of Right and Wrong,* rev. edn. San Diego, CA: Academic Press.

Black-Michaud, J. (1975). *Cohesive Force: Feud in the Mediterranean and the Middle East.* New York: St. Martin's Press (Blackwell).

Blight, J. G., and Lang, J. M. (2005). *The Fog of War: Lessons from the Life of Robert S. McNamara.* Lanham, MD: Rowman and Littlefield.

Bloch, M. H. (1986). *From Blessing to Violence: History and Ideology in the Circumcision Ritual of Madagascar.* Cambridge University Press.

(1998). The Presence of Violence in Religion. In J. Goldstein, Ed., *Why We Watch: The Attractions of Violent Entertainment* (pp. 163–78). New York: Oxford University Press.

Bloch, M., and Parry, J., Eds. (1982). *Death and the Regeneration of Life.* Cambridge University Press.

Bloch, R. H. (1977). *Medieval French Literature and Law.* Berkeley, CA: University of California Press.

Bloomfield, M. W. (1969). Beowulf, Byrhtnoth, and the Judgment of God: Trial by Combat in Anglo-Saxon England. *Speculum,* 64: 545–59.

Blow, C. M. (2011). The Brutal Side of Hazing. *New York Times,* December 9, Comments (www.nytimes.com/2011/12/10/opinion/blow-the-brutal-side-of-hazing.html).

Boas, F., and Codere, F.H. (1966). *Kwakiutl Ethnography*. University of Chicago Press.

Boehm, C. (1999). *Hierarchy in the Forest: The Evolution of Egalitarian Behavior*. Cambridge, MA: Harvard University Press.

Bohannan, P., Ed. (1967a). *African Homicide and Suicide*. New York: Atheneum.

   (1967b). Patterns of Homicide and Suicide. In Bohannan, *African Homicide and Suicide* (pp. 230–66).

Bonanno, G.A., and Kaltman, S. (2001). The Varieties of Grief Experience. *Clinical Psychology Review*, 21: 705–34.

Bourdieu, P. (1966). The Sentiment of Honour in Kabyle Society. In J.G. Peristiany, Ed., *Honour and Shame: The Values of Mediterranean Society* (pp. 191–241). University of Chicago Press.

Bowlby, J. (1973). *Separation: Anxiety and Anger (Attachment and Loss*, vol. II). New York: Basic Books.

   (1989). *The Making and Breaking of Affectional Bonds*. New York: Routledge.

Brandt, R.B. (1954). *Hopi Ethics*. University of Chicago Press.

Brennan, P.A., Mednick, S.A., and Hodgins, S. (2000). Major Mental Disorders and Criminal Violence in a Danish Birth Cohort. *Archives of General Psychiatry*, 57: 494–500.

Brown, P. (1975). Society and the Supernatural: A Medieval Change. *Daedalus*, 104: 133–51.

   (1988). *The Body and Society: Men, Women, and Sexual Renunciation in Early Christianity*. New York: Columbia University Press.

Brown, W.C. (2011). *Violence in Medieval Europe*. Harlow: Longman.

Buell, A.C. (1904). *History of Andrew Jackson: Pioneer, Patriot, Soldier, Politician, Soldier*, vol I. New York: Charles Scribner's Sons.

Bushman, B.J., and Baumeister, R.F. (1998). Threatened Egotism, Narcissism, Self-Esteem, and Direct and Displaced Aggression: Does Self-Love or Self-Hate Lead to Violence? *Journal of Personality and Social Psychology*, 75(1): 219–29.

Butler, M.J. (2005). Elephants of a Feather? The Role of 'Justice' in Canadian and American Cold War Military Interventions. *Canadian Journal of Political Science / Revue Canadienne de Science Politique*, 38: 101–27.

Camilleri, J.A. (2012). Evolutionary Psychological Perspectives on Sexual Offending: From Etiology to Intervention. In T.K. Shackelford and V.A. Weekes-Shackelford, Eds., *The Oxford Handbook of Evolutionary Perspectives on Violence, Homicide, and War* (pp. 173–96). Oxford University Press.

Campbell, A. (1982). Female Aggression. In P. Marsh and A. Campbell, Eds., *Aggression and Violence* (pp. 137–50). Oxford: Basil Blackwell.

Campbell, J. K. (1964). *Honour, Family, and Patronage: A Study of Institutions and Moral Values in a Greek Mountain Community*. New York: Oxford University Press.

(1966). Honour and the Devil. In J. G. Peristiany, Ed., *Honour and Shame: The Values of Mediterranean Society* (pp. 141–70). University of Chicago Press.

Canaan, T. (1931). Unwritten Laws Affecting the Arab Women of Palestine. *Journal of the Palestine Oriental Society*, 11: 172–203.

Canetto, S. S., and Lester, D. (2002). Love and Achievement Motives in Women's and Men's Suicide Notes. *Journal of Psychology: Interdisciplinary and Applied*, 136: 573–6.

Cantor, J. (1998). Children's Attraction to Violent Television Programming. In J. Goldstein, Ed., *Why We Watch: The Attractions of Violent Entertainment* (pp. 88–115). New York: Oxford University Press.

Carlsmith, K. M. (2006). The Roles of Retribution and Utility in Determining Punishment. *Journal of Experimental Social Psychology*, 42(4): 437–51.

(2008). On Justifying Punishment: The Discrepancy Between Words and Actions. *Social Justice Research*, 21(2): 119–37.

Carlsmith, K. M., Darley, J. M., and Robinson, P. H. (2002). Why Do We Punish?: Deterrence and Just Deserts as Motives for Punishment. *Journal of Personality and Social Psychology*, 83(2): 284–98.

Carlsmith, K. M., Monahan, J., and Evans, A. (2007). The Function of Punishment in the "Civil" Commitment of Sexually Violent Predators. *Behavioral Sciences & the Law*, 25(4): 437–48.

Carlsmith, K. M., and Sood, A. M. (2009). The Fine Line Between Interrogation and Retribution. *Journal of Experimental Social Psychology*, 45(1): 191–6.

Carmichael, J. T., and Jacobs, D. (2002). Violence by and Against the Police. In R. G. Burns and C. E. Crawford, Eds., *Policing and Violence* (pp. 25–51). Englewood Cliffs, NJ: Prentice-Hall.

Carroll, J. (2012). The Extremes of Conflict in Literature: Violence, Homicide, and War. In T. K. Shackelford and V. A. Weekes-Shackelford, Eds., *The Oxford Handbook of Evolutionary Perspectives on Violence, Homicide, and War* (pp. 413–34). Oxford University Press.

Castano, E., and Giner-Sorolla, R. (2006). Not Quite Human: Infrahumanization in Response to Collective Responsibility for Intergroup Killing. *Journal of Personality and Social Psychology*, 90(5): 804–18.

Chapleau, K. M., and Oswald, D. L. (2010). Power, Sex, and Rape Myth Acceptance: Testing Two Models of Rape Proclivity. *Journal of Sex Research*, 47: 66–78.

Chelkowski, P. J., Ed. (2010). *Eternal Performance: Ta 'ziyeh and Other Shiite Rituals*. London: Seagull.

Cheney, D. L., and Seyfarth, R. M. (1992). *How Monkeys See the World: Inside the Mind of Another Species*. University of Chicago Press.

(2007). *Baboon Metaphysics: The Evolution of a Social Mind*. University of Chicago Press.

Chenoweth, E., and Stephan, M. J. (2011). *Why Civil Resistance Works: The Strategic Logic of Nonviolent Conflict*. New York: Columbia University Press.

Chirot, D., and McCauley, R. (2006). *Why Not Kill Them All? The Logic and Prevention of Mass Political Murder*. Princeton University Press.

Clarke, J. W. (1998). Without Fear or Shame: Lynching, Capital Punishment and the Subculture of Violence in the American South. *British Journal of Political Science*, 2: 269–89.

Clayton, S., and Opotow, S. (2003). Justice and Identity: Changing Perspectives on What Is Fair. *Personality and Social Psychology Review*, 7: 298–310.

Clinton-Sherrod, A. M., and Walters, J. H. (2011). Marital Rape and Sexual Violation by Intimate Partners. In T. Bryant-Davis, Ed., *Surviving Sexual Violence: A Guide to Recovery and Empowerment* (pp. 48–57). Lanham, MD: Rowman and Littlefield.

Cohen, A. (1965). *Arab Border-Villages in Israel: A Study of Continuity and Change in Social Organization*. Manchester University Press.

Cohen, D. K. (2011). Causes of Sexual Violence During Civil War: Cross-National Evidence (1980–2009). Prepared for the Minnesota International Relations Colloquium, March 28.

(2013a). Explaining Rape During Civil War: Cross-National Evidence (1980–2009). *American Political Science Review*, 107: 461–77.

(2013b). Female Combatants and the Perpetration of Violence: Wartime Rape in the Sierra Leone Civil War. *World Politics*, 65: 383–415.

Cohen, E. (2010). *The Modulated Scream: Pain in Late Medieval Culture*. University of Chicago Press.

Cohen, Y. A. (1964). *The Transition from Childhood to Adolescence*. Chicago: Aldine.

Coid, J., Yang, M.,Ullrich, S., Roberts, A., and Hare, R. (2009a). Prevalence and Correlates of Psychopathic Traits in the Household Population of Great Britain. *International Journal of Law and Psychiatry*, 32(2): 65–73.

Coid, J., Yang, M., Ullrich, S., Roberts, A., Moran, P., Bebbington, P., Brugha, T., *et al.* (2009b). Psychopathy Among Prisoners in England and Wales. *International Journal of Law and Psychiatry*, 32(3): 134–41.

Collins, R. (1974). Three Faces of Cruelty: Towards a Comparative Sociology of Violence. *Theory and Society*, 1: 415–40.

(2008). *Violence: A Micro-Sociological Theory*. Princeton University Press.

Colson, E. (1953). Social Control and Vengeance in Plateau Tonga Society. *Africa: Journal of the International African Institute*, 23: 199–212.

Connole, D. A. (2008). *A "Yankee" in the "Texas Army."* Lanham, MD: Hamilton Books.

Conroy, J. (2000). *Unspeakable Acts, Ordinary People: The Dynamics of Torture.* New York: Knopf.

Cooney, M. (1998). *Warriors and Peacemakers: How Third Parties Shape Violence.* New York University Press.

(2009). *Is Killing Wrong?: A Study in Pure Sociology.* Charlottesville, VA: University of Virginia Press.

Copes, H. (2003). Streetlife and the Rewards of Auto Theft. *Deviant Behavior,* 24: 309–32.

Copes, H., Hochstetler, A., and Forsyth, C. J. (2013). Peaceful Warriors: Codes for Violence Among Adult Male Bar Fighters. *Criminology,* 51: 761–94.

Cottingham, J. (1979). Varieties of Retribution. *Philosophical Quarterly,* 29: 238–46.

Crachiolo, B. (2004). Seeing the Gendering of Violence: Female and Male Martyrs in the *South English Legendary.* In M. D. Meyerson, D. Thiery, and O. Falk, Eds., *'A Great Effusion of Blood'?: Interpreting Medieval Violence* (pp. 147–63). University of Toronto Press.

Crank, J. P. (1998). *Understanding Police Culture.* Belmont, CA: Wadsworth.

Crelinsten, R. D., and Schmid, A. P. (1995). In Their Own Words: The World of the Torturer. In R. D. Crelinsten and A. P. Schmid, Eds., *The Politics of Pain: Torturers and Their Masters* (pp. 35–64). Boulder, CO: Westview Press.

Cuddy, A. J., Rock, M. S., and Norton, M. I. (2007). Aid in the Aftermath of Hurricane Katrina: Inferences of Secondary Emotions and Intergroup Helping. *Group Processes & Intergroup Relations,* 10(1): 107–18.

Daly, M., and Wilson, M. (1988). *Homicide.* New York: Aldine de Gruyter.

Darley, J. M., Carlsmith, K. M., and Robinson, P. H. (2000). Incapacitation and Just Deserts as Motives for Punishment. *Law and Human Behavior,* 24(6): 659–83.

Davis, M. W. (1922). *In the Clutch of Circumstance: My Own Story* (author listed as "A Burglar"). London: D. Appleton.

Deci, E. L., Koestner, R., and Ryan, R. M. (1999). A Meta-Analytic Review of Experiments Examining the Effects of Extrinsic Rewards on Intrinsic Motivation. *Psychological Bulletin,* 125(6): 627–68.

Decker, S. H. (1996a). Deviant Homicide: A New Look at the Role of Motives and Victim–Offender Relationships. *Journal of Research in Crime and Delinquency,* 33: 427–49.

(1996b). Collective and Normative Features of Gang Violence. *Justice Quarterly,* 13: 243–64.

Deibert, G. R., and Miethe, T. D. (2010). Character Contests and Dispute-Related Offenses. *Deviant Behavior,* 24: 245–67.

DeJong, T. M., Overholser, J. C., and Stockmeier, C. A. (2010). Apples to Oranges?: A Direct Comparison Between Suicide Attempters and Suicide Completers. *Journal of Affective Disorders*, 124: 90–7.

Delaney, C. (1987). Seeds of Honor, Fields of Shame. In Gilmore, *Honor and Shame and the Unity of the Mediterranean* (pp. 35–48).

Denig, E. T. (2000/1930). *The Assiniboine*, Ed. J. N. B. Hewitt. Norman, OK: University of Oklahoma Press. Originally published in the Forty-Sixth Annual Report of the Bureau of American Ethnology.

de Waal, F. (1982). *Chimpanzee Politics: Power and Sex Among Apes*. Baltimore, MD: Johns Hopkins University Press.

(1992). Aggression as a Well-Integrated Part of Primate Social Relationships: A Critique of the Seville Statement on Violence. In J. Silverberg and J. P. Gray, Eds., *Aggression and Peacefulness in Humans and Other Primates* (pp. 37–56). Oxford University Press.

DeWall, C. N., Baumeister, R. F., Stillman, T. F., and Gailliot, M.T. (2007). Violence Restrained: Effects of Self-Regulation and Its Depletion on Aggression. *Journal of Experimental Social Psychology*, 43(1): 62–76.

Dieserud, G., Gerhardsen, R. M., Van den Weghe, H., and Corbett, K. (2010). Adolescent Suicide Attempts in Bærum, Norway, 1984–2006. *Crisis*, 31: 255–64.

Dobash, R. E., and Dobash, R. P. (1979). *Violence Against Wives: A Case Against the Patriarchy*. New York: Free Press.

Dolan, T. M., Jr. (2010). Demanding the Impossible: War, Bargaining and Honor. Paper presented at the American Political Science Annual Meeting (http://papers.ssrn.com/sol3/papers.cfm?abstract_id=1644597).

Dollard, J., Doob, L. W., Miller, N. E., Mowrer, O. H., and Sears, R. R. (1939). *Frustration and Aggression*. New Haven, CT: Yale University Press.

Donne, John (1957). A Sermon Preached at White Hall, April 2, 1620. Number 1 in Evelyn Mary Spearing Simpson and George Ruben Potter, Eds., *The Sermons of John Donne*, vol. III. Berkeley, CA: University of California Press. Electronic reproduction by Brigham Young University (http://contentdm.lib.byu.edu/cdm/compoundobject/collection/JohnDonne/id/3151/rec/2).

Donnelly, M. P., and Diehl, D. (2011). *The Big Book of Pain: Torture and Punishment Through History*. Stroud: History Press.

Donnelly, M., and Straus, M. A. (2005). *Corporal Punishment of Children in Theoretical Perspective*. New Haven, CT: Yale University Press.

Douglas, J. D. (1967). *The Social Meanings of Suicide*. Princeton University Press.

Dulaney, S., and Fiske, A. P. (1994). Cultural Rituals and Obsessive-Compulsive Disorder: Is There a Common Psychological Mechanism? *Ethos*, 22: 243–83.

Dumézil, G. (1959). *Gods of the Ancient Northmen*. Berkeley, CA: University of California Press.

Dundas, P. (2002). *The Jains*. Oxford: Routledge.

Dunning, E., Murphy, P., and Williams, J. (1986). 'Casuals', 'Terrace Crews' and 'Fighting Firms': Towards a Sociological Explanation of Football Hooligan Behaviour. In D. Riches, Ed., *The Anthropology of Violence* (pp. 164–83). Oxford: Basil Blackwell.

Durkheim, E. (1951/1897). *Suicide: A Study in Sociology*, Trans. J. A. Spaulding and G. Simpson; Ed. G. Simpson. Glencoe, IL: Free Press.

(1973/1899–1900). Two Laws of Penal Evolution, Trans. T. A. Jones and A. T. Scull. *Economy and Society*, 2: 285–308 (originally published as Deux lois de l'évolution pénal, *Année Sociologique*, 4: 65–95).

(1997/1893). *The Division of Labor in Society*, Trans. L. A. Coser (originally published as *De la division du travail social: Étude sur L'organisation des sociétés supérieures*). New York: Free Press.

(2008/1912). *The Elementary Forms of the Religious Life*. Mineola, NY: Dover.

Eckstein, J. J. (2011). Reasons for Staying in Intimately Violent Relationships: Comparisons of Men and Women and Messages Communicated to Self and Others. *Journal of Family Violence*, 26: 21–30.

Edel, M. M., and Edel, A. (1959). *Anthropology and Ethics*. Springfield, IL: Thomas.

Eidelson, R. J., and Eidelson, J. I. (2003). Dangerous Ideas: Five Beliefs That Propel Groups Toward Conflict. *American Psychologist*, 58: 182–92.

El Dareer, A. (1983). Attitudes of Sudanese People to the Practice of Female Circumcision. *International Journal of Epidemiology*, 2: 38–44.

Eller, J. D. (2010). *Cruel Creeds, Virtuous Violence: Religious Violence Across Culture and History*. Amherst, NY: Prometheus.

Ellison, C. G., Musick, M. A., and Holden, G. W. (2011). Does Conservative Protestantism Moderate the Association Between Corporal Punishment and Child Outcomes? *Journal of Marriage and Family*, 73: 946–61.

Elwin, V. (1950). *Maria Murder and Suicide*. Bombay: Oxford University Press.

Emery, N. J., Seed, A. M., von Bayern, A., M. P., and Clayton, N. S. (2007). Cognitive Adaptations of Social Bonding in Birds. *Philosophical Transactions of the Royal Society of London. Series B, Biological Sciences*, 362: 489–505.

Engelstein, L. (1999). *Castration and the Heavenly Kingdom: A Russian Folktale*. Ithaca, NY: Cornell University Press.

Engh, A. L., Siebert, E. R., Greenberg, D. A., and Holekamp, K. E. (2005). Patterns of Alliance Formation and Postconflict Aggression Indicate Spotted Hyenas Recognize Third-Party Relationships. *Animal Behaviour*, 69: 209–17.

Eronen, M., Hakola, P., and Tiihonen, J. (1996). Mental Disorders and Homicidal Behavior in Finland. *Archives of General Psychiatry*, 53: 497–501.

Evans-Pritchard, E. E. (1937). *Witchcraft, Oracles and Magic Among the Azande*. Oxford University Press.

(1939). Introduction to J. G. Peristiany, *The Social Institutions of the Kipsigis*. London: Routledge.

(1940). *The Nuer: A Description of the Models of Livelihood and Political Institutions of a Nilotic People*. Oxford: Clarendon Press.

Everett, M. W. (1975). American Indian "Social Pathology": A Re-examination. In T. R. Williams, Ed., *Psychological Anthropology* (pp. 249–85). Berlin: Walter de Gruyter.

Fagan, J., and Chin, Ko-lin (1990). Violence as Regulation and Social Control in the Distribution of Crack. In M. De La Rosa, E. Y. Lambert, and B. Gropper, Eds., *Drugs and Violence: Causes, Correlates, and Consequences* (pp. 8–42). National Institute on Drug Abuse Research Monograph. Rockville, MD: US Department of Health and Human Services.

Falk, O. (2004). Bystanders and Hearsayers First: Reassessing the Role of the Audience in Dueling. In M. D. Meyerson, D. Thiery, and O. Falk, Eds., '*A Great Effusion of Blood'?: Interpreting Medieval Violence* (pp. 98–130). University of Toronto Press.

Fallers, L. A., and Fallers, M. C. (1967). Homicide and Suicide in Busoga. In P. Bohannan, Ed., *African Homicide and Suicide* (pp. 65–93). New York: Atheneum.

Fanon, F. (1965). *The Wretched of the Earth*, Trans. C. Farrington. New York: Grove Press.

Farès, B. (1932). *L'Honneur chez les Arabes avant l'Islam*. Paris: Librarie D'Amerique et D'Orient Adrien-Maisionneuve.

Faturechi, R. (2012a). Secret Clique in L.A. County Sheriff's Gang Unit Probed. *Los Angeles Times*, April 20 (http://articles.latimes.com/2012/apr/20/local/la-me-sheriff-clique-20120420).

(2012b). Tattoo in Sheriff's Deputy Clique May Have Celebrated Shootings, Sources Say. *Los Angeles Times*, May 9 (http://articles.latimes.com/2012/may/09/local/la-me-sheriff-clique-20120510).

(2013). L.A. County Sheriff's Department Intends to Fire Seven Deputies. *Los Angeles Times*, February 6 (http://articles.latimes.com/2013/feb/06/local/la-me-jump-out-boys-20130207).

Fehr, E., and Fischbacher, U. (2004). Third-Party Punishment and Social Norms. *Evolution and Human Behavior*, 25: 63–87.

Felson, R. B. (1982). Impression Management and the Escalation of Aggression and Violence. *Social Psychology Quarterly*, 45: 245–54.

(1983). Aggression and Violence Between Siblings. *Social Psychology Quarterly*, 46: 271–85.

(1993). Predatory and Dispute-Related Violence: A Social Interactionist Approach. In R. V. Clarke and M. Felson, Eds., *Routine Activity and Rational Choice* (pp. 103–26). *Advances in Criminological Theory*, vol. V. New Brunswick, NJ: Transaction Books.

(2004). A Rational Choice Approach to Violence. In M. A. Zahn, H. H. Brownstein, and S. L. Jackson, Eds., *Violence: From Theory to Research* (pp. 71–90). Cincinnati, OH: LexisNexis and Anderson.

Felson, R. B., and Russo, N. (1988). Parental Punishment and Sibling Aggression. *Social Psychology Quarterly, 51*: 11–18.

Finkel, E. J. (2007). Impelling and Inhibiting Forces in the Perpetration of Intimate Partner Violence. *Review of General Psychology, 11*(2): 193–207.

Finkel, E. J., DeWall, C. N., Slotter, E. B., McNulty, J. K., Pond, R. S., Jr., and Atkins, D. C. (2012). Using I³ Theory to Clarify When Dispositional Aggressiveness Predicts Intimate Partner Violence Perpetration. *Journal of Personality and Social Psychology, 102*: 533–49.

Finkel, E. J., DeWall, C. N., Slotter, E. B., Oaten, M., and Foshee, V. A. (2009). Self-Regulatory Failure and Intimate Partner Violence Perpetration. *Journal of Personality and Social Psychology, 97*: 483–99.

Fiske, A. P. (1990). Relativity Within Moose ("Mossi") Culture: Four Incommensurable Models for Social Relationships. *Ethos, 18*: 180–204.

(1991). *Structures of Social Life: The Four Elementary Forms of Human Relations*. New York: Free Press (Macmillan).

(1992). The Four Elementary Forms of Sociality: Framework for a Unified Theory of Social Relations. *Psychological Review, 99*: 689–723.

(2000). Complementarity Theory: Why Human Social Capacities Evolved to Require Cultural Complements. *Personality and Social Psychology Review, 4*: 76–94.

(2002). Moral Emotions Provide the Self-Control Needed to Sustain Social Relationships. *Self and Identity, 1*: 169–75.

(2004). Relational Models Theory 2.0. In N. Haslam, Ed., *Relational Models Theory: A Contemporary Overview* (pp. 3–25). Mahwah, NJ: Erlbaum.

(2010). Dispassionate Rationality Fails to Sustain Social Relationships. In A. W. Mates, L. Mikesell, and M. S. Smith, Eds., *Discourse, Sociality, and Frontotemporal Dementia: Reverse Engineering the Social Brain* (pp. 199–241). London: Equinox.

(2011). Metarelational Models: Configurations of Social Relationships. *European Journal of Social Psychology, 42*: 2–18.

Fiske, A. P., and Haslam, N. (2005). The Four Basic Social Bonds: Structures for Coordinating Interaction. In M. Baldwin, Ed., *Interpersonal Cognition* (pp. 267–98). New York: Guilford Press.

Fiske, A. P., and Schubert, L. (2012). How to Relate to People: The Extra-Terrestrial's Guide to *Homo sapiens*. In O. Gillath, G. Adams, and

A. D. Kunkel, Eds., *Relationship Science: Integrating Evolutionary, Neuroscience, and Sociocultural Approaches* (pp. 169–95). Washington, DC: American Psychological Association.

Fiske, A. P., and Tetlock, P. (1997). Taboo Tradeoffs: Reactions to Transactions That Transgress Spheres of Exchange. *Political Psychology, 17*: 255–94.

Flanagan, O., Sarkissian, H., and Wong, D. (2008). Naturalizing Ethics. In W. Sinnott-Armstrong, Ed., *Moral Psychology*, vol. I: *The Evolution of Morality: Adaptations and Innateness* (pp. 1–26). Cambridge, MA: MIT Press.

Flett, G. L., Goldstein, A. L., Hewitt, P. L., and Wekerle, C. (2012). Predictors of Deliberate Self-Harm Behavior Among Emerging Adolescents: An Initial Test of a Self-Punitiveness Model. *Current Psychology, 31*: 49–64.

Flynn, A., and Graham, K. (2010). "Why Did It Happen?" A Review and Conceptual Framework for Research on Perpetrators' and Victims' Explanations for Intimate Partner Violence. *Aggression and Violent Behavior, 15*: 239–51.

Fogel, J. A. (2000). *The Nanjing Massacre in History and Historiography*. Berkeley, CA: University of California Press.

Fox, R. (1977). The Inherent Rules of Violence. In P. Collett, Ed., *Social Rules and Social Behaviour* (pp. 132–49). Totowa, NJ: Rowman and Littlefield.

Frank, R. (1988). *Passions Within Reason*. New York: Norton.

Freud, S. 1913/1899. *The Interpretation of Dreams*, Trans. J. Strachey. New York: Macmillan.

Friedl, E. (1962). *Vasilika: A Village in Modern Greece*. New York: Holt, Rinehart, and Winston.

Friedman, R. E. (1997). *Who Wrote the Bible?* New York: HarperCollins.

Friedrich, P. (1977). Sanity and the Myth of Honor: The Problem of Achilles. *Ethos, 5*: 281–305.

Fulton, R. (2002). *From Judgment to Passion: Devotion to Christ and the Virgin Mary, 800–1200*. New York: Columbia University Press.

Funk, J. B., Baldacci, H. B., Pasold, T., and Baumgardner, J. (2004). Violence Exposure in Real-Life, Video Games, Television, Movies, and the Internet: Is There Desensitization? *Journal of Adolescence, 27*: 23–39.

Gamkrelidze, T. V., and Ivanov, V. V. (1995). *Indo-European and the Indo-Europeans: A Reconstruction and Historical Analysis of a Proto-Language and a Proto-Culture*, Trans. J. Nichols; Ed. W. Winter. Berlin: Mouton de Gruyter.

Gandhi, M. (1998). *The Mind of Mahatma Gandhi*, Ed. R. K. Prabhu and U. R. Rao. Ahemadabad, India: Navajivan.

Garandeau, C. F., and Cillessen, A. H. N. (2006). From Indirect Aggression to Invisible Aggression: A Conceptual View on Bullying and Peer Group Manipulation. *Aggression and Violent Behavior, 11*: 612–25.

Gardner, M. R. (1993). The Mens Rea Enigma: Observations on the Role of Motive in the Criminal Law Past and Present. *Utah Law Review*, 635–750.

Garland, R. (2001). *The Greek Way of Death*, 2nd edn. Ithaca, NY: Cornell University Press.

Geertz, C. (1972). Deep Play: Notes on the Balinese Cockfight. *Daedalus: Myth, Symbol, and Culture*, Winter(1): 1–37. Reprinted in C. Geertz (1973), *The Interpretation of Cultures: Selected Essays* (pp. 412–53). New York: Basic Books.

Gelles, R. J., and Straus, M. A. (1988). *Intimate Violence*. New York: Simon & Schuster.

Gershoff, E. T., Miller, P. C., and Holden, G. W. (1999). Parenting Influences from the Pulpit: Religious Affiliation as a Determinant of Parental Corporal Punishment. *Journal of Family Psychology*, 13: 307–20.

Giangreco, D. M. (2003). "A Score of Bloody Okinawas and Iwo Jimas": President Truman and Casualty Estimates for the Invasion of Japan. *Pacific Historical Journal*, 72: 93–132.

Gibson, J. W. (1986). *The Perfect War: Technowar in Vietnam*. New York: Atlantic Monthly Press.

Gilmore, D. D., Ed. (1967). *Honor and Shame and the Unity of the Mediterranean*. Special Publication of the American Anthropological Association, No. 22.

Ginat, J. (1982). *Women in Muslim Rural Society: Status and Role in Family and Community*. New Brunswick, NJ: Transaction Books.

Ginges, J. (1997). Deterring the Terrorist: A Psychological Evaluation of Different Strategies for Deterring Terrorism. *Terrorism and Political Violence*, 9(1): 170–85.

Ginges, J., and Atran, S. (2009). What Motivates Participation in Violent Political Action: Selective Incentives or Parochial Altruism? *Annals of the New York Academy of Sciences*, 1167(1), 115–23.

(2011). War as a Moral Imperative (Not Just Practical Politics by Other Means). *Proceedings of the Royal Society of London. Series B, Biological Sciences*, 278(1720): 2930–8.

Ginges, J., Atran, S., Medin, D., and Shikaki, K. (2007). Sacred Bounds on Rational Resolution of Violent Political Conflict. *Proceedings of the National Academy of Sciences of the United States of America*, 104(18): 7357–60.

Ginges, J., Atran, S., Sachdeva, S., and Medin, D. (2011). Psychology Out of the Laboratory: The Challenge of Violent Extremism. *American Psychologist*, 66(6): 507–19.

Gintis, H., and Fehr, E. (2012). The Social Structure of Cooperation and Punishment. *Behavioral and Brain Sciences*, 35: 28–9.

Ginzburg, R. (1962). *100 Years of Lynchings*. Baltimore, MD: Black Classic Press.

Giovannini, M. J. (1981). Woman: A Dominant Symbol Within the Cultural System of a Sicilian Town. *Man* (New Series), 16: 408–26.

Glasenapp, H., von (1999). *Jainism: An Indian Religion of Salvation*. Delhi: Motilal Banarsidass.

Glucklich, A. (2001). *Sacred Pain: Hurting the Body for the Sake of the Soul*. New York: Oxford University Press.

Gluckman, M. (1954). Political Institutions. In E. E. Evans-Pritchard, Ed., *The Institutions of Primitive Society: A Series of Broadcast Talks* (pp. 66–80). Oxford: Blackwell.

———— (1963). *Custom and Conflict in Africa*. Oxford: Blackwell.

Godshalk, D. (2000). William J. Northen's Public and Personal Struggles Against Lynching. In J. Dailey, G. E. Gilmore, and B. Simon, Eds., *Jumpin' Jim Crow: Southern Politics from Civil War to Civil Rights* (pp. 140–61). Princeton University Press.

Goetz, A. T., and Romero, G. A. (2102). Intimate Partner Violence: War at Our Doorsteps. In T. K. Shackelford and V. A. Weekes-Shackelford, Eds., *The Oxford Handbook of Evolutionary Perspectives on Violence, Homicide, and War* (pp. 63–76). Oxford University Press.

Goldberg, V. (1998). Death Takes a Holiday, Sort Of. In J. Goldstein, Ed., *Why We Watch: The Attractions of Violent Entertainment* (pp. 27–52). New York: Oxford University Press.

Goldstein, J. (1998). Immortal Kombat: War Toys and Violent Video Games. In J. Goldstein, Ed., *Why We Watch: The Attractions of Violent Entertainment* (pp. 53–68). New York: Oxford University Press.

Goodyear-Smith, F. A., and Laidlaw, T. M. (1999). Aggressive Acts and Assaults in Intimate Relationships: Towards an Understanding of the Literature. *Behavioral Sciences & the Law, 17*: 285–304.

Gough, K. (1972). Nuer Kinship: A Re-examination. In T. L. Beidelman, Ed., *The Translation of Culture* (pp. 79–121). London: Tavistock.

Gould, R. V. (2003). *Collision of Wills: How Ambiguity About Social Rank Breeds Conflict*. University of Chicago Press.

Graham, J., and Haidt, J. (2011). Sacred Values and Evil Adversaries: A Moral Foundations Approach. In M. Mikulincer and P. R. Shaver, Eds., *The Social Psychology of Morality: Exploring the Causes of Good and Evil* (pp. 11–31). New York: APA Books.

Graham, J., Haidt, J., and Nosek, B. (2009). Liberals and Conservatives Use Different Sets of Moral Foundations. *Journal of Personality and Social Psychology, 96*: 1029–46.

Graves, F. P. (1891). *The Burial Customs of the Ancient Greeks*. Brooklyn, NY: Roche and Hawkins.

Graves, J. T. (1906). The Reign of Terror for Southern White Women, *The Atlanta Georgian*, August 21 (www.gpb.org/georgiastories/docs/the_race_riot_of_1906-1).

Gray, K., Young, L., and Waytz, A. (2012). Mind Perception is the Essence of Morality. *Psychological Inquiry*, 23: 101–24.

Greitemeyer, T., and McLatchie, N. (2011). Denying Humanness to Others: A Newly Discovered Mechanism by Which Violent Video Games Increase Aggressive Behavior. *Psychological Science*, 22: 659–65.

Grem, D. (2006). Sam Jones, Sam Hose, and the Theology of Racial Violence. *Georgia Historical Quarterly*, 90: 35–61 (http://www.jstor.org/stable/40584885).

Greven, P. (1977). *The Protestant Temperament: Patterns of Child-Rearing, Religious Experience, and the Self in Early America*. University of Chicago Press.

Grinnell, G. B. (1923). *The Cheyenne Indians*. New Haven, CT: Yale University Press [cited in Benedict, 1932].

Grossman, D. (2009). *On Killing: The Psychological Cost of Learning to Kill in War and Society*. New York: Little Brown.

Gruenbaum, E. (2001). *The Female Circumcision Controversy: An Anthropological Perspective*. Philadelphia: University of Pennsylvania Press.

Guarendi, R. N. (1991). *Back to the Family: Proven Advice on Building a Stronger, Healthier, Happier Family*. New York: Simon and Schuster.

Guillais, J. (1990). *Crimes of Passion*. Oxford: Blackwell.

Guillaumont, A. (1979). *Aux origines du monachisme chrétien: Pour une phénoménologie du monachisme*. Spiritualité Orientale, No. 30. Bégrolles en Mauges (Maine and Loire): Abbaye de Bellefontaine.

Haidt, J. (2001). The Emotional Dog and Its Rational Tail: A Social Intuitionist Approach to Moral Judgment. *Psychological Review*, 108: 814–34.

(2003). The Moral Emotions. In R. J. Davidson, K. R. Scherer, and H. H. Goldsmith, Eds., *Handbook of Affective Sciences* (pp. 852–70). Oxford University Press.

(2007). The New Synthesis in Moral Psychology. *Science*, 316: 998–1002.

Haidt, J., and Bjorklund, F. (2008). Social Intuitionists Answer Six Questions About Moral Psychology. In W. Sinnott-Armstrong, Ed., *Moral Psychology*, vol. II: *The Cognitive Science of Morality: Intuition and Diversity* (pp. 181–217). Cambridge, MA: MIT Press.

Haidt, J., and Joseph, C. (2004). Intuitive Ethics: How Innately Prepared Intuitions Generate Culturally Variable Virtues. *Daedalus*, 133: 55–66.

Halawi, J. (2002). "Honour" Drenched in Blood. *Al-Ahram Weekly*, August 15–21 (http://weekly.ahram.org.eg/2002/599/eg4.htm).

Hale, R. (1997). Motives of Reward Among Men Who Rape. *American Journal of Criminal Justice*, 22: 101–19.

Hales, S. (2002). Looking for Eunuchs: The *Galli* and Attis in Roman Art. In S. Tougher, Ed., *Eunuchs in Antiquity and Beyond* (pp. 87–102). London: Duckworth.

Haliburn, J. (2000). Reasons for Adolescent Suicide Attempts. *Journal of the American Academy of Child and Adolescent Psychiatry*, 39: 13–14.

Hamlin, J. K., Wynn, K., and Bloom, P. (2007). Social Evaluation by Preverbal Infants. *Nature*, 450(7169): 557–9.

Hamlin, J. K., Wynn, K., Bloom, P., and Mahajan, N. (2011). How Infants and Toddlers React to Antisocial Others. *Proceedings of the National Academy of Sciences of the United States of America*, 108(50): 19931–6.

Hamman, A. G. (1977). Les Origines du monachisme chrétien au cours des deux premiers siècles. In C. Mayer, Ed., *Homo Spiritalis: Festgab für Luc Verheijen* (pp. 217–32). Würzburg: Augustinus-Verlag.

Hara, M. (2009). Divine Witness. *Journal of Indian Philosophy*, 37: 253–72.

Haritos-Fatouros, M. (1995). The Official Torturer: A Learning Model for Obedience to the Authority of Violence. In R. D. Crelinsten and A. P. Schmid, Eds., *The Politics of Pain: Torturers and Their Masters* (pp. 129–46). Boulder, CO: Westview Press.

(2003). *The Psychological Origins of Institutionalized Torture*. London: Routledge.

Harkavy, R. E. (2000). Defeat, National Humiliation, and the Revenge Motif in International Politics. *International Politics*, 37: 345–68.

Hartnett, S. M., Bump, N., Dubois, J., Hollon, R., and Morris, D. (2008). *Evaluation of CeaseFire-Chicago*. Chicago: Northwestern University.

Hartung, J. (2012). Chastity, Fidelity, and Conquest: Biblical Rules for Women and War. In T. K. Shackelford and V. A. Weekes-Shackelford, Eds., *The Oxford Handbook of Evolutionary Perspectives on Violence, Homicide, and War* (pp. 77–90). Oxford University Press.

Hasday, J. E. (2000). Contest and Consent: A Legal History of Marital Rape. *California Law Review*, 88: 1373–1505.

Haslam, N. (2006). Dehumanization: An Integrative Review. *Personality and Social Psychology Review*, 10: 252–64.

Haslam, N., and Loughnan, S. (2014). Dehumanization and Infrahumanization. *Annual Review of Psychology*, 65: 399–423.

Hauser, M. (2006). *Moral Minds: How Nature Designed Our Universal Sense of Right and Wrong*. New York: Ecco Books.

Haw, C., and Hawton, K. (2008). Life Problems and Deliberate Self-Harm: Associations with Gender, Age, Suicidal Intent and Psychiatric and Personality Disorder. *Journal of Affective Disorders*, 109: 139–48.

Hawley, J. S., Ed. (1994). *Sati, the Blessing and the Curse: The Burning of Wives in India*. New York: Oxford University Press.

Headley, L. A. (1983). *Suicide in Asia and the Near East*. Berkeley, CA: University of California Press.

Heald, S. (1986). The Ritual Use of Violence: Circumcision Among the Gisu of Uganda. In D. Riches, Ed., *The Anthropology of Violence* (pp. 70–85). Oxford: Basil Blackwell.

Heider, F. (1958). *The Psychology of Interpersonal Relations.* Hillsdale, NJ: Lawrence Erlbaum.

Henberg, M. (1990). *Retribution: Evil for Evil in Ethics, Law, and Literature.* Philadelphia: Temple University Press.

Henrich, J., Heine, S. J., and Norenzayan, A. (2010). The Weirdest People in the World. *Behavioral and Brain Sciences, 33*: 61–83.

Herdt, G. (1987). *The Sambia: Ritual and Gender in New Guinea.* New York: Holt, Rinehart and Winston.

Herzfeld, M. (1980). Honour and Shame: Problems in the Comparative Analysis of Moral Systems. *Man* (New Series), *15*: 339–51.

(1985). *The Poetics of Manhood: Contest and Identity in a Cretan Mountain Village.* Princeton University Press.

(1987). "As in Your Own House": Hospitality, Ethnography, and the Stereotype of Mediterranean Society. In Gilmore, *Honour and Shame and the Unity of the Mediterranean* (pp. 75–94).

Heyman, J., and Ariely, D. (2004). Effort for Payment: A Tale of Two Markets. *Psychological Science, 15*(11): 787–93.

Hinton, A. L. (2002). The Dark Side of Modernity: Toward an Anthropology of Genocide. In A. L. Hinton, Ed., *Annihilating Difference: The Anthropology of Genocide* (pp. 1–40). Berkeley, CA: University of California Press.

Hirshleifer, J. (1987). On the Emotions as Guarantors of Threats and Promises. In J. Dupré, Ed., *The Latest on the Best: Essays on Evolution and Optimality* (pp. 307–26). Cambridge, MA: MIT Press.

Hobbes, T. (2010/1651). *Leviathan: On the Matter, Forme, and Power of a Common-Wealth Ecclesisticall and Civill.* New Haven, CT: Yale University Press.

Homer (1950). *The Iliad,* Trans. E. V. Rieu. New York: Penguin.

Hood, R., and Hoyle, C. (2008). *The Death Penalty: A Worldwide Perspective,* 4th edn. Oxford University Press.

Horowitz, R., and Schwartz, G. (1974). Honor, Normative Ambiguity and Gang Violence. *American Sociological Review, 39*: 238–51.

Huggins, M. K., Haritos-Fatouros, M., and Zimbardo, P. G. (2002). *Violence Workers: Police Torturers Reconstruct Brazilian Atrocities.* Berkeley, CA: University of California Press.

Hughes, D. D. (1991). *Human Sacrifice in Ancient Greece.* New York: Routledge.

Human Relations Area Files. Yale University (http://www.yale.edu/hraf).

Hyams, P. R. (1981). Trial by Ordeal: The Key to Proof in the Early Common Law. In M. S. Arnold, T. A. Green, S. A. Scully, and S. D. White, Eds., *On* the Laws and Customs of England: Essays in Honor of Samuel E. Thorne (pp. 90–126). Chapel Hill, NC: University of North Carolina Press.

Iga, M. (1986). *The Thorn in the Chrysanthemum: Suicide and Economic Success in Japan.* Berkeley, CA: University of California Press.

Ingle, D. (2004). Recreational Fighting. In G. S. Cross, Ed., *Encyclopedia of Recreation and Leisure in America,* vol. II (pp. 198–200). New York: Scribner.

Jackson, L. F. (2008). *The Greatest Silence.* Jackson Films, Inc., in association with The Fledgling Fund and HBO Documentary Films (http://thegreatest silence.org/home/). Excerpt on PBS: Congo Soldiers on Why They Rape (www.pbs.org/wnet/need-to-know/the-daily-need/congo-soldiers-on-why-they-rape/4046/).

Jacobs, B. A., and Wright, R. (2006). *Street Justice: Retaliation in the Criminal Underworld.* Cambridge University Press.

(2008). Moralistic Street Robbery. *Crime & Delinquency, 54:* 511–31.

James, S., director (2011). *The Interrupters* (documentary film). Kartemquin Films, United States.

Jamjoom, M., and Ahmed, A. (2010). Saudi Arabia Urged Not to Paralyze Man as Retribution Punishment. Cable News Network website, August 23 (http://edition.cnn.com/2010/CRIME/08/20/saudi.arabia.paralysis/index. html?iref=allsearch).

Janoff-Bulman, R. (2007). Erroneous Assumptions: Popular Belief in the Effectiveness of Torture Interrogation. *Peace and Conflict: Journal of Peace Psychology, 13*(4): 429–35.

Jaymous, R. (1981). *Honneur et Baraka: Les structures sociales traditionelles dans le Rif.* Cambridge University Press and Paris: Éditions de la Maison des Sciences de l'Homme.

Jeffrey, P. (1979). *Frogs in a Well: Indian Women in Purdah.* London and Atlantic Highlands, NJ: Zed Books.

Jenkins, P. (2010). *Laying Down the Sword: Why We Can't Ignore the Bible's Violent Verses.* New York: HarperCollins.

Jewkes, R. (2002). Intimate Partner Violence: Causes and Prevention. *Lancet, 359:* 1423–9.

Jewkes, R., Fulu, E., Roselli, T., and Garcia-Moreno, C., on behalf of the UN Multi-Country Cross-Sectional Study on Men and Violence Research Team (2013). Prevalence of and Factors Associated with Non-Partner Rape Perpetration: Findings from the UN Multi-Country Cross-Sectional Study on Men and Violence in Asia and the Pacific. *Lancet Global Health, 1*(4), September 10.

Jewkes, R., Sikweyiya, Y., Morrell, R., and Dunkle, K. (2011). Gender Inequitable Masculinity and Sexual Entitlement in Rape Perpetration South Africa: Findings of a Cross-Sectional Study. *PLoS ONE,* December 28. DOI: 10.1371/journal.pone.0029590.

Johnston, D. D. (1995). Adolescents' Motivations for Viewing Graphic Horror. *Human Communication Research*, 21: 522–52.

Jorgensen, J. G. (1972). *The Sun Dance Religion: Power for the Powerless*. University of Chicago Press.

Jost, J. T., Banaji, M. R., and Nosek, B. A. (2004). A Decade of System Justification Theory: Accumulated Evidence of Conscious and Unconscious Bolstering of the Status Quo. *Political Psychology*, 25: 881–920.

Joyce, R. (2007). *The Evolution of Morality*. Cambridge, MA: MIT Press.

Joyce, R., Edging, R., Lorenz, K., and Gillespie, S. (1991). Olmec Bloodletting: An Iconographic Study. In V. Fields, Ed., *Sixth Palenque Roundtable, 1986*. Norman, OK: University of Oklahoma Press (www.mesoweb.com/pari/publications/RT08/Bloodletting.pdf).

Kaeuper, R. W. (1999). *Chivalry and Violence in Medieval Europe*. Oxford University Press.

Kant, I. (1989/1785). *Foundations of the Metaphysics of Morals*, Trans. L. W. Beck. Englewood Cliffs, NJ: Prentice-Hall.

Karatnycky, A. (2005). *How Freedom Is Won: From Civic Resistance to Durable Democracy*. New York: Freedom House.

Katz, J. (1988). *Seductions of Crime: Moral and Sensual Attractions in Doing Evil*. New York: Basic Books.

Kavka, G. S. (1986). *Hobbesian Moral and Political Theory*. Princeton University Press.

(1987). *Moral Paradoxes of Nuclear Deterrence*. New York: Cambridge University Press.

Kelly, J. (2010). Rape in War: Motives of Militia in DRC. Special Report 243, United States Institute of Peace (www.usip.org/files/resources/SR243Kelly.pdf).

Kelman, H. C. (1995). The Social Context of Torture: Policy Processes and Authority Structure. In R. D. Crelinsten and A. P. Schmid, Eds., *The Politics of Pain: Torturers and Their Masters* (pp. 19–34). Boulder, CO: Westview Press.

Kendon, A. (1988). *Sign Languages of Aboriginal Australia: Cultural, Semiotic and Communicative Perspectives*. Cambridge University Press.

Kennedy, D. M. (2002). A Tale of One City: Reflections on the Boston Gun Project. In G. S. Katzmann, Ed., *Securing Our Children's Future: New Approaches to Juvenile Justice and Youth Violence*. Washington, DC: Brookings Institution Press.

(2009). *Deterrence and Crime Prevention: Reconsidering the Prospect of Sanction*. London: Routledge.

(2011). *Don't Shoot: One Man, a Street Fellowship, and the End of Violence in Inner-City America*. New York: Bloomsbury.

Kerr, M., Forsyth, R. D., and Plyley, M. J. (1992). Cold Water and Hot Iron: Trial by Ordeal in England. *Journal of Interdisciplinary History*, 22: 573–95.

Kiefer, T. M. (1968). Institutionalized Friendship and Warfare Among the Tausug of Jolo. *Ethnology*, 7: 225–44.

Kiernan, B. (2007). Blood and Soil: A World History of Genocide and Extermination from Sparta to Darfur. New Haven, CT: Yale University Press.

Kirby, S. L., and Wintrup, G. (2002). Running the Gauntlet: An Examination of Initiation/Hazing and Sexual Abuse in Sport. *Journal of Sexual Aggression*, 8: 49–68 (www.tandfonline.com/doi/abs/10.1080/13552600208413339).

Kleeman, T. F. (1994). Licentious Cults and Bloody Victuals: Sacrifice, Reciprocity, and Violence in Traditional China. *Asia Major*, 7: 185–211.

Klonsky, E. D. (2007). The Functions of Deliberate Self-Injury: A Review of the Evidence. *Clinical Psychology Review*, 27: 226–39.

Knauft, B. M. (1985). *Good Company and Violence: Sorcery and Social Action in a Lowland New Guinea Society*. Berkeley, CA: University of California Press.

　(1987). Reconsidering Violence in Simple Human Societies: Homicide Among the Gebusi of New Guinea. *Current Anthropology*, 28: 457–500.

Knock, M. K. (2009). Why Do People Hurt Themselves? New Insights into the Nature and Functions of Self-Injury. *Current Directions in Psychological Science*, 18: 78–83.

Knox, M. (2010). On Hitting Children: A Review of Corporal Punishment in the United States. *Journal of Pediatric Health Care*, 24: 103–7.

Komter, A. (2004). *Social Solidarity and the Gift*. New York: Cambridge University Press.

Kopytoff, I. (1988). The Cultural Context of African Abolition. In S. Miers, Ed., *The End of Slavery in Africa* (pp. 485–503). Madison, WI: University of Wisconsin Press.

Kopytoff, I., and Miers, S. (1977). African Slavery as an Institution of Marginality. In S. Miers and I. Kopytoff, Eds., *Slavery in Africa: Historical and Anthropological Perspectives* (pp. 3–81). Madison, WI: University of Wisconsin Press.

Korsten, F. W. (2009). Bodies in Pain and the Transcendental Organization of History in Joost van den Vondel. In J. F. van Dijkhuizen and K. A. E. Enenkel, Eds., *The Sense of Suffering: Construction of Physical Punishment in Early Modern Culture* (pp. 377–401). Leiden: Brill.

Kramrisch, S. (1981). *The Presence of Siva*. Princeton University Press.

Kruger, D. J., and Fitzgerald, C. J. (2012). Evolutionary Perspectives on Male–Male Competition, Violence, and Homicide. In T. K. Shackelford and V. A. Weekes-Shackelford, Eds., *The Oxford Handbook of Evolutionary*

Perspectives on Violence, Homicide, and War (pp. 153–70). Oxford University Press.

Kubrin, C. E., and Weitzer, R. (2003). Retaliatory Homicide: Concentrated Disadvantage and Neighborhood Culture. *Social Problems, 50*: 157–80.

La Fontaine, J. (1967). Homicide and Suicide Among the Busoga. In P. Bohannan, Ed., *African Homicide and Suicide* (pp. 94–129). New York: Atheneum.

Langbein, J. H. (2006). *Torture and the Law of Proof: Europe and England in the Ancien Régime*. University of Chicago Press.

Law, R. (1985). Human Sacrifice in Pre-Colonial West Africa. *African Affairs, 84*: 53–87.

Laye-Gindhu, A., and Schonert-Reichel, K. A. (2005). Nonsuicidal Self-Harm Among Community Adolescents: Understanding the "Whats" and "Whys" of Self-Harm. *Journal of Youth and Adolescence, 34*: 447–57.

Lazreg, M. (2008). *Torture and the Twilight of Empire: From Algiers to Baghdad*. Princeton University Press.

Lea, H. C. (1996/1870). *Superstition and Force: Torture, Ordeal, and Trial by Combat in Medieval Law*. Reprint. New York: Barnes and Noble.

Lebow, R. N. (2010). *Why Nations Fight: Past and Future Motives for War*. Cambridge University Press.

Leeson, P. T. (2011). Trial by Battle. *Journal of Legal Analysis, 3*: 341–75.

(2012). Ordeals. *Journal of Law and Economics, 55*: 691–714.

Lefkowitz, M. (2003). *Greek Gods, Human Lives: What We Can Learn from Myths*. New Haven, CT: Yale University Press.

Leidner, B., Castano, E., and Ginges, J. (2013). Dehumanization, Retributive and Restorative Justice, and Aggressive Versus Diplomatic Intergroup Conflict Resolution Strategies. *Personality and Social Psychology Bulletin, 39*(2): 181–92.

Leitenberg, M. (2006). Deaths in Wars and Conflicts in the 20th Century. Cornell University Peace Studies Program Occasional Paper #29, 3rd edn. (www.cissm.umd.edu/papers/files/deathswarsconflictsjune52006.pdf).

Leslie, A. M., Knobe, J., and Cohen, A. (2006). Acting Intentionally and the Side-Effect Effect: 'Theory of Mind' and Moral Judgment. *Psychological Science, 17*(5): 421–7.

Lester, D. (1996). Officer Attitudes Toward Police Use of Force. In W. A. Geller and H. Toch, Eds., *Police Violence* (pp. 180–90). New Haven, CT: Yale University Press.

Lester, D., Wood, P., Williams, C., and Haines, J. (2004). Motives for Suicide – A Study of Australian Suicide Notes. *Crisis, 25*: 33–4.

Lester, R. J. (1995). Embodied Voices: Women's Food Asceticism and the Negotiation of Identity. *Ethos, 23*: 187–222.

Levin, J., and Fox, J. A. (1996). A Psycho-Social Analysis of Mass Murder. In T. O'Reilly-Fleming, Ed., *Serial and Mass Murder: Theory, Research, and Policy* (pp. 55–76). Toronto: Canadian Scholars' Press.

LeVine, R. A. (1961). Anthropology and the Study of Conflict. *Journal of Conflict Resolution*, 5: 3–15.

Levinson, D. (1989). *Family Violence in Cross-Cultural Perspective. Frontiers of Anthropology*, vol. I. Newbury Park, CA: Sage.

Lévi-Strauss, C. (1961/1949). *The Elementary Structures of Kinship*, rev. edn., Trans. J. H. Bell, J. R. von Sturmer, and R. Needham. Boston: Beacon.

Levy, R. I. (1973). *Tahitians: Mind and Experience in the Society Islands*. University of Chicago Press.

Lewis, M. E. (1990). *Sanctioned Violence in Early China*. Albany, NY: State University of New York Press.

Liberman, P. (2006). An Eye for an Eye: Public Support for War Against Evildoers. *International Organization*, 60: 687–722.

(2013). Retributive Support for War and Torture. *Journal of Conflict Resolution*, 57: 285–306.

(2014). War and Torture as "Just Deserts." *Public Opinion Quarterly*, 78(1): 47–70.

Liddle, J. R., Shackelford, T. K., and Weekes-Shackelford, V. A. (2012). Why Can't We All Just Get Along? Evolutionary Perspectives on Violence, Homicide, and War. *Review of General Psychology*, 16: 24–36.

Lienhardt, G. (1961). *Divinity and Experience: The Religion of the Dinka*. Oxford University Press.

Lightfoot, J. L. (2002). Sacred Eunuchism in the Cult of the Syrian Goddess. In S. Tougher, Ed., *Eunuchs in Antiquity and Beyond* (pp. 71–86). London: Duckworth.

Linder, D. O. (n.d.). Los Angeles Police Officers' (Rodney King Beating) Trials. *Famous American Trials* (http://law2.umkc.edu/faculty/projects/ftrials/lapd/lapd.html).

Lindholm, C. (1982). *Generosity and Jealousy: The Swat Pukhtun of Northern Pakistan*. New York: Columbia University Press.

Lindow, J. (2002). *Norse Mythology: A Guide to Gods, Heroes, Rituals, and Beliefs*. New York: Oxford University Press.

Linhares de Albuquerque, C., and Paes-Machado, E. (2004). The Hazing Machine: The Shaping of Brazilian Military Police Recruits. *Policing and Society: An International Journal of Research and Policy*, 14: 175–92 (www.tandfonline.com/doi/full/10.1080/1043946032000143497).

Lisak, D., and Roth, S. (1988). Motivational Factors in Nonincarcerated Sexually Aggressive Men. *Journal of Personality and Social Psychology*, 55: 795–802.

Lison-Tolosana, C. (1983/1963). *Belmonte de los Caballeros: Anthropology and History in an Aragonese Community*. Princeton University Press.

Lodge, H. C., Ed. (1904). *The Works of Alexander Hamilton in Twelve Volumes*, vol. X. New York: G. P. Putnam's Sons.

Löwenheim, O., and Heimann, G. (2008). Revenge in International Politics. *Security Studies*, 17: 685–724 (http://dx.doi.org/10.1080/09636410802508055).

Lowie, R. H. (1919). *The Tobacco Society of the Crow Indians*. Anthropological Papers of the American Museum of Natural History, vol. 21, part 2.

(1922). *The Religion of the Crow Indians*. Anthropological Papers of the American Museum of Natural History, vol. 25, part 2.

Luckenbill, D. F. (1977). Criminal Homicide as a Situated Transgression. *Social Problems*, 25: 176–86.

Lundsgaarde, H. P. (1977). *Murder in Space City: A Cultural Analysis of Houston Homicide Patterns*. New York: Oxford University Press.

MacArthur, D. (1962). Duty, Honor, Country. Thayer Award acceptance address (www.americanrhetoric.com/speeches/douglasmacarthurthayeraward.html).

MacNair, R. M. (2002). *Perpetration-Induced Traumatic Stress: The Psychological Consequences of Killing*. Westport, CT: Praeger.

Malamuth, N. M. (1986). Predictors of Naturalistic Sexual Aggression. *Journal of Personality and Social Psychology*, 50: 953–62.

Malinowski, B. (1922). *Argonauts of the Western Pacific: An Account of Native Enterprise and Adventure in the Archipelagoes of Melanesian New Guinea*. London: Routledge and Kegan Paul.

Mandelbaum, D. G. (1988). *Women's Seclusion and Men's Honour: Sex Roles in North India, Bangladesh, and Pakistan*. Tucson, AZ: University of Arizona Press.

Manning, J. (2012). Suicide as Social Control. *Sociological Forum*, 27: 207–27.

Mark, M. M., Bryant, F. B., and Lehman, D. R. (1983). Perceived Injustice and Sports Violence. In J. H. Goldstein, Ed., *Sports Violence* (pp. 83–109). New York: Springer-Verlag.

Marlantes, K. (2011). *What It Is Like to Go to War*. New York: Atlantic Monthly Press.

Martin, D. D. Jr. (2009). How to Properly Spank My Kids. Message 45, posted April 29 (http://christianblogs.christianet.com/1137709450.htm).

Marvin, C., and Ingle, D. W. (1999). *Blood Sacrifice and the Nation: Totem Rituals and the American Flag*. Cambridge University Press.

Marvin, G. (1986). Honour, Integrity and the Problem of Violence in the Spanish Bullfight. In D. Riches, Ed., *The Anthropology of Violence* (pp. 118–35). Oxford: Basil Blackwell.

Mathew, S., and Boyd, R. (2011). Punishment Sustains Large-Scale Cooperation in Prestate Warfare. *Proceedings of the National Academy of Sciences of the United States of America*, 108: 11375–80.

Mauss, M. (1925). *Essai sur le don. Forme et raison de l'échange dans les sociétés archaïques.* Paris: L'Année Sociologique. Trans. W. D. Halls as *The Gift: The Form and Reason for Exchange in Archaic Societies* (1990). New York: W. W. Norton.

Maxfield, M. G. (1989). Circumstances in Supplementary Homicide Reports: Variety and Validity. *Criminology*, 27: 671–95.

Maybury-Lewis, D. (2002). Genocide Against Indigenous Peoples. In A. L. Hinton, Ed., *Annihilating Difference: The Anthropology of Genocide* (pp. 43–53). Berkeley, CA: University of California Press.

Mayhew, J. (2009). Godly Beds of Pain: Pain in English Protestant Manuals (ca. 1550–1650). In J. F. van Dijkhuizen and K. A. E. Enenkel, Eds., *The Sense of Suffering: Construction of Physical Punishment in Early Modern Culture* (pp. 299–322). Leiden: Brill.

Maynard Smith, J. (1979). Game Theory and the Evolution of Behaviour. *Proceedings of the Royal Society of London. Series B, Biological Sciences*, 205: 475–88.

Mazur, A., and Both, A. (1998). Testosterone and Dominance in Men. *Behavioral and Brain Sciences*, 21: 353–97.

McCall, N. (1995). *Makes Me Wanna Holler: A Young Black Man in America.* New York: Random House Digital.

McCauley, C. R. (2000). How President Bush Moved the U.S. into the Gulf War: Three Theories of Group Conflict and the Construction of Moral Violation. *Journal for the Study of Peace and Conflict*, Annual Edition (2000–1): 32–42.

McKenna, N. D., and Howarth, J. (2009). *The Cutting Tradition* (documentary film). Annual Program, Without Frontiers. Commissioned by the International Federation of Obstetrics and Gynecology. A SafeHands for Mothers production.

McKnight, D. (1986). Fighting in an Australian Aboriginal Supercamp. In D. Riches, Ed., *The Anthropology of Violence* (pp. 136–63). Oxford: Basil Blackwell.

McLoughlin W. G. (1971). Evangelical Childrearing in the Age of Jackson: Francis Wayland's Views on How and When to Subdue the Willfulness of Children. *Journal of Social History*, 9: 20–34.

McNamara, R. P. (2002). From Report Takers to Report Makers: Understanding the Police and Violence. In R. G. Burns and C. E. Crawford, Eds., *Policing and Violence* (pp. 52–72). Englewood Cliffs, NJ: Prentice-Hall.

McVicar, J. (1982). Violence in Prisons. In P. Marsh and A. Campbell, Eds., *Aggression and Violence* (pp. 200–14). Oxford: Basil Blackwell.

Medieval Sourcebook: Charters Relating to Judicial Duels, 11th–12th Century. Fordham University (www.fordham.edu/halsall/source/12Cduels.asp).

Meeker, M. E. (1976). Meaning and Society in the Near East: Examples from the Black Sea Turks and the Levantine Arabs. *International Journal of Middle East Studies*, 7: 243–70, 383–422.

Meinardus, O. (1969). The Upper Egyptian Practice of Making Eunuchs in the XVIIIth and XIXth Century. *Zeitschrift für Ethnologie*, 94: 47–58.

Meisel, A. C., and del Mastro, M. L. (1975). *The Rule of St. Benedict.* New York: Doubleday.

Meloy, J. R., Hempel, A. G., Kris Mohandie, Shiva, A. A., and Gray, B. T. (2001). Offender and Offense Characteristics of a Nonrandom Sample of Adolescent Mass Murderers. *Journal of the American Academy of Child and Adolescent Psychiatry*, 40: 719–28.

Melton, G. B., Petrila, J., Poythress, N. G., and Slobogin, C. (1997). *Psychological Evaluations for the Courts: A Handbook for Mental Health Professionals and Lawyers*, 2nd edn. New York: Guilford Press.

Menand, L. (2013). The Color of Law: Voting Rights and the Southern Way of Life. *New Yorker*, July 8 and 15, pp. 80–9.

Metamura, T. (1970). *Chinese Eunuchs: The Structure of Intimate Politics*, Trans. C. A. Pomeroy. Rutland, VT: Tuttle.

Middleton, J., and Tait, D., Eds. (1954). *Tribes Without Rulers: Studies in African Segmentary Systems.* London: Routledge and Kegan Paul.

Middleton, M. L. (1994). *Cop: A True Story.* Chicago: Contemporary Books.

Miethe, T. D., and Regoeczi, W. C. (2004). *Rethinking Homicide: Exploring the Structure and Process Underlying Deadly Situations.* Cambridge University Press.

Mikhail, J. (2007). Universal Moral Grammar: Theory, Evidence, and the Future. *Trends in Cognitive Sciences*, 11: 143–52.

Milgram, S. (1974). *Obedience to Authority: An Experimental View.* New York: Harper and Row.

Miller, J. D., Zeichner, A., and Wilson, L. F. (2012). Personality Correlates of Aggression Evidence from Measures of the Five-Factor Model, UPPS Model of Impulsivity, and BIS/BAS. *Journal of Interpersonal Violence*, 27: 2903–19.

Millon, T., Simonsen, E., Birket-Smith, M., and Davis, R. D. (1998). *Psychopathy: Antisocial, Criminal, and Violent Behavior.* New York: Guilford Press.

Moio, J. A. (2007). Torture: Advances and Limitations in Explanatory Theories and Implications for Cross Cultural Social Work. *Journal of Ethnic and Cultural Diversity in Social Work*, 15: 1–30.

Moore, G. E. (1903). *Principia Ethica.* Cambridge University Press.

Morinis, A. (1985). The Ritual Experience: Pain and the Transformation of Consciousness in Ordeals of Initiation. *Ethos, 13*: 150–74 (www.jstor. org/stable/639985).

Muehlenkamp, J., Brausch, A., Quigley, K., and Whitlock, J. (2013). Interpersonal Features and Functions of Nonsuicidal Self-Injury. *Suicide and Life-Threatening Behavior, 43*: 67–80.

Muir, J. (2009/1913). The Story of My Boyhood and Youth. In J. Muir, *Journeys in the Wilderness: A John Muir Reader*. Edinburgh: Birlinn.

Muller, E. N. (1979). *Aggressive Political Participation*. Princeton University Press.

Munger, M. (2013). Munger on Sports, Norms, Rules, and the Code. May 31 interview on *EconTalk* by host Russ Robert; podcast posted July 1,2012 (www.econtalk.org/archives/2013/07/munger_on_sport.html).

Murdock, G. P. (1967). *Ethnographic Atlas*. University of Pittsburgh Press.

Nader, L. (1990). *Harmony Ideology: Justice and Control in a Zapotec Mountain Village*. Stanford University Press.

Naimark, N. M. (1995). *The Russians in Germany: A History of the Soviet Zone of Occupation, 1945–1949*. Cambridge, MA: Belknap Press.

Nanda, S. (1998). *Neither Man Nor Woman: The Hijras of India*. Belmont, CA: Wadsworth Publishing.

Nansel, T. R., Overpeck, M., Pilla, R. S., Ruan, W. J., Simons-Morton, B., and Scheidt, P. (2001). Bullying Behaviors Among US Youth: Prevalence and Association with Psychosocial Adjustment. *Journal of the American Medical Association, 25*(16): 2094–2100.

Negron, R., Piacentini, J., Graae, F., Davies, M., and Shaffer, D. (1997). Microanalysis of Adolescent Suicide Attempts and Ideators During the Acute Suicidal Episode. *Journal of the American Academy of Child and Adolescent Psychiatry, 36*: 1512–19.

Nelissen, R., and Zeelenberg, M. (2009). When Guilt Evokes Self-Punishment: Evidence for the Existence of a Dobby Effect. *Emotion, 9*(1): 118–22.

Nesse, R. M., Ed. (2001). *Evolution and the Capacity for Commitment*. New York: Russell Sage Foundation Press.

Nevels, C. S. (2007). *Lynching to Belong: Claiming Whiteness Through Racial Violence*. College Station, TX: Texas A&M University Press.

Nicolson, A. (2005). *Seize the Fire: Heroism, Duty, and the Battle of Trafalgar*. New York: HarperCollins.

Nisbet, R. A. (1993). *The Sociological Tradition*, 2nd edn. New Brunswick, NJ: Transaction Books.

Nisbett, R. E., and Cohen, D. (1996). *Culture of Honor: The Psychology of Violence in the South*. Boulder, CO: Westview Press.

Nivette, A. E. (2011). Violence in Non-State Societies: A Review. *British Journal of Criminology, 51*: 578–98.

Olivola, C. Y., and Shafir, E. (2013). The Martyrdom Effect: When Pain and Effort Increase Prosocial Contributions. *Journal of Behavioral Decision Making*, 26(1), 91–105.

Opotow, S., Ed. (1990). Moral Exclusion and Injustice: An Introduction. *Journal of Social Issues*, 46 (Special Issue): 1–20.

Otterman, M. (2007). *American Torture: From the Cold War to Abu Ghraib and Beyond*. London: Pluto.

Overing, J. (1986). Images of Cannibalism, Death and Domination in a 'Non-Violent' Society. In D. Riches, Ed., *The Anthropology of Violence* (pp. 86–102). Oxford: Basil Blackwell.

Packer, I. K. (2009). *Evaluation of Criminal Responsibility*. Oxford University Press.

Paige, J. M. (1971). Political Orientation and Riot Participation. *American Sociological Review*, 36: 810–20.

Pailing, A., Boon, J., and Egan, V. (2014). Personality, the Dark Triad and Violence. *Personality and Individual Differences*, 67: 81–6. (www.science direct.com/science/article/pii/S0191886913013767).

Papachristos, A. V. (2009). Murder by Structure: Dominance Relations and the Social Structure of Gang Homicide. *American Journal of Sociology*, 115: 74–128.

Parkes, C. M. (1996). *Bereavement: Studies of Grief in Adult Life*. Philadelphia: Taylor and Francis.

Parsons, A. (1969). Is the Oedipus Complex Universal? In A. Parsons, *Belief, Magic, and Anomie: Essays in Psychological Anthropology* (pp. 3–66). New York: Free Press; London: Collier-Macmillan.

Patai, R. (1971). *Society, Culture and Change in the Middle East*, 3rd edn. Philadelphia: University of Pennsylvania Press.

Patrick, C. J., Ed. (2005). *Handbook of Psychopathy*. New York: Guilford Press.

Petee, T. A., Padgett, K. G., and York, T. S. (1997). Debunking the Stereotype: An Examination of Mass Murder in Public Places. *Homicide Studies*, 1: 317–37 (http://hsx.sagepub.com/content/1/4/317).

Peters, E. (1985). *Torture*. New York: Blackwell.

Petersen, R., and Zukerman, S. (2010). Anger, Violence, and Political Science. In M. Potegal, G. Stemmler, and C. Spielberger, Eds., *International Handbook of Anger: Constituent and Concomitant Biological, Psychological, and Social Processes* (pp. 561–81). New York: Springer (http://link.springer. com/chapter/10.1007/978-0-387-89676-2_32).

Petit, O., and Thierry, B. (1994). Aggressive and Peaceful Interventions in Conflicts in Tonkean Macaques. *Animal Behaviour*, 48: 1427–36.

Phang, S. E. (2008). *Roman Military Service: Ideologies of Discipline in the Late Republic and Early Principate*. Cambridge University Press.

Piaget, J. (1965/1932). *The Moral Judgment of the Child*, Trans. M. Gabain. New York: Free Press.

Pinault, D. (1992). *The Shiites: Ritual and Popular Piety in a Muslim Community*. New York: St. Martin's Press.

Pinker, S. (2011). *The Better Angels of Our Nature: Why Violence Has Declined*. New York: Viking.

Pisani, A. L. (1982). Identifying Arson Motives. *Fire and Arson Investigator*, 32(4): 18–25(www.ncjrs.gov/App/Publications/abstract.aspx?ID=84265).

Pitt-Rivers, J. G. (1966a). Honour and Social Status. In J. G. Peristiany, Ed., *Honour and Shame: The Values of Mediterranean Society* (pp. 19–78). University of Chicago Press.

(1966b). Honour and Shame in a Cypriot Highland Village. In J. G. Peristiany, Ed., *Honour and Shame: The Values of Mediterranean Society* (pp. 173–90). University of Chicago Press.

(1977). *The Fate of Shechem or The Politics of Sex: Essays in the Anthropology of the Mediterranean*. New York: Cambridge University Press.

Plate, T. G., and Darvi, A. (1981). *Secret Police: The Inside Story of a Network of Terror*. New York: Doubleday.

Plato (380 BCE). *Gorgias*, Trans. B. Jowett. Internet Classics Archive, MIT. (http://classics.mit.edu/Plato/gorgias.html).

Polanyi, K. (2001/1944). *The Great Transformation: The Political and Economic Origins of Our Time*, rev. edn. Boston: Beacon Press.

Polk, K. (1993). Observations on Stranger Homicide. *Journal of Criminal Justice*, 21: 573–82.

Polybius (second century BCE). *Histories* (http://penelope.uchicago.edu/Thayer/E/Roman/Texts/Polybius/6*.html#36).

Poole, F. J. P. (1982). The Ritual Forging of Identity; Aspects of Person and Self in Bimin-Kuskusmin Male Initiation. In G. H. Herdt, Ed., *Rituals of Manhood: Male Initiation in Papua New Guinea* (pp. 99–154). Berkeley, CA: University of California Press.

Potegal, M. (2006). Human Cruelty Is Rooted in the Reinforcing Effects of Intraspecific Aggression That Subserves Dominance. *Behavioral and Brain Sciences*, 29: 236–7.

Press, I. (1979). *The City as Context: Urbanism and Behavioral Constraints in Seville*. Urbana. IL and London: University of Illinois Press.

Pritchard, J. (1954). *The Ancient Near East in Pictures Relating to the Old Testament*. Princeton University Press.

Quebedeaux, M. (2012). Interviews for class research, Los Angeles, May–June 2012 (personal communication, A. P. Fiske).

Rae, D. W., and Taylor, M. (1970). *The Analysis of Political Cleavages*. New Haven, CT: Yale University Press.

Rai, T. S., and Fiske, A. P. (2011). Moral Psychology is Relationship Regulation: Moral Motives for Unity, Hierarchy, Equality, and Proportionality. *Psychological Review, 118*: 57–75.

(2012). Beyond Harm, Intention, and Dyads: Relationship Regulation, Virtuous Violence, and Metarelational Morality. *Psychological Inquiry, 23*(2), 189–93.

Raine, A. (2013). *The Anatomy of Violence: The Biological Roots of Crime.* New York: Pantheon.

Rapoport, A., and Chammah, A. M. (1966). The Game of Chicken. *American Behavioral Scientist, 10*(3): 10–28.

Rappaport, R. A. (1967). *Pigs for the Ancestors: Ritual in the Ecology of a New Guinea People.* New Haven, CT: Yale University Press.

Richters, J., De Visser, R. O., Rissel, C. E., Grulich, A. E., and Smith, A. M. A. (2008). Demographic and Psychosocial Features of Participants in Bondage and Discipline, "Sadomasochism" or Dominance and Submission (BDSM): Data from a National Survey. *Journal of Sexual Medicine, 5*: 1660–8.

Ricks, T. E. (1997). *Making the Corps.* New York: Touchstone.

Ringrose, K. M. (2003). *The Perfect Servant: Eunuchs and the Social Construction of Gender in Byzantium.* University of Chicago Press.

Robachek, C., and Robachek, C. (2005). Waorani Grief and the Witch-Killer's Rage: Worldview, Emotion, and the Anthropological Explanation. *Ethos, 33*: 206–30.

Robbins, M. M. (2007). Gorillas: Diversity in Ecology and Behavior. In C. J. Campbell, A. Fuentes, K. C. MacKinnon, and M. Panger, Eds., *Primates in Perspective* (pp. 305–21). Oxford University Press.

Roberts, A., and Ash, T. G., Eds. (2011). *Civil Resistance and Power Politics: The Experience of Non-Violent Action from Gandhi to the Present.* Oxford University Press.

Roberts, J. M. (1965). Oaths, Autonomic Ordeals, and Power. *American Anthropologist, 67*: 186–212.

Robertson, C. C., and Klein, M. A. (1983). *Women and Slavery in Africa.* Portsmouth, NH: Heinemann.

Roosevelt, T. (1889). *The Winning of the West: From the Alleghenies to the Mississippi 1769–1776*, vol. I. New York: G. P. Putnam's Sons.

Rosaldo, M. Z. (1980). *Knowledge and Passion: Ilongot Notions of Self and Social Life.* Cambridge University Press.

Rosaldo, R. (1980). *Ilongot Headhunting, 1883–1974: A Study in Society and History.* Stanford University Press.

(1984). Grief and a Headhunter's Rage: On the Cultural Force of Emotions. In S. Plattner and E. Bruner, Eds., *Text, Play and Story: The Construction and Reconstruction of Self and Society* (pp. 178–95). Washington, DC: American Ethnological Society.

Rosenblatt, P. C., Walsh, R. P., and Jackson, D. A. (1976). *Grief and Mourning in Cross-Cultural Perspective*. New Haven, CT: HRAF Press (Yale University).

Rosenfeld, R. and Messner, S. F. (1991). The Social Sources of Homicide in Different Types of Societies. *Sociological Forum, 6:* 51–70.

Ross, M. H. (1993). *The Culture of Conflict: Interpretations and Interests in Comparative Perspective*. New Haven, CT: Yale University Press.

Rosselli, J. (1988). The Castrati as a Professional Group and Social Phenomenon, 1550–1850. *Acta Musicologica, 60:* 143–79.

Rousseau, P. (1985). *Pachomius: The Making of a Community in Fourth Century Egypt*. Berkeley, CA: University of California Press.

Royal Navy Articles of War. The 1749 Naval Act (www.pdavis.nl/NDA1749. htm).

Ruggiero, G. (1985). *The Boundaries of Eros: Sex Crime and Sexuality in Renaissance Venice*. New York: Oxford University Press.

Rule, J. B. (1988). *Theories of Civil Violence*. Berkeley, CA: University of California Press.

Ruthven, M. (1978). *Torture: The Grand Conspiracy*. London: Weidenfeld.

Sahlins, M. (1965). On the Sociology of Primitive Exchange. In M. Banton, Ed., *The Relevance of Models for Social Anthropology*. Association of Social Anthropologists, Monograph 1. London: Tavistock. Reprinted in Marshall Sahlins (1972), *Stone Age Economics*. New York: Aldine.

Sanday, P. R. (2007). *Fraternity Gang Rape: Sex, Brotherhood, and Privilege on Campus*, 2nd edn. New York University Press.

Sansom, B. (1982). The Sick Who Do Not Speak. In D. Parkin, Ed., *Semantic Anthropology* (pp. 183–96). London and New York: Academic Press.

Schelling, T. (1960). *The Strategy of Conflict*. Cambridge, MA: Harvard University Press.

Schieffelin, E. L. (2004). *The Sorrow of the Lonely and the Burning of the Dancers*, 2nd edn. London: Palgrave Macmillan.

Schlegel, A., and Barry, H., III (1979). Adolescent Initiation Ceremonies: A Cross-Cultural Code. *Ethnology, 18:* 199–210.

Schneider, J. (1971). Of Vigilance and Virgins: Honor, Shame and Access to Resources in Mediterranean Societies. *Ethnology, 10:* 1–24.

Schubel, V. J. (1993). *Religious Performance in Contemporary Islam: Shi'a Devotional Rituals in South Asia*. Columbia, SC: University of South Carolina Press.

Scott, A. O., Dargis, M., Stanley, A., and Suellentrop, C. (2013). Big Bang Theories: Violence on Screen. *New York Times*, February 28 (www. nytimes.com/interactive/2013/03/03/arts/critics-on-violence-in-media. html?ref=arts#/#introduction).

Scully, D. (1990). *Understanding Sexual Violence: A Study of Convicted Rapists*. Boston: Unwin Hyman.

Scully, D., and Marolla, J. (1985). "Riding the Bull at Gilley's": Convicted Rapists Describe the Rewards of Rape. *Social Problems*, 32: 251–63.

Sehgal, S. (1999). *Encyclopaedia of Hinduism: C–G*, vol. II (pp. 491–2). New Delhi: Sarup and Sons.

Sen, M. (2001). *Death by Fire: Sati, Dowry Death, and Female Infanticide in Modern India*. New Brunswick, NJ: Rutgers University Press.

Senechal de la Roche, R. (1996). Collective Violence as Social Control. *Sociological Forum*, 11: 97–128.

Serres Güiraldes, A. M. (1979). *La Estrategia de General Roca*. Buenos Aires: Pleamar [quoted passage translated by D. Maybury-Lewis].

Sharma, S. K. (1989). *Hijras: The Labelled Deviants*. New Delhi: Gian.

Shils, E. A., and Janowitz, M. (1948). Cohesion and Disintegration in the Wehrmacht in World War II. *Public Opinion Quarterly*, 12: 280–315.

Shover, N. (1996). *Great Pretenders: Pursuits and Careers of Persistent Thieves*. Boulder, CO: Westview.

Shover, N., and Honaker, D. (1992). The Socially Bounded Decision Making of Persistent Property Offenders. *Howard Journal of Criminal Justice*, 31: 276–93.

Shweder, R. A. (2002). "What About Female Genital Mutilation?" and Why Understanding Culture Matters in the First Place. In R. A. Shweder, M. Minow, and H. Rose Markus, Eds., *Engaging Cultural Differences: The Multicultural Challenge in Liberal Democracies* (pp. 216–51). New York: Russell Sage.

Sidanius, J., and Pratto, F. (1999). *Social Dominance: An Intergroup Theory of Social Hierarchy and Oppression*. New York: Cambridge University Press.

Silk, J. (2003). Practice Random Acts of Aggression and Senseless Acts of Intimidation: The Logic of Status Contests in Social Groups. *Evolutionary Anthropology*, 11: 221–5.

Simão, C., and Seibt, B. (2014). Gratitude Depends on the Relational Model of Communal Sharing. *PLoS ONE*, 9(1): e86158. doi:10.1371/journal.pone.0086158.

Simmel, G. (1955). *Conflict, and the Web of Group-Affiliations*. "Conflict," Trans. K. H. Wolff; "The Web of Group-Affiliations," Trans. R. Bendix. Glencoe, IL: Free Press.

Singer, A. (film maker) and Ryle, J. (anthropologist) (1981). *Witchcraft Among the Azande* (film). Disappearing Worlds Series (UK).

Singer, P. (1981). *The Expanding Circle: Ethics and Sociobiology*. New York: Farrar, Straus and Giroux.

Slack, A. T. (1988). Female Circumcision: A Critical Appraisal. *Human Rights Quarterly*, 10: 437–86.

Slotter, E. and Finkel, E. (2011). I³ Theory: Instigating, Impelling, and Inhibiting Factors in Aggression. In P. R. Shaver and M. Mikulincer, Eds., *Human*

Aggression and Violence: Causes, Manifestations, and Consequences (pp. 35–52). Herzilya Series on Personality and Social Psychology. Washington, DC: American Psychological Association.

Smith, P., Stager, L. E., Greene, J. A., and Avishai, G. (2013). Age Estimations Attest to Infant Sacrifice at the Carthage Tophet. *Antiquity*, 87: 1191–9.

Spencer, B., and Gillen, F. J. (1904). *The Northern Tribes of Central Australia*. London: Macmillan.

Spencer, P. (1965). *The Samburu: A Study of Gerontocracy in a Nomadic Tribe*. Berkeley, CA: University of California Press.

Sontag, S. (2003). *Regarding the Pain of Others*. New York: Picador.

Stark, R. (1972). *Police Riots: Collective Violence and Law Enforcement*. Belmont, CA: Wadsworth.

Staub, E. (1989). *The Roots of Evil: The Origins of Genocide and Other Group Violence*. Cambridge University Press.

(1990). Moral Exclusion, Personal Goal Theory, and Extreme Destructiveness. *Journal of Social Issues*, 46: 47–64.

(2000). Genocide and Mass Killings: Origins, Prevention, Healing, and Reconciliation. *Political Psychology*, 21: 367–82.

(2006). Reconciliation After Genocide, Mass Killing, or Intractable Conflict: Understanding the Roots of Violence, Psychological Recovery, and Steps Toward a General Theory. *Political Psychology*, 27: 867–94.

Stephan, M. J., and Chenoweth, E. (2008). Why Civil Resistance Works: The Strategic Logic of Nonviolent Conflict. *International Security*, 33: 7–44.

Stevenson, W. (1995). The Rise of Eunuchs in Greco-Roman Antiquity. *Journal of the History of Sexuality*, 5: 495–511.

(2002). Eunuchs in Early Christianity. In S. Tougher, Ed., *Eunuchs in Antiquity and Beyond* (pp. 123–42). London: Duckworth.

Stouffer, S. A. (1949). *The American Soldier*: vol. I, *Adjustment During Army Life*. Princeton University Press.

Strasser, M. (2013). Social Motives and Relational Models: Empirical Studies on Drivers and Structures. Ph.D. dissertation, Faculty of Economics, Technische Universität München (http://mediatum.ub.tum.de?id=1166695).

Straus, M. A. (1980). The Marriage License as a Hitting License: Evidence from Popular Culture, Law, and Social Science. In M. A. Straus and G. T. Hotaling, Eds., *Social Causes of Husband–Wife Violence* (pp. 39–50). Minneapolis, MN: University of Minnesota Press.

(2000). Corporal Punishment by Parents: The Cradle of Violence in the Family and Society. *Virginia Journal of Social Policy and the Law*, 8: 7–60.

Straus, M. A., and Donnelly, D. A. (2001). *Beating the Devil Out of Them: Corporal Punishment in American Families and Its Effects on Children*. New Brunswick, NJ: Transaction Books.

Stroebe, W., and Stroebe, M. S. (1987). *Bereavement and Health: The Psychological and Physical Consequences of Partner Loss*. Cambridge University Press.

Swidler, A. and Watkins, S. C. (2007). Ties of Dependence: AIDS and Transactional Sex in Rural Malawi. *Studies in Family Planning, 3*: 147–62.

Tam, T., Hewstone, M., Cairns, E., Tausch, N., Maio, G., and Kenworthy, J. (2007). The Impact of Intergroup Emotions on Forgiveness in Northern Ireland. *Group Processes & Intergroup Relations, 10*(1): 119–36.

Tatai, K. (1983). Japan. In L. A. Headley, Ed., *Suicide in Asia and the Near East*. Berkeley, CA: University of California Press.

Tatar, M. (1998). "Violent Delights" in Children's Literature. In J. Goldstein, Ed., *Why We Watch: The Attractions of Violent Entertainment* (pp. 69–87). New York: Oxford University Press.

ter Haar, B. J. (2011). Violence in Chinese Religious Culture. In A. R. Murphy, Ed., *The Blackwell Companion to Religion and Violence* (pp. 249–62). New York: Blackwell.

Thalmann, W. G. (2004). "The Most Divinely Approved and Political Discord": Thinking About Conflict in the Developing Polis. *Classical Antiquity, 23*: 359–99.

Thatcher, M. (1993). *Downing Street Years*. New York: HarperCollins.

Throop, C. J. (2010). *Suffering and Sentiment: Exploring the Vicissitudes of Experience and Pain in Yap*. Berkeley, CA: University of California Press.

Thurston, R. W. (2011). *Lynching: American Mob Murder in Global Perspective*. Burlington, VT: Ashgate.

Tiedens, L. Z., Unzueta, M. M., and Young, M. J. (2007). An Unconscious Desire for Hierarchy? The Motivated Perception of Dominance Complementarity in Task Partners. *Journal of Personality and Social Psychology, 93*: 402–14.

Tolnay, S. E., Glenn, D., and Beck, E. M. (1996). Vicarious Violence: Spatial Effects on Southern Lynchings, 1890–1919. *American Journal of Sociology, 102*: 788–815.

Toohey, P. Death. In M. Gagarin, Ed., *The Oxford Encyclopedia of Ancient Greece and Rome*, vol. II (pp. 363–7). Oxford University Press.

Tougher, S. F. (1997). Byzantine Eunuchs: An Overview, with Special Reference to Their Creation and Origin. In L. James, Ed., *Women, Men and Eunuchs* (pp. 168–84). New York: Routledge.

(2008). *The Eunuch in Byzantine History and Society*. London: Routledge.

Traninger, A. (2009). Whipping Boys: Erasmus' Rhetoric of Corporeal Punishment and Its Discontents. In J. F. van Dijkhuizen and K. A. E. Enenkel, Eds., *The Sense of Suffering: Construction of Physical Punishment in Early Modern Culture* (pp. 39–58). Leiden: Brill.

Trigger, B. G. (2003). *Understanding Early Civilizations: A Comparative Study.* Cambridge University Press.

Trivers, R. L. (1971). The Evolution of Reciprocal Altruism. *Quarterly Review of Biology, 46:* 35–57.

Tsai, Shih-shan H. (1996). *The Eunuchs in the Ming Dynasty.* Albany, NY: State University of New York Press.

Tsang, J. A. (2002). Moral Rationalization and the Integration of Situational Factors and Psychological Processes in Immoral Behavior. *Review of General Psychology, 6(1):* 25–50.

Turiel, E. (1983). *The Development of Social Knowledge: Morality and Convention.* Cambridge University Press.

Turner, B. J., Chapman, A. L., and Layden. B. K. (2012). Intrapersonal and Interpersonal Functions of Non Suicidal Self-Injury: Associations with Emotional and Social Functioning. *Suicide and Life-Threatening Behavior, 42:* 36–55.

Tyler, T., and Lind, E. (1992). A Relational Model of Authority in Groups. In M. Zanna, Ed., *Advances in Experimental Social Psychology,* vol. 25 (pp. 115–91). New York: Academic Press.

Tzu, Han Fei (1964) (original *c.* 235 BCE). *Basic Writings,* Trans. B. Watson. New York: Columbia University Press.

Ullrich, S., Paelecke, M., Kahle, I., and Marneros, A. (2003). Kategoriale und dimensionale Erfassung von "psychopathy" bei deutschen Straftätern. *Nervenarzt, 74:* 1002–8.

Valdez, A., Cepeda, A., and Kaplan, C. (2009). Homicidal Events Among Mexican American Street Gangs: A Situational Analysis. *Homicide Studies, 13:* 288–306.

Valeri, V. (1985). *Kingship and Sacrifice: Ritual and Society in Ancient Hawaii,* Trans. P. Wissing. University of Chicago Press.

Vandello, J. A., and Cohen, D. (2003). Male Honor and Female Fidelity: Implicit Cultural Scripts that Perpetuate Domestic Violence. *Journal of Personality and Social Psychology, 84:* 997–1010.

(2008). Culture, Gender, and Men's Intimate Partner Violence. *Social and Personality Psychology Compass, 31:* 652–67.

van Dijkhuizen, J. F. (2009). Partakers of Pain: Religious Meanings of Pain in Early Modern England. In J. F. van Dijkhuizen and K. A. E. Enenkel, Eds., *The Sense of Suffering: Construction of Physical Punishment in Early Modern Culture* (pp. 189–220). Leiden: Brill.

van Gennep, A. (1960/1909). *The Rites of Passage.* University of Chicago Press.

Varshney, A. (2003). *Ethnic Conflict and Civic Life: Hindus and Muslims in India.* New Haven, CT: Yale University Press.

Veblen, T. (2007/1899). *The Theory of the Leisure Class.* Oxford University Press.

Veilleux, Armand (1986). Monasticism and Gnosis in Egypt. In B. A. Pearson and J. E. Goehring, Eds., *The Roots of Egyptian Christianity* (pp. 271–306). Studies in Antiquity and Christianity. Philadelphia: Fortress Press.

Vera Institute of Justice (1977). Felony Arrests: Their Prosecution and Disposition in New York City's Courts. New York: Vera Institute of Justice.

Viki, G. T., Osgood, D., and Phillips, S. (2013). Dehumanization and Self-Reported Proclivity to Torture Prisoners of War. *Journal of Experimental Social Psychology*, 49(3): 325–8.

Vittrup, B., and Holden, G. W. (2009). Children's Assessments of Corporal Punishment and Other Disciplinary Practices: The Role of Age, Race, SES, and Exposure to Spanking. *Journal of Applied Developmental Psychology*, 31: 211–20.

Volk, A., Camilleri, J. A., Dane., A., and Marini, Z. (2102). If, When, Why Adolescent Bullying Is Adaptive. In T. K. Shackelford and V. A. Weekes-Shackelford, Eds., *The Oxford Handbook of Evolutionary Perspectives on Violence, Homicide, and War* (pp. 270–88). Oxford University Press.

Vossekuil, B., Fein, R., Reddy, M., Borum, R., and Modzeleski, W. (2002). *The Final Report and Findings of the Safe School Initiative: Implications for the Prevention of School Attacks in the United States*. Washington, DC: United States Secret Service and United States Department of Education.

Waegel, W. B. (1984). How Police Justify the Use of Deadly Force. *Social Problems*, 32: 144–55.

Waldron, J. J., Lynn, Q., and Krane, V. (2011). Duct Tape, Icy Hot & Paddles: Narratives of Initiation Onto US Male Sport Teams. *Sport, Education and Society*, 16: 111–25.

Walker, J. S. (2004). *Prompt and Utter Destruction: Truman and the Use of Atomic Bombs Against Japan*, rev. edn. Chapel Hill, NC: University of North Carolina Press.

Waller, A. L. (1988). *Feud: Hatfields, McCoys, and Social Change in Appalachia, 1860–1900*. Chapel Hill, NC: University of North Carolina Press.

Watkins, C., Ed. (2000). *The American Heritage Dictionary of Indo-European Roots*, 2nd edn. Boston: Houghton Mifflin.

Waytz, A., and Epley, N. (2012). Social Connection Enables Dehumanization. *Journal of Experimental Social Psychology*, 48(1): 70–6.

Weekes-Shackelford, V. A. (2012). Why Can't We All Just Get Along? Evolutionary Perspectives on Violence, Homicide, and War. *Review of General Psychology*, 16: 24–36.

Weinberg, T. S., Ed. (1995). *S and M: Studies in Dominance and Submission*, rev. edn. New York: Prometheus Books.

Welch, D. A. (1993). *Justice and the Genesis of War*. New York: Cambridge University Press.

Westermarck, E. (1908). *The Origin and Development of the Moral Ideas*, 2 vols. London: Macmillan.

Westley, W. A. (1953). Violence and the Police. *American Journal of Sociology*, 38: 34–41.

Whitman, J. Q. (2012). *The Verdict of Battle: The Law of Victory and the Making of Modern War*. Cambridge, MA: Harvard University Press.

Wilcox, M. B. (2004). *Soft Patriarchs, New Men: How Christianity Shapes Fathers and Husbands*. University of Chicago Press.

Wilkinson, D. L., and Fagan, J. (1996). The Role of Firearms in Violence "Scripts": The Dynamics of Events Among Adolescent Males. *Law and Contemporary Problems*, 59: 55–90.

Wilkinson, S. J. (2009). Riots. *Annual Review of Political Science*, 12: 329–43.

Wilson, M. (1951). *Good Company and Violence: A Study of Nyakyusa Age-Villages*. Boston: Beacon.

(1957). *Rituals of Kinship Among the Nyakyusa*. Published for the International African Institute. London: Oxford University Press.

Wilson, T. A. (2002). Sacrifice and the Imperial Cult of Confucius. *History of Religions*, 41: 251–87.

Winerip, M. (2012). When a Hazing Goes Very Wrong. *New York Times*, April 12 (www.nytimes.com/2012/04/15/education/edlife/a-hazing-at-cornell.html?partner=rssandemc=rss).

Winkler, G. (1982). The Origins and Idiosyncrasies of the Earliest Forms of Asceticism. In W. Skudlarek, Ed., *The Continuing Quest for God: Monastic Spirituality in Tradition and Transition* (pp. 9–43). Collegeville, MN: Liturgical Press.

Witt, R. (2002). The Other Castrati. In S. Tougher, Ed., *Eunuchs in Antiquity and Beyond* (pp. 235–60). London: Duckworth.

Wong, L., Kolditz, T. A., Millen, R. A., and Potter, T. M. (2003). *Why They Fight: Combat Motivation in the Iraq War*. Carlisle Barracks, PA: Strategies Studies Institute of the United States Army War College.

Wood, E. J. (2009). Armed Groups and Sexual Violence: When Is Wartime Rape Rare? *Politics and Society*, 37: 131–61.

Woodworth, M., and Porter, S. (2002). In Cold Blood: Characteristics of Criminal Homicides as a Function of Psychopathy. *Journal of Abnormal Psychology*, 111: 436–45.

Wright, R. T., and Decker, S. H. (1997). *Armed Robbers in Action: Stickups and Street Culture*. Boston: Northeastern University Press.

Wyatt-Brown, B. (1982). *Southern Honor: Ethics and Behavior in the Old South*. New York: Oxford University Press.

Wyman, L., and Thorne, B. (1945). Notes on Navaho Suicide. *American Anthropologist*, 47: 278–88.

Xella, P., Quinn, J., Melchiorri, V., and van Dommelen, P. (2013). Phoenician Bones of Contention. *Antiquity*, 87: 1199–1207.

Xygalatas, D., Mitkidis, P., Fischer, R., Reddish, P., Skewes, J., Geertz, A. W., Roepstorff, A., *et al.* (2013). Extreme Rituals Promote Prosociality. *Psychological Science*, 24: 1602–5.

Yamagata, N. (1994). *Homeric Morality*. Leiden and New York: E. J. Brill.

Young, F. (1985). *Initiation Ceremonies: A Cross-Cultural Study of Status Dramatization*. New York: Macmillan.

Yu, J. (2012a). Self-Inflicted Violence. In R. L. Nadea, Ed., *The Wiley-Blackwell Companion to Chinese Religions* (pp. 461–80). Malden, MA: Wiley-Blackwell.

(2012b). *Sanctity and Self-Inflicted Violence in Chinese Religions, 1500–1700*. Oxford University Press.

Yuki, M., and Schug, J. (2012). Relational Mobility: A Socioecological Approach to Personal Relationships. In O. Gillath, G. Adams, and A. Kunkel, Eds., *Relationship Science: Integrating Evolutionary, Neuroscience, and Sociocultural Approaches* (pp. 137–51). Washington, DC: American Psychological Association.

Zaibert, L. (2006). *Punishment and Retribution*. Aldershot: Ashgate.

Zeid, A. A. M. (1966). Honour and Shame Among the Bedouins of Egypt. In J. G. Peristiany, Ed., *Honour and Shame: The Values of Mediterranean Society* (pp. 243–59). University of Chicago Press.

Ziegler, V. L. (2004). *Trial by Fire and Battle in Medieval German Literature*. Rochester, NY: Camden House.

Zillmann, D. (1998). The Psychology of the Appeal of Portrayals of Violence. In J. Goldstein, Ed., *Why We Watch: The Attractions of Violent Entertainment* (pp. 179–211). New York: Oxford University Press.

INDEX

CPSIA information can be obtained at www.ICGtesting.com
Printed in the USA
LVOW02*1725090415

433931LV00010B/102/P